THE DEFINITIVE Guitar HANDBOOK

Publisher and Creative Director: Nick Wells
Project Editor: Sara Robson
General Editor: Rusty Cutchin
Consultant Editor: Michael Leonard
Art Director and Layout Design: Mike Spender
Digital Design and Production: Chris Herbert
Notation: Alan Brown of Take Note

Special thanks to: Chelsea Edwards, Sarah Goulding, Rebecca Kidd, Victoria Lyle, Geoffrey Meadon, Sonya Newland,
Ross Plotkin, Valerie Powell, Polly Prior, Melinda Revesz, Paul Robson, Julia Rolf and Claire Walker

First published 2008 by
FLAME TREE PUBLISHING
Crabtree Hall, Crabtree Lane
Fulham, London SW6 6TY
United Kingdom

www.flametreepublishing.com

Music information site: www.musicfirebox.com

08 10 12 11 09

1 3 5 7 9 10 8 6 4 2

Flame Tree is part of The Foundry Creative Media Company Ltd

Every effort has been made to contact copyright holders. We apologize in advance for any omissions and
would be pleased to insert the appropriate acknowledgment in subsequent editions of this publication.

The CIP record for this book is available from the British Library.

ISBN 978-1-84786-391-1

Printed in China

THE DEFINITIVE Guitar HANDBOOK

Rusty Cutchin, Cliff Douse, Hugh Fielder, Mike Gent,
Adam Perlmutter, Richard Riley, Michael Ross, Tony Skinner

Foreword by Paco Peña

General Editor:
Rusty Cutchin

Consultant Editor:
Michael Leonard

FLAME TREE
PUBLISHING

Contents

4

Foreword

For a young musical person in the 1950s in Andalucía, southern Spain, Flamenco was, inevitably, the only form of self-expression. Whether one wanted to sing, dance or play music it was the obvious vehicle and the road we followed. Of course, the guitar trapped me very early on!

There was little money around so you couldn't have any lessons; it sure would have been nice, at that time, to be able to lay your hands on a book such as this! No, you mostly learned by joining groups of other amateurs and accompanying their songs and dances. It was a great time and I loved it, not only for the music but also for the opportunity the guitar offered me of mixing socially with other kids.

Solo flamenco guitar was a rarity at that time. A solo concert was unheard of. So when I arrived in London in the 1960s, I discovered a whole new atmosphere with audiences and aficionados generally; the guitar was hugely popular in so many different disciplines and I mixed and played with countless other young guitarists of every definition, who were as captivated as I was by the beauty and allure of the instrument. I discovered how little I knew and I learned such a lot from them. Having been immersed in my own musical world, I saw then that the guitar can be used to express yourself in whatever musical culture you belong to; or to project the personal message that you most deeply identify with emotionally. So many styles of guitar playing....

There was also in London a great culture and activity of Spanish classical guitar from which I learned a great deal. But I discovered, as well, an openness to accept and appreciate other less familiar contributions, like what I had to offer. It was a great surprise to find that flamenco could be popular in a place so far removed from its roots. That realization spurred me greatly onto the mad, but at the same time, sweet adventure of launching into a solo career. And London and the world has been kind to me ever since.

Very soon after my first concert at the Wigmore Hall I was asked to take part in a gig called 'Guitar-In' at the Royal Festival Hall on London's South Bank, a show about the versatility of the guitar offering four different styles of playing: flamenco, by myself; classical by the duo Tim Walker–Sebastian Jorgensen; folk blues by Bert Jansch and, top of the bill, one Jimmy Hendrix doing his own thing. Wow!!!

Since then, it has been my great privilege to meet and play with many wonderful guitarists in a variety of fields. To have had the opportunity of sharing the stage with the likes of John Williams, Joe Pass, Leo Kottke, Eduardo Falú, as well as Hendrix, Jansch, Manuel Barrueco, Eliot Fisk, Benjamin Verdery and other great musicians has indeed been a serious honour and a lot of fun.

And yet the guitar has given me much more than that. It has shaped my life and made me whoever I have become. It has taken me to every place I have been to. It has given me the chance to discover the world. And above all it has been the means by which I have met most of my friends. When I started the International Guitar Festival of Córdoba, I was able to bring there my greatest lifelong idol, Sabicas and show him off to the people of my hometown, where he had never been or played before. Likewise, I brought Mario Escudero, Paco de Lucía and many other big names, and I was immensely proud of that. But it is for me much more pointed and significant that, when earlier on I had asked my friend John Williams if he would come and add his name to 'my' event in Córdoba, he said that, of course, he would; that way John contributed overwhelmingly to place the festival on the map of serious guitar events. To get John to go anywhere professionally at that time would have been as difficult, as it was irrelevant to discuss payment of any kind. He just did it as a friend.

And so, the journey has been wonderful as has been the music making and the fun throughout all those years. But I feel, deep down, that I am most grateful to the guitar for having helped me find the people that I hold most dear in my life. All of them, I think....

Paco Peña

Paco Peña

Renowned flamenco guitarist Paco Peña was born in Córdoba, Spain in 1942. A traditionalist who sees his role as promoting flamenco culture, rhythms and traditional sounds, Peña began to take guitar lessons from his brother at the tender age of six. By age 12 he was appearing professionally on the concert stage.

After moving to London in the late Sixties, Peña began to tour the world both as a soloist and an accompanist to top flamenco singers and dancers. As a soloist, he performed in some of the most prestigious music venues in the world, including London's infamous Ronnie Scott's Jazz Club and the Royal Albert Hall, Carnegie Hall in New York and the Concertgebouw in Amsterdam.

Authenticity and Innovation

In 1970 Peña founded the 'Paco Peña Flamenco Company', consisting of himself, dancers, singers and another musicians – the company has since given concerts worldwide. He signed to the Decca label, resulting in *The Art Of Flamenco Guitar* (1972), *The Flamenco World Of Paco Peña* (1978, from the BBC TV documentary *The World Of Paco Peña*), and *The Paco Peña Flamenco Company Live At Sadler's Wells, London* (1980), amongst others.

In 1981 he founded the Centro Flamenco Paco Peña in Córdoba, a centre from which he hosted an annual festival, the Festival Internacional de la Guitarra, a month-long celebration of the guitar with concerts and master-classes from flamenco and classical musicians such as his good friend John Williams, Ben Verdery and Serranito. In 1985 Peña was appointed the world's first Professor of Flamenco at the Rotterdam Conservatory, and in 1997 was awarded 'the Cross of the Order of Merit' by the King of Spain. He favours a guitar built by Almerian Gerundino Fernández.

7

Introduction

'Sometimes you want to give up the guitar, you'll hate the guitar. But if you stick with it, you're gonna be rewarded.'
Jimi Hendrix

Today, some 40 years after Jimi Hendrix offered that sage advice, it seems fantastic that anyone would need to be convinced of the satisfaction one feels in becoming a practised guitarist, and not because the instrument is unduly hard to learn or tedious, but because the power of the guitar seems only to increase with time. In the 50 years since it began to replace the piano as the instrument most popular with beginner musicians, the guitar has reached into every style of music, every culture and every corner of the earth.

Anyone who has been playing, even for a short time, knows the rewards that the guitar brings to a player and, eventually, his or her audience. But where can a beginner get all the information needed for a solid grounding in fundamentals, advanced techniques, technology and history? This book will provide all of that and enhance the joy you get from playing your favourite songs.

Everyone hears music before they contemplate picking up an instrument, so this handbook begins with an overview of the various styles with which you're already familiar from radio, CDs, downloads or live shows. All of the most popular guitar

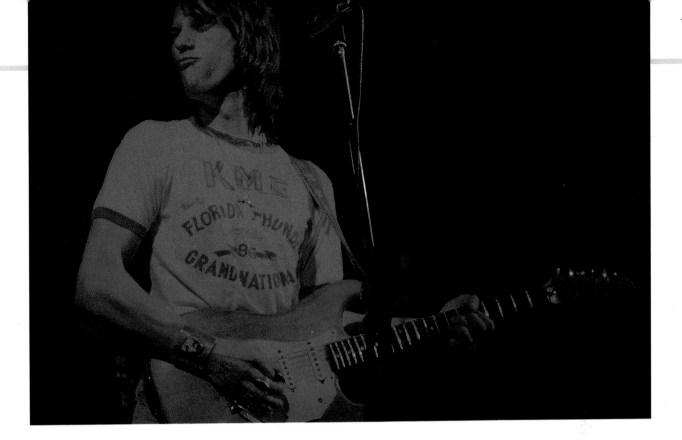

styles are discussed, from rock to jazz and from Latin to reggae (*see* Musical Styles, pages 12–51). The artist profiles here are augmented later in the book by in-depth discussions of your favourite players, from Chet Atkins to Frank Zappa (*see* The Guitarists, pages 266–97).

In between you'll find the details of choosing, playing and taking care of your guitar. You'll learn the basics of musical notation (*see pages* 104–05) and essential harmonic tools, like chords, notes and scales. You'll master vibrato and string bends and, when you're ready, you'll move on to modes, arpeggios and the other advanced techniques that can lead you towards becoming an accomplished jazz or classical player.

For those about to rock, we salute you with great tips on playing a rock solo, choosing an amp, how and when to use effects and lots of other info that will help you handle the rock stardom that awaits you. And even if you just want to jam in your bedroom, you'll learn about new effects boxes and home recording tools that will help you rock out without going on the road or setting your gear afire.

Nothing beats the joy of getting your first guitar or graduating to an axe that you've only seen on TV or on stage. In the Guitars section (*see pages* 298–313), you'll find a comprehensive list of the most popular and important guitars in history, with descriptions of the players who made these axes famous. You'll be able to choose a model (or at least a type) of guitar that will help you fulfil your dreams, whether it's to shred in front of millions with Eddie Van Halen's Frankenstrat or return to those thrilling days of yesteryear astride a horse with Gene Autry's Martin D-45.

Whatever guitar, style or level at which you play, you'll find something useful in this book to help move you along the path to guitar satisfaction. As the saying goes, there's only one way to get to Carnegie Hall (or Wembley, or the Sidney Opera House, or the Tokyo Dome): practise, practise, practise. Becoming a respectable guitar player is no walk in the park, but to paraphrase the founder of Taoism, the journey of a thousand miles begins with a single chord, or riff, or lick. Turn the page and enjoy the journey.

Rusty Cutchin (General Editor)

The Essentials

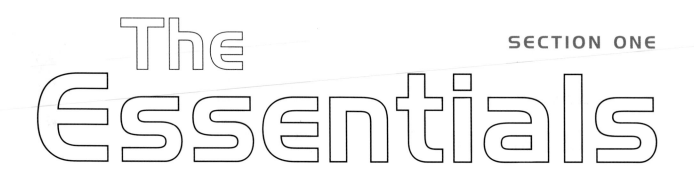

Here you meet the challenge of becoming a guitar player with the essentials — the nuts and bolts of fretting, picking, and producing a cool and proper guitar sound. First we explore the sounds of guitar, from rock to reggae and beyond, with examples you can practise now or later. Then we look at the instrument itself and its component parts. Next are the tools to build your playing vocabulary — chords, notes, hand positions, strumming patterns and much more. Then you'll be ready to develop your chops as a rhythm or lead guitarist. Which kind of player are you?

Musical

Blues

Styles

The blues has played a larger role in the history of popular music than any other genre. It is a direct ancestor to music styles as diverse as rock'n'roll, rock, heavy metal, soul, funk and pop. Without the blues there would have been no Beatles, Jimi Hendrix, Led Zeppelin, James Brown, Stevie Wonder or Oasis, to name but a few!

The blues emerged out of the hardships endured by generations of African–American slaves during the late nineteenth and early twentieth centuries. By 1900, the genre had developed into a three–line stanza, with a vocal style derived from southern work songs. These 'call and response' songs were developed further by early blues guitar players, who would sing a line and then answer it on the guitar. By the 1920s, rural African-Americans had migrated to the big cities in search of work, bringing their music with them. Early street musicians such as Blind Lemon Jefferson, a guitar-playing blues singer, started to make recordings and these inspired the next generation of blues guitar players.

blues performers Charley Patton, Son House and Robert Johnson travelled throughout the southern states, singing about their woes, freedom, love and sex to community after community. Johnson, who, the legend goes, made a mysterious pact with the devil to become a better guitar player, was the first true blues performance artist. Over on the East Coast, musicians such as Blind Boy Fuller, Sonny Terry and Gary Davis developed a more folky blues style.

Chicago Blues

By the 1940s, Chicago bluesmen took Mississippi Delta ideas and played them on electric guitars. Lone performers became scarcer while small bands sprang up everywhere. By the 1950s, electric blues was in full swing, with B.B. King, Muddy Waters, John Lee Hooker, T–Bone Walker and Howlin' Wolf all playing to packed houses in major cities. King pioneered across–the–string vibrato and note–bending techniques on his beloved guitar, 'Lucille', and these techniques are now used by all blues lead–guitar players. Hooker developed a completely different style, in which he stomped continuously with his right foot while singing and playing. Wolf injected more power and frustration into the blues, and Walker jazzed things up,

Delta Blues

The 1930s were a crucial period in the development of the blues, for it was then that acoustic Mississippi Delta

RIGHT: **Blind Lemon Jefferson's lack of sight resulted in expressive playing and vocals.**

LEFT: **Blues legend Howlin' Wolf contributed to the post-war Chicago blues explosion.**

BELOW: **Stevie Ray Vaughan had a stunning, high-energy blues style.**

British Blues

The 1960s witnessed a musical and cultural revolution when British guitar players such as Eric Clapton and Peter Green started to mimic American bluesmen. They used solid–body guitars and more powerful amplifiers to get a harder, more driving sound than their American mentors. Clapton's electric guitar sound led to the birth of a number of other styles, including blues rock, hard rock and even heavy metal.

but it was perhaps Muddy Waters' passionate singing and biting guitar tones that popularized the style more than anyone else from this period. Some bluesmen, such as Big Bill Broonzy, visited England, where their performances inspired British musicians to adopt the style.

From the 1970s onwards, artists including Stevie Ray Vaughan, Robert Cray and Robben Ford have added more voices and sounds to the blues repertoire, and the genre is still thriving today.

Playing the Blues

Blues is based around the blues scale (see page 110), which is a pentatonic minor scale with an added flat fifth note (the 'blue' note). Blues music is usually played in the keys of A, D, E and G as they are all easy keys to play on the guitar. The style has an odd harmonic structure, as the blues scale is usually played or sung over chords that are all dominant sevenths (e.g. A7, D7 and E7 in the key of A) or chords derived from them.

Acoustic Blues

There are two main blues styles: traditional acoustic blues and urban electric blues. Acoustic blues normally requires a 'finger-style' approach, in which the thumb of the right hand – assuming the player is right-handed – plays a steady bass-note groove while the melody or licks are picked out by the first and second fingers. Most of this is performed quite forcefully, although acoustic blues players rest the side of their picking hand across the strings at times to make sure the bass notes don't ring out too loudly. Son House, Leadbelly and Big Bill Broonzy were all masters of this style, so if you want to play it you should familiarize yourself with their recordings. It is important to realize, however, that a lot of their guitar playing was improvised and designed to accompany their own vocal phrasings.

Electric Blues

Urban electric blues guitar is usually played within the context of a band, so it is normally restricted to lead or rhythm playing at any one time. Some electric guitar players use a plectrum (pick) to achieve better articulation, while others favour a more earthy finger-style approach. Electric blues guitarists play in a wider range of keys than their acoustic counterparts, as they often work with horn players who prefer to play in B♭ and C. Lauded electric blues guitar players include B.B. King, Freddie King, Albert Collins, Buddy Guy, Eric Clapton, Robben Ford and Stevie Ray Vaughan.

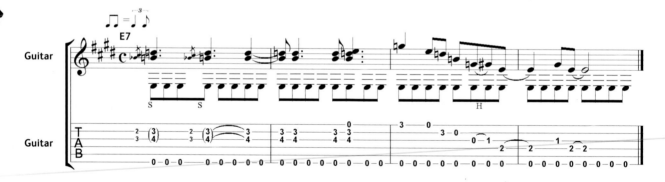

Acoustic blues finger-style playing. The low E string is played repeatedly with the thumb, establishing a traditional blues rhythm.

An example of an electric blues solo. A 'lead-in' before the bar and the use of string bends make this a typical Chicago-style solo.

Playing Electric Blues

Electric blues stylists often embellish their phrases with
expressive techniques such as string bending, sliding and vibrato.
String bending should simply be thought of as another way of
moving from one pitch to another on the fretboard. To bend
a string accurately, you must know your target note – this will
usually be a note pitched a half step, a whole step or a step

and a half above your unbent note. If your target note is a half
step higher, for example, you can play the note behind the next
fret up on the same string to hear what it should sound like.
When you perform the bend, push the string over towards the
bass strings until you hear your target note.

ABOVE: **Buddy Guy was a leading exponent of the Chicago blues sound.**

ABOVE: **Bending strings is one of the oldest techniques of lead-guitar playing. You can bend one, two or even three strings at the same time.**

You can produce a blues slide effect by playing a note on a string and, while holding the string firmly down, slide along the fingerboard to another note. You can even slide across two or more strings at a time by barring your fretting finger across the strings and moving it along the neck in the same way. To obtain a vibrato effect, play a fretted note and move the string from side to side – across the fingerboard – with your fretting finger. This makes a sustained note sound more expressive or even aggressive.

Going Solo

There are many different approaches to soloing over a blues progression, but the simplest way to learn is to target the root notes of each chord in the progression. In the key of C, for example, the main blues chords are C7, F7 and G7. You can begin by playing the C pentatonic minor scale and targeting the notes C, F and G (which are all in the scale) over their respective chords. Try bending or sliding to these notes to make things sound more bluesy.

|| C7 | C7 | C7 | C7 |

| F7 | F7 | C7 | C7 |

| G7 | F7 | C7 | G7 :||

Tens of thousands of blues songs are based around the most common chord progression in the history of popular music: the 12-bar blues sequence.

It is also a good idea to practise blues lead phrasing by using the 'call and response' approach favoured by early blues musicians; sing a phrase and then reply to it with a guitar line, and so on. This should help you to get an authentic blues feel. It will enable you to put comfortable, natural rests between your phrases and notes so it all ends up sounding more musical and logical. You should also jam with other like-minded musicians, as this is not only fun but will also motivate you to become a better player.

(Call)   (response)   (Call)

O   grave - yard,   O   grave - yard,   I'm

(response)

walk - in troo de grave - yard;   lay dis bod - y down

Work songs such as this retain a strong African influence, with irregular rhythms that often follow speech patterns.

Using a Bottleneck

Some blues players, including Elmore James and Duane Allman, have used a bottleneck made out of glass or metal to obtain a distinctive sliding effect between notes. Bottlenecks are inexpensive and fun to play with, but you'll need a little patience to master the technique properly. Special tunings such as D A D F♯ A D are often used for bottleneck pieces, as they enable the guitarist to play whole chords up the guitar neck with just one finger!

Getting a Blues Sound

To get an authentic blues sound you'll need an appropriate guitar. Almost any acoustic instrument will do for acoustic blues, although resonators – guitars that use thin aluminium cones to mechanically amplify their sound – will give you a particularly 'bluesy' tone. If you're after an authentic electric blues sound, you should pick an instrument similar to one played by your favourite blues artist. If you want to sound like B.B. King, for example, you should consider a Gibson ES–335, as this is the guitar he has favoured over the years, while a Fender Stratocaster will enable you to sound more like Robert Cray or Stevie Ray Vaughan, and a Telecaster would be essential for that biting Albert Collins sound.

Amplification is important too, and most blues artists favour valve amplifiers such as the Marshall Bluesbreaker combo or Fender's Twin and Deluxe models, as they give a warm, fat sound with a wide dynamic range.

RIGHT: **The wings on a Gibson 335 allow for a rich, warm tone.**

ABOVE: **The IK Multimedia AmpliTube, an amplifier-simulator plug-in.**

Transistor amplifiers are cheaper but they sound more synthetic. If you're just playing guitar in your bedroom you should consider getting an amp-modelling device such as a Line 6 POD, or a virtual amp software package such as IK Multimedia's AmpliTube or Native Instruments' Guitar Rig. Each of these comes armed with a surprisingly authentic set of blues presets, and you can use them without upsetting the neighbours.

Tone control settings are important as well; boosting an amplifier's bass and mid-range will give a fat B.B. King sound, while boosting the treble will help to emulate the 'icy' tones of Albert Collins. All in all, it is important to find a guitar tone that you feel comfortable with – if you like your sound, you'll play well!

Musical Jazz Styles

Eddie Lang is widely acknowledged as the first significant jazz guitarist. His single-note playing with jazz orchestras during the 1920s marked the beginning of the guitar as a solo instrument in the genre.

18

Born in Philadelphia in 1902, Lang was the son of a guitar maker. He started learning the violin at an early age but had switched to the guitar by the time he was 10. After working with bands in his hometown, he joined the Mound City Blue Blowers in 1924. They toured the US and Europe, and Lang quickly earned a reputation as 'America's best jazz guitarist'. He joined Paul Whiteman's orchestra in 1929 before becoming Bing

LEFT: **Before musicians such as Eddie Lang began to play single-line lead solos, guitars were just part of the rhythm section.**

Crosby's accompanist. He was soon one of the best-paid musicians of the day but, tragically, he died at the peak of his career in 1933, after a 'routine tonsillectomy operation' went wrong.

Lang's Legacy

Lang's pioneering guitar work in the 1920s paved the way for the two jazz-guitar giants of the 1930s: Django Reinhardt and Charlie Christian.

Reinhardt lost the use of two fingers in his left hand after a horrific caravan fire. Astonishingly, he overcame the disability and developed a way of playing the guitar with just the first two fingers of his left hand. He formed the Quintette du Hot Club de France with violinist Stephane Grappelli and other musicians in 1933. They were a resounding success, recording more than 100 songs and touring all over Europe. Django's soloing set new standards in jazz lead guitar and influenced practically every other jazz guitarist from the 1930s through to the 1950s. Charlie Christian was also hugely influential; he emerged in the early 1940s as the first electric-guitar virtuoso, playing saxophone-like lead lines at a volume that could compete with other jazz instruments.

LEFT: **Django Reinhardt developed a unique style of playing after damaging two fingers.**

ABOVE: **Acclaimed bop guitarist Tal Farlow has influenced everyone from Al Di Meola to Scotty Moore and John McLaughlin.**

Bebop

By the 1950s, the more complex bebop style was well established and a number of exciting guitarists began to appear: Barney Kessel was an acclaimed 'bop' soloist who became a session ace and played in bands fronted by Chico Marx and Oscar Peterson; Tal Farlow expanded the jazz–guitar chord vocabulary and was one of the first guitarists to be able to play a harmonic note from every fret of the instrument. Johnny Smith developed a subtle chord-oriented style and had a hit with the mellow 'Moonlight In Vermont' (1952).

Jazz Superstars

Jim Hall, Wes Montgomery and Kenny Burrell were the big jazz guitar names during the 1960s. Hall, unlike most other virtuosos, did not play lots of notes in his solos. In fact, he took the opposite approach and his phrases were usually thoughtful and lyrical, displaying a depth and subtlety that few other guitarists have ever been able to achieve. Wes Montgomery developed an unusual style by using his thumb as a pick. He was one of the first solo guitar players to effortlessly mix single notes with octaves and chords. Kenny Burrell forged a cool, tasteful bop style that established him as one of the most popular instrumental voices in jazz. It was also during the 1960s that the first jazz–guitar supergroup, Great Guitars, was born. Featuring Charlie Byrd, Herb Ellis and Barney Kessel,

Great Guitars was an eclectic mainstream band that pitted Byrd's Latin and classical style against the other two players' straight-ahead bop.

Joe Pass was another great jazz-guitar player to emerge during the 1960s, although he didn't become truly popular until the following decade. Using a phenomenal right-handed finger technique, he was able to play melodies, chords and bass lines all at the same time, and usually performed as a solo player. His album *Virtuoso* (1973), recorded for Norman Granz's Pablo label, made him a jazz star and he later accompanied the likes of Ella Fitzgerald, Count Basie, Duke Ellington and Oscar Peterson.

Jazz Fusion

During the 1970s, a number of guitar players began to fuse jazz with rock; the most influential of these were John McLaughlin, Al Di Meola and Allan Holdsworth. McLaughlin was the lead guitar player on Miles Davis's pioneering jazz-rock album *Bitches Brew* (1969), and he took the direction further with his own band the Mahavishnu Orchestra. Al Di Meola developed a formidable picking technique and fused jazz with Latin and rock styles on his critically acclaimed albums *Elegant Gypsy* (1977) and *Casino* (1978). Allan Holdsworth developed a truly unique and idiosyncratic style, characterized by spectacular chord voicings and fleet, legato solos. He became one of the decade's most sought-after fusion players.

A number of other great jazz-guitar players have emerged during the past 30 years, including Pat Metheny, Larry Carlton, Martin Taylor, Stanley Jordan, John Scofield, Bill Frisell and Scott Henderson. Of all these, Pat Metheny has enjoyed the most commercial success. He has forged an earthy and mellow jazz style that appeals to both hardcore jazzers and easy listeners. Few other jazz players have made their music so accessible without sacrificing their integrity.

LEFT: **Joe Pass began playing the guitar aged nine and covered a huge range of styles, including jazz, bebop, blues and Latin.**

ABOVE: **Jazz guitarist Stanley Jordan employs a unique, two-handed picking style to create his sound.**

Playing Jazz Guitar

All accomplished jazz musicians have a thorough knowledge and understanding of chords and scales, and you will need this too if you want to want to progress with this most demanding of musical styles. Most jazz tunes are based around extended chords (sevenths, ninths, 11ths and 13ths) so make sure you know how to play these all over the fingerboard. Jazz composers also like to raise or lower the fifth and ninth intervals in chords to create more colour within a piece, so it is a good idea to learn these chords as well. Another jazz trick is chord substitution,

which is often done by taking a chord with a dominant seventh note, and replacing it with another chord with a root note a tritone (a flattened fifth) higher – for example, substituting a D–flat 7 chord for a G minor chord.

‖ C	Am	Dm	G ‖

can become:

‖ Cmaj9	Am11	Dm9	G13 ‖

‖ Cmaj9	Am7♯5	Dm7♭5	G 7♯5♯9 ‖

‖ Cmaj9	E♭7	A♭9	D♭13 ‖

Try playing through these examples of jazz chord extensions, substitutions and altered jazz chords.

Chord Progression

The most common chord progression in jazz is the II–V–I, which uses chords based on the second, fifth and first notes of the major scale respectively. The II chord is a minor 7 chord, while the V is a dominant 7 and the I is a major 7 chord. So in the key of C, the basic II–V–I progression is Dm7, G7, CMaj7. You should familiarize yourself with this chord progression in different keys and in different positions on the fingerboard.

Improvisation

Jazz soloing involves a fair degree of improvisation, and to do this you will need to know a variety of scales and understand which chords they complement. All the major scale modes can be used, but the Dorian, Mixolydian and Ionian modes are of particular importance as they complement the minor 7, dominant 7 and major 7 chords and extensions that are so frequently used in jazz. Most jazz tunes also feature key changes, so the big challenge in jazz improvisation is to play over these changes without interrupting the melodic flow of a solo.

Other scales featured in jazz improvisation include the melodic and harmonic minor scales, the whole tone scale, the diminished scale and the chromatic scale. The latter is often used as it contains notes outside the key scale, which can be used to create extra tension in a melody or solo. Chromatic notes are usually played briefly in phrases that resolve on to key notes, although they can also be sustained to create more tension in the music.

Improvisation within a set piece is best approached by starting with the basic melody of a tune and playing around with variations of it. You should also jam regularly with other musicians as this will make you comfortable with playing over different chord progressions. Start with simple progressions that allow you to improvise with one or two scales, and then work at jamming over key changes. If you like a real challenge, you can also try 'free improvisation' – trying to create music on the spot with other improvisers without any obvious chord progressions or grooves.

Comping

Another important jazz–guitar skill you should work on is 'comping' – playing chord progressions as an accompaniment while others improvise. When you're comping, try substituting different chords and using different strum patterns to create more harmonic and rhythmic interest. The challenge here is to make the rhythm section sound as cool and varied as possible without losing the underlying groove.

Getting a Jazz Sound

Although jazz can be played on just about any type of guitar, you might want to try an electric archtop model such as the Gibson ES–175, as this produces a warm, mellow tone. A relatively clean amplifier such as a Polytone Mini Brute or Roland Jazz Chorus will complement this guitar perfectly. Set your amplifier to boost the low and mid-range frequencies, and cut back on the high frequencies to accentuate the warmth of the guitar.

Play through this example of chromatic playing in jazz improvisation, and then see if you can come up with your own.

If you want to play jazz rock, try a solid–body or semi–solid guitar with a rock amplifier as this will allow you to play soaring, sustained solos with minimal feedback. You can also use a chorus pedal to smoothen your chords, and an overdrive unit to make your solos sound more dynamic. Another effect worth trying is the ring modulator, a pedal that produces metallic, atonal sounds, and is great for creating a really 'out there' vibe!

RIGHT: **Gibson ES-175 guitars were developed in the 1940s. Archtop guitars like this are the favourite instruments of many jazz-guitar players.**

LEFT: **A Roland Jazz Chorus amplifier works well with a Gibson ES-175.**

You can also use an amp–modelling box like the Line 6 POD, or a virtual amp software package such as IK Multimedia's AmpliTube to create a realistic jazz–amp sound. If you're using a software sequencer package such as Cubase SX, Logic or Sonar to make recordings on your computer, you can also use the sequencer's built-in effects to add more colour and spice to your guitar sound.

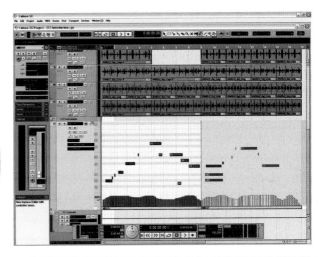

ABOVE: **Cubase has long been one of the most popular MIDI and audio sequencers for home recording.**

Rock

Musical Styles

By the late 1960s, many popular acts had grown tired of producing chart songs, and injected more attitude, experimentation and social conscience into their music. 'Rock' was born. The pioneers of this new style included Eric Clapton, the Rolling Stones and Jimi Hendrix, and their music appealed to record buyers who saw mainstream pop as tame.

Clapton first made a name for himself with John Mayall's Bluesbreakers in 1965 when he turned his amp up loud to get a more aggressive, sustained guitar tone. He formed Cream two years

later with bassist Jack Bruce and drummer Ginger Baker, and they were the first popular group to feature extended virtuoso solos in their music. By 1967, Hendrix had also extended the range of the electric guitar by coaxing sounds out of it that hadn't been heard before. Clapton and Hendrix based their playing around the blues scale and their solos were often long improvisations. Pop-guitar solos were usually brief instrumental fills between vocal passages, but 'classic rock' solos would often take up half of the song.

Birth of the Riff

Another prominent feature in early rock music was the riff – a repeated note or chord phrase over which the vocals and solos were projected. A classic example of this is Cream's 'Sunshine Of

BELOW: **In the 1970s, the Rolling Stones moved from their blues roots to a more polished rock sound.**

ABOVE: **Ritchie Blackmore of Deep Purple was famous for his complex and lengthy guitar solos.**

Your Love' (1968), a whole song based upon a simple, grinding riff. Other players such as Jimmy Page, Ritchie Blackmore and Tony Iommi latched on to the sheer power of this device and started to create even more powerful riffs, such as Led Zeppelin's 'Whole Lotta Love' (1969), Deep Purple's 'Speed King' (1970) and Black Sabbath's 'Paranoid' (1970).

Rock music marked a shift away from singles and towards albums; projects such as Led Zeppelin's acclaimed *Led Zeppelin II* (1969), Pink Floyd's psychedelic *Dark Side Of The Moon* (1973) and Mike Oldfield's instrumental *Tubular Bells* (1973) were all bestselling albums by artists who rarely recorded singles.

RIGHT: **For many, the Clash were the ultimate punk-rock band.**

Punk

In 1976, punk suddenly appeared and bands like the Sex Pistols, the Clash and the Damned introduced a basic rock style that relied more on attitude than technique. However, it was a short-lived trend and by the late 1970s rock began to fragment into a number of sub-genres, including new wave (an offshoot from punk), stadium rock (the likes of Bruce Springsteen and Queen) and the various strands of heavy metal that were beginning to develop in the US and UK.

New wave was essentially a generic term used for the wide range of British bands that followed on from punk. These included idiosyncratic artists such as Elvis Costello and XTC, straight-ahead rockers like the Pretenders and the Cars, white reggae or ska-pop bands including Madness and the Police, and a legion of synthesizer-driven bands. The genre died out when new bands such as the Smiths and REM began to appeal to more alternative rock fans.

Indie

The Smiths were the dominant British 'indie' rock band of the 1980s, and this was mainly down to the unique combination of singer Morrissey's forlorn crooning and the uncluttered rhythm guitar work of Johnny Marr. They recorded a number of hit singles and albums that laid down the foundations for the next generation of British guitar bands, before splitting up in 1987. REM also boasted a unique singer/guitarist combination – Michael Stipe's cryptic vocals and the ringing guitar hooks of Peter Buck. They are still going strong today.

Grunge

Despite the influx of fresh indie bands into the album and singles charts during the 1980s, most of the popular bands from this period, including Bon Jovi and Guns N' Roses, were purveyors of straight-ahead rock. By the end of the decade, however, grunge – a vibrant mixture of punk and heavy metal – became a prominent movement with Nirvana, a Seattle-based band, at the helm. Nirvana's success was down to a combination of strong material, stop-start dynamics, and the manic intensity of singer-guitarist Kurt Cobain. Unfortunately, Cobain suffered from drug addiction and manic depression, a combination that ended in suicide.

Variety of Rock Styles

A number of major song-orientated rock styles emerged during the 1990s including Britpop, which mixed songwriting – inspired by bands like the Beatles – with the more indie vibe of the Smiths. Suede, driven by the quasi-glam vocals of Brett Anderson and

RIGHT: **Bernard Butler helped to make Suede a huge success with his virtuoso riffs and squalls.**

sweeping guitar of Bernard Butler, pioneered this style, and they paved the way for the huge success of Oasis and Blur, bands from the north and south of England respectively. The decade also saw the rise of inventive alternative-rock bands including Radiohead, who combined intense guitar sounds with electronic drones and angst-driven lyrics. Today there is an unprecedented variety of rock styles and this range is still growing.

Playing Rock

If you want to be a proficient rock guitarist, you'll need to know a variety of basic chord shapes. The most common open chords (ones that include open strings as well as fretted ones) are A, Am, B7, C, C7, D, Dm, D7, E, E7, F, G and G7, which will allow you to play songs in the popular rock keys of A, C, D, E and G. The barre chords you should know are the barred versions of the A and E shapes (major barre chords) and Am and Em shapes (minor barre chords). These will allow you to play in any key you want, as barre shapes can be played anywhere on the fingerboard. Open chords are good for earthy strumming and would suit, for example, an Oasis-style song, while barre chords can be used to create a more powerful, aggressive sound for punk and hard-rock styles. Major chords are ideal for upbeat rock riffs, while minor ones are more suitable for ballads.

Power Chords

You should also familiarize yourself with the basic 'power chords' used in grunge and hard rock. These are two-note chords consisting of the first and fifth notes of the major scale, played on any two adjacent strings (such as the sixth and fifth strings, or fourth and third strings) with your index finger fretting the root note (on the thicker string) and your third finger fretting the fifth note (on the lighter string) two frets further up the fingerboard. To play an A power chord on the sixth and fifth

RIGHT: Fifth chords are often referred to as 'power chords' because of their solid sound.

C5

strings (E and A strings), for example, place your index finger behind the fifth fret on the sixth string and your third finger behind the seventh fret on the fifth string and then strum those strings only. To play a B power chord on the same two strings, simply move the shape two frets further up the guitar neck and so on.

Strumming and Picking

Rhythmically, rock is fairly straightforward, with emphasis mainly on the first and third beats of the bar. Strumming is usually performed with downstrokes, as these supply more power, although more intricate rhythms might require alternating downstrokes and upstrokes. Many rock guitarists also play chords as arpeggios (playing all the separate notes in ascending or descending order) with a plectrum or the fingers of the picking hand, to produce a more melodious sound. This is used to great effect in rock classics such as Led Zeppelin's 'Stairway To Heaven' and the Animals' 'House Of The Rising Sun'.

Most rock solos feature the pentatonic minor and blues scales (pages 108–10), and you should familiarize yourself with these scales if you want to play basic rock lead guitar. If you want to take things further, the major scale and the Mixolydian mode (pages 106–07 and 113) will add greater depth to your upbeat solos, and the Aeolian mode will come in handy for those haunting rock ballads.

Chords in grunge rhythm playing are largely played as fifth chords in order to achieve a controlled, tighter sound.

In classic rock repetitive guitar riffs, such as this one, often open and then form the basis of the songs.

Getting an Authentic Rock Sound

If you want to get a good rock-guitar sound you'll need an electric guitar and some sort of amplifier. The guitar can be a solid-body instrument (one made out of solid wood) or a semi-solid model (hollowed out). Solid-body guitars are great for producing a clear, sustained tone with minimal feedback, while semi-solid instruments produce a fat, warm sound but tend to feedback more when used at higher volumes.

Choosing the Right Amplifier

When it comes to amplifiers, you have a number of options, the most traditional of which would be a hardware, or freestanding, amp. These come in two flavours: valve (tube) amps, which are expensive but produce a fat, warm sound; and transistor amps, which are more affordable and reliable but not ideal if you're after a 'vintage' tone. If you choose to buy a hardware guitar amp, consider one with built-in effects capabilities (see below).

Hardware amps can get loud, and playing through one at home might upset your neighbours. In such a case, you should consider using an amplifier-modelling box such as a Line 6 POD, or a virtual amp software package such as IK Multimedia's AmpliTube. These come with an arsenal of realistic and ready-to-go rock presets, and you can use them at any volume you like. You can even gig with them, as long as the venue at which you're playing has a PA system.

The Right Effects

Effects pedals have been used extensively by rock players over the years and you too can use them to colour your guitar sound. A wah-wah pedal will come in handy for Hendrix-style soloing, while a phaser or flanger can be used to create rich textures and unique tones. An overdrive pedal might be useful for adding extra distortion during solos, and a compressor can be great for ironing out excessively loud sounds so that you end up with a more consistent volume. Most virtual amps come with a selection of built-in effects that you can use.

Metal

S
E
C
T
I
O
N

30

O
N
E

Although the term 'heavy metal' did not become firmly established until the late 1970s, the roots for this popular genre were firmly planted when Led Zeppelin and Black Sabbath were formed a decade earlier in the UK. Led Zeppelin was born when the Yardbirds split up and their guitarist, Jimmy Page, assembled a band of his own.

Influenced by the high-volume electric blues-rock guitar styles of Clapton and Hendrix, Page worked on his own ideas and came up with a heavy riff style that featured heavily – alongside Robert Plant's screaming vocals – in Zeppelin's 'Whole Lotta Love' (1969). Black Sabbath were formed that same year in Birmingham when guitarist Tony Iommi, singer Ozzy Osbourne, bassist Geezer Butler and drummer Bill Ward decided to start their own band.

ABOVE: **Van Halen revived interest in hard rock after a period of punk music.**

They developed a heavy-riff style that they used on 'Paranoid' and 'Iron Man' (both 1970). Although critics of the time mocked the band's obsession with death, destruction and mental illness, these themes were soon adopted by other bands such as Motörhead, Rainbow and the leather-clad Judas Priest – heavy metal was born!

NWOBHM

By the late 1970s, a number of new British bands had begun to emerge, including Iron Maiden, Saxon, Def Leppard and Samson. Although their music exuded less depth, range and invention than that of their predecessors, the style was a huge commercial success, and later categorized as a distinct sub-genre: the New

ABOVE: **Iron Maiden's trademark galloping rhythms and lyrics about fantasy or the devil have changed little over the years.**

ABOVE: **Metallica were the most successful of the thrash-metal bands, gradually developing their sound into heavy metal.**

Wave Of British Heavy Metal (NWOBHM). Meanwhile in the US, Van Halen introduced a new style of technically oriented heavy rock, showcasing the pioneering two-handed tapping techniques of guitarist Eddie Van Halen and dazzling showmanship of extrovert singer David Lee Roth, while over in Australia, school uniform-clad guitarist Angus Young and his pals had already forged their own heavy brand of 'no-nonsense rock'n'roll' in AC/DC.

Thrash

By the middle of the 1980s, the various hard-rock and metal styles had evolved further into other styles. Guitarists bored with the NWOBHM style decided they wanted to spice things up by playing harder and faster; thrash metal was born. The six primary thrash bands were Metallica, Slayer, Anthrax, Megadeth, Sepultura and Pantera. Metallica were by far the most successful of these. Their first few albums, *Kill 'Em All* (1983), *Ride The Lightning* (1984) and *Master Of Puppets* (1986), expanded the limits of metal by introducing intricately structured compositions played at an unheard-of speed.

Despite this, their attitude was refreshingly down-to-earth and unpretentious – they had street cred. Slayer developed an even faster style, delivering a stream of full-throttle metal with formidable chops, manic solos and deranged lyrics. Their fifth album, *Reign In Blood* (1986), is widely regarded as a metal classic. Various other sub-styles later evolved out of thrash, including death metal and black metal.

A Solo Effort

While Kirk Hammett of Metallica and Kerry King of Slayer
were thrashing their way around the globe, a handful of other
heavy-rock soloists such as Steve Vai and Yngwie Malmsteen
adopted a more 'arty' approach to their soloing. Vai played
for Alcatrazz, David Lee Roth and Whitesnake during the 1980s,
while releasing a series of solo albums showcasing his then
unheard-of whammy bar pyrotechnics and sublime modal
soloing. Along with his former mentor, Joe Satriani, Vai raised
the standard for rock-guitar virtuosity and, while neither of
them is considered to be a heavy-metal player, both have been
emulated by lead guitarists within the genre. Malmsteen fused
metal with the classical styles of Bach and Paganini, and became
the main pioneer of a style that later earned the amusing tag
'baroque and roll'.

Nu-metal

As the 1980s drew to an end, young audiences veered away from
thrash and 'flash' and opted for grunge bands like Nirvana and
Pearl Jam, but the early 1990s saw a new style emerge: nu-metal
bands such as Korn and Slipknot took the best elements of metal
and grunge, donned seven-string guitars, with the extra string
tuned down to a low B, and played a new style of subversive riff
that was hugely popular by the middle of the decade. The novelty
of all this wore off after a few years, although offshoot bands
including System of a Down, who mix quirky syncopations with
political lyrics, and Linkin Park, a rap-influenced nu-rock band,
have had success well into the new millennium.

ABOVE: **Krist Novoselic, Dave Grohl and Kurt Cobain of Nirvana,
the band that epitomized the grunge movement.**

RIGHT: The unpredictability and sheer energy of bands like Lamb of God ensures their continuing appeal.

Return of Thrash

As nu-metal began to wane, the thrash style suddenly became cool again, and the metal genre seemed to turn full circle as new American bands such as Shadows Fall, Chimaira, Killswitch Engage and Lamb of God fronted the unimaginatively named New Wave Of American Heavy Metal, while across the Atlantic, the likes of Rhapsody, Soilwork, Lacuna Coil, In Flames and Nightwish have kept the European metal flag flying.

Playing Metal

Although most metal guitarists know a variety of chord shapes, you can play a lot of music in this style with power chords. The most basic of these are two-note chords consisting of the first and fifth notes of the major scale, played on any two adjacent strings (such as the sixth and fifth strings, or fourth and third strings) with your index finger fretting the root note (on the thicker string), and your third finger fretting the fifth note (on the lighter string) two frets further up the fingerboard. To play a G power chord on the sixth and fifth strings (E and A), for example, place your index finger behind the third fret on the sixth string and your third finger behind the fifth fret on the fifth string and

RIGHT: The unpredictability and sheer energy of bands like Lamb of God ensures their continuing appeal.

C5

then strum those strings only. To play an A power chord on the same two strings, simply move the shape two frets further up the guitar neck, and so on.

LEFT: Power, or fifth, chords are often used in heavy-metal and rock music, along with distortion.

Add Power to Power Chords

You can strengthen your power chords further by adding an extra note, one that is an octave higher than your root note, on the next adjacent string. This is easy to do as it is in the same fret as the fifth interval note; to play a three-note G power chord on the sixth, fifth and fourth strings, adopt the fingering position already described, and place your fourth (little) finger behind the fifth fret on the fourth string to get that octave note. Bear in mind, though, that when you're playing any power chords, you should only strum the strings you are fretting – strumming any of the others will almost certainly produce a dreadful sound!

You should also learn the barred versions of the open A and E shapes and the open Am and Em shapes. These will allow you to play full major or minor chords in any key you want, as the shapes can be used anywhere on the fingerboard. Diminished and augmented chords can also be useful for metal as they produce a dissonant, disturbing effect – ideal for making threatening music!

ABOVE: **Strumming is an essential technique for the rhythm guitarist to master.**

Getting in Rhythm

Rhythmically, metal is usually relentless, with emphasis on insistent eighth- or sixteenth-note rhythms and a heavy accent on the first and other beats. Strumming is usually performed with downstrokes as these supply more power, although more intricate rhythms will sometimes require alternating downstrokes and upstrokes. Metal guitarists also perform muted versions of their riffs by resting the side of their picking hand against the strings. This creates a great dynamic effect when combined with unmuted versions of the riffs.

Scale-wise, you should learn the pentatonic scales and all the common major scale modes. If you want to play a thrash-related style you will have to learn to play them fast with alternate picking – realistically this might take a couple of years. If you want to get quicker results, practise hammer-ons and pull-offs (see pages 130–31), as these can easily be combined with picked notes to create rapid phrases within a solo. Another technique often used in metal is sweep-picking (also called economy-picking). By applying this technique to notes on adjacent strings, you can play an ascending line with a downstroke or a descending line with an upstroke. This works best for arpeggios, which are often one note per string.

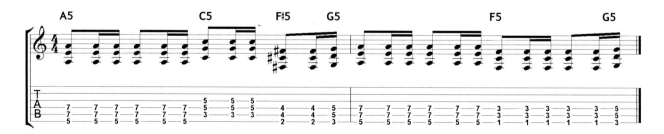

Try this example of metal rhythm playing, which uses sixteenth notes and power chords.

Getting an Authentic Metal Sound

If you want to get an authentic metal guitar sound you'll need a solid-body electric guitar and an amplifier with preamp distortion capabilities. Solid-body guitars are essential for producing a sustained, overdriven tone with minimal feedback at reasonably high volumes. All the classic Gibson models are great for this purpose but there is also a range of dedicated metal instruments available, including the ESP JH2, BC Rich Warlock, PRS Singlecut, Jackson Kelly and Washburn Dime models. All these guitars have humbucking pickups, which are ideal for an aggressive metal sound. You can also use guitars fitted with traditional single-coil pickups if you use an extra distortion pedal.

A thick pick is essential for metal music. A wide one (0.9 mm/0.003 in or thicker) will make a firmer contact with your strings than a thin one, making it easier to play riffs accurately and severely. Try several different picks out before you decide which one is best for you.

Which Amplifier is Best?

There are a number of dedicated metal amplifiers which can deliver a truly mean sound. These include valve-style (tube) models such as the Mesa Boogie Dual Rectifier, Marshall Mode 4, Hughes & Kettner Warp 7, Peavey 5150 and Randall Warhead models.

RIGHT: **Buying the right equipment is vital if you're trying to achieve an authentic metal sound. Pictured here is a Washburn Special Edition guitar.**

Metal can get rather loud, and if you want to play it without upsetting your neighbours, try an amp-modelling box such as a Line 6 POD, or a virtual amp software package like IK Multimedia's AmpliTube, Native Instruments' Guitar Rig or Steinberg's Warp VST. All of these feature some great metal presets, and you can use them at any volume you like. Get moshing!

BELOW: **No logo is more synonymous with heavy rock than the white-on-black Marshall stamp.**

Folk

Musical Styles

Folk music can be described as 'the natural expression of a people'. It exists in every country, whether it comes in the form of African tribal chants, Irish reels or Native American ceremonial songs.

Folk music is rarely written for profit and it is passed down from generation to generation, musician to musician. Popular folk music, as we know it today, can be traced directly back to the singer–songwriter Woody Guthrie. Born in 1912 in Okemah, Oklahoma, Guthrie grew up in a poor but musical family. During the drought and devastation of the Dust Bowl in the 1930s, Guthrie hitchhiked to California, writing songs like 'This Land Is Your Land' about his experiences. Guthrie became a famous champion for oppressed migrant workers, and a controversial social critic.

UK Folk Scene

In the UK, Renaissance lute music and American folk styles inspired the likes of Martin Carthy, Bert Jansch and John Renbourn to write strong, original guitar material during the 1960s. Ralph McTell also helped to popularize English folk with his hit 'Streets Of London' (1974). John Martyn and Christy Moore had developed unique and earthy folk styles by the 1970s and influenced many other singer–songwriters.

Guthrie's Influence

Guthrie made a number of recordings during the 1940s that influenced the likes of Pete Seeger, Bob Dylan and Joan Baez. The growing acceptance of these artists led to an explosion of folk–style pop music in the early 1960s, making stars of guitar-based groups like the Kingston Trio, the New Christy Minstrels and Peter, Paul & Mary. Such was their influence that the singer-songwriters of the late 1960s and early 1970s, such as Paul Simon, James Taylor, and Joni Mitchell were often called folk singers.

RIGHT: **Joan Baez and Bob Dylan helped to kick-start the folk revival of the 1960s.**

Playing Folk Music

In folk music, acoustic guitar can be either finger–picked or strummed with a plectrum. Typical finger–pickers will normally play the bass strings with the thumb and the treble strings with the index, middle and third fingers of their picking hand. Some players just use their index and middle fingers for the treble strings, and rest their other two fingers on the guitar body for support.

Guitarists often use the same finger–picking pattern for the whole song. Some virtuoso players adopt a more elaborate style, using all four fingers to play the treble strings or separate contrapuntal harmonies on the bass (with the thumb) and treble strings at the same time.

RIGHT: **Flat-picking is a playing style in which all notes, scalic and chordal, are articulated with a plectrum or thumb pick.**

Then stroke the plectrum across the strings, making sure that all the notes in the chord ring out cleanly.

Some acoustic flat-pickers can play extremely fast solos with a plectrum by alternating between upstrokes and downstrokes of the picking hand, while the fretting hand is fingering the notes. Accomplished bluegrass and 'crossover' guitarists like Ricky Skaggs and Steve Morse have used this style.

Flat-picking

A number of folk flat-pickers use a plectrum to play chord arpeggios across the strings, along with scales and licks. When accompanying vocals, these players tend to strum the same rhythm for an entire song. To strum with a plectrum, finger your chord with your fretting hand and angle the plectrum, pointing slightly upwards, in towards the strings with your picking hand.

Amplification

While most traditional folk music can be performed without any amplification, modern folk musicians will use a microphone or electronic pickup to amplify their acoustic guitars. They might also play an acoustic-electric guitar, which can be plugged into a specialized acoustic amp. Dedicated acoustic amplifiers bring out the rich tones of an acoustic guitar.

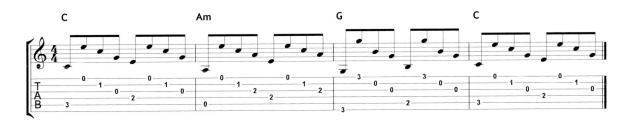

With any folk song, the words are the main focus, leaving the melody and structure simple, as in this example.

Typically, most traditional folk-guitar playing is based on finger-picking. The bass strings are usually picked by the thumb, whilst the index, middle and ring fingers are used to pick the treble strings. It is very rare for the little finger to be used.

Soul & Funk

Soul music emerged from rhythm and blues (R&B) during the 1950s, and Ray Charles is widely acknowledged to be the first soul star. Blind from the age of six, Charles became interested in gospel and blues music, and developed a unique singing and songwriting style.

Atlantic Records signed the young singer, who produced an almost instant hit with 'I Got A Woman' (1955). This was followed by a string of hits that combined his soulful vocal delivery with R&B rhythms. Soon, Atlantic and other labels, notably Memphis's Stax, began to penetrate the pop market with artists like Otis Redding, Jackie Wilson and Aretha Franklin.

The Motown Sound

By the mid-1960s, Berry Gordy had established Motown in Detroit, with artists such as Smokey Robinson, the Four Tops, Marvin Gaye, the Supremes and Stevie Wonder. Gordy used an in-house team of producers and composers, plus a formidable house band, the Funk Brothers, to forge the famous 'Motown sound' that has since been mimicked by countless soul producers worldwide.

ABOVE: **James Brown was key in turning soul music into funk and disco.**

developed a rhythm style so powerful that the melody and harmony were forced to take a back seat. It was popularized even further during the 1970s by acts such as the Isley Brothers, Earth Wind & Fire, Funkadelic and Chic.

Funk

Funk also emerged out of R&B and soul during the 1960s, when artists such as James Brown and his guitarist Jimmy Nolan

RIGHT: **This album sold a million copies and proved to be Funkadelic's breakthrough.**

Guitars in Funk

Guitars played a more prominent part in funk music than they did in soul, and many funk guitarists, including Ernie Isley, Prince and Johnny 'Guitar' Watson also became popular. Other guitar heroes of the funk movement

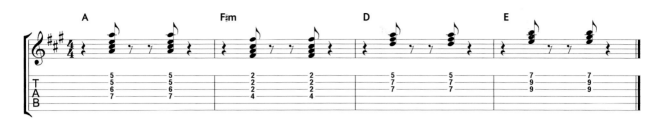

Playing guitar in a soul music context is all about timing and the interaction between instruments

Rather than playing long, elaborate solos, funk players tend to play short, rhythmic riffs, repeated throughout the song.

included Eddie Hazel of Parliament/Funkadelic and the tandem of Al McKay and Johnny Graham, who defined pop–funk guitar with Earth, Wind & Fire's hit 'Shining Star' (1975).

Playing Soul Guitar

Although soul and funk are both played by electric guitarists, the styles are different. Soul guitar is usually simple guitar chords or repetitive licks that fit in with a groove but don't interfere with the vocals. Funk guitar is usually a series of short licks that form a part of the groove upon which the song is based. These syncopated licks, along with the bass line, give the tune a funk 'edge'.

Playing Funk Guitar

Funk guitar tends to be played on treble strings and away from the chord root notes, as the bass player usually has the job of playing these. Funk guitarists often play extended chords such as ninths, minor ninths and 11ths to give the groove an almost jazzy feel. Guitarists usually play these chords with simple shapes that can be moved all around the guitar neck.

Another funk technique uses rhythmic strumming on strings muted by the fretting hand. Funk players alternate this with ringing extended chords or simple licks. Isaac Hayes' 'Shaft' (1971) features an example of this style.

Funk'n'Soul Effects

Both soul and funk music require a clean rhythm–guitar sound, and this is best obtained by playing a single coil guitar such as a Fender Stratocaster through an amplifier with the bass and mid-range trimmed down and a little bit of compression added. Wah-wah pedals have often been used to add more interest.

Other effects that have been commonly used with funk-guitar styles include phasers and flangers. You can easily get these sounds today with the current range of pedals and virtual effects available with computer music programs. Remember, however, the most important ingredient to make your guitar sound really funky is the rhythmic way you play it.

ABOVE: **Wah-wah pedals can be used to create a 'wack-wacka' funk rhythm.**

Country

Country music grew out of American folk music and now encompasses a variety of styles, including bluegrass, traditional C&W (country and western), western swing, country rock and Americana. Most country songs are built around simple chord progressions and melodies.

The country genre was 'born' in the late 1920s when Jimmie Rodgers and the Carter Family recorded for Victor Records. Rodgers had a unique voice and the Carters had an impressive repertoire of American folk tunes. They appeared regularly on the Grand Ole Opry, a legendary Nashville-based national radio show.

ABOVE: **Gene Autry had one of the most visually stunning Martin guitars, the D-45, made for him in 1932.**

By the 1930s, 'cowboy' singers such as Roy Rogers and Gene Autry appeared in popular films; western-swing bands like Bob Wills & his Texas Playboys successfully fused country folk with big band, blues, Dixieland and Hawaiian sounds; and Bill Monroe introduced a more Celtic-influenced bluegrass style. In the 1940s, country spawned its first superstar, Hank Williams, whose 'Lovesick Blues' (1949), 'Cold, Cold Heart' (1951) and 'Jambalaya (On the Bayou)' (1952) would be covered by country and pop artists alike for decades.

Nashville

Another development was 'the Nashville sound', a blend of country and pop that appeared during the 1950s. It propelled artists such as Jim Reeves, Eddy Arnold and Patsy Cline into the limelight with lush, densely arranged ballads and honky-tonk stories. In reaction to the Nashville sound, artists like Buck Owens, Johnny Cash and Merle Haggard got a foothold in the 1960s, emphasizing country's roots and singing about societal outcasts, such as prisoners. Willie Nelson, Waylon Jennings and others parlayed these attitudes into the 'Outlaw' movement of the 1970s , while bands like Lynyrd Skynyrd and Alabama fused country with rock.

BELOW: **Willie Nelson and Waylon Jennings were the 'most wanted' of the outlaw movement.**

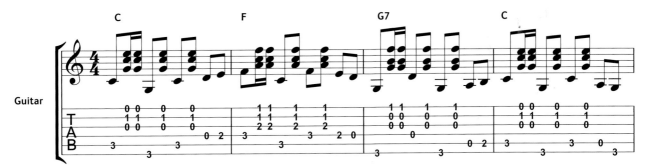

The classic country-music guitar figure would be played on an acoustic instrument, providing a simple but steady melodic and rhythmic structure.

RIGHT: **Violining: the little finger of the picking hand adjusts the volume while playing.**

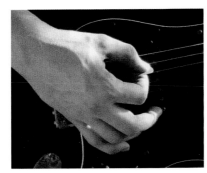

Modern Country

During the 1980s, artists such as Ricky Skaggs, the Judds and Randy Travis spearheaded a neotraditionalist movement that grew into the phenomenal crossover success enjoyed by Garth Brooks, Reba McEntire, Alan Jackson, Vince Gill, the Dixie Chicks and others in the 1990s and beyond.

Country–guitar virtuosos have included finger–picking pioneers like Merle Travis and Doc Watson; and dynamic electric players like Albert Lee, Danny Gatton and Steve Morse. Some versatile players, like Chet Atkins, Vince Gill and Brad Paisley, have become international superstars.

Playing Country

Country–music acoustic guitarists employ the same techniques as folk players. However, country electric–guitar players use a lot of note bends in their solos. Of particular importance is the 'harmony bend', a pedal–steel type effect where some notes are held while another is bent. Country players also use double–stops (two–note chords), hammer–ons, pull–offs and slides to add further colour to their solos. Another specialist country technique is 'chicken picking', a damped, staccato right–hand style employed by James Burton and others for fast, funky phrases.

Another neat country trick is to use the guitar's volume control (or a volume pedal) to fade chords and notes in from nothing to give a nice, soft attack to the tone – a technique known as 'violining'.

The Right Guitar

The Fender Telecaster produces a clean, twangy sound and has probably been favoured by more country players than any other electric guitar. If you haven't got a Telecaster, you can approximate its sound by choosing the bridge pickup on any single-coil guitar, selecting a clean amplifier sound and cutting back on your mid-range. However, modern Nashville guitarists can be seen playing everything from a Fender Strat to dual-humbucker shredders more closely associated with heavy metal.

RIGHT: **A Fender Telecaster, the first production-made solid electric guitar.**

Musical **Styles**

Classical

Although guitar-like instruments have been around since the Middle Ages, the 'classical' guitar as we know it today didn't appear until the middle of the nineteenth century. Its repertoire was non-existent until Andrés Segovia started performing guitar arrangements of pieces by Bach, Handel and others some 50 years later.

BELOW: **Self-taught, Andrés Segovia plucked the strings with a combination of flesh and nail that helped him produce a wide range of tones.**

Segovia put the classical guitar on the map as a 'serious' instrument and personally taught a further generation of classical virtuosos, including Alirio Diaz, Julian Bream, Christopher Parkening, Eliot Fisk, John Williams and Alexandre Lagoya. These players took the classical technique to new heights and broadened its repertoire further by performing contributions from other new composers.

Playing Classical Guitar

To adopt the correct classical guitar posture, sit on a chair and rest the centre of your instrument's body on your left leg. Angle the neck upwards so that your left arm (assuming you're a right-handed player) can reach the fingerboard without any obstructions. Rest your right arm on the upper edge of the guitar's body so that you can position your right hand's fingers directly over the strings near the sound hole. You might also want to place your left foot on a small footstool, bringing your left leg up a little to support the instrument. Practise picking up the guitar and getting into playing position so that it feels natural and easy. Make sure you feel relaxed and there is no tension in your limbs.

ABOVE: **Taught by Andrés Segovia, Julian Bream also studied piano, cello, harmony and composition at the Royal College of Music, London.**

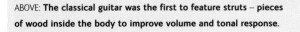

ABOVE: **The classical guitar was the first to feature struts – pieces of wood inside the body to improve volume and tonal response.**

Classical Techniques

The classical guitar is picked by the tips/nails of the thumb and first three fingers of the right hand (or left hand for left-handed players) so it is important to keep these tidy. These fingers are labelled as follows after their Spanish names: P = pulgar (thumb), I = indice (index finger), M = medio (middle finger) and A = anular (third finger).

RIGHT: **Classical guitarists use their thumb and first three fingers to pick strings, as opposed to a plectrum.**

To get a basic idea of how it all works, start to play the open sixth string (the thickest string) with a downward movement of the tip of your thumb, and then, while this low note is still ringing out, strike the open third, second and first strings consecutively with upward movements from your index, middle and third fingers respectively. Repeat this series of movements again and again

so that you are following the pattern PIMA PIMA PIMA PIMA. Now start to reverse the order of your finger movements so that your thumb stroke is followed by your third finger, your middle finger and then your index finger: PAMI PAMI PAMI PAMI. Then combine the two exercises so that you alternate between the two: PIMA PAMI PIMA PAMI. Once you feel comfortable with these variations, you'll be in a position to start learning classical guitar music.

The fretting hand is equally important as it has to articulate the notes you are picking. With your thumb behind the neck, position your fingers so that they arch around and their fingertips are perpendicular to the strings. You must have very short fingernails on this hand so that you can press down on the strings and articulate notes cleanly and accurately. The fretting hand switches between chordal positions (for playing arpeggios) and a one-finger-per-fret style (for scalar melodies).

Classical guitarists employ a tremolo technique which involves the I, M and A fingers playing a continuous, repeating pattern on a single note, a 'ligato' technique that involves striking a note and then hammering on to another note on the same string with a finger, and rubato, a technique involving the use of subtle tempo changes to accentuate and embellish specific parts of the music.

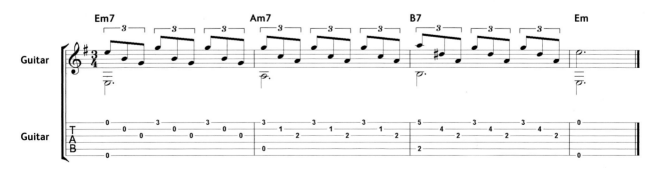

If you can read music, try playing through this excerpt from Francisco Tárrega's Étude in E Minor, for a true idea of how music for the classical guitar can sound.

Musical Styles

Reggae

Reggae is a Jamaican style of music characterized by four beats to the measure with the off-beats (beats two and four) strongly accented. It evolved from ska, a music style born in the early 1960s when Jamaican musicians changed the emphasis of the basic R&B rhythm from the first and third beats in the measure to the second and fourth.

Ska

The most influential ska group was the Skatalites, a collection of classically trained musicians who played to dancehall crowds in Jamaica's capital, Kingston. They adopted a tight, disciplined and steady rhythm, designed to whip the dancers into a frenzy.

Rocksteady

During the late 1960s, producers slowed the beat down to create a more soulful, laid-back reggae style called rocksteady. The main exponents of this style included Desmond Dekker, who had the No. 1 hit 'Israelites' (1969), and Jimmy Cliff, singer of 'Wonderful World' (1969). Many of their hits featured charismatic guitar lines from Ernest Ranglin, a renowned reggae session guitarist.

Roots

Roots reggae introduced an even more laid-back rhythm with a prominent bass line in the 1970s. Eric Clapton's cover of Bob Marley's 'I Shot The Sheriff' (1974) helped to introduce the style to the world, and Marley later became a megastar with songs like 'No Woman No Cry' (1975), 'Jamming' (1977) and 'Is This Love' (1978),

before he died of cancer in 1981. Formed with Bunny Wailer and Peter Tosh, Marley's group, the Wailers, were the most prominent group to record in the ska, rocksteady and reggae periods.

Reggae Today

The popularity of ska, rocksteady and roots reggae spawned a number of other sub-genres: dub, an instrumental style with all the vocals (except voice effects) removed; ragga, a harsher, more jagged style; and dancehall, a stripped-down version with just drums, bass and vocals. Ska and reggae also influenced groups like Madness, UB40, Aswad, the Police and Musical Youth, who all had considerable chart success during the 1980s. Even pop, punk and alternative artists as diverse as 10cc, the Clash and Frank Zappa have employed catchy reggae rhythms for songs.

ABOVE: **Hugely popular in the 1980s, Madness revived the ska style for a new audience.**

Reggae music is characterized by the emphasis on the off-beat, which pulls the tempo back and gives the music a laid-back feel.

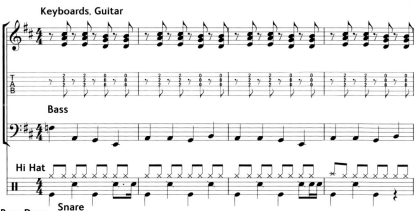

Ska features a very simple bass on the beat with the keyboards and guitar bouncing off the beat. The resulting um-ska sound, which gave ska its name, is the basis for virtually all reggae styles that followed.

chords in an entire song. There is rarely any lead guitar in the style, although a second guitarist will often play repetitive note phrases with note damping (with the palm of the picking hand) to enhance the groove.

You can use just about any electric solid-body guitar and any reasonable amp to play reggae, but you will probably want to keep the sound clean and turn down your bass and mid-range controls, so that your guitar doesn't end up fighting against that heavy bass! Reggae rhythms can be very repetitive, so you might want to use some effects pedals, such as digital delay, wah or chorus to create more interest in the rhythm-guitar parts.

Playing Ska Guitar

While reggae uses two skanks per bar, ska uses four, and each of these is between the beats, so you need to be accurate with your strumming and use only upward strums over the guitar's thinner strings.

Playing Reggae Guitar

Reggae rhythm guitar is usually played as clean 'skanks' (downstrokes), with the strings damped as soon as the chord is sounded, although double-skank rhythms, where the downstrokes are swiftly followed by upstrokes, are sometimes employed. The chord progressions are simple; sometimes there are only two

RIGHT: Aswad have a unique sound combining jazz, funk, soul and fusion layered over a rock-steady reggae beat.

Your playing should complement the grooves of the bassist and drummer in your band, so that you're creating a steady, even rhythm. Listen to recordings by the Wailers, Desmond Dekker, Peter Tosh, Duke Reid or Aswad and you'll soon get the idea!

Flamenco

Musical Styles

46

Flamenco music can be traced back to mid-nineteenth-century Spain, when Andalucian musicians developed a 'café cantante' guitar style to accompany singers and dancers at local cafés. Although the earliest Spanish guitar players had relatively unrefined skills, the style evolved over the next half-century, until Ramon Montoya emerged in the early twentieth century as the first celebrated modern flamenco player.

Montoya made more than 700 recordings with top singers and was a huge influence on the next generation of flamenco guitarists, including his nephew Carlos Montoya, who developed the style further between the 1940s and 1960s. His influence was also felt by flamenco greats Paco Peña, Juan Martín and Paco de Lucía.

ABOVE: **Renowned flamenco guitarist Paco de Lucía has one of the fastest, most intricate finger-picking techniques in the world.**

Flamenco Today

Today a number of talented flamenco guitarists are recognized worldwide, but perhaps the most well known is Paco de Lucía. In addition to a brilliant recording and performing career, de Lucía was the first flamenco player to cross over into other styles of music. He made a number of critically acclaimed acoustic guitar trio recordings with jazz–rock maestros

RIGHT: **Flamenco dancing was developed by Spanish gypsies in the fifteenth century.**

Al Di Meola and John McLaughlin, including *Friday Night In San Francisco* (1980) and *The Guitar Trio* (1996). Despite this, de Lucía's style has always remained decidedly flamenco.

Playing Flamenco

While classical guitarists aim for a clean, elegant style, flamenco players tend to favour a more earthy, powerful and dynamic sound. Flamenco guitarists use a number of specialist techniques, including rasgueado, tremolo and golpe. A rasgueado is a unique strumming technique created by fanning or brushing the fingers

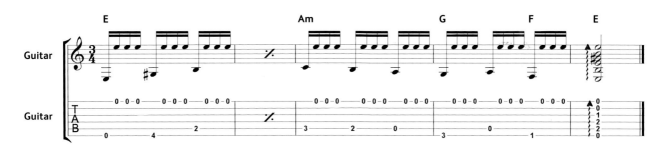

In flamenco, the exact guitar lines played are normally improvised and developed from a standard theme.

across the strings to generate a circular effect. A tremolo involves playing a single note repeatedly and swiftly with the picking-hand fingers to produce long, sustained notes. A golpe is a percussive effect performed by tapping the instrument's body with the picking hand to reinforce rhythms and accents in the music.

There are dozens of different flamenco styles defined by characteristic melodic, rhythmic and harmonic structures. The most popular include bulerías, soleares, alegrías, fandangos, rondeñas and tanguillos. Each one has a distinctive mood, although many are actually regional variants of each other. Flamenco guitarists also play a number of other folk- and Latin-influenced styles including garrotín, farruca, guajiras and rhumba. The traditional flamenco posture has the guitar resting against the upper part of the body and held tightly between thigh and upper right arm.

Techniques

While the capo is rarely used in classical-guitar playing, it is commonly used in flamenco music as it allows the guitarist to change keys while preserving his or her favourite chord voicings. Flamenco players also use the capo because it shortens the vibrating string length and can thus brighten the instrument's sound. Flamenco guitarists make greater use of their thumbs and fingers than classical players: in classical music, the thumb is usually limited to playing the bass notes, while the next three fingers concentrate on the higher strings; in flamenco, the thumb

can range over all six strings and all four picking-hand fingers are usually employed. Flamenco players also mute the strings with their left hand while strumming with the right to produce a percussive, rhythmic style.

LEFT: **A capo is a simple device that allows the pitch of the guitar's open strings to be changed.**

Flamenco Guitar

Although flamenco guitars look similar to classical instruments, they are actually quite different; classical guitars tend to have deep rosewood bodies while flamenco instruments are thinner and usually constructed from cypress. Flamenco guitars tend to produce a louder, more penetrating sound than classical instruments. They also have their strings set lower and feature a plastic shield on the soundboard to protect the body from damage caused by the energetic finger rasgueados and golpes employed by the players.

RIGHT: **A flamenco guitar is deceptively similar to – but slightly smaller than – a typical classical guitar.**

Latin

Musical Styles

'Latin' music is a generic term used to describe a diverse range of musical styles from various regions of Central and South America. These include well-known dance rhythms such as the tango, samba, bossa nova, rhumba, mambo, cha-cha and salsa, as well as Latin pop and rock.

The Tango

The first popular Latin dance rhythm to achieve worldwide recognition was the tango. Characterized by long, gliding steps and sudden pauses, the style was popular with working-class Argentinians during the 1890s and it became internationally established by 1910. The stop-start choreography was erotic and employed close contact between the male and female dancers.

Bossa Nova

By the middle of the twentieth century, a number of more 'regular' Afro-Cuban rhythms, such as the mambo, samba and cha-cha had been established, but the guitar did not become a prominent instrument in the genre until Antonio Carlos Jobim helped to popularize the laid-back bossa nova rhythm.

ABOVE: Rio de Janeiro, Brazil, is home to the world-famous carnival, as well as to rhythms such as the samba.

Jobim became an international star when Stan Getz and Charlie Byrd scored a surprise hit with his laid-back bossa nova tune 'Desafinado' (1962). The whole world suddenly went mad for the new Brazilian rhythm and Jobim recorded a number of successful easy-listening albums during the early to mid-1960s. The hit trend ran out of commercial steam in the late 1960s, but the bossa nova rhythm remains a popular device in many styles of music.

With his self-named band Carlos Santana created a unique blend of blues rock, Latin grooves and psychedelia and brought Latin music rhythms to a wider rock audience. Other notables who have fused rock- and blues-guitar sounds with

BELOW: **Santana in 1968. Their music is a fusion of Latin styles and blues rock.**

ABOVE: **Brazilian band Trio Mocoto have been around since the late 1960s, and have created a distinctive samba-soul-rock sound.**

Latin grooves include Ry Cooder, an acclaimed multi-genre electric guitarist; Sepultura, the most popular heavy-metal band to emerge from Brazil; and Iconoclasta, an influential Mexican prog-rock band.

The Samba

The samba is another hugely popular Afro-Cuban rhythm. Unlike the laid-back bossa nova, samba is upbeat and associated with parties and celebrations. It is heavily featured at the annual Rio de Janeiro carnivals and has been employed by artists as diverse as Latin band Trio Mocoto, fusion guitarist Pat Metheny and prog-rock keyboardist Patrick Moraz. Latin rhythms have also featured in many pop hits during the past 40 years, and artists such as Astrud Gilberto, Edmundo Ros, Ruben Blades, Los Lobos, Gloria Estefan and Ricky Martin have all enjoyed successful careers as Latin pop stars.

Playing Latin Guitar

Latin guitar music can be played on both acoustic and electric instruments. Jobim's bossa nova tunes should be approached on a mellow-sounding guitar, preferably with gut or nylon strings. If you are playing by yourself, you probably won't need an acoustic amplifier, unless you are performing live. However, if you want to play this music with a band, you will need a decent acoustic amplifier to help your instrument stand out among other instruments. Bossa nova tunes tend to be intimate and understated affairs, so care is needed not to ruin a piece by overplaying!

If you want to get a Santana-style electric sound, you'll need a solid-body guitar with humbucking pickups and a reasonably powerful amplifier that will allow you to add just enough distortion to give your sound an edge. The most important thing to bear in mind while playing any Latin style is to articulate and phrase in a way that emphasizes or complements the underlying groove – because it is this groove that gives all Latin music its distinct vibe.

RIGHT: **Emulate Carlos Santana's distinctive sound with a guitar such as this solid-body Fender Stratocaster.**

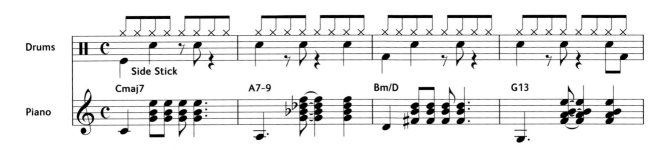

An example of a typical bossa nova rhythm. The drum pattern is played over the top of an off-beat counter rhythm. The guitar chords are given along with the piano music.

African

LEFT: **Biggie Tembo**, lead singer of Zimbabwean guitar band the Bhundu Boys, named the group after his experiences as a runner – or 'bhundu boy' – for the rebels in his country's struggle for liberation.

Their mixture of complex rhythms, spoken language and natural sounds may sound cacophonous to the uninitiated, but their music does have a meaning.

Soukous

A number of guitar-based African music styles have appeared since the beginning of the twentieth century and one of the most documented is soukous, a style which emerged from the Congo region 100 years ago. This music style was originally performed on guitar, likembe ('thumb piano') and bottle at European work camps during the first quarter of the twentieth century. From these humble beginnings it evolved into a popular 'rhumba' style played by extended band line-ups featuring numerous guitars, bass, keyboards, brass, drums and vocals (sung in Lingala, the trade

Although African music clearly laid down the foundations for the guitar-based genres of blues and rock, relatively few African guitar players have been celebrated outside their own continent. This is mainly because the harmonies and melodies in African musical styles are often different to those that 'western' ears are used to hearing.

The African concept of music is different from that in the West; while western musicians make music that is intended to be pleasing to a listener's ear, traditional African musicians are expressing life as they know it through the medium of sound.

RIGHT: **Kanda Bongo Man** emigrated to Paris from the Congo region to achieve recognition away from the competition.

LEFT: **Ali Farka Toure is a blues guitarist often compared to John Lee Hooker.**

in 1939 in Mali and started to learn the guitar at the age of seven. He practised obsessively and developed his own blues style, characterized by a rhythmic, foot-stomping guitar style and a low vocal delivery. He has often been called the 'African John Lee Hooker' because of similarities between his style and that of the legendary American bluesman. Toure has recorded and performed with many other internationally acclaimed musicians including Ry Cooder, Taj Mahal and the Chieftains.

Playing African Guitar

Most African guitarists play electric instruments with regular tuning, and a typical African band will have two, three or even four guitar players. A clear tone with a fair amount of treble and mid-range is essential for African popular music.

A number of African players with limited financial resources made their own guitars out of oilcans, and the idea caught on after it became clear that these guitars produced a surprisingly charismatic sound. Most African guitar playing is rhythm guitar, and this can range from simple strumming to two or three contrapuntal rhythm melodies being played at the same time by different players. Major chords are used extensively and sometimes even in places where you might expect to hear minor chords. This approach lends a bright, optimistic, 'carnival' vibe to the material that makes it very infectious. African pop melodies also tend to be major-scale oriented and this contributes towards the lively, celebratory sound of the music.

language of the Congo region). Modern performers of this style include Souzy Kasseya, Kanda Bongo Man, Theo Blaise, Fidele Zizi, Victoria and Orchestre Virunga.

The best-known guitarist to hail from the Congo region was Franco (Francois Luambo Makiadi). Born in 1938, Franco began playing a home-made guitar made out of tin cans and stripped electrical wire. He formed the group OK Jazz and became well-known for his social commentary and satire as much as his dexterous guitar playing. His most notable releases include 'Jackie' (1974), a sexually explicit song for which he was briefly sent to jail, and 'Tailleur' (1980), a dance piece lampooning the prime minister of Congo. Franco died of an AIDS-related illness in 1989.

Ali Farka Toure

Ali Farka Toure is the continent's most celebrated electric guitarist. Toure was born

LEFT: **'Afri-can' guitars produced by the African Guitars company are high-specification models made out of oilcans.**

The Acoustic Guitar

History of the Guitar

The ancestor of the modern guitar emerged in the Middle East and shared a common origin with Asian and Indian instruments. The oldest known image of a guitar precursor is a 3,300–year–old stone carving. The word guitar comes from the Spanish *guitarra*, and traces back to the Latin *cithara*.

Around 40 AD, Romans brought the cithara to Hispania, where it shared space with the four–string Moorish oud and the six–string

RIGHT: **The European lute is an early ancestor of the acoustic guitar. Much Renaissance lute music can be played on a guitar by tuning the guitar's third string down by a half-tone.**

Scandinavian lut (lute). By 1200 AD, the four–string 'guitar' had evolved into two types: the guitarra morisca (Moorish guitar), which had a rounded back, wide fingerboard and several soundholes; and the guitarra latina (Latin guitar), which had one soundhole and a narrower neck.

Ultimately, the Spanish vihuela, with its lute–style tuning and guitar–like body, spawned the modern guitar. Antonio Torres Jurado (1817–92), of Seville, and Louis Panormo (active 1820s–40s), of London are credited with standardizing the guitar's dimensions and improving its bracing.

Anatomy of an Acoustic Guitar

The wood used for the body, top and neck of an acoustic guitar significantly affects the tone and performance of the instrument.

ABOVE: **The shape of the vihuela is very similar to that of the modern guitar.**

1 Top

The top of the guitar can be made from spruce, maple or koa wood, each of which produces a unique sound. Rosewood, alder, poplar, basswood and even bamboo may also be used. The top is usually made from one piece of close-grained wood, split in two and laid in halves. This process is called 'book-matching'. A rosette may be inlaid around the soundhole or a thin strip of darker wood may sometimes be inlaid to enhance the guitar's appearance.

2 Bridge

Steel-string guitars have non-adjustable bridges fixed to the guitar top. The bridge transmits the string vibrations to the top, which in turn vibrates and amplifies the sound of the guitar. The bridge is often made of rosewood or ebony and is fitted with a bone or plastic saddle.

3 Bracing

Braces, or 'ribs', are thin pieces of wood that support the top and back of the guitar inside the body. The braces strengthen the guitar and can greatly affect the guitar's tone. The steel-string acoustic guitar uses the traditional 'X' brace pattern, with the centre of the X positioned just below the soundhole.

4 Body

The acoustic guitar has a hollow body, usually made of mahogany. The body has waisted sides and may also have a cutaway on the upper bout to enable access to the higher frets. Binding is inlaid around the body at the point where the top and back meet the sides of the guitar. The guitar is finished with polyester, polyurethane or nitro-cellulose lacquer.

5 Neck

Necks are usually made of the same wood as the guitar's back and sides. The neck has an adjustable truss rod inside, which helps to keep the neck properly aligned. On an acoustic guitar the neck normally meets the body at the 14th fret.

6 Frets and Fingerboard

A rosewood or ebony fingerboard is attached to the neck and fitted with 20 or 21 frets. Position markers are laid into the fingerboard at the 3rd, 5th, 7th, 9th and 12th frets to aid the guitarist. Corresponding markers are usually laid into the edge of the fingerboard.

7 Strings

On a steel-string acoustic guitar, strings one, two and three are plain lengths of wire, usually nickel, of different thicknesses (gauges). Strings four, five and six have an additional winding of copper throughout the length of the strings. On a classical guitar, strings four, five and six are also 'wound', but strings one, two and three are made of nylon, a softer material that creates the mellow sound of the classic guitar, often erroneously called gut-string guitar.

SECTION ONE

53

The Electric Guitar

The electric guitar is a marriage of twentieth-century technology to the time-honored convenience and playability of the classical and Spanish guitar. The first electric versions of the acoustic guitar were made in the early 1900s, a result of ongoing efforts by inventors, tinkerers and musicians. In the 1950s, Leo Fender developed the first mass-produced and affordable electric guitar.

The modern electric guitar is the result of a half-century of ideas and imagination. Yet the first commercially successful electric guitars – the Fender Stratocaster and Telecaster – are still produced today. Anyone transported in time from 1950 to today would see nothing unusual in a Fender Telecaster built in a South Korean factory just the day before. The design classic has stood the test of time.

LEFT: First created in 1954 by Leo Fender, the Stratocaster is a design classic.

How Do They Work?

Electric guitars make sound by creating electromagnetic induction through pickups containing copper wire wrapped around a magnet. The discovery by Michael Faraday and Joseph Henry in 1831 of electro-magnetic induction brought about many technological benefits, including the invention of the telephone some 45 years later. Some say that it was not long before guitar players were experimenting with telephone receivers attached to acoustic guitars in an effort to become amplified.

The First Electric Guitars

Some of the earliest electric guitars adapted hollow-bodied acoustic instruments and used tungsten pickups. This type of guitar was first manufactured in 1931 by the Electro String Instrument Corporation under the direction of Adolph Rickenbacher and George Beauchamp. The guitar was called a Rickenbacker.

Another early solid-body electric guitar was designed and built by musician and inventor Les Paul in the early 1940s. His 'log guitar' consisted of a simple 4 x 4 wood post with a neck attached to it and home-made pickups and hardware. The instrument was patented and is often considered to be the first of its kind, although it shares nothing in design or hardware with the solid-body 'Les Paul' model sold by Gibson.

BELOW: The Rickenbacker, the world's first electric guitar, was later nicknamed the 'Frying Pan'.

LEFT: **The Esquire was the first solid-body electric guitar manufactured by Fender in 1950.**

In 1946, radio repairman and amplifier-maker Clarence Leonidas Fender, better known as Leo Fender, designed the first commercially successful solid-body electric guitar with a single magnetic pickup, which was initially named the Esquire. This was a departure from the typically hollow-bodied Jazz-oriented instruments of the time and immediately found favor with country & western artists in California. The two-pickup version of the Esquire was called the Broadcaster. However, Gretsch had a drum set marketed with a similar name (Broadkaster), so Fender changed the name to Telecaster.

Modern Pickups

A magnetic pickup consists of a permanent magnet wrapped with a coil of a few thousand turns of fine enamelled copper wire. The single-coil pickup can have subtle variances in tone, even when mass-produced successfully, as were the classic pickups of the original Telecaster and Stratocaster. That's why some Strats may sound magnificent and others merely acceptable. One problem with single-coil electromagnetic pickups is that they pick up hum along with the musical signal.

The desire for a guitar that could reject this unwanted hum led to the development of the humbucking pickup concurrently and independently by Gibson and Gretsch. A humbucking pickup generally comprises two standard pickups wired together with identical coils bathed in fields of opposite magnetic polarity. The two coils are wired to cancel the

ABOVE: **Single-coil pickups on a Fender Stratocaster. These are used to detect the vibrations of a guitar string that can then be amplified.**

hum produced by each. The signal from the vibrations of the guitar strings is captured by both pickups and added together, doubling the output. Side effects are a rounder tone with fewer highs than that produced by a Strat or Tele, and a hotter signal more easily able to overdrive an amp for a warm distortion effect.

BELOW: **A super humbucker V2 pickup on an Ibanez Studio electric guitar. Humbucking pickups are generally made up of two single pickups wired together.**

Anatomy of an Electric Guitar

The electric guitar is not complex, but the pieces of the electric guitar must fit together and match each other perfectly or the guitar will never reach its potential. Here are some of the most important ingredients:

① Fingerboard

The fingerboard covers the face of the neck and provides a playing surface for the guitarist. The fingerboard can be made of any suitable material but they are usually made of rosewood

BELOW: **Maple is a hardwood commonly used in the manufacture of guitars, particularly the fingerboards and necks of Fender solid-bodies, such as the Telecaster or Stratocaster.**

or maple. Frets are set into the fingerboard to enable the guitarist to find and stop the string at the desired point quickly.

The fingerboard can have 21, 22 or 24 frets, depending on the model of guitar. Fingerboard material also influences the tone of the guitar. Maple and ebony produce a brighter tone while rosewood has a darker tone. These days, some manufacturers are making fingerboards from synthetic materials such as graphite.

② Body

This is usually wooden, made of ash, elder or basswood depending on the origin of the instrument. Expensive US-produced guitars are made of rare hardwoods such as mahogany and maple. As good-quality wood becomes harder to obtain, guitars are nearly always made of one or more pieces of wood sandwiched together to create a body of the required depth. Modern guitar manufacturers such as Ibanez have created guitars with no wooden parts, while Gibson has a range of 'Smart Wood' guitars made from wood cut from sustainable forests.

③ Nut and Frets

The nut of the guitar is placed at the end of the fingerboard just below the headstock, where it provides one of the two anchor points (the other being the bridge saddle) for the string. Nickel silver frets are fitted to the fingerboard underneath the strings. The frets are placed at precise points on the fingerboard to enable the guitarist to play in tune. Frets wear down over time and change the tone of the guitar. The distance between the nut and the bridge saddle is extremely important and dictates the scale of the guitar. Fender instruments have a 25-in (63.5-cm) scale while Gibson instruments have a slightly smaller 24-in (61-cm) scale.

4 Hardware

Pickups, bridge and electronics are fundamental to the tone of the electric guitar. Single-coil pickups produce a very bright sound; twin-coil pickups have a warmer, less defined sound. Bridges are usually adjustable, which lets you adjust the action (height) of the strings and help keep the guitar's intonation true. Bridge assemblies may be either fixed or vibrato (tremolo) models. Vibrato models enable the player to produce amazing sounds by pressing on the vibrato arm to lower the tension in the strings. Tension is returned when the player releases the arm and springs pull the bridge back into place. Certain guitars also have a hardware tailpiece, where the strings terminate, rather than a string-through design, in which strings are fed through the back of the guitar and over the bridge before being stretched to the tuners on the headstock.

5 Neck

The neck of the guitar is often made from dense maple or ash. The wood needs to be hard and stable as the neck is under tension. Depending on the model of guitar the neck may either be joined to the body with three or four long screws, or by a traditional wood joint and string glue. If the neck is screwed to the body it is called a 'bolt-on neck'. Necks that are jointed to the body are called 'set-in'. Bolted and jointed necks have different tonal characteristics: bolted necks are thought to be brighter, while set-in neck guitars have a rounded tone.

Tuning

Tuning is the first skill any guitarist has to master: No matter how well you play, it won't sound any good if the guitar is out of tune.

Pitch

A guitar can be tuned so that all the strings are 'in tune' with one another, and this can sound fine if you are playing alone or unaccompanied. However, if you intend to play with other musicians or along to a recording, then you'll need to make sure that your guitar is tuned to 'concert pitch'. Technically, that means that the note A, when played on the fifth fret of the first string (the A above middle C on a piano), is vibrating at 440 hertz (cycles per second). In practice, guitarists in a band will usually tune up to a keyboard

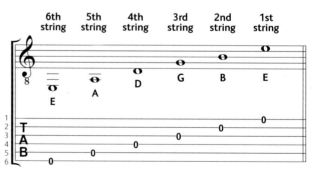

LEFT: **Some electronic tuners are fitted with an internal microphone to allow an acoustic guitar to be tuned.**

or use an electronic tuner for reference. Acoustic guitarists sometime still use a tuning fork to find a 'true' pitch.

The open strings of the guitar, from the lowest note (thickest string) to the highest (thinnest string) should be tuned as shown below.

Tuning at the Fifth Fret

Once you have tuned the low string to the pitch of E you can use this as the starting point from which to tune all the other strings.

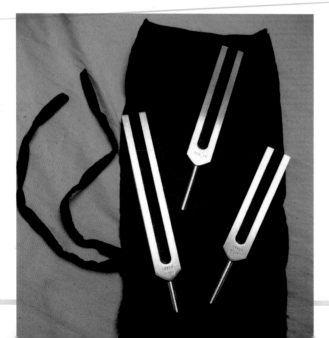

LEFT: **A tuning fork is normally used to find the 'true' pitch.**

6th string	5th string	4th string	3rd string	2nd string	1st string
E	A	D	G	B	E

1. Begin by playing a note on the fifth fret of the low E string; this will produce the note A. You should then turn the fifth string machine head (tuning peg) until the pitch of this open string matches the fretted note on the lower string. If the open fifth string sounds higher than the fretted A note then you should rotate the machine head to slacken the string; if the open fifth string sounds too low then you should tighten the string.

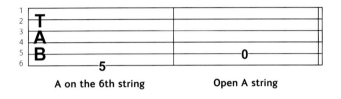

A on the 6th string   **Open A string**

2. Once you have tuned the A string, you can produce the note of D by picking a note at the fifth fret; this will provide you with the pitch you need to tune the open D string accurately. You can then use the same method for tuning the open G string, i.e. by adjusting it to match the note played on the fifth fret of the D string.

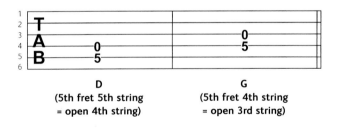

D   **G**
(5th fret 5th string   (5th fret 4th string
= open 4th string)   = open 3rd string)

3. The procedure changes slightly when you come to the B string. You need to tune this to the pitch of the note on the fourth fret of the G string. Once the B string is in tune, fretting it at the fifth fret will produce the note E; you should adjust the open first string to match this pitch.

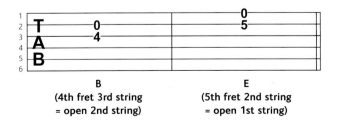

B   **E**
(4th fret 3rd string   (5th fret 2nd string
= open 2nd string)   = open 1st string)

Once you've completed this process, listen closely to various chords at different positions on the neck and make any final tuning adjustments.

It's important to remember that a guitar is not a synthesizer, and characteristic imperfections in a guitar's components can affect its intonation (the accuracy of its pitch at all positions) as well as its tone. These characteristics are not necessarily bad things and can give a guitar a unique personality. They can also make it easier or harder to keep a guitar in tune.

> **Tip**
> Unless you are fitting new strings, you will not need to make large turns on the machine heads. If you tune your guitar regularly, then a few small tuning adjustments should be all it normally needs.

BELOW: **You should now be able to have a go at tuning your guitar.**

Hand Positions

If you don't position your hands in the optimum way, learning to play guitar might prove to be an uphill struggle; playing with a good technique from the start, by positioning your hands correctly, will make learning new techniques relatively easy.

Fretting Hand

1. Regardless of whether you are playing chords or single notes, you should always press the fretting-hand fingers as close to the fretwire as possible. This technique minimizes the unpleasant 'fretbuzz' sounds that can otherwise occur. Pressing at the edge of the fret also greatly reduces the amount of pressure that is required, enabling you to play with a lighter and hence more fluent touch.

ABOVE: **The optimum position for your hand when you are fretting a note: fingers are close to the frets, which minimizes any fretbuzz.**

2. Try to keep all the fretting-hand fingers close to the fingerboard so that they are hovering just above the strings ready to jump into action. This minimizes the amount of movement required when moving from one chord or note to another.

3. Unless you are playing more than one note with the same finger, you should always use the tips of your fingers to fret notes; this will produce the sound more directly and cleanly than using the fleshier pads of the fingers.

BELOW: **CORRECT hand position: your thumb should be placed at the centre of the back of the guitar neck, your fingers arching over the fretboard to descend more or less vertically on the strings.**

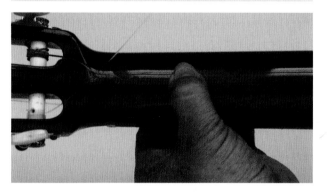

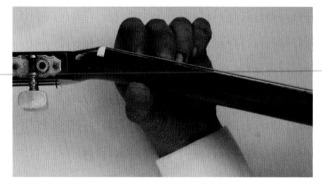

BELOW: **INCORRECT hand position.**

ABOVE: **Avoid holding the plectrum at right angles to your index finger, otherwise your wrist may lock.**

make sure that the amount of plectrum that extends beyond the index finger is not excessive: this would result in a lack of pick control, making the plectrum liable to flap around when striking the strings – reducing both fluency and accuracy. Alternatively, if you find that when you try to pick a string you often miss it completely, the cause is most likely to be not enough plectrum extending beyond the fingertip.

2. Although you need to hold the plectrum with a small amount of pressure so that it doesn't get knocked out of your hand when you strike the strings, be very careful not to grip the plectrum too tightly. Excessive gripping pressure can lead to muscular tension in the hand and arm, with a subsequent loss of flexibility and movement.

Picking Hand

1. If you're using a plectrum (pick), grip it between the index (first) finger and the thumb. Position the plectrum so that its tip extends only just beyond the fingertip, by about $\frac{1}{10}$ in (25 mm). Whilst this measurement doesn't have to be exact,

3. The most efficient way to pick single notes is to alternate between downstrokes and upstrokes. Unless you want to achieve a particular staccato sound, this 'alternate picking' technique should be used for all melodies or lead-guitar playing. (For information on finger-picking, see pages 66–67.)

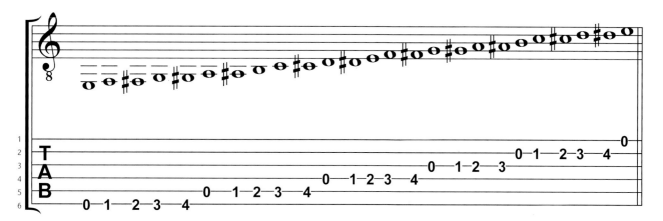

The E chromatic scale consists of a continual series of half steps, which means that every note in 'open position' is played. This makes the scale ideal for building technique as it uses all four fingers to fret notes. It should be played using alternate down and up plectrum strokes.

First Chords & Simple Sequences

Chords form the backbone of all music. As soon as you've mastered a few chord shapes you'll be well on the road to music-making. The really great thing about chords is that once you've learnt them they'll last you a lifetime: you'll still be using any chord you learn today 20 years from now.

Chord Name	Chord Symbol
G major	G
D major	D
E minor	Em
A minor	Am

Chord Symbols

There are two main types of chords that form the core of most popular music: 'major chords' and 'minor chords'.

1. The chord symbol that tells you when to play a major chord is simply the letter name of the chord written as a capital. For example, the chord symbol for the G major chord is 'G' and the chord symbol for the D major chord is 'D'. Major chords have a bright, strong sound.

2. Minor chord symbols consist of the capital letter of the chord name followed by a lowercase 'm'. For example, the chord symbol for the E minor chord is 'Em' and the chord symbol for the A minor chord is 'Am'. Minor chords have a mellow, sombre sound.

Starting Chords

Begin with E minor, as this involves only two fretted notes and uses plenty of open strings. Place your fingers on the strings, pressing lightly yet securely with the fingertips, and then strum across all six strings. Once you're familiar with this chord, move your two fretting fingers from E minor on to the adjacent higher strings, and add the first finger on the first fret of the B string – this is A minor. Notice that the low E string should be omitted when you strum A minor.

Next try some major chords. If G major seems like too much of a stretch between the second and third fingers, allow your thumb to move down to the centre of the back of the guitar neck until the chord feels comfortable. Notice that only the top four strings should be strummed when playing D major.

Em

Am

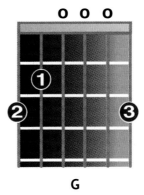

G

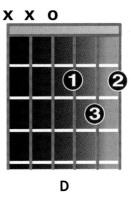

D

Fretboxes

Guitar chord fingerings are written in diagrams known as 'fretboxes'. These indicate the strings and frets that are used for the chord, and which fingers should be used for fretting the notes.

1. In this book, fretboxes are written with vertical lines representing the strings: the low E string is represented by the line on the far left and the high E string by the line on the far right.
2. The thick line at the top of the fretbox represents the nut of the guitar, and the remaining horizontal lines represent the frets.
3. The recommended fret-hand fingering is shown in numbers: 1 = the index finger and 4 = the little finger.
4. An 0 above a string line means this string should be played open (unfretted).
5. An X above a string line means this string should not be played.

Simple Chord Sequences

Many songs consist of a short chord sequence that is repeated throughout. Once you have learnt a couple of basic chord shapes you can start playing a chord sequence by changing from one chord to another. It's then only a short step before you can play the chords to a complete song.

Minor Chords

Begin by strumming downwards four times on an E minor chord, then without stopping change to A minor and play another four strums, keeping the same tempo. Without stopping or hesitating, move your fingers back to E minor and continuing strumming so that the whole sequence begins again.

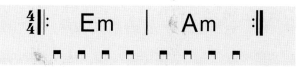

Notice the similarity of the E minor and A minor chord shapes: the second and third fingers are used at the second fret in both chords, the only difference being that they move from the A and D strings in E minor to the adjacent D and G strings in A minor. Try to keep this in mind when you change between these chords, so that you can minimize the amount of finger movement you make – this will make changing between the chords easier and quicker.

Major Chords

Begin by playing four downstrums on a G major chord then, without stopping, move your fingers to D major and play another four strums. Repeat the sequence from the beginning by changing back to G major. Try to keep an even tempo throughout and practise slowly until you are able to change between the chords without pausing or hesitating.

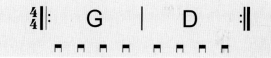

Notice how the third finger stays at the third fret for both G and D major. Use this as a pivot point to lead the chord change. Try to move all three fretting fingers as one shape when changing chord, rather than placing the fingers on one at a time; this will make the chord changes smoother.

Combining Chords

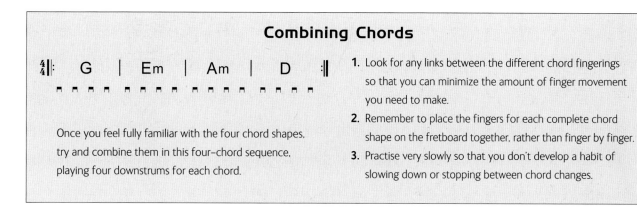

Once you feel fully familiar with the four chord shapes, try and combine them in this four-chord sequence, playing four downstrums for each chord.

1. Look for any links between the different chord fingerings so that you can minimize the amount of finger movement you need to make.
2. Remember to place the fingers for each complete chord shape on the fretboard together, rather than finger by finger.
3. Practise very slowly so that you don't develop a habit of slowing down or stopping between chord changes.

Strumming

Strumming chords forms the foundation of any guitar player's range of techniques. Strumming can be used to accompany your own or some else's singing; it can also be used to provide a backing for lead-guitar playing. Being able to strum in a variety of styles will enable you to play rhythm guitar in a wide range of musical genres.

BELOW: **Strumming is an essential technique to master.**

Strum Technique

For the music to flow smoothly it's essential to develop a relaxed strumming action. It will aid the fluency of rhythm playing if the the action comes from the wrist: a fluid and easy strumming action is best achieved this way, with the wrist loose and relaxed. If the wrist is stiff and not allowed to move freely then excessive arm movement will occur, as the strumming action will be forced

smashing pumpkins ★ siamese dream

LEFT: **One of the best ways to practise strumming is to play along to records you like. Try learning songs that are fairly easy, with mostly open chords, such as 'Disarm' from the Smashing Pumpkins' 1993 album *Siamese Dream*.**

Tip

You don't need to strum all the strings, particularly when playing upstrums. You'll often get a much clearer sound if you only strum the top three or four strings.

---

to come from the elbow instead. As this can never move as fluently as the wrist, there will be a loss of smoothness and rhythmic potential.

2. Progress to adding two upstrums per bar: one between beats two and three, and one after the fourth beat. After the first two bars, try changing the chord to A minor and see if you can keep the strumming pattern going. If you can't change the chord quickly enough then start again from the beginning, playing at a much slower tempo.

Strumming Exercises

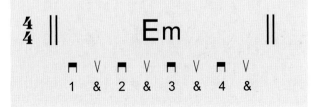

1. Begin by strumming an E minor chord using four downstrums per measure, and then experiment by inserting a quick upstrum between the second and third beats. The upstrum should be played by an upwards movement generated from the wrist, as though the strumming hand is almost effortlessly bouncing back into position ready for the next downstrum. Keep practising this technique until it feels natural, always making sure that the arm itself isn't moving up and down when you're strumming.

3. To really get the strumming hand moving try adding an upstrum after every downstrum. Although this strumming style would be too busy for most songs, this exercise does provide practise in building a fluent strumming technique. Make sure that you have the plectrum positioned correctly, with its tip extending only just beyond the index fingertip, so that it does not drag on the strings as you strum.

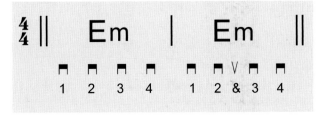

Finger-picking

Finger-picking can provide a really interesting alternative to strumming. The technique is not just confined to classical or folk guitarists – many rock and pop players also use finger-picking as a method of bringing melodic interest to a chord progression and as a way of introducing musical subtleties to a song.

Fingering

In music notation, each picking finger is identified by a letter: 'p' represents the thumb, 'i' the index finger, 'm' the middle finger and 'a' the third finger. (As it is much shorter than the others, the little finger is rarely used in finger-picking.)

The thumb is mostly used for playing the bass strings (the lowest three strings), while the fingers are used for playing the treble strings. There are many different ways of finger-picking, but one of the easiest is to use the 'a' finger for picking the first string, the 'm' finger for the second string and the 'i' finger for the third string.

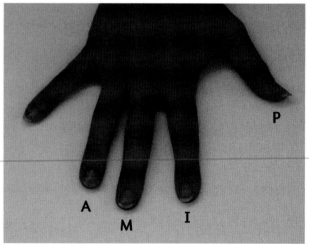

Picking Patterns

Many guitarists use a repetitive finger-picking pattern throughout a song to create a continuity of sound. Picking patterns nearly always begin by playing the root note of the chord (i.e. the note that gives the letter name to the chord) on the bass string using the thumb. For example, the low E string would be the first note

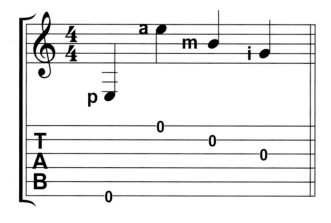

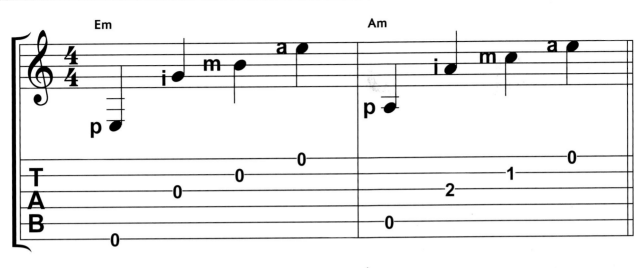

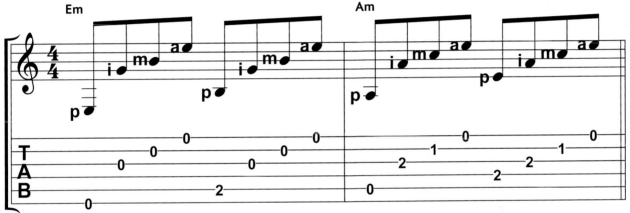

of a pattern when finger-picking on a chord of E minor, and the open A string would be the first note when finger-picking on a chord of A minor.

If the picking pattern on a chord is repeated then sometimes a different bass is used the second time. This will normally be another note from the chord, usually the adjacent bass string. This technique can completely transform a simple chord progression, making it sound quite complex because of the moving bass line. This style of finger-picking is known as 'alternating bass'.

In some musical styles, more complex picking patterns might be used on the treble strings. It is best to practise these types of patterns on one chord until the picking pattern feels totally comfortable. Once you are familiar with a pattern it's relatively easy to apply it to a chord progression. You just need to take care about which bass note to pick on each chord, ensuring you use the root note as your starting point.

Tip
It's easier to finger-pick if you let your fingernails grow a little. Using nails to pick the strings will also give you a crisper, clearer and stronger sound.

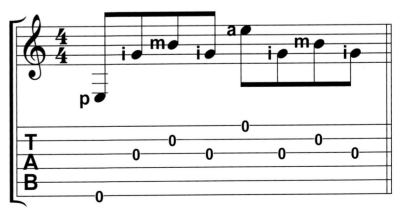

More Chords

The more chords you learn, the more songs you'll be able to play. Developing knowledge of only the 10 most common chords will enable you to play literally thousands of songs, providing you practise them enough so that you can change fluently from chord to chord.

Main Chord Types

Although there are dozens of different chord types, all of these can be considered as just variations of the two core types of chords: major chords and minor chords. For example, if you come across a chord chart that includes Am7, playing a simple

A minor chord will work almost as well. Consequently, developing a good knowledge of the most popular major and minor chords will provide a firm foundation for all future chord playing.

Major Chords

In addition to the G and D major chords that were covered on page 62, some other important major chords to start with are A, C, E and F.

Notice that all the strings can be strummed on the E major chord, whereas the sixth string should be omitted when the A or C chords

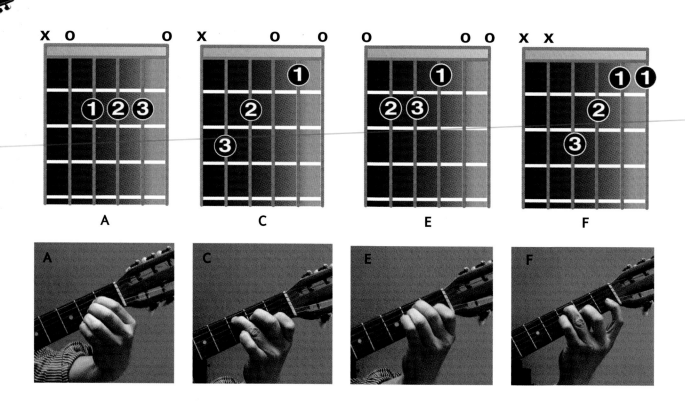

A   C   E   F

are strummed. The F major chord is different from the other chord fingerings in that the first finger needs to lie flat across both the first and second strings. You will find this easier if you ensure that your thumb is positioned quite low at the back of the guitar neck; this will help you keep your first finger flat while the second and third fingers press with the fingertips. Make sure that you only strum the top four strings when playing the F major chord.

Minor Chords

In addition to the Am and Em chords that were covered on page 62, the other most important minor chords to learn at first are Dm and F♯m.

Both Dm and F♯m are four-string chords (i.e. the fifth and sixth strings should be omitted when playing these chords). The F♯m chord is a development of the technique that you gained when learning to play the F major chord, but this time the first finger needs to fret all the top three strings. If you find this tricky, you might like to try resting the second finger on top of the

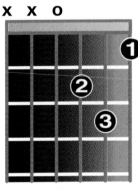

first finger; this will add extra weight and strength to help the first finger hold down all three strings. Positioning the fretting finger as close as possible to the fretwire will reduce the amount of finger pressure required.

ABOVE: **Jazz guitarist Barney Kessel added variety to his music by experimenting with many different chords.**

Keys

The 'key' of a song refers to its overall tonality, and dictates which scale will be used as the basis of the melody and which chords fit naturally into the arrangement. Understanding which chords go together in a key will help you work out the chord structure of songs, and will provide a framework to begin writing your own songs.

Major Keys

In each major key, three major chords occur – as shown below:

Key	Major Chords in the Key
C major	C F G
G major	G C D
D major	D G A
A major	A D E

A song or chord progression will normally begin with the tonic (keynote) chord. This is the chord that has the same name as the key. For example, in the key of C major, C is the tonic (keynote) chord.

Minor chords also occur in major keys. Some of the most commonly used minor chords in the keys of C and G major are shown right.

Key	Minor Chords in the Key
C major	Dm Em Am
G major	Am Bm Em

Although there are no fixed rules about which chords can be combined when you are composing a song or chord progression, if you select chords from the same key they will always fit together well. Below is an example of a chord progression using chords in the key of C major.

‖ C | Dm | Em | F | Am | G | F | C ‖

Minor Keys

In each minor key, three minor chords are closely related, and most commonly occur in popular songs. For example, in the key of A minor the chords of Am, Dm and Em are the most important. Three major chords also occur in each minor key. For example, in the key of A minor, C, F and G major chords occur. As all these chords are within the same key they can be combined in any order (after starting with the tonic/keynote chord) to make a pleasant-sounding chord sequence. An example is shown below, but you can experiment with rearranging the chords in a different order and then playing them through to hear the musical result.

Here are a few chord progressions demonstrating some of the most common chord sequences used in a few of the most popular major and minor keys.

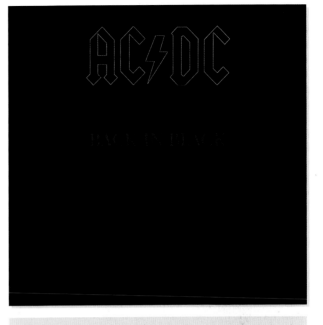

ABOVE: **Most AC/DC songs are in A minor, which is C major's relative minor.**

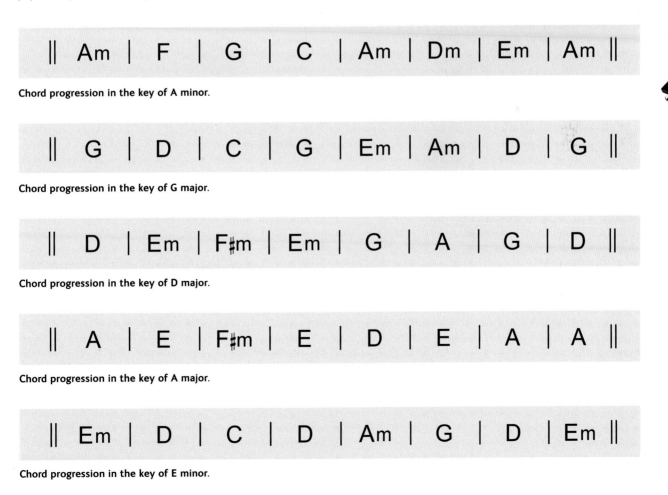

‖ Am | F | G | C | Am | Dm | Em | Am ‖

Chord progression in the key of A minor.

‖ G | D | C | G | Em | Am | D | G ‖

Chord progression in the key of G major.

‖ D | Em | F♯m | Em | G | A | G | D ‖

Chord progression in the key of D major.

‖ A | E | F♯m | E | D | E | A | A ‖

Chord progression in the key of A major.

‖ Em | D | C | D | Am | G | D | Em ‖

Chord progression in the key of E minor.

Introduction

Knowledge of a wide range of chord types will enable you to play songs from almost any musical genre, and will provide a platform for writing your own songs. Understanding the music theory behind chord construction means that you'll be able to explore chord fingerings that suit your playing style, without reliance on a chord book.

ABOVE: **Johnny Marr adds texture to his playing by making full use of a huge variety of chords.**

Exploring Chords

While some players prefer the simplicity of sticking to common major and minor chords, others have made their music unique by exploring the range of chordal variations that can be played on the guitar. Some of the most experimental chord players include Barney Kessel, Pat Metheny, Peter Buck, Johnny Marr, Joe Pass and John McLaughlin.

Chord Fingerings

Because the guitar has a three to four octave range, and some notes can be played at exactly the same pitch in several fingerboard positions, the harmonic possibilities on the instrument are almost endless: even simple major or minor chords can be played in numerous fingerboard positions – each with a multitude of possible fingerings. It's important to remember this, because no instruction books will have space to illustrate all the possible fingering options available for every chord type. Therefore, gaining an understanding of how chords are formed will allow you to devise your own chord fingerings – using shapes that suit your fingers and that work well with the other chord shapes you're playing in the song. Often you'll find that, rather than having to jump around the fingerboard to play the next chord in a song, you can devise an alternative fingering near to the previous chord.

Building Chords

Although there are dozens of different chord types that exist in music, all of them stem from the basic major and minor triads (illustrated on pages 76–79). Once you have a good knowledge

LEFT: **Peter Buck provides the complex chordal structure that is integral to REM's sound.**

Tunings

Using alternative tunings opens up a whole new world of harmonic possibilities on the guitar. You'll be able to discover chords that might be difficult or even impossible to play in standard tuning, yet which fall easily under the fingers in a new tuning. Of course, the main disadvantage is that none of the chord or scale shapes you've learnt in standard tuning will produce the same results when played in a different tuning. This means that a lot of effort will have to be put into exploring the possibilities of any new tuning – but, given the tremendous musical potential, you might just decide it's worth it (see pages 140–41).

of the basic triads and an understanding of chord construction, you'll realize that all other chords are merely extensions or variations of these foundation chord types.

RIGHT: **Pat Metheny is a true pioneer and one of the most important guitarists in the history of jazz. His experimentation with chord variations is legendary.**

Intervals

Intervals are the spaces between notes from the major scale, or other scales. Chords are constructed by combining various intervals. The name of a chord is often based upon the largest interval contained within that chord.

Major Second

A major second is the interval from the first to the second note of the major scale (e.g. in the key of C, from C to D).

If you play the major second note an octave higher it forms a major ninth interval. This interval is included in all major, minor and dominant ninth chords.

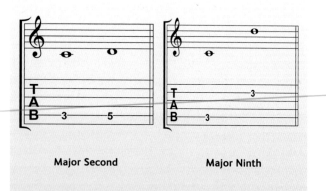

Major Second　　　　Major Ninth

Major Third

A major third is the interval from the first to the third note of the major scale (e.g. in the key of C, from C to E). This interval is important in that it defines the tonality of a chord; a chord that

is constructed with a major third interval from its root note will always be a type of major chord.

If you lower the major third interval by a half step it becomes a minor third. Just as the major third interval determines that a chord has a major tonality, the minor third interval determines that a chord is minor.

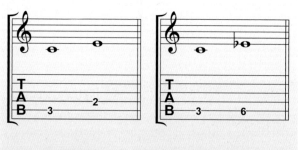

Major Third　　　　Minor Third

Perfect Fourth

A perfect fourth is the interval from the first to the fourth note of the major scale (e.g. in the key of C, from C to F).

Perfect Fourth

Perfect Fifth

A perfect fifth is the interval from the first to the fifth note of the major scale (e.g. in the key of C, from C to G). The perfect fifth occurs in nearly all chords, apart from diminished or augmented chords.

If you lower the perfect fifth interval by a half step it becomes a diminished (flattened) fifth. This interval occurs in diminished chords and any chords labelled with a flattened fifth note.

If you raise the perfect fifth interval by a half step it becomes an augmented (sharpened) fifth. This interval occurs in augmented chords and any chords labelled with a sharpened fifth note.

Perfect Fifth

Diminished Fifth

Augmented Fifth

Major Sixth

A major sixth is the interval from the first to the sixth note of the major scale (e.g. in the key of C, from C to A). The major sixth occurs in both major and minor sixth chords.

If you add an octave to a major sixth it becomes a major 13th interval. This interval is used in all 13th chords.

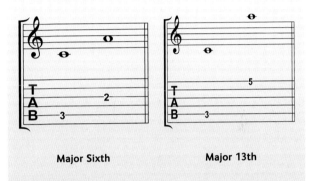

Major Sixth   **Major 13th**

Major Seventh

A major seventh is the interval from the first to the seventh note of the major scale (e.g. in the key of C, from C to B). The major seventh interval occurs in major seventh chords.

If you lower the major seventh interval by a half step it becomes a minor seventh. This interval occurs in both minor seventh and dominant seventh chords.

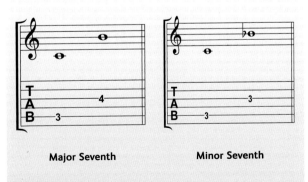

Major Seventh   **Minor Seventh**

Major Triads

Chords that contain three different notes are known as 'triads'. All standard major chords are triads. All other chords, no matter how elaborate, can be considered simply as variations or extensions of these triads. Therefore, learning all the major triads will provide a firm foundation for learning any other chords.

Cmaj

	C Major Scale	C Major Triad
1	C	C
2	D	
3	E	E
4	F	
5	G	G
6	A	
7	B	
8	C	

The first, third and fifth notes of the major scale make up a major triad. For example, the C major triad is formed by taking the first, third and fifth notes of the C major scale.

You can work out which notes are in any major triad by selecting the first, third and fifth notes from the major scale with the same starting note as the chord. This would give the following results:

Although major triads only contain three different notes, strumming three-string chords could result in quite a thin sound, so quite often major chords are played with some of the notes doubled so that five or six strings can be strummed. For example, in this open position G major chord, the G note is played three times (on the sixth, third and first strings), the B note is played twice (on the fifth and second strings) and the D note is played once.

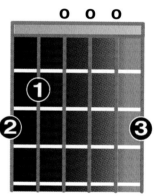

G   G Major
1st (G), 3rd (B), 5th (D)

Now that you know the notes contained in each major triad you can devise as many different fingerings for each chord as you wish. To help you get started, there follows one fretbox example for each major triad. Other shapes are shown in the chord dictionary at the back of this book.

Major Triads	Notes in Triad
C	C E G
G	G B D
D	D F♯ A
A	A C♯ E
E	E G♯ B
B	B D♯ F♯

Major Triads	Notes in Triad
F♯	F♯ A♯ C♯
F	F A C
B♭	B♭ D F
E♭	E♭ G B♭
A♭	A♭ C E♭
D♭	D♭ F A♭

A   A Major
1st (A), 3rd (C#), 5th (E)

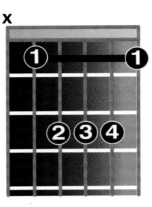

B♭/A#   B♭ Major
1st (B♭), 3rd (D), 5th (F)

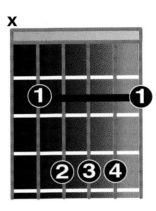

B   B Major
1st (B), 3rd (D#), 5th (F#)

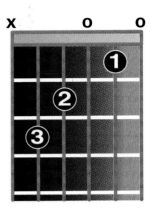

C   C Major
1st (C), 3rd (E), 5th (G)

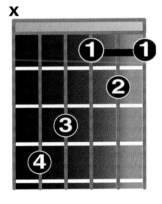

C#/D♭   C# Major
1st (C#), 3rd (E#), 5th (G#)

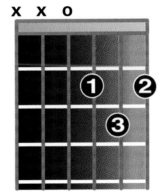

D   D Major
1st (D), 3rd (F#), 5th (A)

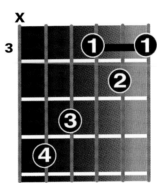

E♭/D#   Eb Major
1st (E♭), 3rd (G), 5th (B♭)

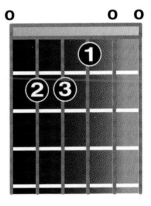

E   E Major
1st (E), 3rd (G#), 5th (B)

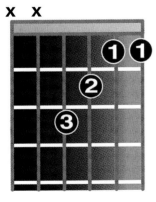

F   F Major
1st (F), 3rd (A), 5th (C)

F#/G♭   F# Major
1st (F#), 3rd (A#), 5th (C#)

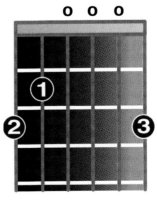

G   G Major
1st (G), 3rd (B), 5th (D)

A♭/G#   Ab Major
1st (A♭), 3rd (C), 5th (E♭)

SECTION ONE

77

Minor Triads

Minor triads have a more mellow, mournful sound than major triads but, just like major triads, they also contain only three different notes. All other minor chords are built on the foundation of these minor triads, so learning at least the most common minor triads is essential for any rhythm-guitar player.

C Natural Minor Scale		C Minor Triad
1	C	C
2	D	
3	E♭	E♭
4	F	
5	G	G
6	A♭	
7	B♭	
8	C	

Minor triads contain the first, flattened third and fifth notes of the major scale. (The flattened third note can be found one fret lower than the major third note.) For example, the C minor triad contains the notes C E♭ and G. Taking the first, third and fifth notes from the natural minor scale will give the same results.

You can work out which notes are in any minor triad by selecting the first, third and fifth notes from the natural minor scale with the same starting note as the chord.

Remember that although triads consist of only three different notes, you can repeat one or more of the notes when playing them as chords on the guitar.

Minor Triads	Notes in Triad
Am	A C E
Em	E G B
Bm	B D F♯
F♯m	F♯ A C♯
C♯m	C♯ E G♯
G♯m	G♯ B D♯

Minor Triads	Notes in Triad
D♯m	D♯ F♯ A♯
Dm	D F A
Gm	G B♭ D
Cm	C E♭ G
Fm	F A♭ C
B♭m	B♭ D♭ F

Other Triads

As well as major and minor triads, there are other triads: diminished, augmented and suspended (see pages 80–83). There are also some chords, known as 'diads', that contain only two different notes (see 'Fifth Chords' page 81).

Cm

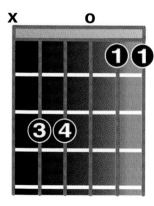
Csus4 C Suspended 4th
1st (C), 4th (F), 5th (G)

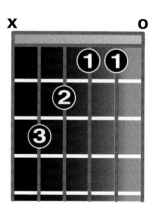
C+ C Augmented
1st (C), 3rd (E), ♯5th (G♯)

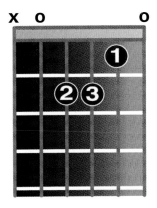

Am   A Minor
1st (A), ♭3rd (C), 5th (E)

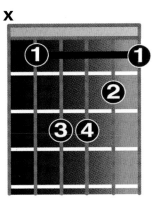

B♭m/A#m   B♭ Minor
1st (B♭), ♭3rd (D♭), 5th (F)

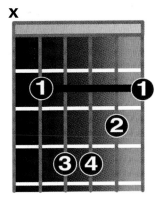

Bm   B Minor
1st (B), ♭3rd (D), 5th (F#)

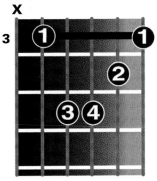

Cm   C Minor
1st (C), ♭3rd (E♭), 5th (G)

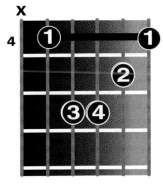

D♭m/C#m   C# Minor
1st (C#), ♭3rd (E), 5th (G#)

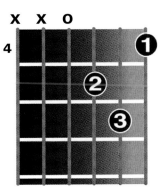

Dm   D Minor
1st (D), ♭3rd (F), 5th (A)

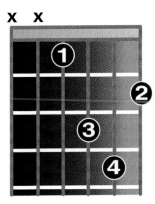

E♭m/D#m   E♭ Minor
1st (E♭), ♭3rd (G♭), 5th (B♭)

Em   E Minor
1st (E), ♭3rd (G), 5th (B)

Fm   F Minor
1st (F), ♭3rd (A♭), 5th (C)

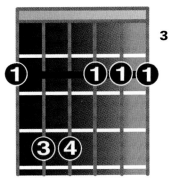

F#m/G♭m   F# Minor
1st (F#), ♭3rd (A), 5th (C#)

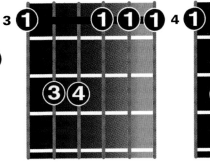

Gm   G Minor
1st (G), ♭3rd (B♭), 5th (D)

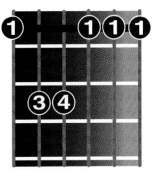

A♭m/G#m   A♭ Minor
1st (A♭), ♭3rd (C♭), 5th (E♭)

Chord Construction

When you've studied the basic major and minor chords on the previous pages, you'll find that there's good news: all other chords can be viewed as variations or extensions of the basic chords. To convert the basic triads into other chords, all that's normally required is to add to the triad a note from the major scale.

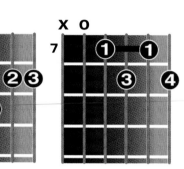

A6

Sixth Chords

To work out how to play any major sixth chord you just play through the major scale until you reach the sixth note in the scale. Find the name of this note and then add this note to the basic major triad – thereby converting it into a major sixth chord. For example, to play A major 6 (A6) you should add F♯ (the sixth note of the A major scale) to the A major chord. (You will find an F♯ note on the second fret of the first string.)

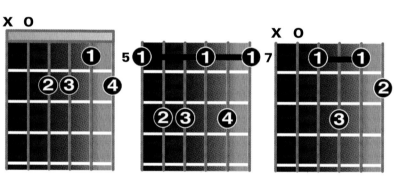

Am6

Minor sixth chords are formed in the same way, by adding the sixth note of the major scale to the minor triad. Notice that you always use the major scale – even if the chord is minor!

Seventh Chords

There are three main types of seventh chord: major seventh (maj7), dominant seventh (7) and minor seventh (m7). Only the major seventh chord uses the seventh note of the major scale; the other two types use the flattened seventh note of the scale.

The major seventh chord is formed by taking the basic major chord and adding the seventh note of the major scale to it. For example, Amaj7 contains the notes A C♯ E G♯.

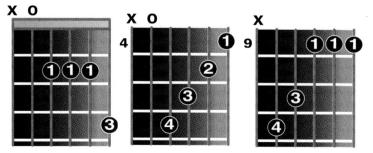

Amaj7

The dominant seventh chord is formed by taking the basic major chord and adding the flattened seventh note of the major scale to it. For example, A7 contains the notes A C♯ E G.

The minor seventh chord is formed by taking the basic minor chord and adding the flattened seventh note of major scale to it. For example, Am7 contains the notes A C E G.

Sus Chords

Some chords are formed by replacing a note, rather than adding one. Sus chords are a good example of this, as the chord's third is replaced by the fourth note of the major scale in sus4 chords, and by the second note of the scale in sus2 chords. For example, Asus2 contains the notes A B E, and Asus4 contains the notes A D E.

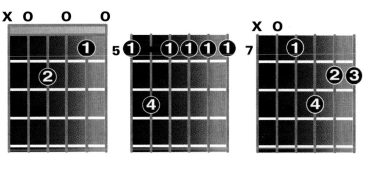

A7

Am7

Asus4   Asus2

Fifth Chords

Fifth chords are unusual in that they do not include a major or minor third. They consist only of the root note and the fifth. For example, A5 contains the notes A and E. In rock music, a prime example of the fifth chord is the 'power chord', where the root note and the fifth above it are played on the sixth and fifth, or fifth and fourth strings. With the right combination of electric guitar, amp and effects, this powerful sound characterizes hard rock and heavy metal.

A5

Tip
When adding notes to chords, it's normally best if you can find the note in a higher register, such as on the first string, before looking for it on the lower strings. Sometimes you might need to take a finger off a string to allow the new note to sound.

Extended & Altered Chords

Using extended chords, containing five or six notes, helps to create a rich sound and to extend your chordal vocabulary. Altered chords provide an ideal method of creating a sense of tension and adding harmonic dissonance to a chord progression.

Extended Chords

Just as seventh chords are built by adding an extra note to a basic triad, extended chords are built by adding one or more extra notes to a seventh chord. The most common types of extended chords are ninths, 11ths and 13ths. Each can be played in either a major, minor or dominant form.

Ninth Chords

Major ninth chords are extensions of major seventh chords. They are formed by adding the ninth note of the major scale (with the same starting note) to a major seventh chord. The interval spelling is 1 3 5 7 9. For example, Cmaj9 contains the notes C E G B (the notes of Cmaj7) plus the note of D (the ninth note of the C major scale). Major ninth chords have a delicate sound that makes them highly suitable for use in ballads.

Dominant ninth chords are formed by adding the ninth note of the major scale to a dominant seventh chord.

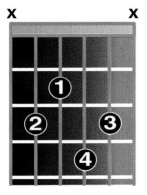

Cmaj9

For example, C9 contains the notes C E G B♭ (the notes of C7) plus D (the ninth note of the C major scale). The interval spelling is 1 3 5 ♭7 9. Dominant ninth chords have a rich, bluesy sound.

Minor ninth chords are extensions of minor seventh chords, formed by adding the ninth note of the major scale. For example, Cm9 contains C E♭ G B♭ (the notes of Cm7) plus D (the ninth note of the C major scale). The interval spelling is 1 ♭3 5 ♭7 9. Minor ninth chords have a suave, mellow sound and are often used in soul and funk music.

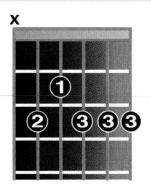

C9

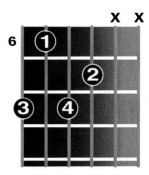

Cm9

Eleventh Chords

There are three main types of 11th chord as shown here. You'll notice that each incorporates some form of ninth chord, plus the 11th note of the major scale. In practice, the ninth note is normally omitted when playing 11th chords on the guitar.

Dominant 11th:	1 3 5 ♭7 9 11
Minor 11th:	1 ♭3 5 ♭7 9 11
Major 11th:	1 3 5 7 9 11

Thirteenth Chords

There are three main types of 13th chord, as shown in the table below. In practice, it is not possible to play all seven notes of a 13th chord on guitar, therefore some notes (normally the 9th, 11th and sometimes the 5th) are omitted.

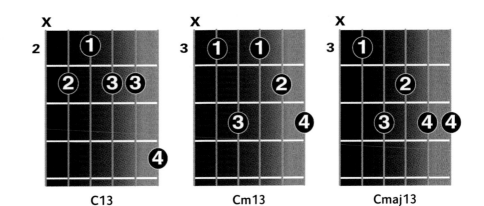

C13

Cm13

Cmaj13

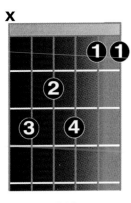

C11

C11

Dominant 13th:	1 3 5 ♭7 9 11 13
Minor 13th:	1 ♭3 5 ♭7 9 11 13
Major 13th:	1 3 5 7 9 11 13

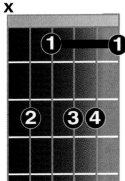

Cmin11

Cm11

Altered Chords

These are chords in which the fifth and/or ninth has been 'altered' – i.e. either raised or lowered by a half step. Altered chords are most commonly used in jazz. These are examples of commonly used altered chords. See the chord dictionary for sample chord fingerings.

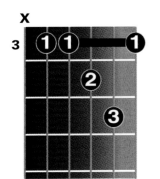

Cmaj11

Cmaj11

Augmented triad:	1 3 ♯5
Diminished triad:	1 ♭3 ♭5
Diminished 7th chord:	1 ♭3 ♭5 ♭♭7
Dominant 7th ♭5:	1 3 ♭5 ♭7
Dominant 7th ♭9:	1 3 5 ♭7 ♭9
Dominant 7♯ 9:	1 3 5 ♭7 ♯9

Chord Substitution

You can make your own interpretations of chords in a songbook by using chord inversions, embellishments and substitutions instead of the original chords. You can also use this approach when songwriting, by starting with a simple chord progression and turning it into something quite elaborate.

Chord Embellishment

Chord embellishment consists of varying a chord by substituting a note within it for a new note, or by adding an extra note. Whichever method is used, the new note should be taken from the 'key scale' of the chord: for example, you could add any note from the C major scale to the C major chord without changing the fundamental harmonic nature of the chord. By sticking to notes from the key scale, the new embellished chord can normally be used as a direct replacement for the simpler basic chord without causing any clashes with the melody of the song.

Chord embellishments are often easier to play than the basic major or minor chords. If you lift the finger off the first string

when playing an open position D major chord shape, it will become a Dsus2 chord.

Adding an extra note to a chord is also an effective way of creating an embellishment. The ninth note of the major scale is often used, as this creates a certain warmth when added to a basic major chord.

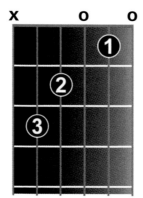 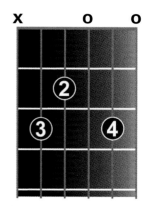

C major is extended to become Cadd9 by the addition of the ninth note, D.

The same approach can be taken with minor and dominant seventh chords. The table below gives examples of the most commonly used chord embellishments – none of which will cause problems within an existing chord progression as the basic chord's harmonic nature will not be changed.

Basic Chord	Possible Embellishments
Major	major 6th, major 7th, major 9th add 9, sus2, sus4, major 6th add 9
Minor	minor 7th, minor 9th, sus2, sus4
Dominant 7th	dominant 9th, dominant 13th dominant 7th sus4

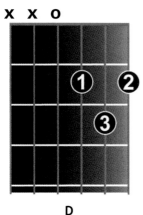

D   Dsus2

Chord Inversions

Rather than play every chord starting from its root note, you can play an 'inversion' by choosing another chord tone as the lowest note. There are three main types of inversion:

- First inversion: the third of the chord is played as the lowest note.
- Second inversion: the fifth of the chord is played as the lowest note.
- Third inversion: the extension of the chord is played as the lowest note.

Inversions are normally notated as 'slash chords':
C/E is 'C major first inversion'.

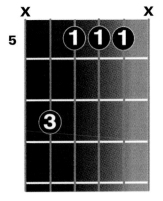

C/E (C major first inversion)

C/G (C major second inversion)

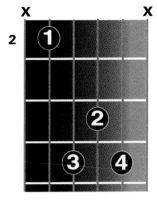

Cmaj7/B (C major seventh third inversion)

Chord Substitution

An interesting effect can be achieved by substituting one chord for another. For example, a major chord might be replaced by its 'relative minor' (i.e. the minor chord with a root note three half steps lower). For example, A minor might be substituted for C major. Alternatively, a minor chord could be replaced by its 'relative major' (i.e. the major chord with a root note three half steps higher). For example, C major might be substituted in place of A minor.

C/E

Introduction

Knowing a number of chord shapes is useful, but it's only when you can put some of these chords together with an interesting strumming pattern, and change fluently between them, that you'll really start making music by playing rhythm guitar.

Importance of Rhythm

Rhythm-guitar playing is rarely given as much attention as lead playing, but it's important to remember that it's rhythm playing that forms the backbone of most songs. If you join a band, regardless of the musical style, you'll almost certainly spend more time playing rhythm guitar than lead guitar.

Notable rhythm-guitar specialists are Bo Diddley, John Lennon, Pete Townshend, Noel Gallagher, Paul Weller, Peter Buck of REM, Fran Healy of Travis and Badly Drawn Boy (a.k.a. Damon Gough).

Good Rhythm

1. The first essential of becoming a good rhythm-guitar player is the ability to keep in time: practising with a metronome, drum machine or backing tracks will provide the ideal preparation; always listen closely to the drums and bass and try to stay in time with them. Remember that as a rhythm-guitar player you are part of the 'rhythm section' of any band, and you should try to interact closely with the other rhythm section musicians. (See pages 88–89.)

LEFT: One of the features of Damon Gough's unique sound is his rhythm-guitar playing, which underpins the majority of his tracks.

ABOVE: **Pioneering guitarist Pete Townshend was a master of rhythm guitar.**

these could appear in a variety of formats, from a simple handwritten list of chords to a fully typeset chart with time signatures, notated rhythms and interpretation markings included. (See pages 94–99.)

BELOW: **Inspired by the Who's Pete Townshend and Dr Feelgood's Wilko Johnson, Paul Weller picked up an axe and strummed his way to becoming a rhythm-guitar specialist.**

2. Another core skill is the ability to change fluently from one chord to another: always look for links, or common notes, between consecutive chords – so that you can minimize the amount of finger movement needed when changing chords; you may be able to keep some fingers on, or at least slide them along a string to the next chord. Leaving gaps between chords when strumming through a song or chord progression is a recipe for musical disaster – the performance will sound fragmented and can make it difficult for you to keep in time. (See pages 120–21.)

3. Developing a reliable strumming technique is an essential part of becoming a good guitar player. Once you have mastered basic rhythm–playing skills, then it's time to become inventive with your strumming patterns. It's the quality and inventiveness of strumming that distinguishes great rhythm players from the rest. (See pages 100–01.)

4. Being able to understand and follow chord charts is another required skill for any rhythm–guitar player. Depending on the style of music and who has prepared the chord chart,

Timing

Rhythm Guitarist

The most important skill any rhythm-guitar player needs is the ability to maintain an even tempo and keep in time with other band members. It's essential that your rhythm playing sits in the same groove as the other members of the rhythm section.

Developing Timing Skills

88

Some people have a natural sense of rhythm and timing that just needs nurturing, while others have to concentrate on developing a secure sense of timing. A simple test to evaluate your sense of

BELOW: As a rhythm guitarist it's vital that you play along to the groove of the drums.

timing is to try and clap along to a recording by one of your favourite bands. While listening to the recording, focus your attention on the drums and try to clap a regular beat that matches the main rhythmic pulses within the song. Listen carefully to your clapping and see if you can stay in time

ABOVE: **Nile Rodgers is known for the crisp timing of his rhythm chops.**

throughout the whole song –
stamina is an important aspect
of rhythm playing. Before you
try to play through a song make
sure that you have mastered
any technical challenges, such
as awkward chord changes,
in advance. Otherwise, the
temptation will be to slow down
when approaching the difficult
bits and perhaps speed up on the
easy bits. You should try to avoid
developing poor timing habits
from the start by always choosing
a slow practice tempo at which
you can master the whole song –
difficult bits and all! Once you can
play the song without any mistakes
or hesitations, it's relatively easy
to gradually increase the tempo
each time you practise.

LEFT: **A metronome – a tried and tested device to help you keep in good time.**

your strumming style. You
can program the machine,
or use preset patterns, so that it
emulates different musical genres.

Playing along to records is also
a good method of developing
a secure sense of timing: the
band on the recording won't
wait around if you lose time
or hesitate over a chord change.
Because there will be a longer
space between beats, playing
along with songs at a slow
tempo emphasizes any timing
inconsistencies – so don't
forget to practise a few ballads
alongside the thrash metal!

Timing Aids

Ideally you should always try to practise your rhythm playing
with a device that keeps regular time. The simplest method
is to practise with a metronome. This is a small mechanical
or electronic device that sounds a click on each beat. You can
set it to click in increments from a very slow to a super-fast
tempo. It's always best to practise anything new at a slow tempo,
increasing the metronome setting by a couple of notches each
time you've successfully played it the whole way through.

A drum machine can be used instead of a metronome.
The advantage of the drum machine is that you can set
it to play back interesting drum patterns to help inspire

RIGHT: **A drum machine can help you play in time.**

Tip
Record yourself playing along to a CD or a drum machine. Listen carefully to hear if your playing is exactly in time.

S
E
C
T
I
O
N

89

O
N
E

Time Signatures

The time signature is the most important element in setting the musical feel and mood of a piece of music. It provides the framework for the rhythmic structure of a song and plays a large part in establishing the character of the music.

Recognizing Time Signatures

The symbol indicating the time signature is always written at the start of the music or chord chart. The time signature is normally written as two numbers, one above the other. The top number represents the number of beats per measure (bar), while the bottom number refers to the type of beats.

The most common time signature used in all styles of popular music is $\frac{4}{4}$ time. This indicates that there are four beats in a measure, and that these are quarter notes (crotchets). Sometimes the $\frac{4}{4}$ symbol is replaced with **C**, meaning 'common time'.

Note that the time signature only tells you the number and type of 'beats' that will occur in a measure; this is not the same as the number of 'notes' you can play in the measure. For example, a measure of music in $\frac{4}{4}$ time will last for the equivalent duration of four quarter beats, but in this space you might play less

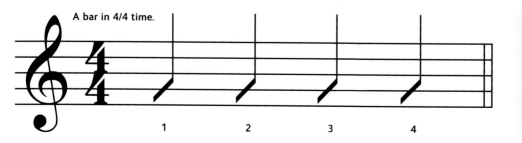

A bar in 4/4 time.

1   2   3   4

ABOVE: **Country star Chet Atkins would have been familiar with** $\frac{3}{4}$ **time, a common feature of country ballads. Pictured is his signature Gretsch model.**

THE RHYTHM GUITARIST: PLAYING RHYTHM GUITAR

longer-lasting notes or more shorter notes. In fact, you can play any combination of long, medium or short notes providing the duration per measure is equivalent to four quarter-note beats. (See pages 92–93 for more information on understanding notation.)

Other commonly used time signatures:

$\frac{2}{4}$: this has two quarter-note beats per measure. This time signature tends to give a march-like feel to the music. Sometimes the $\frac{2}{4}$ symbol is replaced with a ₵ symbol, meaning 'cut time'.

$\frac{3}{4}$: this has three quarter-note beats per measure. This time signature gives a waltz-like character to the music and is often used in country and folk ballads.

$\frac{2}{2}$: this has two half-note beats per measure. This is equivalent in length to $\frac{4}{4}$ time, but with two long beats per measure instead of four quarter-note beats.

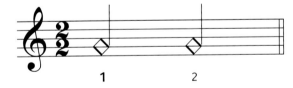

$\frac{6}{8}$: this has six eighth-note beats per measure. However, these are normally played as two groups of three.

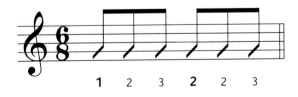

$\frac{12}{8}$: this has 12 eighth-note beats per measure. These are normally played as four groups of three. $\frac{12}{8}$ is commonly used in blues and jazz.

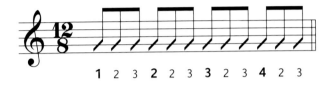

Establishing the Time Signature

If you were just to play a long series of chords all of equal strength it would be hard for the listener to recognize any rhythmic structure in the music – in other words, they wouldn't be able to 'feel the groove'. So normally the first beat of each measure is slightly accented, as this helps the sense of rhythm in a piece of music. In $\frac{6}{8}$ and $\frac{12}{8}$ time, an accent is normally played on the first of each group of three notes. (If you're playing in a band it might be the drums or other instruments that emphasize these accents.)

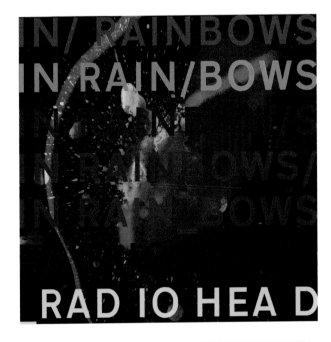

ABOVE: '15 Steps' from Radiohead's 2007 album *In Rainbows* has a $\frac{5}{4}$ time signature, unusual in Western music.

SECTION ONE

91

Rhythm Notation

Understanding how rhythms are written down will help you play through notated chord charts. The ability to notate your own rhythms is useful for passing the information to other players and as a memory aid. Even if you intend to rely mainly on tablature, a knowledge of rhythm notation will help you get the most out of the many song transcriptions that provide the full notation with the tab.

Note Values

Rhythm notation consists of pitchless notes and rests. The type of note used tells you how many beats a chord lasts; the type of rest used tells you how many beats a silence lasts. The diagram below shows the names of the most common types of notes, their symbols and how many of each type of note can occur in a single measure in $\frac{4}{4}$ time.

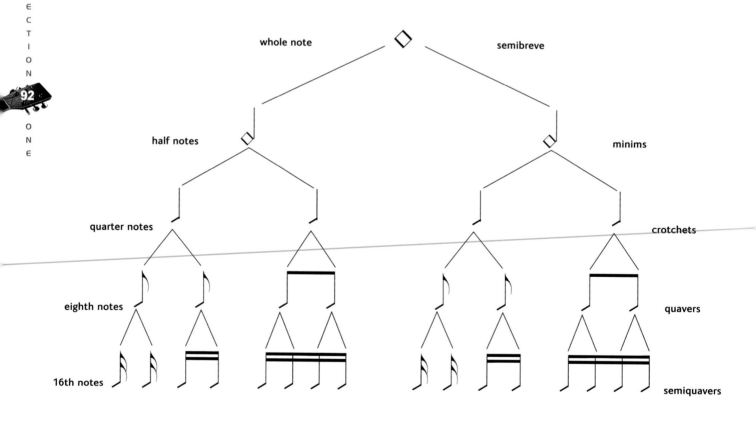

whole note — semibreve
half notes — minims
quarter notes — crotchets
eighth notes — quavers
16th notes — semiquavers

The terminology that is widely used in North America (and increasingly amongst pop, rock and jazz musicians in the UK and elsewhere) is different from that traditionally used by classical musicians in many parts of the world. In the diagram the modern names are shown on the left and the traditional names are shown on the right.

LEFT: Beatles' guitarist John Lennon was one of the great rock rhythm guitarists. His signature was a rest-one-two-and-rest.

Rests

The table below shows the names of the most common types of rests, their symbols, their note equivalents, and the duration of each type of rest in $\frac{4}{4}$ time.

Name	Rest symbol	Note equivalent	Duration in $\frac{4}{4}$ time
semibreve rest (whole rest)			4 beats
minim rest (half rest)			2 beats
crotchet rest (quarter rest)			1 beat
quaver rest (eighth rest)			1/2 beat
semiquaver rest (16th rest)			1/4 beat

Dotted Notes

A dot after a note or rest means that the note or rest lasts for half as long again. This chart shows the values of dotted notes and dotted rests in $\frac{4}{4}$ time.

Name	Note	Rest	Duration in $\frac{4}{4}$ time
dotted minim (dotted half note)			3 beats
dotted crotchet (dotted quarter note)			1 1/2 beats
dotted quaver (dotted eighth note)			3/4 of a beat

Ties

A curved line known as a 'tie' is used to join together two notes of the same pitch in order to increase the duration of the note.

In this example, the first chord would be allowed to sustain for the equivalent of five eighth notes. It is not possible to use a dot after the initial chord as this would have increased the duration of the note to the equivalent of six eighth notes.

Another common instance where ties are used is across bar lines as a method of sustaining a note beyond the end of a measure.

In this example, a tie is used so that the chord at the end of measure one can sustain into measure two.

Triplets

A triplet sign indicates where three notes should be played in the space of two notes of the same value.

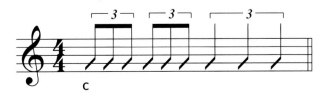

Chord Charts

Simple chord charts are the most commonly used way of notating the chord structure of a song or progression. If you audition for a pop or rock band, the music you'll be asked to play will most likely be presented as a simple chord chart.

Reading Chord Charts

A chord chart normally has the time signature written at the very beginning. If there is no time signature then it's usually safe to assume that the music is in $\frac{4}{4}$ time.

Each measure is separated by a vertical line, with two vertical lines indicating the end of the piece. Chord symbols are used to show which chords should be played.

Split Measures

When more than one chord appears in a single measure it can be assumed that the measure is to be evenly divided between the chords that appear within it. In a song in $\frac{3}{4}$ time, if three chords all appear in the same measure then you can assume that the measure is to be divided equally – with one beat per chord.

LEFT: **Noel Gallagher's songwriting skills are perhaps best showcased on Oasis's 2006 compilation album *Stop The Clocks*.**

‖ $\frac{4}{4}$ C | Am | Dm | G | F | Em | G | C ‖

‖ $\frac{3}{4}$ C | Am | Em F G | C ‖

In the penultimate measure, each chord lasts for one beat.

LEFT: **Gallagher's song-writing technique is based on a good understanding of chords.**

In many chord charts, in order to make the intention clear and avoid confusion, any division within a measure is shown by either a dot or a diagonal line after each chord: each dot or diagonal line indicates another beat.

Interpreting Chord Charts

In standard chord charts, while the duration of each chord is clearly shown, the rhythm style that should be played is left to the discretion of the performer. In theory this means that you could interpret the chart in any way you wish in terms of the number of strums per beat, however you should make sure that your rhythm playing relates to the musical style and mood of the song.

‖ 4/4 C ╱ Am ╱ |Dm ╱ G ╱ |F ╱ Em ╱ |G ╱ C ╱ ‖

Each chord lasts for two beats: one beat indicated by the chord symbol and an additional beat indicated by the diagonal line.

‖ 4/4 C Em ╱ ╱ |F G ╱ ╱ |Am Em ╱ ╱ |G C ╱ ╱ ‖

In this example, the first chord in each measure lasts for just one beat and the second chord lasts for three beats.

‖ 4/4 C . . Dm |Em . . F |Dm . . G |F . . C ‖

In this example, instead of diagonal lines, dots are used to show the rhythmic divisions within each measure. The first chord in each measure lasts for three beats and the second chord lasts for one beat.

Following Chord Charts

If every bar of a whole song were written out in a chord chart it would take up several pages and become cumbersome to read. Instead chord charts are normally abbreviated by using a number of 'repeat symbols'. In order to follow a chord chart accurately it is essential to understand what each repeat symbol means.

Repeat Symbols

/. This symbol is used when one bar is to be repeated exactly.

//. This symbol is used when more than one bar is to be repeated. The number of bars to be repeated is written above the symbol.

Here is an example of these symbols in use.

‖ 4/4 G | ⁄ | C | D | ²⁄⁄ | Em | ⁄ ‖

should be played as

‖ 4/4 G | G | C | D | C | D | Em | Em ‖

Section Repeats

The symbol of a double bar-line followed by two dots indicates the start of a section, and the symbol of two dots followed by a double bar-line indicates the end of the section to be repeated. If there are no dots at the start of

the section, then repeat the music from the beginning of the piece. If the section is to be repeated more than once, the number of times it is to be played is written above the last repeat symbol.

‖ 4/4 Em | D ‖: G | C | Am | Em :‖ (x 4)

SECTION ONE

If two sections of music are identical, except for the last measure or measures, repeat dots are used in conjunction with first-time and second-time ending directions, as shown here.

$$\| : \quad \frac{4}{4} \quad Am \quad | \quad G \quad | \quad F \quad | \quad \overset{1.}{Em} \quad : | \quad \overset{2.}{Dm} \quad | \quad Am \quad \|$$

should be played as

$$\| \quad \frac{4}{4} \quad Am \quad | \quad G \quad | \quad F \quad | \quad Em \quad | \quad Am \quad | \quad G \quad | \quad F \quad | \quad Dm \quad | \quad Am \quad \|$$

As well as repeat dots there are several other commonly used repeat signs:

- D.C. (an abbreviation of Da Capo) means play 'from the beginning'. For example, if the entire piece of music is to be repeated, D.C. can be written at the end to instruct you to play it again from the beginning.

- D.S. (an abbreviation of Dal Segno) means play 'from the sign': 𝄋. For example, if the verse and chorus of a song are to be repeated, but not the introduction, D.S. can be written at the end of the music with the D.S. sign written at the start of the verse. This instructs the performer to start again from the sign.

- Coda is the musical term for the end section of a piece of music. The start of the coda is marked by the sign.

- Fine is the musical term for the end of a piece of music.

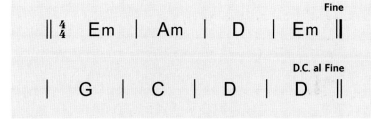

In this example, after eight measures repeat from the beginning and then end after measure four where the sign 'Fine' appears.

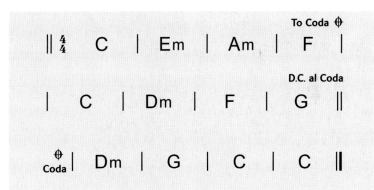

In this example, after eight measures repeat from the beginning and then after measure four jump to the coda section.

Some of the above repeat signs might be combined in a chord chart.

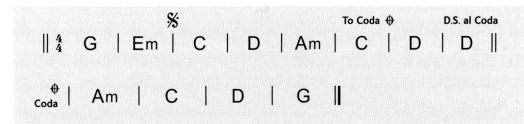

In this example, after eight measures repeat from the start of measure three to the end of measure six, then jump to the coda section.

Rhythm Charts

While standard chord charts are commonly used by pop and rock bands, more detailed and complex charts known as 'rhythm charts' are often presented to guitarists involved in recording sessions and those who play in theatre and function band settings. Learning to read rhythm charts will help expand your employability as a guitarist.

Chart Styles

Some rhythm charts can be quite elaborate and may include a fully notated rhythm part, as well as detailed instructions about dynamics and tempo. Others may contain notated rhythms only at the beginning, in order to establish the feel of the song, with further rhythm notation only being used where specific rhythmic accents or features occur. The type of rhythm charts you come across will depend on the context and the transcriber's personal preferences.

Dynamic Markings

Symbols are often used in rhythm charts to indicate changes in volume – e.g. when you should play softly and when you should strum strongly. The symbols do not refer to any precise decibel volume level, instead their main function is to highlight changes in overall volume. The most common dynamic markings are shown on

LEFT: A good session guitarist needs to understand rhythm charts. In his pre-Led Zeppelin days, virtuoso guitarist Jimmy Page was a full-time session man, then known as 'Little Jim'.

the right. Accents, where certain individual beats are played stronger than others, are marked by this sign: >. The letters 'sfz' (*sforzando*) may be also used to indicate an accent.

Tempo

Most rhythm charts will contain an indication of the speed at which the music should be played, and is usually written at the start of the music. The tempo indication may appear in either traditional Italian musical terms or their English equivalents. Alternatively, a metronome marking may be shown to indicate the exact number of beats per minute (b.p.m.). The most common tempos are shown in the table on the right.

Some music may contain changes in tempo. These are usually indicated through the use of Italian terms. The most widely used are:

- **Accel.** (an abbreviation of accelerando) means play gradually faster.
- **A tempo** indicates that you should resume the normal tempo after a derivation.
- **Meno mosso** (less movement) means that you should slow down at once.
- **Rall**. (an abbreviation of rallentando) means play gradually slower.
- **Rit**. (an abbreviation of ritenuto) means to hold back the tempo.

Symbol	Name	Meaning
pp	pianissimo	very soft
p	piano	soft
mp	mezzo-piano	medium soft
mf	mezzo-forte	medium loud
f	forte	loud
ff	fortissimo	very loud
◁	crescendo	getting louder
▷	diminuendo	getting softer

Italian Term	Meaning	Approximate speed
Largo	very slow	40–60 b.p.m.
Adagio	slow	50–75 b.p.m.
Andante	walking pace	75–100 b.p.m.
Moderato	moderate tempo	100–120 b.p.m.
Allegro	fast	120–160 b.p.m.
Presto	very quick	160–200 b.p.m.

Playing Rhythm Charts

Below you'll see a sample rhythm chart, incorporating some of the terms and symbols described above. Refer to pages 92–93 if you need to be reminded of the note values.

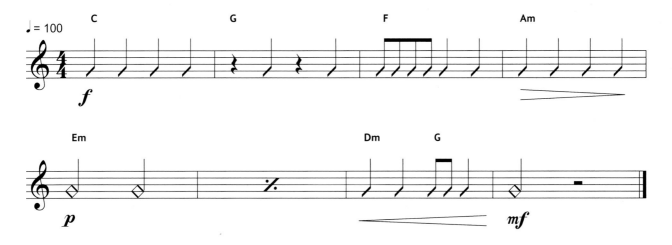

Strumming Patterns

Building up a repertoire of useful strumming patterns is a good way of developing your rhythm-guitar playing. Once you've mastered the core patterns used in rock and pop you can easily expand these by adding variations.

Strum Technique

Playing with a loose wrist action is an essential ingredient of developing a good strumming technique. Keeping the wrist tight and strumming by using the whole forearm will severely restrict the potential speed and fluency of your rhythm playing – so make sure that the strumming action comes from your wrist. It's a good idea to practise in front of a mirror, or record a video of yourself playing guitar, so that you can see if you're using the right technique.

Chord Technique

Be careful not to over-grip with the fretting-hand thumb on the back of the neck as this will cause muscle fatigue and tend to limit freedom of the thumb to move. The fretting-hand thumb must move freely when changing chords. If the thumb remains static this restricts the optimum positioning of the fingers for the next chord, which may result in unnecessary stretching and the involuntary dampening of certain strings (as the fingers are not positioned upright on their tips). Be aware that for the fingers to move freely the wrist, elbow and shoulder must be flexible and relaxed: Make sure your standing or sitting position doesn't restrict the movement of your hands and arms.

RIGHT: **Bo Diddley played a key part in the transition from blues to rock'n'roll due to his more insistent, driving rhythms.**

Strum Patterns

On the right you'll find several examples of popular strumming patterns. It's a good idea to start by playing all the progressions using just four downstrums per measure – this way you'll become familiar with the chord changes before tackling the strum patterns. In nearly all styles of music, there is no need to strum all the strings on every beat – feel free to add variety, particularly by omitting some bass strings on upstrokes and some treble strings on downstrokes.

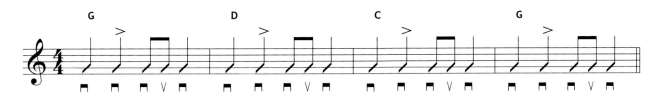

The second beat of the measure is accented to create dynamic variety. An upstroke is used after the third beat of the measure.

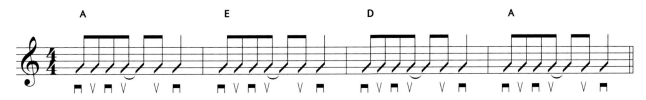

This pattern uses a mixture of down and upstrokes, but notice how the fourth strum and the last strum are held longer than the others. This variety creates an effective rhythm.

A simple down-up strum pattern, but the use of rests creates a very distinctive rhythmic effect.

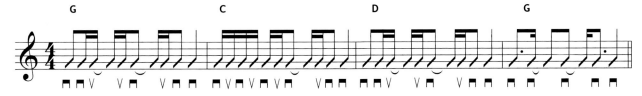

This 'Bo Diddley' type pattern is a good example of how to use rhythmic variations: notice that measure 1 and 3 are the same, while measures 2 and 4 are each variations on the first measure.

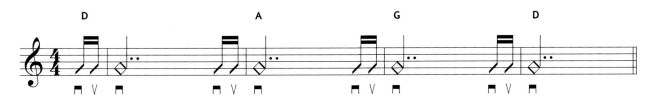

This typical rock strumming pattern is essentially just one strum per measure. What makes it distinctive is the rapid down-up 'pre-strum' before the main beat. These 'pre-strums' do not need to be played across all the strings, and open strings can be used on the second of them to help get to the main chord quickly.

Introduction

Whether you're playing a fiery rock solo or a subtle blues line, lead-guitar playing is a great way to express your emotions through your instrument. However, underlying every great guitar solo is a foundation of scale knowledge and fingerboard technique that enables players to turn their musical ideas into reality.

Influential Players

Some of the early pioneers of modern lead-guitar styles are B.B. King, Buddy Guy, Eric Clapton, Jimmy Page, Jeff Beck,

Ritchie Blackmore and Carlos Santana. If you've never heard these players, check out some of their recordings.

Improvisation

Later in this chapter all the essential scales that underpin lead-guitar playing will be illustrated, but it's important to remember that playing scales up and down in itself doesn't make a solo.

Scales simply set the range of notes that will be in tune in any key. It's how well you improvise with a scale that dictates how good

LEFT: **Buddy Guy has inspired thousands over the years with his strong and inventive lead-guitar playing.**

your solo will be. To get a feel for the song, it's always a good idea to play through the chord sequence before you play any lead guitar.

Six Stages to Improvising

1. When you first start playing lead guitar you could begin by simply playing the correct scale up and down over the chord progression. This way you can begin to hear the overall sound and tonality of the key, but always bear in mind that just playing scales up and down isn't enough to make a good solo.

2. As the first stage in learning to improvise, rather than playing the scale in straight time, experiment by playing some notes quickly while allowing others to ring on; you'll notice that this

sounds more musical and inventive, even though you're still playing the same notes in the same order.

3. Next, try repeating a series of notes, so that you begin to establish licks or phrases that will stick in the listener's ear. Once you have a phrase that you like, try to vary it slightly when you repeat it – that way it will sound fresh, while still giving the listener something recognizable to latch on to.

4. Leave some gaps between your phrases so that the music has space to breathe. There's no need to fill every second of the solo with notes.

5. Try to make your lead playing fit the musical style and mood of the song, so that the solo complements the groove and vocals.

6. The most important thing is to let your ears, rather than your fingers, guide you. Listen carefully to the musical effect of every note you play.

LEFT: **The opening to 'Stairway to Heaven', as first played by Jimmy Page of Led Zeppelin, is one of the most-copied intro riffs of all time.**

BELOW: **Joe Satriani and Steve Vai are just two of today's artists whose work with improvisation is legendary.**

Basics of Notation

There are three ways in which scales, licks and solos are written down: traditional notation, tablature and fretboxes. While you don't need to be a great sight-reader to play lead guitar, having a good understanding of each of the notation systems will help you learn lead guitar relatively easily.

Tablature

Tablature (TAB) uses six lines to represent the six strings of the guitar, with the top line representing the high E string and the bottom line representing the low E string. Numbers are written on the lines to indicate which fret to play at. A zero indicates that the string is played open. TAB is great for notating scales or chords and, although it doesn't usually include any rhythm notation, its simplicity makes it ideal for learning music that you have heard before.

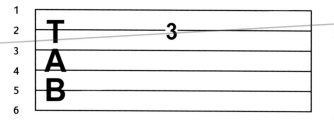

This means play at the third fret on the second string.

Music Notation

Traditional music notation is written on a staff of five lines. Each line, and each space between the lines, represents a different note. For guitar music, a treble clef is written at the start of each line of music. Temporary extra lines (ledger lines) are used for any notes that are either too high or too low to fit on the staff.

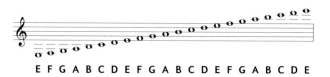

E G B D F F A C E

Notes on the lines and spaces in the treble clef.

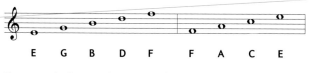

E F G A B C D E F G A B C D E F G A B C D E

Using ledger lines, this diagram shows the notes from the open low E string to the E at the 12th fret on the first string.

A sharp sign (♯) is written in front of a note, on the same line or space, to raise its pitch by a half step (semitone) i.e. equivalent to one fret higher.

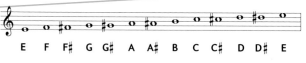

E F F♯ G G♯ A A♯ B C C♯ D D♯ E

A flat sign (♭) is written in front of a note, on the same line or space, to lower its pitch by a half step (semi-tone). Any sharps or flats affect all the notes of the same pitch within the bar. A natural sign (♮) on the same line or space is used to cancel the previous sharp or flat.

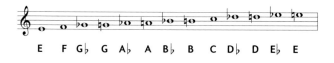

E F G♭ G A♭ A B♭ B C D♭ D E♭ E

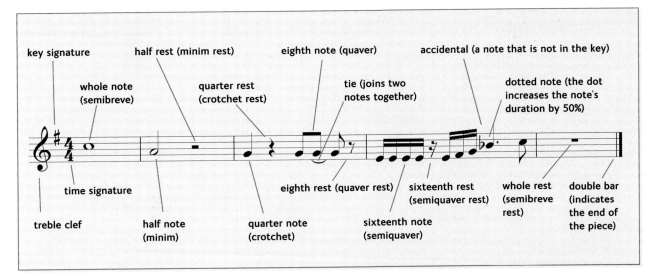

Reading music: being able to read music is a useful skill, especially when learning new songs or jamming with new people.

Key Signatures

The key of a piece of music determines the main notes that will be included in it. In music notation a key signature is written at the beginning of every line of music to indicate the key. Key signatures make music easier to read because any sharps or flats in the key need only be written at the start of each line and will then apply to all those notes throughout the piece, rather than needing to write a sharp or flat sign every time such a note occurs. Each major key has a unique key signature, consisting of a collection of sharps or flats written in a set order; these sharps and flats match those that occur in the major scale for that key. The key of C major is unusual in that no sharps or flats occur in the keyscale, and therefore the key signature is blank.

Minor keys share key signatures with their relative major keys (i.e. major keys that have a keynote three half steps higher than that of the minor key).

F major   Bb major   Eb major   Ab major   Db major   Gb major
D minor   D minor   C minor   F minor   D minor   Eb minor

Flat key signatures

Fretboxes

See page 62 for a description of fretboxes.

G major   D major   A major   E major   B major   F# major
E minor   B minor   F# minor   C# minor   G# minor   D# minor

Sharp key signatures

Major Scales

By far the most important scale in music is the major scale. All other scales, and even all chords, can be considered as stemming from the major scale. The major scale is used as the basis for the majority of popular melodies. When used in lead playing it gives a bright and melodic sound.

Scale Construction

The major scale is constructed by using a combination of whole steps/whole tones (W) and half steps/semitones (H). Regardless of the key, the pattern of tones and semitones is as follows: W W H W W W H.

For example, the C major scale, is constructed as follows:

C	plus a **whole** step	=	D
D	plus a **whole** step	=	E
E	plus a **half** step	=	F
F	plus a **whole** step	=	G
G	plus a **whole** step	=	A
A	plus a **whole** step	=	B
B	plus a **half** step	=	C

C major scale.

Transposing Scales

All the scales illustrated in this chapter are 'transpositional': they can be played in other keys simply by starting the finger pattern at a different fret. For example, to play the D major scale, use the exact fingering shown for C major but start two frets higher. For some keys, for example G major, you might prefer to start the scale pattern on the low E string in order to avoid high fingerboard positions.

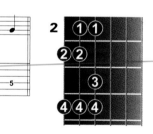

D major scale.

G major scale.

Pentatonic Major Scale

The term 'pentatonic' means 'five-note'; the pentatonic major scale is a five-note abbreviation of the standard major scale, with the fourth and seventh degrees of the major scale omitted. For example, the notes in the C major scale are C D E F G A B. To convert this into the C pentatonic major scale omit the notes F (the 4th) and B (the 7th), resulting in C D E G A.

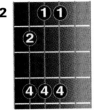

C pentatonic major scale.

The pentatonic major scale has none of the overtly sugary sound often associated with the standard major scale – instead it has a great combination of brightness with a cutting edge. It is a very useful scale for improvising in major keys; because it contains fewer notes than the standard major scale there is less chance of any of the notes clashing with the accompanying chords.

Traditionally, pentatonic major scales have been used in country music, but many rock bands – from the Rolling Stones and Free to Travis and Supergrass – have used them frequently on their recordings.

Brit-rock bands were great fans of the pentatonic major scale, particularly Noel Gallagher, who relied on them almost exclusively for his solos on the first few Oasis albums. Some of its greatest exponents were country-rock players like Danny Gatton and Albert Lee.

LEFT: Oasis's debut album *Definitely Maybe* (1994) features a number of solos that are based on the pentatonic major scale.

Minor Scales

There are a variety of minor scales to suit all musical styles, from the soulful natural minor scale to the exotic harmonic minor scale. But it is the rock-edged pentatonic minor scale that is by far the most widely used scale in lead-guitar playing.

Natural Minor Scale

The natural minor scale is constructed using a combination of whole steps/tones (W) and half steps/semitones (H) in the following pattern: W H W W H W W. For example, C natural minor scale, is constructed as follows:

C	plus a **whole** step	=	D
D	plus a **half** step	=	E♭
E♭	plus a **whole** step	=	F
F	plus a **whole** step	=	G
G	plus a **half** step	=	A♭
A♭	plus a **whole** step	=	B♭
B♭	plus a **whole** step	=	C

The interval spelling for the natural minor scale is 1 2 ♭3 4 5 ♭6 ♭7 8, meaning that, in comparison to the major scale with the same keynote, the third, sixth and seventh notes are flattened by a

half step. The natural minor scale is widely used in rock- and blues-based music. The scale has a soulful, yet melodic sound. Carlos Santana and Gary Moore are two of its best-known exponents.

C natural minor scale.

LEFT: **Many of the solos by blues and hard-rock guitarist Gary Moore use the natural minor scale.**

Pentatonic Minor Scale

In all forms of rock music, the pentatonic minor scale is the most commonly used scale for lead–guitar playing. The interval spelling is 1 ♭3 4 5 ♭7 8. It is a popular scale for improvising in minor keys because it contains fewer notes than the natural minor scale – this makes the scale easy to use and means that there is little chance of any of the notes clashing with the accompanying chords.

C pentatonic minor scale.

Harmonic Minor Scale

The harmonic minor scale is very similar to the natural minor scale. The only difference is that, in the harmonic minor scale, the note on the seventh degree is raised by a half step. This results in a large interval between the sixth and seventh degrees of the scale, giving the scale its distinctive, exotic sound. The interval spelling is 1 2 ♭3 4 5 ♭6 7 8. Ritchie Blackmore was one of the first rock guitarists to exploit the melodic potential of this scale.

C harmonic minor scale.

Melodic Minor Scale

The step pattern of this scale alters depending on whether it is being played ascending or descending. When played descending it has the same notes as the natural minor scale; when played ascending the sixth and seventh degrees are each raised by a half step. The interval spelling is 1 2 ♭3 4 5 6 7 8 ascending and 1 2 ♭3 4 5 ♭6 ♭7 8 descending. The scale is mostly used in jazz rock and fusion.

C melodic minor scale ascending.

Jazz Melodic Minor Scale

The jazz melodic minor scale is the same as the ascending version of the standard melodic minor scale. The sixth and seventh degrees of the scale are raised by a half step in comparison to the natural minor scale, giving it a much brighter tonality that is well suited to some forms of jazz music. The interval spelling is 1 2 ♭3 4 5 6 7 8.

Further Scales

Expanding your knowledge of scales beyond the common major and minor scales will broaden your musical vocabulary, enabling you to play lead guitar in a wide range of musical styles. A grasp of a broad collection of scales will also facilitate improvisation over complex chord progressions.

Blues Scale

The blues scale contains all the notes of the pentatonic minor scale, but with the addition of a ♭5 note. It is this note that gives the blues scale its distinctive blues flavour. All blues lead–guitar playing uses the blues scale as its foundation. The interval spelling of the blues scale is 1 ♭3 4 ♭5 5 ♭7. C blues scale contains the notes C E♭ F G♭ G B♭.

C blues scale.

Chromatic Scale

This scale contains every half step between the starting note and the octave. It is the only 12–note scale in music and does not relate to any particular key. Instead, when improvising, notes from the chromatic scale can be added to introduce notes that are not in the key of the backing. Including these 'outside' notes as chromatic passing notes within a lead-guitar solo can help provide moments of harmonic tension.

C chromatic scale.

Country Scale

The country scale contains all the notes of the pentatonic major scale, but with the addition of a minor 3rd note. This gives it a slightly bluesy edge that suits 'new country' and 'country rock' guitar styles. The interval spelling is 1 2 ♭3 3 5 6 8.

C country scale.

Diminished Scales

These are eight-note scales made up of alternating whole-step and half-step intervals. Diminished scales can start either with a whole step or a half step. Diminished scales that start with a whole step are described as whole/half diminished scales. These are generally used to improvise over diminished seventh chords. The interval spelling is 1 2 ♭3 4 ♭5 ♭6 ♭♭7 7 8.

Diminished scales that start with a half step are described as half/whole diminished scales. These are widely used in jazz and fusion to create a sense of musical tension and colour when improvising over dominant seventh chords. The interval spelling is 1 ♭2 #2 3 #4 5 6 ♭7 8.

C whole/half diminished scale.

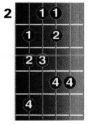

C half/whole diminished scale.

Whole-tone Scale

The whole-tone scale is constructed using only whole steps. Between any note and its octave there are six whole steps, therefore the whole-tone scale contains six different notes. Whole-tone scales are rarely used as key scales, but instead tend to be used for improvising over dominant altered chords (such as 7#5). The interval spelling is 1 2 3 #4 #5 ♭7 8.

C whole-tone scale.

Modes

Modes are scales that are formed by taking the notes of an existing scale but starting from a note other than the original keynote. This results in each mode having a unique tonality. The most common modes played on the guitar are those of the major scale, in particular the Dorian, Lydian and Mixolydian modes.

Dorian Modal Scale

Taking the notes of the major scale starting from its second degree creates the Dorian modal scale. For example, the notes of the B♭ major scale are B♭ C D E♭ F G A B♭. The second note in the B♭ major scale is C, so the C Dorian modal scale contains the notes C D E♭ F G A B♭ C. The interval spelling is 1 2 ♭3 4 5 6 ♭7 8.

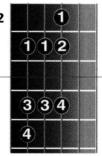

C Dorian modal scale.

Even though the B♭ major scale and the C Dorian mode derived from it contain the same notes, they have a very different sound and character. For example, the major scale has a major third interval from the first to the third note and a major seventh interval from the first to the seventh note. In contrast, the Dorian modal scale contains minor third and minor seventh intervals – making it a type of 'minor' scale. Compared to the

natural minor scale, the Dorian modal scale has a brighter, less melancholic, sound and is often used in funk, soul and jazz styles.

Lydian Modal Scale

The Lydian modal scale has a laid-back sound that is well-suited to jazz, fusion and soul music. The mode is formed by taking the notes of the major scale starting from its fourth degree. For example, the notes of the G major scale are G A B C D E F♯ G. The fourth note in the G major scale is C, so the Lydian modal scale that is generated from the G major scale is the C Lydian modal scale – comprising the notes C D E F♯ G A B C. The interval spelling is 1 2 3 ♯4 5 6 7 8.

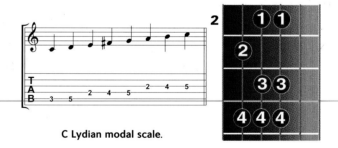

C Lydian modal scale.

You might notice that when compared to the 'tonic major' (the major scale with the same starting note) the only difference is the inclusion of the ♯4 note in the Lydian modal scale.

Tip
The Ionian modal scale is an alternative name for the major scale, and the Aeolian modal scale is another name for the natural minor scale.

Mixolydian Modal Scale

The Mixolydian modal scale is used in blues and rock music. It is formed by taking the notes of the major scale starting from its fifth degree. For example, the notes of the F major scale are F G A B♭ C D E F. The fifth note in the F major scale is C, so the Mixolydian modal scale that is generated from the F major scale is the C Mixolydian modal scale – comprising the notes C D E F G A B♭ C. The interval spelling is 1 2 3 4 5 6 ♭7 8.

C Mixolydian modal scale.

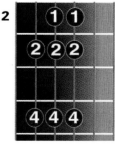

ABOVE: **Tal Farlow and George Benson jazzing it up with modal scales.**

When compared to the 'tonic major' (the major scale with the same starting note) the only difference is the inclusion of the ♭7 note in the Mixolydian modal scale. This gives the scale a bluesy, yet melodic sound.

Further Modes

Learning some of the more esoteric modal scales can be a useful method of making your playing more individual. It can lead you to investigate musical styles and create sounds that you might otherwise leave unexplored; your playing might begin to include elements of Spanish flamenco or avant-garde jazz that you'd never even dreamed of.

Phrygian Modal Scale

The Phrygian modal scale is quite unusual in that it starts with a half-step interval between the first two degrees. This gives it

BELOW: **The Phrygian mode is one of the most important scales in flamenco music. It is often referred to as the Flamenco scale.**

a typically Spanish flamenco sound. The scale is formed by taking the notes of the major scale starting from the third degree. For example, the notes of the A♭ major scale are A♭ B♭ C D♭ E♭ F G. The third note in the A♭ major scale is C, so the Phrygian modal scale that is generated from the A♭ major scale is the C Phrygian modal scale – containing the notes C D♭ E♭ F G A♭ B♭ C. The interval spelling is 1 ♭2 ♭3 4 5 ♭6 ♭7 8.

from the D♭ major scale is the C Locrian modal scale. The C note becomes the keynote of the Locrian modal scale and the remaining notes in the D♭ major scale make up the rest of the C Locrian modal scale. The interval spelling is 1 ♭2 ♭3 4 ♭5 ♭6 ♭7 8.

The Locrian modal scale is a minor scale with a diminished tonality, making it well suited for improvising over half-diminished chords.

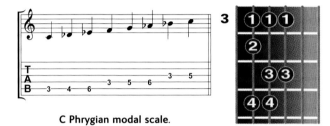

C Phrygian modal scale.

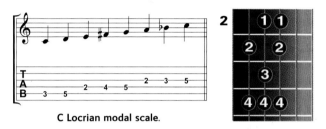

C Locrian modal scale.

Phrygian Major Modal Scale

The Phrygian major modal scale is actually the fifth mode of the harmonic minor scale, but it can be considered as a variation of the Phrygian modal scale: all the notes are the same except that the Phrygian major modal scale contains a major (rather than flattened) third. The interval spelling is 1 ♭2 3 4 5 ♭6 ♭7 8.

As well as flamenco, it is commonly used in heavy-metal guitar styles.

Lydian Dominant Modal Scale

The Lydian dominant modal scale is actually the fourth mode of the jazz melodic minor scale. However, the scale is often referred to as the Lydian ♭7 modal scale. This is because, apart from containing a ♭7 interval, it contains the same notes as the Lydian modal scale. The interval spelling is 1 2 3 ♯4 5 6 ♭7 8.

The scale is mostly used in jazz and fusion styles.

C Phrygian major modal scale.

C Lydian dominant modal scale.

Locrian Modal Scale

The Locrian modal scale is the mode that starts on the seventh degree of the major scale. For example, C is the 7th note in the scale of D♭ major, so the Locrian modal scale that is generated

---

Tip

Modes can be treated as key centres in their own right, with a group of chords to accompany each modal scale. Alternatively, modes can be used as chord scales – using a different mode over each chord.

Pitch

Melodic Guitarist

In this chapter, scales have been shown with a starting note of C. You can alter the pitch of any scale easily by starting the same finger pattern at a different fret. However, you may need to change the fingering for each scale to play it in a higher or lower octave – or simply in a different fingerboard position.

Fingerboard Positions

One of the interesting things about the guitar fingerboard is that the same note can be played at exactly the same pitch in several different places on the fingerboard.

If you play through the example below, you'll notice that each E note has a slightly different tonal quality even though they all have the same pitch. The same applies to scales and riffs – they will have a slightly different tone depending upon the chosen fingerboard position. You will also find that some riffs or licks might be easier to play in one fingerboard position compared to another.

The note of E can be played at exactly the same pitch in five different fingerboard positions.

If you're really serious about studying the guitar, you should make it a long-term aim to learn as many different fingerboard positions as possible for all your scales, because this will provide you with the maximum amount of flexibility in your playing.

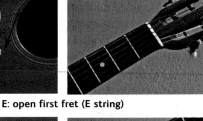

E: open first fret (E string)

E: fifth fret (B string)

E: 9th fret (G string)

E: 14th fret (D string)

E: 19th fret (A string)

To start you on your way, here are three positions of the C major scale – all at the same pitch.

Changing Octave

As well as learning scales of the same pitch in different fingerboard positions, you also need to be able to play them in different octaves. This will give you a wider sonic range to play across – from deep bassy riffs to high-pitched screaming solos. This fingerboard knowledge will help you play sympathetically with other elements in a song, for example, playing in a range that will merge well with the vocals or other instruments in some sections of the song, while moving to an octave that will make the guitar jump out of the mix in other sections.

Practising scales in a variety of fingerboard positions and octaves will help you develop a good knowledge of the location of notes on the fingerboard; this in turn will enable you to target notes that match the chord structure when improvising.

Ideally, you should aim to develop a practice regime that will enable you, over a period of time, to learn all the scales in this book in all keys and in all possible octaves and fingerboard positions.

As a starting point, the fretboard diagrams below show the same C major scale that is illustrated above, but this time in a higher octave and in five different fingerboard positions.

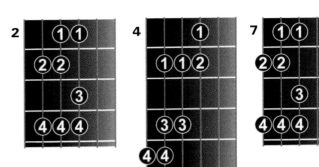

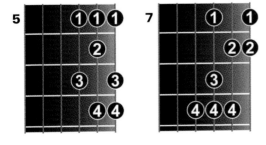

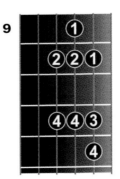

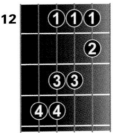

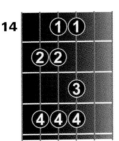

SECTION ONE

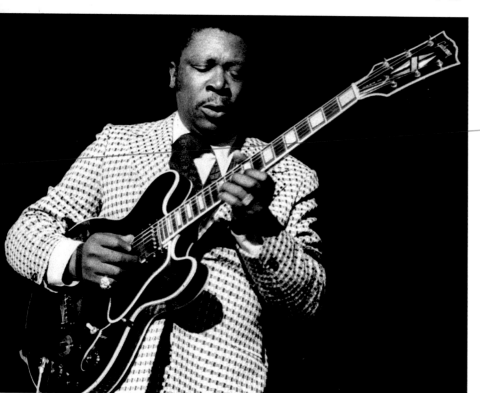

Introduction

Once you've learnt the fundamentals of guitar playing, such as scales and chords, it's time to put these into action in a practical music-making setting. Applying specialist guitar techniques, such as string bending and vibrato, will enhance the sound of your performance and enable you to add individuality to both lead and rhythm playing.

Lead Techniques

Throughout this chapter the most essential lead-guitar techniques will be explained in some depth. Some of these techniques, such as hammer-ons and pull-offs, will help you develop fluency and smoothness in your playing. Others, such as vibrato and string bending, will enable you to make your lead playing more expressive and personal. Guitarists who are renowned for their skill in using string bends include David Gilmour, Gary Moore, Eric Clapton and Buddy Guy.

Blues guitarist B.B. King is widely acknowledged as the master of vibrato playing. Other guitarists who excel with this technique include Peter Green, Albert Collins and Paul Kossoff.

An arpeggio is created by playing the notes contained within a chord individually rather than simultaneously. When playing licks or solos, arpeggios can provide just as important a role as scales, in fact, some players – such as Yngwie Malmsteen, Albert Lee and Mark Knopfler – rely very heavily on arpeggios in their lead-guitar playing.

Rhythm Techniques

Techniques that can make your rhythm-guitar playing more creative and exciting are also covered in this chapter. These include topics such as using string damping as a method of extending the dynamic range of your rhythm playing, and playing riffs using chord shapes rather than just single notes. Listen to the guitar playing of Dave Davies

LEFT: **Blues legend B.B. King uses a well-practised vibrato technique to add richness to his playing.**

ABOVE: **Dave Davies (far left) used chords in the introductory riff of the Kinks' hit song 'You Really Got Me'.**

of the Kinks, Mick Ronson, Angus Young and Paul Weller for some of the best examples of rhythm–guitar techniques in action.

Specialist Techniques

Exploring some advanced techniques, such as octave playing and harmonics, can really add range and variety to your playing. If your guitar is fitted with a tremolo arm, experimenting with this can lead to some interesting sonic discoveries. Compare the subtle use Hank Marvin makes of the tremolo arm with the wild sounds made by Steve Vai and Jeff Beck.

If you don't already own one, try to get hold of a bottleneck (slide). Using one of these will provide you with musical possibilities unobtainable through normal playing. Although their use originated in blues and country music, many rock players also regularly use slides as an alternative to their usual solo styles. Some great slide players include Duane Allman, Ry Cooder, Muddy Waters and George Thorogood.

RIGHT: **Southern-rock guitarist Duane Allman was renowned for his slide technique.**

Changing Chords

It's one thing to know some chord shapes, but it's a far more difficult skill to change fluently between them without leaving any gaps in between. Luckily, there are a few short cuts you can take to make your chord changes easier and faster.

Minimum Movement Principle

It's essential that chord changes are crisp and prompt. This might not be too hard when using chords that you're very familiar with, but it can seem daunting with chords that are new to you.

However, changing between any chords can be made much easier if you follow the 'minimum movement principle'. This involves making only the smallest finger movement necessary between chords, and avoiding taking fingers off strings or frets only to put them back on again for the next chord. Excess movement between chords is what slows chord changes down; the less your fingers move, the faster your chord changes will be.

Some chords have one or more notes in common. For example, the open position A minor and F major chords both include the note C (first fret on the B string). The C major chord also includes this note and, in addition, has another note in common with the

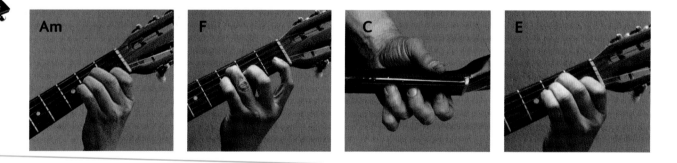

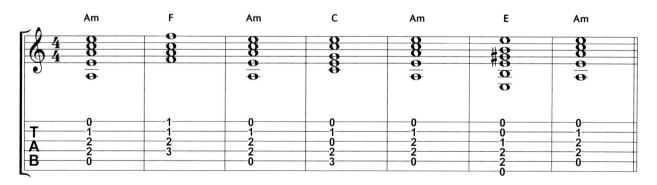

When moving from Am to F, keep the first finger on the second string first fret, but flatten it to cover the first string as well. Between Am and C only move the third finger; keep the others in place. Notice how E major is the same 'shape' as Am – just on different strings.

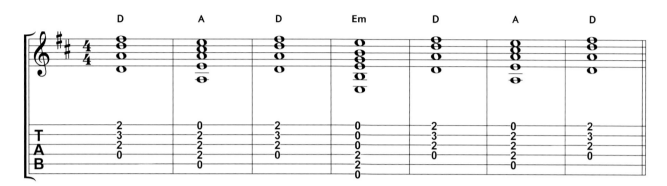

Try to spot the common links between consecutive chord shapes. For example, between the D and A chords the third finger could just slide along the second string, while the first and second fingers move up or down across the strings.

A minor chord (E on the second fret of the D string). The chord progression shown below uses the chords Am, F, C and E: notice the common fingering between each chord change; in particular, how the first finger stays on the first fret and how the second finger stays on the second fret throughout.

Even if different chords don't contain too many common notes, changing between them can still be made easier if you look out for any possible links. For example, when changing between the D and A major chords the third finger can be slid along the second string (between frets two and three) rather than being taken off the string only to be put back on a fret higher a moment later.

Following the principle of minimum movement saves time and makes the chord changes smoother. No matter how remote a

chord change appears to be, there will always be some kind of link between the chords; once spotted, this will make changing between them easier.

'Open Vamp' Strum

If all else fails, there is a 'pro-trick' you can use that will mask any gap between chord changes: using an 'open vamp' strum. This simply involves strumming the open strings while your fingers move between the chord change. While not ideal, it does mean that the overall fluency and momentum of the performance is maintained. In fact, some players actually make a feature of this technique to bring out accents within their rhythm playing. Whatever technique you use, the golden rule in rhythm playing when you come across difficult passages is 'never stop – always keep strumming'.

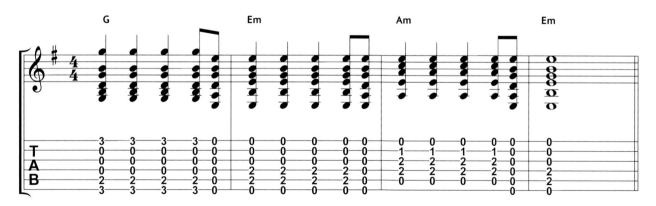
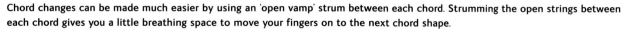

Chord changes can be made much easier by using an 'open vamp' strum between each chord. Strumming the open strings between each chord gives you a little breathing space to move your fingers on to the next chord shape.

Power Chords

Playing only selected notes from a chord can actually give a stronger sound than playing the whole chord – especially when you add a touch of distortion. You can get a tighter and more easily controlled sound by just using two or three notes from a chord.

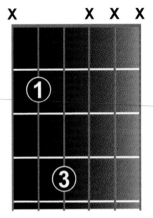

X   X X X

①

③

C5 power chord

Fifths

In rock music, instead of full chords, abbreviated versions just using the root and fifth note are often played. These 'fifth chords' are commonly called 'power chords'. Apart from the tone, one of the main advantages of using fifths is that it's much easier to move quickly from chord to chord because there are only a couple of fingers involved. To play a fifth power chord, simply fret a note on any bass string and add a note two frets up on the adjacent higher string.

Songs that use fifths are normally in minor keys, so learn a minor scale in fifths as this will prepare you for the type of progressions commonly used.

To hear the differences in sound between fifths and standard chord shapes, play through a short chord sequence, first using normal open position chords and then with the chords as fifths. Once you've done this, you could experiment by converting songs that you already play with open chords into a version using fifths.

C5

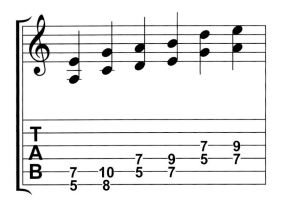

A pentatonic minor scale in fifths.

Seventies rock bands like Judas Priest and Black Sabbath (the heavy–metal pioneers) specialized in writing songs based upon riffs played in fifths – often adding an octave note to the chord to get a more powerful sound.

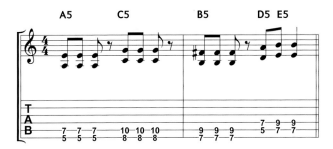

A typical 1970s rock riff. Octave notes could be used as well as the fifth to give a heavier sound.

Eighties heavy–metal bands like Iron Maiden and Metallica used plenty of fifths in their songs, but often varied the fifth shape a little by using augmented or diminished fifths to create a more foreboding sound.

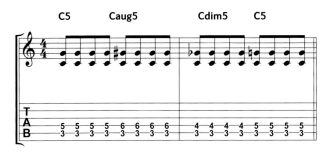

A 1980s metal riff, using variations on the standard fifth chord.

In the early Nineties, the Seattle grunge sound was based on the use of fifths. Bands like Pearl Jam and Nirvana tended to use a less distorted sound than their metal predecessors and also tended to strum using down and up strokes.

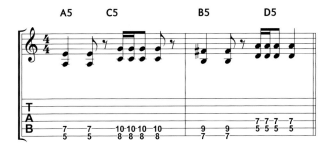

Down and up strums capture the grunge spirit.

More recent rock bands such as Slipknot and Blink–182 base much of their rhythm playing on fifth power chords, often using dropped tunings to create an even stronger sound.

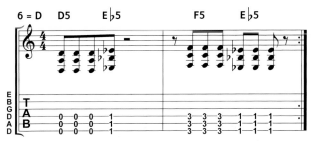

The low E string is de-tuned to D, enabling fifth power chords to be played on the 6th and 5th strings on a single fret – making fast chord changes much easier.

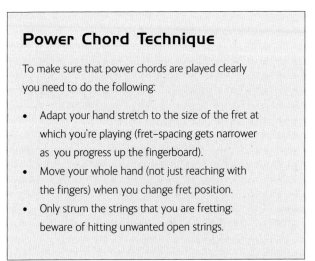

Power Chord Technique

To make sure that power chords are played clearly you need to do the following:

- Adapt your hand stretch to the size of the fret at which you're playing (fret-spacing gets narrower as you progress up the fingerboard).
- Move your whole hand (not just reaching with the fingers) when you change fret position.
- Only strum the strings that you are fretting; beware of hitting unwanted open strings.

Barre Chords

Playing open position chords is a great way to begin learning the guitar, but if you take a careful look at any professional players you'll soon notice that most of their chord positions are further up the fretboard; more often than not they'll be playing shapes known as 'barre chords'.

Advantages of Barre Chords

Playing a barre chord involves re-fingering an open position chord so as to leave the first finger free to play the barre by fretting all six strings. The whole chord can then be moved up the fingerboard to different pitches. The main advantage of using barre chords is that you can move the same shape up or down the fingerboard to create new chords without the need to memorize a whole host of different fingerings for each chord. Using barre chords will allow you to play more unusual chords (like B♭ minor or F♯ major), which are unobtainable in open position.

Major Barre Chords

To play major chords in barre form, begin by re-fingering an open position E major chord using the second, third and fourth fingers. Then move this up to different fingerboard positions, with the first finger fretting all the strings on the adjacent lower fret.

BELOW: **Barre chords are useful because a single hand position can be used for all of the 12 different keys simply by moving it up or down the neck of the guitar.**

A♭/G♯ major

Most guitars have marker dots on frets three, five and seven, and moving the barre of the E major shape to these positions will give the chords of G, A and B major.

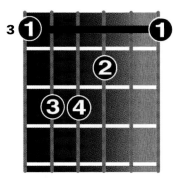

G major barre chord – based upon an E major shape. Move this shape to the fifth fret for A major and to the seventh fret for B major.

In theory, you could play all major chords with just this one barre chord shape. In practice, however, this would involve leaping around the fingerboard too much when changing from one chord to another. Therefore, knowing at least two shapes for each chord type will enable you to play through most songs without ever having to shift more than a couple of frets for each chord change. The second major shape you can convert to a barre chord is the open position A major shape; moving this shape with the barre on the marker dots on frets three, five and seven of the A string will give the chords of C, D and E major.

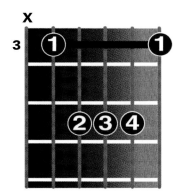

C major barre chord – based upon an A major shape. Move this shape to the fifth fret for D major and the seventh fret for E major.

Minor Barre Chords

Open position minor chords can also be converted to barre chords. The E minor and A minor shapes can be re-fingered to leave the first finger free to make the barre. When the E minor shape is moved up, the pitch of the chord should be taken from the barre position on the E string. When the A minor chord

is moved up, the pitch should be taken from the barre position on the A string.

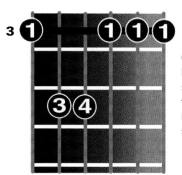

G minor barre chord – based upon an E minor shape. Move this shape to the fifth fret for A minor and to the seventh fret for B minor.

Mixing Barre Chords

Most songs will combine a mixture of major and minor chords. Whether you decide to use an E or A shape barre chord will depend on the position of the previous and the following chord; the trick is to choose the shape that will avoid any large fingerboard shifts.

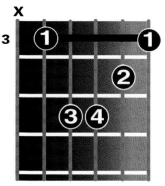

C minor barre chord – based upon an A minor shape. Move this shape to the fifth fret for D minor and to the seventh fret for E minor.

Barre Chord Technique

- Keep the first finger straight and in line with the fret.
- The creases between the joints of the barring finger should not coincide with strings.
- Position all the fretting fingers as close to the fretwire as possible.
- Press down firmly, but avoid using excessive pressure.
- When you move between barre chords ensure that your thumb also shifts, so that your whole hand position is moving with each chord change.

Chord Riffs

Don't assume that chords are used purely for strumming an accompaniment – in some musical styles chords are quite frequently used to create the main riffs within songs. Some of the strongest and most memorable riffs in the history of rock music have been created using chords rather than single notes.

AC/DC or the White Stripes to hear some fine examples of chordal riffing. When creating riffs with chords, you'll normally need to use more than one chord per measure in order to give a sense of movement. This might mean changing quickly to a totally different chord, or the riffs may just consist of chordal variations (such as major chords changing to suspended chords).

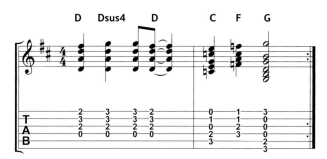

Example of a riff using open position chords.

Using Rests

Using rests (silences) between chords will help to add a well-defined rhythm to your riff, giving it musical shape and character. Place the strumming hand against the strings when you wish to mute them. The opening to the Rolling Stones' 'Brown Sugar' is a classic example of this technique.

ABOVE: 'Black Math' from the White Stripes' 2003 album *Elephant* is an excellent example of chordal riffing.

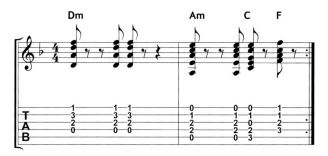

The rests give this riff its distinct rhythmic character.

Creating Riffs

A riff is a short musical phrase that is repeated many times throughout a song. Using chords to play riffs will nearly always result in a much more powerful sound than a riff played just using single notes. Listen to anything by the Rolling Stones,

Separating Strings

An effective technique for chord riffing is to separate the bass and treble strings when a chord is played. This will allow you to create a piano-like effect, with the bass part clearly separated from the treble.

Begin the E and G major chords by striking only the bass strings, followed by just the treble strings of each chord.

Using Power Chords

When playing chord riffs it's not always necessary to strum all of the strings – often just strumming the root and fifth notes of a chord (normally the bottom two strings of the chord) will suffice.

In fact, for riffing, playing 'power chords' often sounds better than strumming all the strings of the complete chord shape as the sound will be tighter and better defined. Deep Purple's 'Smoke On The Water' is probably the best-known example of a power chord riff.

Example of a riff using power chords.

Adding Single Notes

Chord riffs do not need to consist exclusively of chords: adding an occasional single note, particularly an open bass string, can add variety to a riff and often make it easier to play.

On the A major chord the bass and treble strings are strummed separately; the E and F♯ bass notes then facilitate the change to the G major chord.

Tip
Playing chord riffs will inevitably involve the need for some fast chord changes. Practise the chord changes very slowly at first – only speeding up once you are totally secure in moving between the chords.

String Damping

Nearly all rock and blues players use string damping as a way of controlling the guitar's volume and tone. By resting the side of the strumming hand lightly on the strings, close to the saddle, a choked or muted sound can be achieved by deadening the sustain of the strings.

Damping Technique

String damping is an essential technique for varying the tone and volume of your guitar playing. The technique can be used after a note or chord has been played to achieve a short and detached 'staccato' effect. The technique can also be used to bring out accents in a rhythm, by maintaining the muting effect throughout and releasing only intermittently on the beats to be accented.

ABOVE: **String damping, using 'palm muting' technique: the edge of the fretting hand rests against the strings next to the bridge; the hand stays in position when you strum, to mute the strings.**

Strumming-hand Damping

To learn this technique, first strum slowly across all the open strings to hear the natural sound of the guitar. Then, place your strumming hand at a 90-degree angle to the strings, close to the saddle, with the side of the hand (in line with the little finger) pressing lightly against all six strings. Maintain contact with the strings with the edge of your hand, and then rotate the hand towards the strings and strum again. The pressure of the hand against the strings will dampen the volume and sustain – this is known as 'palm muting'. Notice how this is very different from the normal sound of strummed open strings. Now try this again with an E minor chord. When you use string damping it's not

LEFT: **One of the most famous examples of string damping is the Police's 'Every Breath You Take' from their 1983 album** *Synchronicity*.

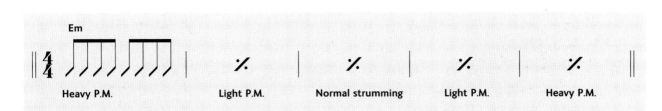

Em

Heavy P.M.   Light P.M.   Normal strumming   Light P.M.   Heavy P.M.

Palm muting. Measure 1: press firmly against the strings. M. 2: lighten the pressure. M. 3: release damping hand. M. 4: re-apply damping hand, increasing pressure in the final measure.

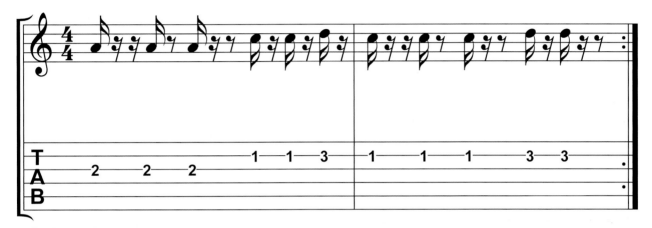

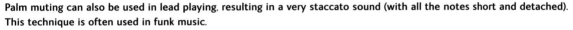

Palm muting can also be used in lead playing, resulting in a very staccato sound (with all the notes short and detached). This technique is often used in funk music.

necessary to always strum all the strings of the chord; often – particularly in rock styles – it's better just to strum the bass string and a couple of others. Vary the amount of pressure with which the side of the hand rests on the strings: if you press too hard the notes will just become dead thuds, but if you press too lightly the strings will start to ring and sustain again. Be aware that it's all too easy at first to pull the damping hand away from the strings as you begin to strum, so losing the muting effect. Although it may take a while to gain control of this technique, and to strike the right balance of pressure and release, it's well worth the effort as string damping is an essential tool that will broaden your technique.

Fretting-hand Damping

You can also mute the strings by slightly relaxing the pressure on the strings that you are fretting: the fingers still touch the strings, but do not press them all the way down to the fretboard. This technique can be used after a note has been picked to achieve a

staccato effect, or after a chord has been strummed to achieve a chord 'chop'. The technique can also be used to bring out accents, by damping the fretting hand continuously while the strumming hand plays a rhythm – the fretting hand only pressing the chord intermittently, so that it sounds only on the beats to be accented.

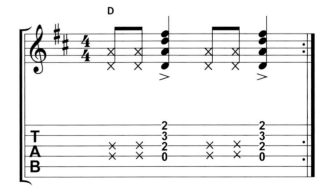

Fretting-hand damping: the fretting hand begins by touching, rather than pressing, the strings. This causes the notes to be muted. On the accented beats, the notes of the chord are fretted normally so that the chord sounds clearly when strummed strongly.

Slurs

Slurring is a method that not only enables you to play much faster than with normal picking, but also provides a much smoother (legato) sound. There are two slurring techniques: 'hammering-on' and 'pulling-off'.

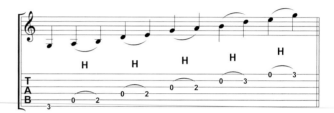

G pentatonic major scale played ascending using hammer-ons. The curved slur line and the H sign indicate which notes should be hammered-on.

Hammer-ons

When moving from one note to a higher note on the same string it's not always necessary to pick the string again. By forcefully bringing down your finger on to the new fret while the previous note is sounding you create a hammer-on. You may need to pick the first note a little harder than other picked notes, as its vibrations will need to carry over to the hammered-on note. The notes may sound more even on an electric guitar because of natural or added sustain, but acoustic guitarists use hammer-ons just as frequently.

Pull-offs

Similarly, when moving from one note to a lower note on the same string you may not want to pick the string again. By removing your finger from the higher note with a slight pulling motion,

BELOW: **Hammer-on technique: a hammer-on with three fingers.**

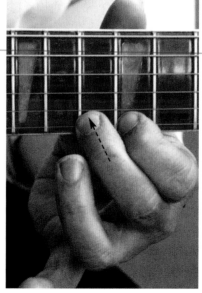

LEFT: **Pull-off technique: a pull-off with two fingers.**

you essentially pluck that string with your fretting hand, thus creating a pull-off.

Hammer-ons and pull-offs of two fretted notes are limited by the distance you can stretch the fingers of your fretting hand, but you can also hammer-on from (or pull-off to) open strings, creating whatever intervals sound good to you.

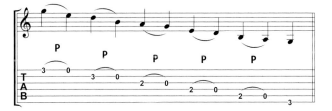

G pentatonic major scale played descending using pull-offs. The curved slur line and P sign indicate which notes should be pulled-off.

Combining Hammer-ons and Pull-offs

Once you've mastered the basic techniques described above, try the slurring exercises below, which combine both hammer-ons and pull-offs.

Combination slur, Exercise 1. Two pull-offs lead to an open string, then hammer back on and start again, so that only the very first note is picked.

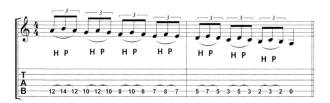

Combination slur, Exercise 2. Use a hammer-on, then a pull-off, on each note of the A natural minor scale descending along the fifth string – picking only the first of each three notes.

Trill

If you repeatedly hammer-on and pull-off between the same two notes it is known as a 'trill'. This is a technique favoured by many rock guitarists, from Jimi Hendrix to Steve Vai.

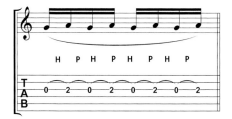

Trill: alternately hammering-on and pulling-off rapidly between the notes G and A.

Tip

On an electric guitar slurring is much easier if your guitar is adjusted to have a low action. Using a compressor (usually with a distortion effect) will help your slurs sound uniform and even.

Slides

Sliding from one note or chord to another is a great way of creating a seamless legato sound that can make your playing sound relaxed and effortless. The technique also provides an easy way of adding passing notes to make your playing unique and inventive.

Slide Technique

To slide a note means to fret it and then, while maintaining the fretting pressure, to move the finger to another fret on the same string without picking the note again. The second note is sounded only because of the continued pressure of the fretting hand; it is not picked again.

In a standard slide you only hear the first and last notes. However, you can also play a 'glissando' type of slide, in which all the intervening notes are also sounded.

Controlling the amount of grip with the fretting hand is the secret to good sliding. You should try to ensure that the thumb at the back of the guitar neck relaxes its grip when you are in the process of sliding a note up or down. This doesn't mean that the thumb needs to be released totally, but simply that it shouldn't be squeezing tightly against the back of the guitar neck. However, just as your hand reaches the note that you want to slide into, the thumb should squeeze the neck slightly harder to act as a brake, preventing your fingers sliding beyond the destination fret.

Sliding Chords

The guitar is one of the few instruments on which you can slide chords up and down, changing their pitch easily and smoothly; the technique creates a fluidity and smoothness of sound that piano players can only dream of! Because slides are so natural to the guitar they form a core component of any good rhythm-

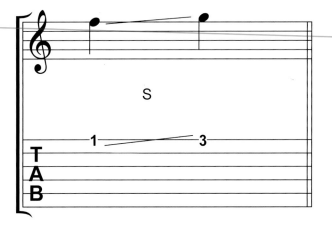

Slide: pick the F note then, using the force of the fretting finger alone, sound the G note by quickly sliding the first finger along the E string.

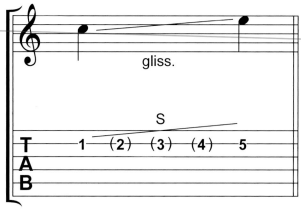

Glissando slide: pick the C note then, using the force of the fretting finger, slide along the B string up to the E note, allowing the notes in between to sound.

guitarist's technique. Slides are used by guitarists in nearly all musical styles, from metal and blues to country and ska.

ABOVE: **Slide technique: a slide from a high note to a low note using heavy sustain.**

When sliding chords it's important to ensure that the chord shape is maintained, so that one finger doesn't end up a fret ahead of the rest! The trick is to achieve a neutral balance whereby the chord shape is kept under control, yet at the same time the fingers are relaxed enough to slide up or down the fingerboard.

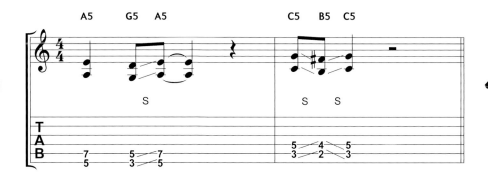

Example of using slides with power chords. Start with an ascending slide, from two frets below the destination chord, followed by a double slide (sliding down and then back up one fret).

Playing fifth 'power chords', where only two notes are fretted, is the ideal introduction to sliding chords. Playing power chords with a copious amount of distortion is the easiest way to begin chord sliding: the distortion will provide sustain which will encourage you not to grip too hard when sliding the chords. Using ascending slides (raising the pitch of a chord) is easier at first – the volume tends to disappear quite quickly with descending slides.

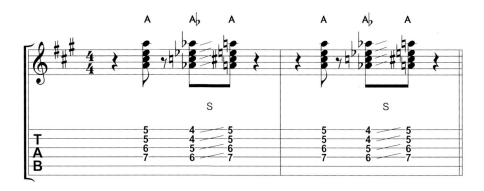

Example of using slides with major chords. Note that the first finger frets the top two strings. You'll need to keep a strong pressure with the fretting finger in order to maintain volume.

Vibrato

By repeatedly varying the pitch of a note very slightly you can achieve an effect known as 'vibrato'. This is used on most string instruments, but it is particularly useful on electric guitar because of the instrument's potentially long sustain – especially if an overdriven sound is used.

RIGHT:
Vibrato technique.

Using vibrato can turn a plain solo into something that sounds really classy. Vibrato can help you make the most of the guitar's sustain, and make your playing more expressive.

Vibrato is often confused with string bending (see page 136), but in fact they are two completely different techniques (although the two are sometimes played together within a lick). The main difference between the two techniques is that string bending involves substantially changing the pitch of a note (usually by a half step or more), whereas vibrato is more subtle, with the note being only 'wavered' with a very small variation in pitch (always returning to, and alternating with, the original pitch).

Vibrato Types

There are three main types of vibrato.

1. Horizontal vibrato: rock the fretting hand from side to side, along the direction of the string. Keep the fretting finger in contact with the string, but release the pressure of the thumb on the back of the neck. This type of vibrato will give you

LEFT: **Paul Kossoff is well known for his excellent use of vibrato.**

LEFT: **Rock guitarist Carlos Santana often incorporates vibrato into his melodic blues-influenced style.**

sure that you return the string to its starting position. This type of vibrato is ideal for adding to a string bend. Once a note is bent you can add vibrato to it to add a subtle enhancement to the bend and add sustain. Peter Green and Paul Kossoff were two of the classic exponents of this technique. Other guitarists employed their own variations on the technique: Buddy Guy and Ritchie Blackmore for example, often prefer to use a very fast 'stinging' vibrato after a bend, while Gary Moore and Yngwie Malmsteen tend to use wider, more extreme vibrato.

increased sustain with just the tiniest variation in pitch. You can rock the hand either slowly or quickly, and for as short or long a time as you wish, depending upon the sound you want to achieve. Classic exponents of this type of vibrato include Mike Oldfield, Mark Knopfler, Dominic Miller, Carlos Santana and John Williams.

2. Wrist vibrato: while the first finger frets a note, the pitch can be wavered by rotating the wrist away from the fingerboard and back again repeatedly. This is one of the best-sounding vibratos, and can result in a sweet singing tone. However, it can only be used on notes that are fretted by the first finger. The undisputed master of this technique is blues legend B.B. King. Modestly he states: 'I won't say I invented it, but they weren't doing it before I started.' This style of vibrato has been an everyday tool of blues and rock guitar players. B.B. King tends to keep his thumb pressed on the back of the neck to get a fast but short pitch-range, 'stinger' vibrato. Other players, such as Eric Clapton, prefer to release the thumb in order to achieve a slower, wider-ranging vibrato.

3. Vertical vibrato: while fretting a note, repeatedly waggle the tip of the fretting finger to move the string up and down slightly. You don't need to move it too far and you should always make

Vibrato Notation

In music notation, vibrato is indicated by a horizontal wavy line. Sometimes the abbreviation 'vib.' is also written. Occasionally, the word 'wide' might be written to indicate wide vibrato, but generally the type of vibrato used is left to the discretion of the performer.

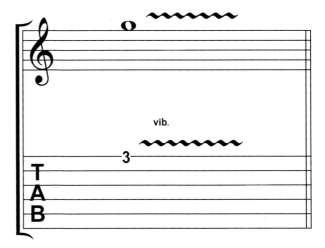

String Bends

String bending is one of the most essential techniques for any electric guitarist. Nearly every rock or blues guitarist since the Fifties has used string bending as part of their technique, and as a way of expressing emotion through their playing. Acoustic guitarists use bends too, but electronic instruments and effects have greatly extended the range of string-bending possibilities.

String bending is the perfect vehicle for adding emotion, expression and individuality to your lead playing. By carefully pushing a string upwards while fretting it you can alter the pitch of the note that you are playing without needing to move to another fret. Classic exponents include Jimi Hendrix, Eric Clapton, B.B. King, David Gilmour and Ritchie Blackmore, but listen to any guitar–based band today and you'll still hear the technique in regular use in almost every solo.

Bending Technique

In theory, you can bend any note in any scale as long as you bend it up to reach another note in that scale. In practice, most bends will

be restricted to the next note in the scale – i.e. a half step (the equivalent of one fret) or a whole step (the equivalent of two frets) higher than the fretted note. You can use any finger to bend a note but, so as not to move out of position and lose fluency, it's best to use the finger that you would normally use to fret the note within the scale. If you're executing the bend with the third or fourth finger, it's really important that you use the remaining fingers, on the same string, to give you added strength when bending. Ignoring this advice will mean that your bends won't go high enough to be in tune, or if they do, then you could end up straining your finger.

Bending in Tune

There are several ways to begin mastering string bends. If you're a good singer you can practise making the string bend until its pitch matches the note you're singing. Another method is to repeatedly pick the string while bending it up very slowly so that

LEFT: **Bending technique: two-string and single-string bends. (Use two fingers to strengthen the control.)**

you can hear the note gradually bend into tune. The essential thing is to listen as you bend, because not much sounds worse than badly out-of-tune string bending! It's important to practise string bends in a range of keys, because the amount of pressure that you need will vary greatly depending upon your position on the fingerboard. For instance, bending a note on the third fret of the third sting will be much harder than bending on the 12th fret on the same string.

Once you feel confident that you are able to bend a note in tune, try playing through these examples, which start with third-finger half-step bends, before progressing to third- and fourth-finger whole-step bends.

Third-finger half-step bend: using the A blues scale, the D note on the G string is bent up a half step to Eb, then let down to D, using the third finger.

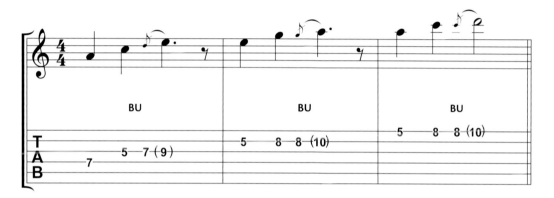

Third- and fourth-finger whole-step bend: using the A pentatonic minor scale, all the bent notes are raised up a whole step. Bend each note slowly until it's in tune, and then hold it there. Use the fourth finger to bend the notes on the second and first string; when doing so, make sure that the second and third fingers are also on the string to give extra strength and support to the fourth finger.

Types of String Bends

- **Choke:** bend the note, and then quickly choke the sound by letting the right hand touch the strings.
- **Hold:** bend the note slowly until it's in tune – then just hold it there.
- **Release:** bend the note up without picking it – then pick it and slowly release it.
- **Up-and-down:** bend the note up and then without re-picking let it down.
- **Double:** bend the note up, let it down, and then bend it up again – but only pick the string the first time.

- **Unison:** while bending a note, fret and play the same note on the next string – or alternate between the two.
- **Vibrato:** bend the note up and then add vibrato by lowering and raising the note repeatedly.
- **Rising:** rapidly pick the string while bending it up very slowly.
- **Harmony:** bend a note while playing or holding a note higher in the scale.
- **Teasing bend:** use several very small bends before fully bending the note into tune. This creates almost a speaking effect – much used by blues players.

Plectrum Technique

that if you show too little plectrum you might end up missing the string altogether. Experiment until you get just the right balance. Also, be mindful of how you grip the plectrum. If you use too much pressure your hand muscles will tighten and so reduce your fluency, but if you hold it too loosely you'll keep dropping it.

Hold the plectrum so that it's in line with your fingernail. Avoid holding it at right angles to your index finger, as this will cause your wrist to lock.

Most electric guitarists want to play fast, and developing great speed starts with having proper control over your plectrum. If you start by holding the plectrum the wrong way you can develop habits that will make it hard to become a fast and accurate player.

Gripping the Plectrum

The best method is to grip the plectrum between the thumb and index finger. Position the plectrum so that its point is about half a centimetre ($\frac{1}{4}$ of an inch) beyond the fingertip. Use only the tip of the plectrum to pick the strings or you will create a physical resistance that will slow down your playing. However, bear in mind

BELOW: **How to hold your plectrum. Notice the angle and amount of plectrum tip showing.**

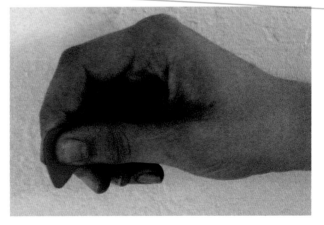

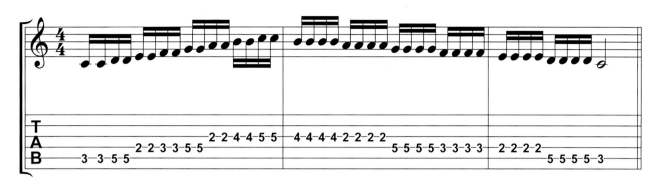

C major scale, played ascending with double picking and descending with quadruple picking.

Alternate Picking

If you want to achieve any degree of speed with the plectrum for lead playing then it's best to use 'alternate picking' as the mainstay of your plectrum technique. This involves alternating downstrokes and upstrokes. Alternate picking is the most logical and economical way of playing, since once you have picked a string downwards, the plectrum will then be ideally positioned to pick upwards, whereas if you try to play two downstrokes in a row you will need to raise the plectrum back up before you can strike the string again.

When alternating down- and upstrokes, make sure that the picking action is generated by swivelling the wrist; try to avoid moving the elbow up and down as this will make your picking style much too cumbersome and will hamper your fluency. For fast lead playing, alternate picking and a relaxed wrist action are the fundamental requirements.

Picking Exercises

Begin by practising alternate picking on the open sixth string. Once you have a secure plectrum technique you can make your licks sound faster by doubling, or even quadrupling, your picking on some notes.

The fretting hand may be moving quite slowly, but the lick will sound more mobile because of the activity of the picking hand. Practise this technique at first by playing scales with double and quadruple picking.

A fast rock sound can be achieved by mixing fretted notes with an open string – while the right hand keeps picking with alternate down- and upstrokes.

Triplet Picking

A great way of making your playing sound super-fast is to use triplet picking patterns. Because these patterns cut across the standard 4/4 rhythm, they give the impression of being much faster than they really are. This repeated 'down-up-down' picking style can give a rolling or galloping effect to a piece of music. (The term 'triplet' here refers only to the three-part picking action; the rhythm doesn't have to be a triplet in the traditional musical sense.)

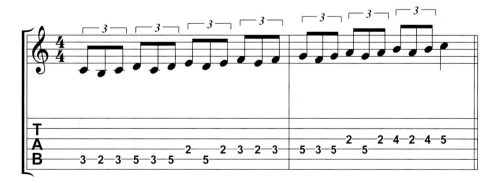

Use a 'down-up-down' picking pattern for each triplet.

Alternative Tunings

Discover a new range of beautiful chordal harmonies by simply tuning your guitar in a different way. If you sometimes start to feel restricted by sticking to the same chord shapes you've played before, then experimenting with alternative tunings is a great way of generating some fresh sounds and ideas.

Dropped D Tuning

There are numerous ways in which a guitar can be retuned, but the simplest and most commonly used is 'dropped D tuning'. All you need to do is lower the pitch of the low E string by a whole step until it reaches the note of D (an octave lower than the open fourth string). You can check that you've retuned correctly by playing on the seventh fret of the sixth string and comparing the note to the open fifth string – they should produce exactly the same pitch.

Dropped D tuning is perfect for playing songs in the keys of D major or D minor. Having the low D bass string is almost like having your own built-in bass player – it can add great solidity and power to your sound. To make the most of this bass effect many guitarists use the low D string as a 'drone' – i.e. they repeatedly play this low

D note while moving chord shapes up and down the fingerboard. Moving a simple D major shape up the fingerboard while playing a low D drone produces a very effective sound.

BELOW: 'With Or Without You' from U2's 1987 album *The Joshua Tree* is a good example of a song in the key of D major.

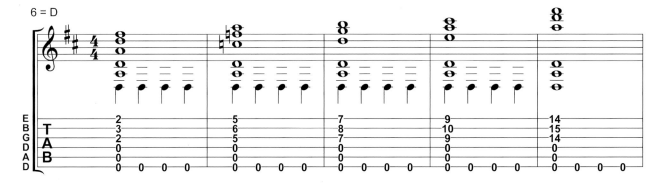

D Modal Tuning

Tuning the sixth, second and first strings down a whole step creates what is known as 'D modal tuning': D A D G A D. When you need to reach this tuning unaided just remember that the A, D and G strings are tuned as normal. Playing the open D string will give you the pitch for the lowered sixth string when it is played at the 12th fret. Playing the A string at the 12th fret will give you the pitch to tune the second string down to, and playing the D string at the 12th fret will give you the pitch to tune the first string down to. Once the guitar is correctly tuned it will give you a Dsus4 chord when the open strings are all strummed, thus creating instant ambiguity and a sense of interest. When first using this tuning, playing in the key of D will prove the easiest: by placing the first finger on the second fret of the G string you will make a nice deep–sounding D major (D5) chord. Traditional chord shapes will not work in the same way with any altered tuning, so it's really a case of experimenting to find chord sounds that you like. The secret is to be adventurous and see what ideas you can come up with when freed from the restrictions of conventional chord shapes.

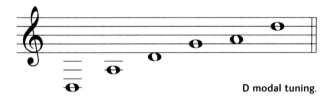

D modal tuning.

Other Tunings

If the two altered tunings described above have given you the taste for experimentation, then here are a few other tunings you can try (all shown starting with the low sixth string).

Slack key tuning – D G D G B D (the first, fifth and sixth strings are 'slackened' down a whole step to form a G major chord).

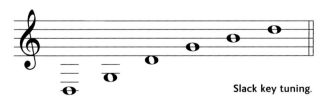

Slack key tuning.

Open E tuning – E B E G♯ B E (the third, fourth and fifth strings are tuned higher than normal to make an E major chord).

Open E tuning.

Open D tuning – D A D F♯ A D (the first, second, third and sixth strings are tuned down so that the open strings form a D major chord).

Open D tuning.

Bottleneck or Slide Guitar

A bottleneck (also known as a 'slide') is a tubular device that can be used instead of the fingers for sounding notes. Using a bottleneck is a great technique for musical styles such as blues, country and rock music when you want to slide between notes and achieve smooth glissandos.

LEFT: When using a bottleneck, the centre of the tube must rest over the centre of the fret, rather than just behind it.

finger being large enough to support the bottleneck. To reach the correct pitch, the middle of the bottleneck should be held directly over the fret, rather than behind it as when fretting a note. The bottleneck only needs to touch the strings; you should not try to press against the frets with the bottleneck as this will cause fretbuzz and result in the notes being out of tune.

Bottleneck is usually played using some vibrato. This is achieved by moving the bottleneck slightly backwards and forwards along the strings above the target fret.

BELOW: Legendary Delta bluesman Robert Johnson was an early exponent of slide guitar.

Originally, the bottleneck guitar sound was created by running a glass neck from a bottle along the strings. Early blues players sometimes used other objects, such as whiskey glasses and knives. Nowadays guitarists can benefit from specially manufactured metal, glass or plastic tubes. The metal versions are technically known as 'slides', although in practice the terms 'slide' and 'bottleneck' are often interchanged. Glass bottlenecks give a more rounded tone, but they create less sustain than the metal versions.

Using the Bottleneck

Most players tend to place the bottleneck on the third or fourth finger: using the fourth finger enables the third finger to remain free for normal fretting, but this is dependent upon the fourth

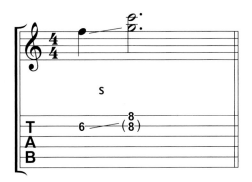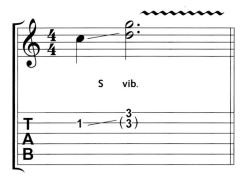

Bottleneck guitar lick in standard tuning. A slide movement is made on the second string from two frets below up to a two-note chord. Be sure to mute unused strings with either the side of the picking hand or with the lower fingers of the bottleneck hand.

Vibrato is essential for any bottleneck guitarist. It can be achieved by keeping the bottleneck vertical and moving slightly from left to right above the fret, but always returning to the correct pitch.

Tuning

So that a full chord can be played with the bottleneck over just one fret, altered tunings are often used. The most common bottleneck tunings are D tuning (D A D F♯ A D) and G tuning (D G D G B D). Using a D tuning and placing the bottleneck across all strings over the 12th fret will produce a D major chord.

Doing the same on the seventh and fifth frets will produce the two other major chords in the key: A and G. By picking the strings one at a time as arpeggios you can make interesting melodic licks.

To take advantage of the chord–based tuning, quite often block chords are used in bottleneck playing – usually sliding into a chord from a fret below, as shown below.

Bottleneck arpeggio lick using D tuning.

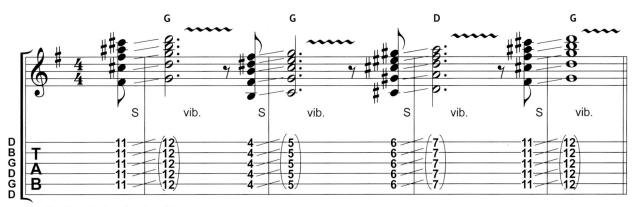

Bottleneck chords using G tuning.

Lap Steel & Resonator Guitars

The techniques you employ when playing bottleneck or slide guitar also apply to instruments like the lap steel and resonator guitars. Resonator guitars are often referred to generically by the brand name Dobro, although many companies, including Dobro's ancestor and competitor, National Stringed Instrument (later National Reso-phonic), have made different versions of the instrument through the years.

Horizontal Playing

A resonator may have six or eight strings and either a square or rounded neck. The round-neck version may be played like a traditional guitar, but the square-neck kind is played in your lap (or on a stand) facing up. A lap steel may have anywhere from six to 12 strings. (Six- and eight-string models are the most common.) Lap steel is normally played while seated but can be mounted on legs or a stand.

RIGHT: **The National Style O is the most famous style of guitar produced by the National (Dobro) company.**

The lap steel evolved from the hugely popular sound of Hawaiian guitar in the 1910s and 1920s. With the addition of more strings, an additional neck, and footpedals and knee levers for changing pitches, the lap steel turned into the modern pedal-steel guitar.

Dobro and lap steel have much in common. They can be tuned the same way, and the basic techniques for playing are the same. Lap steel is an electric instrument with lighter string gauges, and so you can use a lighter touch.

Tunings

The tunings used for lap steel and resonator are different from standard-guitar tunings. However, you can play in standard guitar tuning if you stick to single-note melodies. Steve Howe of Yes has recorded lap steel with standard tunings as well as an open E tuning.

LEFT: **Four legs normally support the pedal-steel guitar, with the performer sitting on a stool. The right foot is used to control the volume while the left leg controls the pedals, using both the foot and knee to move the pedals.**

You can also use a capo with a lap steel. A capo allows you to change keys without re-tuning and apply open position runs in odd keys.

Basic Tunings

The most common tuning in lap-steel and resonator playing is the open G (G B D G B D). Hawaiian players often use the open A (A C# E A C# E), a whole step higher.

To get minor chords in the open G or A tunings, you can play notes selectively, such as playing the open third and second strings (G and B) for an Em in G tuning. A variation on this tuning is D G D G B D, which extends the low range and is very useful when you're playing a solo. An open E tuning (E B E G# B E) is also used frequently.

Using the Bar

With lap steel your fretting hand creates notes and chords by laying a steel bar over the strings. The two types of steel bars are the Stevens and the bullet. The Stevens bar has ridges along the sides (for a good grip) and a blunt, snub nose.

Electric steel players usually use the bullet bar, which has smooth, rounded sides with no ridge, and a rounded tip ('bullet'). You can use various tricks to sound additional notes not in the chord created by the bar.

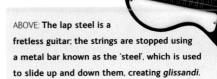

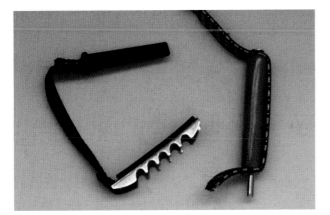

ABOVE: **The lap steel is a fretless guitar; the strings are stopped using a metal bar known as the 'steel', which is used to slide up and down them, creating *glissandi*.**

For example, while holding the bar in position, use your left middle finger to pull a string behind the bar to raise the pitch. Try this: play a D chord at the seventh fret in G tuning, then pull the third string a half step and you have a B seventh chord.

Picks

A common setup is to use a plastic thumb pick and two metal finger picks. Some players prefer lighter gauge metal (.020) and heavier gauge (.025) for acoustic playing. Some players use picks on all five fingers.

The thumb is often used for melody playing in Hawaiian music, while bluegrass and country players often play faster streams of notes by alternating the thumb with the middle (or index) finger.

ABOVE: **A capo is a gripping device applied to the guitar neck. It's used to shorten the fretboard in the same way as an index finger in a barre chord changes the pitch of all the strings.**

Basic Arpeggios

Learning arpeggios is a good way of developing a comprehensive knowledge of the guitar fingerboard. But arpeggios aren't just technical exercises – they're great for soloing and can make your lead playing more melodic by emphasizing the harmonic structure of the underlying chord progression.

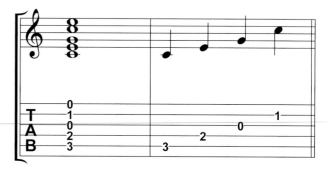

C major chord   C major arpeggio

Constructing Arpeggios

An arpeggio is simply the notes of a chord played individually. Standard major and minor chords, and therefore their arpeggios, contain only three different notes. For example, if you look closely at the open position C major chord you'll notice that although you're playing five strings, there are in fact only three different notes (C E G) in the chord. If you play these notes consecutively, rather than strum them simultaneously, then you've created a C major arpeggio.

When you're first learning arpeggios it's helpful to practise them in the set order (1st, 3rd, 5th, 8th), but once you know them you can improvise freely by swapping the notes around, or repeating some, to make up an interesting lick or riff, just as you would

BELOW: **Playing a C major arpeggio.**

ABOVE: **C major fingerboard position.**

A string, C bass note

G string, G note

B string, C note

E string, E note

when improvising with a scale. The really useful thing is that, because the C major arpeggio contains exactly the same notes as the C major chord, whatever notes you play from the C major arpeggio when improvising will always be totally in tune with a C major chordal accompaniment.

To work out minor arpeggios flatten the third note of the major arpeggio by a half step (e.g. C minor arpeggio contains the notes C E♭ G).

Aim to acquire knowledge of all major and minor arpeggios in as many fingerboard positions as possible. Here are some fingerboard positions for C major and C minor arpeggios. They can be transposed to other pitches by moving them up or down the fingerboard.

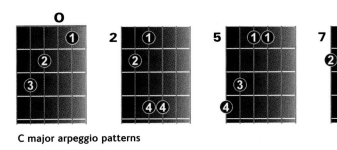

C major arpeggio patterns

  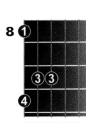

C minor arpeggio patterns

Major and Minor Arpeggios

Each basic major or minor arpeggio will only contain three notes; you can work out which notes these are by analyzing the relevant chord shape. A major arpeggio always contains the first, third and fifth notes of the major scale with the same starting note (for example, C E G are the 1st, 3rd and 5th notes of the C major scale and so form the C major arpeggio).

Using Arpeggios

You can use arpeggios for riffs and lead playing. When you use a scale for a lead solo you'll notice that some notes sound more resolved against certain chords than other notes. This problem disappears when you use arpeggios; because the notes of each arpeggio are taken from the chord they will all sound completely 'in tune' – providing you're playing the right arpeggio for each chord. If you've only used scales before, this takes a little getting used to as you'll need to change arpeggio every time there is a chord change.

In a normal playing situation guitarists rarely use arpeggios throughout a whole solo, as this approach can tend to sound almost too 'in tune'. Instead, arpeggios are used to add colour over just a couple of chords, and the normal key scale is used for the majority of the solo.

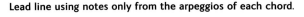

Lead line using notes only from the arpeggios of each chord.

More Arpeggios

Once you've learnt the basic major and minor arpeggios it's not too difficult to extend these to learn the arpeggios for other chords, such as sevenths and even extended and altered chords. A secure knowledge of arpeggios will mean that you'll always be able to improvise over any chord progression.

Seventh Arpeggios

These are formed by taking the notes of the relevant seventh chord and playing them in a scale–like pattern. There are three main types of seventh chord arpeggios: dominant seventh, minor seventh and major seventh. Although they have some notes in common, the sound varies considerably between each one: dominant seventh arpeggios are great for blues and R&B, minor sevenths are used a lot in both rock and funk, and major sevenths give a very melodic sound suited to ballads.

Sixth Arpeggios

Major and minor sixth arpeggios are commonly used for creating riffs. The typical rock'n'roll riff below is taken directly from the C major sixth arpeggio.

C6

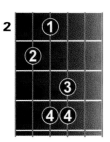

C dominant 7th
arpeggio
C E G B♭

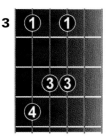

C major 7th
arpeggio
C E G B

C minor 7th
arpeggio
C E♭ G B♭

Altered Arpeggios

One of the most useful applications of arpeggios is over altered chords, such as diminished or augmented chords. Although you may have difficulty choosing a scale to improvise over such chords, arpeggios will always work – because they contain exactly the same notes as the chords you cannot fail to play in tune. Therefore, a thorough knowledge of altered arpeggios will prove highly useful if you wish to improvise over advanced chord progressions, such as those used in jazz and fusion. Here are some of the most useful altered arpeggios. They are all illustrated with a root note of C, but can be easily transposed simply by starting at a different fingerboard position.

**C diminished 7th
arpeggio
C E♭ G♭ B♭♭**

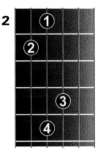

**C augmented 5th
arpeggio
C E G#**

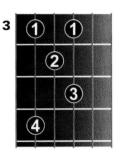

**C minor 7th ♭5
arpeggio
C E♭ G♭ B♭**

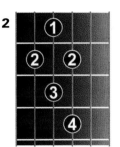

**C dominant 7th ♭5
arpeggio
C E G♭ B♭**

**C dominant 7th #5
arpeggio
C E G# B♭**

Extended Arpeggios

When improvising or creating riffs, using arpeggios over extended chords, such as ninths or 13ths, is an ideal way to explore the full melodic potential of these chords. Scale–based lead playing, unlike arpeggio playing, will rarely be able to exploit the full range of chord tones that these extended chords have available. Below you'll find some of the most frequently used extended arpeggios. Remember to shuffle the notes around and play them in a musical and improvised way when using arpeggios in your lead playing. This way they won't sound like a series of technical exercises.

**C major 9th
arpeggio
C E G B D**

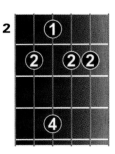

**C dominant 9th
arpeggio
C E G B♭ D**

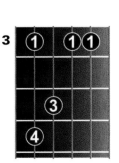

**C minor 9th
arpeggio
C E♭ G B♭ D**

**C dominant 11th
arpeggio
C E G B♭ D F**

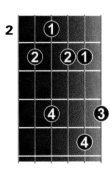

**C dominant 13th
arpeggio
C E G B♭ D F A**

Octaves

Advanced techniques

Octave playing is an instant way of giving more power and solidity to your playing, and because of this it is a technique that is often used by jazz and rock musicians alike. Learning octaves is also one of the quickest ways of getting to know all the notes on the fretboard.

Playing octaves involves playing two of the same notes together (e.g. C and C), but with one of those notes at a higher pitch (i.e. an octave above). The fact that the two notes are the same is what gives octave playing its powerful sound and avoids the excessive sweetness that is often associated with other pairings of notes.

Bass Octaves

There are various ways in which octaves can be played, but for notes on the bass strings by far the most common way is to add a note two frets and two strings higher. For example, if your original note is A on the fifth fret of the sixth string, then the octave A will be on the seventh fret of the fourth string. Similarly, if your original note is D on the fifth fret of the fifth string, then the octave D will be on the seventh fret of the third string. This system, of finding the octave two frets and two strings higher than the original note,

will work for all notes on the sixth and fifth strings. The lower note should be played with the first finger, while the octave can be fretted with either the third or the fourth finger.

Octave shape based upon the 6th string

Octave shape based upon the 5th string

The most important technique when playing bass octaves is to ensure that the string between the lower note and the octave is totally muted. This should be done by allowing the first finger to lie across it lightly – not fretting the string but just deadening it. You should also be careful not to strum the strings above the octave note, and as a precaution it's a good idea to mute them by allowing the octave–fretting finger to lightly lie across them.

A bass octave can also be achieved by moving your hand up or down two frets along one string.

Treble Octaves

The easiest way of playing octaves on the treble strings is to use a similar approach to that described above. but with the octave note requiring a further one-fret stretch. For the fourth and third strings the octave notes can be found by playing three frets and two strings higher. For example, if your original note is G on the fifth fret of the fourth string then the octave G will be on the eighth fret of the second string. This system of finding the octave three frets and two strings higher than the original note will work for all notes on the fourth and third strings.

A treble octave based upon the fourth string.

A treble octave based upon the third string.

Octave shape based upon the 4th string

Octave shape based upon the 3rd string

Playing Octaves

Once you're familiar with the octave shapes shown above, try to play through the examples of octave use given below.

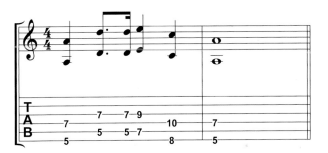

Sixth and fifth string octaves. Using octaves starting from two strings can minimize the amount of fingerboard movement needed. Just be careful to strum the correct strings and make sure that unwanted strings between the fretted notes are fully muted.

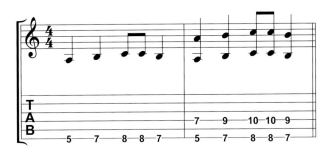

Sixth string octave riff. Notice how much stronger this riff sounds when it is played the second time with the octave note added.

Fingerboard Knowledge

Once you're familiar with the octave shapes you can use them to learn the notes all across the fingerboard. For example, assuming that you can memorize the notes on the sixth string you can then use your octave shape to work out instantly where the same notes will appear on the fourth string.

Harmonics

Harmonics can add interesting bell-like chimes to your guitar playing, and are a useful way of sustaining notes. Harmonics are also a great way of adding an extended pitch range to your playing by enabling you to play notes that are much higher than the pitch you can normally reach on the fingerboard.

Natural Harmonics

There are various forms of harmonics that can be played on the guitar, but natural harmonics are the easiest to learn at first. Natural harmonics occur on all strings on frets 12, seven and five (and 12 frets up from these). Natural harmonics also occur on frets nine and four, although making these ring clearly is a bit harder.

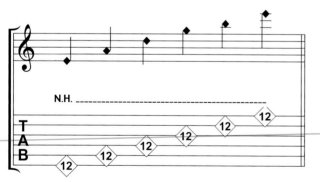

Natural harmonics at the 12th fret.

The best way to start playing natural harmonics is to pick the low E string and then touch that string right above the 12th fret. Don't fret the note in the normal way by pressing down onto the fingerboard; instead just lightly touch the string directly over the fretwire.

The harmonics on fret 12 produce the same notes (although with a different tone) as the 12th–fret fretted notes,

but harmonics at all other fingerboard positions affect the pitch of the note produced: the harmonic notes on fret seven are an octave higher than the fretted notes; the harmonic notes on fret five are the same as the 12th fret fretted notes but an octave higher; the harmonic notes on fret four are two octaves higher than the fretted notes. Natural harmonics also occur on fret nine, and 12 frets up from the previously mentioned fret numbers (e.g. 17, 19, 24).

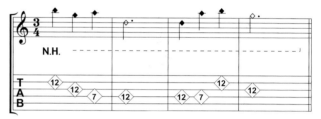

Natural harmonics have a chiming bell-like quality.

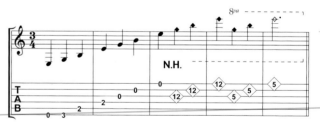

The E minor arpeggio is extended to four octaves by the use of harmonics. Unless you have a 24-fret guitar, the last note would be impossible without using harmonics.

Tip
Harmonics are easier to execute if you select the treble pickup and turn the treble up on the amplifier. Playing near the bridge (for natural harmonics) and adding some sustain with a compressor or distortion device will also help.

ABOVE: **Harmonics enable notes higher than those fretted to be played.**

Other Harmonics

- 'Tapped harmonics' (also known as 'touch harmonics') are most easily played by fretting and picking a note as normal and then touching the same string 12 or seven frets higher.

- 'Artificial harmonics' are similar to tapped harmonics, in that you touch the string 12 frets higher than the fretted note. However, in this technique, instead of picking the fretted note first, you pick the string with the third finger of the picking hand after you have positioned the first finger over the 'harmonic note'.

- 'Pinched harmonics' are often used in rock for making screeching high notes appear out of nowhere in the middle of a lick. The effect is achieved by fretting a note normally and then picking the string with the side edge of the plectrum while allowing the side of the thumb to almost immediately touch the string – so creating a harmonic. The quality and pitch of the sound that you achieve depends upon where you pick the string. Start by trying to locate the 'nodal point' – that is the equivalent of 24 frets (i.e. two octaves) higher than the note you are fretting.

LEFT: **ZZ Top guitarist Billy Gibbons is widely known for his use of pinched harmonics.**

Tremolo Arm

The tremolo arm can be one of the most expressive tools available to the electric guitarist. Note that tremolo means a variation in volume, so the arm – which produces a variation in pitch – should really be called a vibrato arm.

To compound the confusion, the device is often referred to amongst rock guitarists as a 'whammy bar'. The arm or bar can be used in a wide variety of ways, from very subtle vibrato to extreme variations in pitch.

LEFT: **The tremolo arm (or whammy bar) on an American Deluxe Stratocaster HSS.**

No matter what style of music you're playing, using the tremolo arm can add a new element to your sound, enabling you to spice up your playing. Duane Eddy and Hank Marvin (of the Shadows) were two of the first guitarists to pioneer the use of the tremolo arm – putting it to good use in their many instrumental hit records of the 1960s. Marvin remains one of the true experts of the technique – often called 'the master of the melody' because of his ability to use the tremolo arm to make his guitar lines expressive and almost vocal–like.

BELOW: **As part of the Shadows, Hank Marvin (pictured on the right) used the tremolo arm to great effect, giving the band a distinctive sound.**

154

Tremolo Arm Techniques

1. The tremolo arm can be used simply as a way of adding vibrato (either subtle or wide) to a note, by gently but repeatedly raising the bar up and down. In fact, this was what the bar was first invented for. This technique generally works best on notes either at the start or end of a phrase, or on any individual notes that you might wish to emphasize – but, just as with a vocal performance, too much vibrato can sound contrived, so use this technique with care and thought.

Shake the tremolo arm up and down very slightly to get a typical Shadows-style vibrato.

2. By pushing or pulling the bar a little further you can actually change the pitch of the note – rather like bending a string. You can lower a note by pushing the bar inwards or you can raise a note by pulling the bar upwards. It takes some practice, but you'll soon begin to get a feel for the amount of pressure required in order to reach the exact pitch of the note you require; notice that less tremolo arm movement is required to alter the pitch of notes higher up the fingerboard compared to lower-fretted notes.

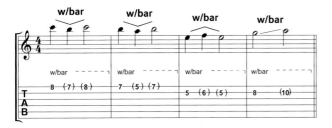

Depress the tremolo arm bar to achieve the downwards dips in pitch, and then release the bar back to return each note to its original pitch. Pull the tremolo arm upwards to raise notes.

3. Use of the tremolo arm need not be restricted to single notes – it also works really well with chords, giving a keyboard-like effect to a single strummed chord.

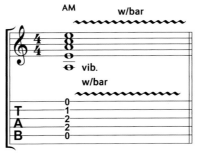

When striking a single chord, a quite strong but steady movement of the tremolo arm will result in a powerful sweeping sound.

4. Rock players from Jeff Beck to Eddie Van Halen and Steve Vai have extended the range of whammy bar techniques with effects like the 'dive bomb' (depressing the bar to lower the note fully until the strings are completely slack).

The tremolo arm is gradually fully depressed to create a 'dive-bombing' effect.

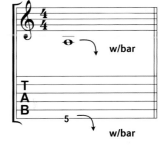

Tapping

Rather than using a plectrum to pick a note, you can play it by tapping the string firmly against the fretboard using a picking-hand finger. Rock guitarists such as Eddie Van Halen, Randy Rhodes, Nuno Bettencourt and Joe Satriani use tapping as a regular part of their lead playing.

one of the pioneers of tapping. His straightforward approach was 'since you've got fingers on both hands why not use both of them to fret notes?' The world of rock guitar has never looked back, and today tapping is a widely used technique in rock circles.

Tapping allows the guitarist to change between low and high notes on the same string, making possible large interval leaps that are unobtainable in normal playing. Eddie Van Halen was

Tapping Techniques

If you intend to play an entire solo with nothing but tapping, you could jettison your plectrum and use your first finger to tap. However, most guitarists prefer to keep the plectrum ready for use between the first finger and thumb, and instead use the

BELOW **Tapping technique: examples of vertical tapping using the second or middle finger to tap the notes.**

second finger to tap notes. Whichever finger you use, make sure that you tap with the bony tip of the finger, rather than the soft fleshy pad, to get the clearest sound.

You can angle your tapping finger so that it is in line with the fretboard (horizontal tapping, or position the tapping finger at right angles to the fretboard (vertical tapping) – either method will suffice for basic tapping patterns, but a vertical tapping technique will provide you with more possibilities as your playing develops. To get a good tone, tap the fingerboard with a fast, strong action just behind the fretwire.

Although you can perform tapping with a clean sound, it's easier at first to use some distortion because the extra sustain means that you don't need to tap so hard to fret each note.

Taps and Slurs

Tapping is often combined with pull–offs to create fast legato licks. These are often based upon arpeggio patterns, with the high tapped notes taken from the same arpeggio as the fretted notes.

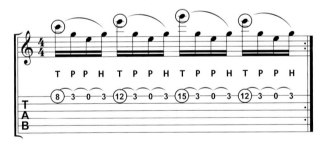

Tapping, Example 1. The tap hand moves, while the fret hand plays the same phrase. The tapped notes are circled.

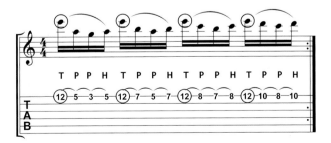

Tapping, Example 2. The tap hand plays the same note, while the fret hand moves along the fretboard.

ABOVE: **Eddie Van Halen's tapping technique is well showcased on 'Eruption' and 'Spanish Fly'.**

Guitar Set-up

The lower the action on your guitar the easier you'll find it to produce notes clearly when tapping. Make sure that your guitar's intonation is set up accurately, as the large interval leaps that tapping allows will highlight any intonation problems. Many tap specialists use a string damper near the nut in order to minimize the unwanted ringing of adjacent strings. Tapping is easiest on an electric guitar with powerful pickups; try adjusting your pickups so that they are close to the strings. Using compression will help to disguise any volume imbalances between notes.

Constructing Solos

The real benefit of having studied all the scales and lead-playing techniques covered in the earlier pages of this book can be realized when you begin to put all this knowledge into action by constructing your own lead guitar solos.

Using Scales

To solo over any chord sequence you'll need a scale, as this will set the range of notes that will fit with the backing chords. For example, if a song uses chords from the key of C major, all the notes of the C major scale can be used as the basis for your solo. However, you don't need to play all the notes of the scale, or play them in any set order. You should always aim to make your solo sound fresh and inventive, rather than scale-like.

ABOVE: 'Comfortably Numb' from Pink Floyd's 1977 album *The Wall*: best rock guitar solo of all time? Whatever your opinion on this, listening to some great guitar solos may just give you the inspiration to write your own epic!

Phrasing

Once you've spent hours practising a scale it's all too easy to keep playing it in a continuous way when soloing. The best method of breaking this habit is to leave spaces between notes so that you start to create short phrases. Within these phrases use notes of different lengths: some long notes that you sustain, balanced by some very quick short notes. This rhythmic variety will add interest and shape

to your phrases. To start with, experiment with the C major scale; instead of playing it in strict time, vary the length of some notes and leave some gaps.

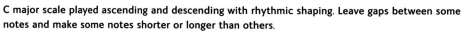

C major scale played ascending and descending with rhythmic shaping. Leave gaps between some notes and make some notes shorter or longer than others.

Sample melody using the C major scale.

Use intervals to make a solo less scale-like.

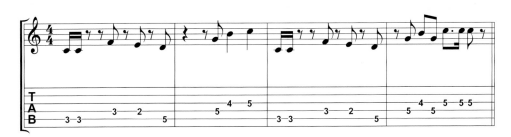

Use repetition of phrases to give your solo structure.

Try to incorporate rhythmic variety into your improvisations, remembering that you should also vary the direction in which you play: there's no need to play up the whole range of the scale before you play some descending notes. Adopt a melodic approach in which your improvisation can weave up and down the scale.

Using Intervals

One thing that always makes a solo sound too scale-like is using notes that are adjacent to each other in a scale. This type of playing gives the game away to the listener – they can hear,

almost instantly, that the improvisation is derived from a scale. Using interval gaps when playing a scale is a perfect way to break away from this scalic sound.

Repetition

By repeating short series of notes you will begin to establish phrases that will give your solo a sense of structure. By repeating these phrases, or variations on them, you will give the listener something recognizable to latch on to, instead of a seemingly random series of notes with no direction.

Specialist Techniques

Don't forget to use some of the specialist guitar techniques that have been covered in this and the preceding chapter. String bends, vibrato, slides or slurs will all help give your solo an individual character and will turn it from a melody into a true guitar solo.

> **Tip**
> **Listen carefully to what is being played on other instruments and try to make your solo relate to the overall musical style of the song.**

Stagecraft

Once you feel confident that you can cope with the technical challenges of rhythm- and lead-guitar playing covered so far in this book, then it's time to think of joining a band and playing your first gig. Spending a little time thinking about stagecraft will mean you are fully prepared.

ABOVE: **Buy the best cables you can afford to suit your needs, and ensure that they are long enough.**

Cables

Avoid cost-cutting when it comes to buying guitar cables. For stage work you need a cable you can rely upon: one in which the connections won't pull loose as you leap across the stage. Choose a cable long enough to allow you freedom of movement around a stage. If you're planning a really boisterous stage act you should consider investing in a wireless system – this will eliminate the need for a cable between the guitar and amplifier.

Tuning

Once you set foot on the stage the show begins – so always get your guitar in tune before you come on stage. Obtain an electronic tuner so that you can tune-up easily in noisy environments. You can even set up the tuner in line between the guitar and amplifier so that you can check the tuning between songs.

Noise

Consider buying a noise gate (some compressors have these built in), or even a volume pedal, so that you can cut down on unwanted signal noise from distortion pedals or high amp settings, both between songs and during quiet passages.

ABOVE: **Using a footswitch will allow you to change sounds without stopping playing.**

Feedback

Unless you want to attract feedback (a high-pitched screaming sound) for special effect, try not to stand right next to and facing into the amplifier if the volume is set very high. If your guitar feeds back too easily, ask a guitar technician to check it out, or consider a different instrument.

Balance

Adjust the volume of your amplifier and guitar so that it blends well with the other instruments, but don't be scared of turning it up for solos so that you can be heard when playing single notes.

Listening

It's essential that you listen to what other musicians in the band are playing, so that you can play together as a cohesive unit. Listen to how your guitar tone and volume blends with or stands out from the band, and adjust this to make it musically appropriate for each song.

ABOVE: **Marshall amps are the ideal piece of kit for pumping out a good, old-fashioned hard-rock solo. Crank up that volume!**

Foldback

Get to the venue early and conduct a soundcheck so that levels can be set. If possible, use monitors (small wedge-shaped speakers that face towards the musicians) so that you can hear the vocals clearly. At large venues a sound engineer may provide you with a full foldback mix – if so, make sure the sound is adjusted so that you can hear not only your guitar, but also the rest of the band clearly.

Safety

As a gigging musician you may encounter dubious wiring in clubs or concert halls. Use circuit breakers and surge protectors – they could save your equipment!

LEFT: **Be prepared and organize all your gear before you go so that it functions flawlessly onstage.**

Introduction

ABOVE: **Jimi Hendrix's pioneering approach came to define the guitar sound of the 1960s.**

Music starts with sound; the thoughts and emotions you feel when hearing a live performance or recording are influenced by the sound of the voice or the instruments as much as by the notes they are producing. The sound of much modern guitar music depends on the proper use of electronic effects.

Proper use of effects can add emotional impact to your music. But improper use can detract from it, and so there are a few things to keep in mind when confronting the wealth of sound-altering devices available. For one, a certain effect may sound great when you're playing alone in your room, but that same effect might not sound great in a mix of instruments. As the variety of processors available can be daunting, you should try to have an idea of the sound you want, and then look for an effect to create it.

RIGHT: **U2's The Edge favours effects such as delay, compression and pitch-shifting to achieve his band's trademark sound.**

The Great Masters

Many famous guitarists achieved their marvellous tone with surprisingly little use of effects. Jeff Beck usually uses just a little distortion and delay to wrest an amazing number of tones out of his Stratocaster. Jimi Hendrix used much less distortion than you might think; tunes like 'Little Wing' were built on clean or only mildly distorted tones. At the other end of the spectrum the effects used by Pink Floyd's David Gilmour and U2's The Edge would take a book to describe. Similarly, Adrian Belew's style is largely informed by his use of a car-load of effects. They allowed Belew to make his guitar sound like an elephant, rhinoceros, cello, trumpet or seagull, as well as a guitar.

In the following sections we will look at how effects work, how to use them and how some well-known artists make magic with them.

ABOVE: **Jeff Beck uses minimum effects for maximum impact.**

Compression

You may have wondered how professional guitarists get their notes to resound so clearly and evenly. Along with developing solid technique, a pro guitarist may use compression to make a guitar's tone more uniform and to increase its sustain.

LEFT: **Adrian Belew's sound with King Crimson and the Bears, as well as with his solo material, has made heavy use of compression.**

To understand the use of compressors it helps to understand the difference between distortion and sustain. Distortion is a quality of sound; sustain refers to how long the note, clean or distorted, remains audible. Compression can be used to increase 'apparent' sustain without any distortion.

It helps if you think of a compressor as an automatic volume pedal; first, the compressor restricts the guitar signal to a pre-set level. Then, as the string vibration slows and the guitar volume drops, an amplifier in the compressor raises it back to the same level as the initial attack.

loud notes). A heavily compressed guitar signal sounds 'squeezed', because its normal dynamic range has been limited. Yet this compression helps a guitar sound 'pop out' in a mix, and the sustain created adds warmth to distortion effects.

RIGHT: **Pedal compressors such as this are used to control volume levels and reduce dynamic range.**

Compressor Applications

1. For clean rhythms, or country 'chicken picking', you can create a squeezing effect by setting a quick attack.
2. The added sustained volume helps to make chorusing and flanging effects much more dramatic.
3. It can provide controlled feedback with minimal distortion and volume.

You can hear these applications used to great effect by Adrian Belew and Andy Summers.

What Does it Sound Like?

Compressors make uneven audio levels more consistent, and the best ones do their job silently. In the studio, bass, drums and vocals are almost always compressed, with little audible evidence. On guitar, however, a compressor's effect is easy to hear, because a guitar, like a piano, has a wide 'dynamic range' (the difference between soft notes and

LEFT: **Andy Summers' sparse, tasteful rhythm guitar reveals a mastery of effects, including compression, delay and chorus.**

Distortion

LEFT: **Away from rock, even the horn-like tone of Charlie Christian's jazz solos was the product of an amplifier driven to its limits.**

Distortion is the sound of rock guitar, created originally, and still optimally, by sending a signal that is 'too hot' into an amplifier not designed to take it. This is called overdriving the amp. (See Amplifiers, pages 192–207).

Another way of getting a distorted guitar tone is with an effects unit or 'stomp box' pedal. Different pedals may be labelled with terms like distortion, overdrive or fuzz, which describe different levels of distorted sound.

LEFT: **The sound from an overdrive pedal maintains the character of the original signal.**

Fuzztones

Early distortion boxes were dubbed 'fuzztones' due to their buzzsaw-like tone. They have been used creatively by Jeff Beck,

Jimi Hendrix and Adrian Belew, who showed that you could process non–guitar sounds with a fuzz unit. Fuzz has been used for every kind of pop music, from psychedelia to swamp.

Getting the Right Effect

Modern stompboxes create a more natural-sounding distortion. Some pedals use an actual tube, while others use increasingly sophisticated chips to offer the feel and sound of an overdriven amp. Most distortion devices come with controls marked distortion, drive or gain; level or volume; and tone.

To get the most out of your distorted sound, remember that the level of the input signal will affect the distorted sound. For example, single-coil pickups will create a sound different from that generated by higher–powered humbucking pickups plugged into the same pedal. A Strat, therefore, will need a higher dose of distortion than a Les Paul to achieve a similar effect. Too much distortion, however, can make your notes indistinct, especially if you are playing fast. Check out Van Halen or Hendrix; they use less distortion than you might think. If your amplifier is already slightly distorted when your guitar volume is fully up, adding just a little gain on the pedal will make it sing.

ABOVE: **A distortion pedal produces a grittier, crunchier sound than an overdrive pedal.**

Chorus

Think about the full, rich sound of a 12-string guitar, or the sound of two guitars playing identical parts at the same time. To emulate that sonic girth when you are playing live and alone, with only six strings, you'll need a chorus effect.

RIGHT: **Many double-neck guitars have a 12-string neck, so that guitarists can switch tones during performances, for example, Jimmy Page when playing 'Stairway To Heaven'.**

The big sound and chiming characteristics described above are created by notes that are slightly out of sync and out of tune. It is the delay of the pick hitting one of the doubled strings after the other, and the slight tuning variations, that give a 12-string its distinctive sound. The timing inconsistencies and tuning differences of two guitarists, or an overdubbed part, similarly expand the sonic field. The chorus pedal emulates this effect and uses delay and pitch-shifting to achieve its end.

many strings being played slightly out of time and tune. Chorus pedals are provided with rate and depth controls. The depth control increases the amount of pitch fluctuation, while the rate knob determines how quickly it fluctuates.

BELOW: **A chorus pedal works by mixing a delayed signal with the original sound.**

How Does it Work?

A chorus device delays the original signal by approximately 20 milliseconds, varying the delay by plus or minus about five milliseconds to create a pitch shift. (You can hear this effect on a standard delay pedal by playing a note while turning the delay time control knob back and forth.) A chorus mixes the sound caused by the delay fluctuation with the original signal, thus emulating the effect of twice as

Some pedals include a blend or level control that allows you to mix the amount of affected signal with the original 'dry' signal. This is handy for controlling the chorus effect, which can be undesirable on solos. Sometimes a feedback control is included to send the delayed signal back, delaying it again for a more intense effect.

BELOW: **A digital chorus unit such as this allows you to control the exact amount of delay time you want.**

Flanging & Phasing

Supposedly the term flanging was created when an engineer placed a thumb on a recording-tape reel, or 'flange', as they are known in the UK, and liked the whooshing sound that it produced. This whoosh became a favourite sound of the psychedelic era – think 'Itchycoo Park' by the Small Faces.

That effect is simulated in flanger devices by sweeping a short delay (about five to 10 milliseconds) over a wide range (from one to 10, or two to 20 milliseconds) with a certain amount of feedback, or recycling of the delay.

A Distinctive Sound

In addition to speed or rate controls, flangers often have an added control marked feedback or regeneration. This recycles the delay back through itself and increases the 'metallic' sound of the effect. A flanger set for a medium rate, lower depth, and minimal feedback can mimic a mild chorus effect. That setup helped to define Andy Summers' sound in the Police. A slow sweep with more intense depth and feedback settings will get closer to the Hendrix or Van Halen sound. Eddie also uses a phaser for this type of effect.

Phaser vs. Flanger

Flangers are confused with phasers (phase shifters) due to the similar sweeping sound. Phase shifters use an even shorter delay and almost no feedback, continually sweeping the dry and delayed signals in and out of phase. A phase shifter produces a more subtle, musical effect than a flanger with its more edgy, metallic sound.

ABOVE: **The Small Faces made use of the distinctive 'jet-taking-off' flanging effect that was perfected in the early 1960s.**

Advanced Functions

Some more upscale flanging and phasing units will allow you to tap in the time of the sweep to match the tempo of the song that you are playing; some even have a 'trigger' setting that starts the sweep anew each time you strike the strings; this can work well for funk applications.

RIGHT: **As well as producing a whooshing sound, the flanger also produces a metallic warbling reminiscent of sci-fi ray guns.**

Ambient Effects: Delay & Reverb

Sometimes the spatial environment in which you play your guitar is not ideal, and that can hurt your sound. Luckily, engineers have invented electronic methods of modifying the ambience (literally, the 'surrounding air') that accompanies your sound.

RIGHT: **Some ambient effects will make it sound as if you are playing in a concert hall, even if you are in your bedroom.**

Ambience

In audio, room ambience is affected by the time delay between a sound leaving its source (the amplifier) and the effect from obstacles in the sound's path. The ear hears the sound first from its source and then again – after various echoes – bounced off walls, ceiling and floors. These echoes allow the brain to gauge the size and nature of the room in which the sound is produced. Eventually, engineers invented effects such as reverb that help to restore a natural room ambience. These effects allow the guitar to sound like it is being played in a huge empty hall, even in a small club or basement studio.

Tape Delay

Les Paul was one of the first to discover tape delay. Running a signal into a reel-to-reel tape recorder, he recorded it on the machine's 'record' head and played it back as it passed over the 'playback' head milliseconds later. Combining the two signals created a delay effect. Recycling the delayed signal created additional repeats.

To vary the delay, the speed of the tape can be increased, causing the delay to get shorter; or the playback head can be moved further away from the record head to lengthen the delay. Multiple playback heads can also be used, allowing multiple delays. Recycling the repeats and mixing them back is one way of creating the illusion of a much larger room.

The 'slap' echo used on early rockabilly recordings was also produced in this way. This is one of the earliest examples of using 'effects' in recording.

LEFT: **Elvis's early singles were noted for their slap-back echo.**

167

Delays

As with flanging, the discovery of the tape-delay effect in the studio created a tremendous demand for a unit that could recreate the effect live. Thus the Echoplex, a portable tape echo, was born. Alternatives quickly appeared in the form of analogue and digital delays.

Analogue Delay

Tape-based machines are cumbersome and require maintenance. Eventually, engineers developed 'analogue' delays, which passed the signal along a series of IC chips. This 'bucket-brigade' technology allowed tape-type effects to be generated by smaller devices, including stompbox-size units.

LEFT: You can hear The Edge's use of delay on 'Where The Streets Have No Name'.

The Edge and Andy Summers used analogue delays to set up rhythmic patterns, while Adrian Belew used them to simulate insect sounds. Bucket-brigade chips have become increasingly rare, so newly manufactured analogue delays can be quite expensive.

Digital Delay

Digital technology solved some of the problems inherent in analogue delays. While analogue delays repeat the signal electronically, digital delays sample the original signal, turning it into digital code. The code is then processed and translated back into a signal again before sending it to the output. Since the encoded signal is less subject to degradation, it allows for longer delays with less distortion.

In analogue delays the sound quality of the echoes diminishes significantly as the delay times and number of repeats increase. After about a half-second of delay these units add significant noise and unpleasant distortion. Still, many guitarists value analogue delays for their warmth, and the fact that the degradation of the signal with each repeat avoids conflict with the dry signal, sounding more natural to some guitarists.

ABOVE: Analogue delays appeared in the 1970s and are the link between tape and digital delays.

Digital delays allow for extremely long delay times and applications like playing along with yourself. Robert Fripp's effects-laden guitar style makes uses of these features. The signals generated by digital delays are extremely clean; the delayed signal can be virtually indistinguishable from the original.

RIGHT: Digital delays sample the guitar's sound and play it back after a defined period.

Using Delay

Delays can be used for ambience, for doubling, for creating rhythmic patterns, and for many other effects. Delay plays a subtle but distinct role in the sound of artists like Jeff Beck, David Gilmour, Eddie Van Halen and Robben Ford.

RIGHT: **Robben Ford makes use of a small amount of delay, as well as volume and wah-wah pedals.**

Most delays have three controls. One is delay length; this can be called delay time, effect, range or simply delay. Another control affects the number of repeats, from a single repetition of the signal to 'runaway' feedback; this knob can be called feedback, regen (regeneration) or repeat. The third controls the amount of effect added to the original or 'dry' signal. This may be called mix or blend depending on the unit. Many delays will also have a dry output and an effect output, which lets you send them to separate channels or amps and create your own mix of the two signals.

Artificial Ambience

Increasing the delay time increases the apparent room size, but remember that repeats can obscure your original signal. Decrease the number of repeats as you increase the length of the delay unless you want to sound like you are playing in a cave.

Too much delay can make your instrument indistinguishable in a mix. However, be prepared to add delay to your signal when

BELOW: **When you are trying to create a natural ambience remember that delay is never louder than the direct signal.**

other instruments enter a mix or as a club fills up, since bodies will absorb the ambience.

Digital delays work well for a doubling effect. For this you need the delay to be as clean as possible since it will be mixed equally, or almost equally, with the original. The delay should be long enough to fatten the sound, but short enough so that it is not a rhythmic pattern. Use a single repeat or it will start to sound like reverb.

BELOW: **Ensure that you tailor the amount of delay you use to suit the room in which you are playing, and monitor this during the performance.**

Rhythmic Delays & Looping

Digital delays let you set up rhythmic repeat patterns. These can produce uniformly 'retro' or 'spacey' sounds, or result in polyrhythmic patterns like those created by Andy Summers or The Edge. Looping delays can provide a single guitarist with extra parts, or can create highly textured, atmospheric pads.

SECTION ONE

170

To use rhythmic delays with a live drummer requires planning, because one of you must set the tempo while the other attempts to match it. Some digital delays allow you to set the delay length by tapping a switch, so you can make adjustments on the fly if the drummer wavers.

Looping Effects

Digital delays with longer delay times (two seconds or more) allow you to create 'looping' effects by playing along with yourself, in the manner of Robert Fripp, Bill Frisell and others. One way to do

LEFT: **Listen to *Exposure* by Robert Fripp to hear the first recorded evidence of his pioneering looping technique.**

this is to set a very long delay time, with an even mix and the feedback high. This way, as old patterns fade, you can overlay new ones. Another way is to use the hold button (present on almost all digital delays) to lock in what you have played up to that point and then improvise over the repeats. Some delays include specific 'looping' functions, and some devices are meant for looping alone.

Dedicated loopers or combination looper/delay pedals often permit the player to slow the recorded loop or speed it up. Some devices also allow the signal to be reversed, for 'backwards guitar' effects.

ABOVE: **A looping device can add texture to your playing.**

Time-based Delays

To create rhythmic delays you need to understand the relationship between tempo, in beats-per-minute (BPM), and delay time, in milliseconds (ms). For example, at 120 BPM (two beats per second) one beat equals 500 ms. A sixteenth-note delay is one-quarter of this, or 125 ms. Faster tempos mean shorter delay times; slower tempos mean longer delay times.

LEFT: **If you're using rhythmic delays, you and your drummer must remain in sync.**

Reverb

From surf music to jazz records, reverb plays a major role in defining a guitarist's sound. Even a lack of reverb makes a statement about the kind of music you are making. In general, it is an effect that moves the sound further away from the listener the more it is applied.

ABOVE: **Early recordings by the Beach Boys are great examples of the all-time classic use of reverb.**

What is Reverb?

Natural ambience is not the result of a single delay length or evenly spaced repeats. Sound is being constantly echoed back at us at various delay times, and the echoes are heard not as repeats, but as the ambience, size, type and emptiness or fullness of the room.

Delay units are limited in their ability to reproduce the natural ambience of a space due to the distinction and the identical nature of their repeats. Although they are adequate for sounds with little or no attack, like volume swells and lightly picked or strummed chords, the repeats become too distinct and the regularity of their spacing too pronounced when any hard picking or tight, funky chord work is required. The creation of a space around your sound is more the provenance of reverb.

from electrical energy to mechanical energy, then sends it down a spring or springs to another transducer, where it is converted back to electrical energy. The time it takes to travel the length of the spring adds delay. The spring degrades the frequency response in a more uneven manner than analogue or digital delays, creating a more natural effect. More springs means a more natural effect, and longer springs create longer delays.

Digital Reverb

Digital reverbs can simulate virtually any size and type of room, and place the sound anywhere in it. Similarly to digital delays, digital reverbs take the signal and convert it to digital code, then add delays and frequency changes to simulate the desired room size and to place the sound in the desired location within it.

Spring Reverb

An early type of mechanical reverb was the spring reverb. Found in many guitar amplifiers, it employs a transducer to convert the signal

RIGHT: **The spring reverb's sound is created from the physical reverberations of a spring built into the amplifier.**

ABOVE: **As well as simulating the sound of different room spaces, digital reverb can also mimic the sound of artificial reverb devices, such as reverb plates and chambers used in studios.**

Volume & Wah-wah Pedals

By placing volume and tone controls, like those on your guitar, into pedals, manufacturers transformed those tools into creative effects. George Harrison and Larry Carlton turned the simple volume pedal into an expressive tool, while Isaac Hayes and Jimi Hendrix used the wah-wah pedal (essentially a tone pedal) to produce rhythmic and vocal-like effects.

Volume Pedal

The volume pedal has myriad uses. At its most basic, it allows you to adjust your volume without interrupting play, maintaining the proper mix with the band.

Many guitarists were inspired to explore volume pedals by pedal-steel players, who constantly manipulate one while playing. You will find that your pedal-steel licks sound more authentic if you swell into them with a pedal. You can also create lush pads with a volume pedal and a delay: add distortion and play single low notes for a cello effect, or higher ones for a violin sound.

Getting Pedal-steel Effects
1. Plug your guitar into a volume pedal.
2. Plug the pedal into your amplifier.
3. Play a chord and gradually increase the volume with the pedal from zero to full.
4. If your guitar has a vibrato arm, gently rock it.
5. Add a long delay for a richer effect.

RIGHT: **George Harrison: master of the volume pedal?**

Wah-wah

Unlike a guitar's tone control, a wah-wah pedal has active circuitry that boosts the highs at one end and the lows at the other. Often rocked in time for rhythmic effect, it can also be used for expressive tonal effects. The riff on the Dire Straits' hit 'Money For Nothing' (1984) is the sound of a partially backed-off wah-wah pedal. Accenting the treble on bent notes gives a distinct vocal effect, while slow sweeping through the range as you play a rhythmic part can emulate a synthesizer filter.

BELOW: **Mark Knopfler and Dire Straits had great success with a wah-wah pedal.**

Combining Effects

Once you understand the workings of individual effects you will want to combine them to create sounds you have heard, or to make some exciting new sounds of your own.

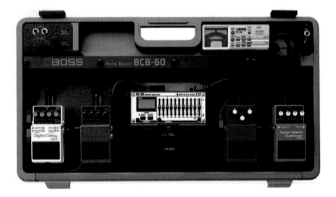

ABOVE: **Securing your pedals to a board makes it easy to see exactly what you are working with.**

Effects can be combined in a number of ways. Pedals can be attached to a pedalboard, or placed in a rack pedal drawer and triggered remotely along with rack devices. Or, you may want to use one of the many multi-effects units available in either rack or pedal form.

Multi-effects Units

Many manufacturers offer multi-effects units containing all those

ABOVE: **Pedalboard cases are a good idea if you are on the move: your effects will be far more portable as well as secure.**

Pedals on a Board

No matter which pedals you use, where you place them in the 'signal chain' will determine your final sound. Dynamics processors, like compressors, should do their work earlier while a volume pedal would be one of the last devices in the chain. Here is a possible sequence of effects that would work well in most cases:

1. Compressor
2. Tuner
3. Fuzz
4. Wah-wah
5. Distortion or overdrive
6. Chorus/flanger/tremolo
7. Volume
8. Delay
9. Reverb

effects that we have discussed – and more. These can come in a floorboard system or a rack unit that requires a separate controller, usually using MIDI, a protocol that allows devices to communicate with one another. The advantage of a multi-effects unit is that you can program it to switch numerous effects on and off simultaneously. Thus, with one motion you could conceivably turn your distortion and delay on and your chorus and compressor off. The disadvantage is that modifying the settings of the effects is not as easy as bending down and turning a knob on a pedal. A common compromise is a rack with a drawer for pedals and a switcher that brings the pedals in and out of the signal path in pre-set combinations.

RIGHT: **A multi-effects unit can be useful if you don't have a lot of space.**

Moving On

You've worked hard to become proficient (if not quite yet masterful) on guitar. You're proud of your work and of what you can do with your axe. Now you come to the crossroads – one perhaps not as ominous as Robert Johnson's or Eric Clapton's, but one with life-changing potential nonetheless. Will you continue to play guitar solely for your own enjoyment, or will you make the leap toward playing for others, playing in a band and becoming a professional guitarist? If you choose the latter (and even if you don't), there is still much to be learned. Read on....

Practising at Home

Much has changed since the days when Paul McCartney impressed John Lennon by playing Eddie Cochran's 'Twenty Flight Rock' and George Harrison impressed them both by playing 'Raunchy'. What hasn't changed is that musicians want to impress other musicians, and all guitarists want to be at their best when showing off their skills. It all starts with practise, and practising remains a constant throughout any serious guitarist's life.

Skill Sets

If you've developed a solid practising routine by regularly repeating the examples in the opening section of this book, then you're well on your way to being ready for any performance situation. There are, however, certain aspects of your playing that may require special attention if you're looking to play with other people.

Pay particular attention to timing when playing lead or rhythm. Yes, you must pick the notes and voice the chords properly, but playing out of time will ruin a piece of music and hurt your reputation with those who are hearing you play for the first time.

You should practise picking notes cleanly at different tempos and at different rhythms. Playing the various scales and modes described in the previous sections may feel tedious and redundant at first, but they will make your playing fluid and give you confidence in short order. Seek out the myriad exercises and tips available from guitarists you admire.

RIGHT: **It is Yngwie Malmsteen's speed combined with his incredible technical ability that makes him one of the world's top guitarists. Speed alone just wouldn't cut it!**

Walk, Don't Run

All guitarists want to impress with their speed, but speed without accuracy is meaningless. To be an accurate player, you must play phrases slowly and then gradually increase your speed.

This is true even when you've become a fluid guitarist. If you want to create a new lick that no one's heard before, you will have to articulate it slowly and then build up speed.

RIGHT: **Digital metronomes, such as this Korg BeatLab, have different rhythms built-in so you can practise to more than a click track.**

Tools

The most valuable modern tools you can own to help your playing are some sort of metronome and a recording device. Both can easily be implemented in your home computer, or you can use dedicated (and portable) tools for each. A separate electronic tuner is equally important when you begin playing away from home or in a band.

A metronome will tell you if you are playing too fast ('rushing') or too slow ('dragging'). These flaws (faced by all beginning guitarists) sometimes evolve into more subtle timing issues such as playing 'on top of' or 'behind' the beat, which may even be desirable in some situations. Practising with a metronome will help you to always know when you are 'locked in' to the beat and 'in the pocket'.

Likewise, a digital audio recorder (see Recording, pages 208–35) will tell you things about your playing that you may not pick up on your own. You can record yourself playing along with a solo

ABOVE: **A digital audio recorder is an essential bit of kit for anyone looking to improve their playing.**

you've learned or to pre-recorded tracks with intentionally missing guitar parts. Playing these back will show you what aspects of your playing need work.

The Home Front

There was a time when practising electric guitar at home was a sure invitation of parental, neighbour or roommate wrath. But modern digital-effects boxes and headphones have eliminated that problem, along with the previously required amplifier. Devices like the Line 6 Pod and software like Native Instruments' Guitar Rig let you blast away without fear of reprisal.

Advancing to a performing level, however, will require you to 'play out' in a space where you can really hear your sound and gauge your performance skills. For many young guitarists, a spacious basement or garage (and accommodating parents, of course) can fit the bill. Older, independent musicians will need other solutions.

BELOW: **By plugging a set of headphones into a Line 6 Floor Pod you can silently strum away and create sounds through a number of different amp models and effects.**

Playing with Others

Practising alone in your room will make you a good player, especially if you are able to concentrate and stay focused on your work. But your guitar education, not to mention enjoyment, will rise to another level when you begin to play with other people.

Roles

Getting together with other players doesn't necessarily mean facing off with another headbanger, your Marshall stacks placed speaker to speaker and turned up to eleven while you shred each other into oblivion (at least not in the beginning). Initially, you might just be getting together with another acoustic-guitar player to see what will happen.

Beginner guitarists will discover that two instruments strummed in exactly the same fashion (with or without two voices singing the same melody and lyrics) can get tiresome rather quickly. More likely, two guitarists will instinctively begin to assume different roles, playing complementary parts, and perhaps harmonizing vocally. When this happens to you, you've begun to create an arrangement.

Playing Your Part

The list of classic acoustic-guitar songs with interesting guitar parts is practically endless. There are simple strumming duets

like the Stones' 'Wild Horses' and 'Patience' by Guns N' Roses. There are more complex two-guitar intros like the Beatles' 'I've Just Seen A Face', and hundreds more. What the best songs have in common is that players cooperate to create a sound that works, either because of well-written parts that don't clash or because of a mood or tone that conveys something unique to the listener.

The best tools for creating something good with other musicians are your ears and your communication skills. When working on your own songs, let your creativity emerge without being overly critical of other players' ideas. You'll know when you have the right partner and the right nucleus for a band.

Building the Band

How many famous bands do you know of that had the exact same personnel when they hit it big as they did when they started out? A few did, but more often bands go through several personnel changes before the right combination begins to gel. Yet if your skills have developed to the point where you need a certain level of proficiency in your band mates, you may need

ABOVE: 'Wild Horses' from the Rolling Stones' 1971 album *Sticky Fingers* is an easy duet to practise with another guitarist.

RIGHT: **Like most bands, the Rolling Stones have been through a few line-up changes over the years.**

to search beyond your circle of friends to find the right pieces to the puzzle.

Shopping Around

Many bands begin as groups of neighbourhood chums or schoolmates who share a common musical interest. If you're a beginner, however, you'll find that your choices are broadened by checking out players at other schools and in other areas. Go to events outside your local town where musicians are playing. Ask about players who are available and sit in with other bands that you like. Let it be known that you're a serious player (you are, aren't you?) and

that you're looking to put a serious band together. If you're businesslike and methodical, that seriousness will shine through and other players will want to check you out. Just be ready to play well, so the word doesn't go around that you're not as serious as you say.

Getting Serious

More advanced players will scout local music papers and the Web for auditions or advertise for needed players. If your band is already established, then players will come to you. Insist that your new partners be as dedicated as you are, but treat every player with respect, even if you're not interested in working with him or her. Eventually, you'll have a crew that you know will sound great or at least have a lot of fun and grow together. And then you're ready for serious rehearsal.

LEFT: **Websites like Join My Band are free online resources for musicians, and an excellent place to start if you're looking to join a band or recruit a new band member.**

The Garage Band

Countless musicians began their careers playing with schoolmates in bands that set up their gear and rehearsed their songs in a garage or basement, and the term 'garage band' has come to mean many things, including a genre of music and a software application. Today a garage band might just as easily be a bunch of aging baby-boomers getting together on weekends for recreational head-banging. If you've managed to entice a bass player, drummer and keyboardist, or second guitarist to start rehearsing with an eye towards performing live, here are some tips.

The Space

Pick a room with enough space to stretch out. Every player needs ample room to play comfortably (you won't always have this luxury on stage). Try to have comfortable seating beyond a drum stool or piano bench. Players need breaks from playing, but don't let relaxation take the focus away from the music.

The Gear

In every band, someone is always more gear-oriented than someone else. Be prepared to help with gear, but first make sure your own gear is well maintained and ready for action. For example, poor cables and wiring that creates a constant buzz will destroy a good vibe at a rehearsal. And nothing kills a rehearsal faster than a guitar player who breaks a string and doesn't have a spare. Be prepared!

BELOW: **When you rehearse with your band, it's important to find a space that allows your creativity to shine through. Can you image Nirvana writing their 1991 album _Nevermind_ in a cramped basement?**

has a recording in advance or charts (lead sheets) ready for rehearsal. Equally, if you're playing 'originals', the songwriter should provide a demo or written music in advance whenever possible. Record your rehearsals, even if it's with an old cassette player.

Developing these habits will save you hours of wasted time in the long run. Young musicians sometimes think this approach takes the fun out of music, turning it into work instead of play, but in time you'll be glad you stayed organized.

ABOVE: **Take the time to make sure all of your equipment is in tip-top condition – your rehearsal time is better spent playing than fixing your gear.**

The Attitude

Decide before you join a band if you want to play for fun or profit, and don't get involved with players who don't share your attitude. If you do commit, remember the adage that a chain is only as good as its weakest link, and don't be the weak link! To get paying jobs is hard work, and to keep them coming is even harder. Help your band strengthen its links by being flexible and supportive.

The Goals

Many guitarists can be satisfied learning songs they love and playing for friends. If, however, you've decided to play live and make money, you must become businesslike in your approach, even if someone else in the band is the main 'business person'.

Set regular rehearsal times that don't work hardships on band members and try to have an agenda for each rehearsal. If you're covering other musicians' songs, be sure everyone

The Gigs

At some point, all your hard work will pay off – literally! But first you must convince someone to hire your band. It is rarely enough just to love the music you play and think you're a great band, all bands feel the same way. You have to sell your band with your performance or business skills.

Take advantage of auditions or 'Battle of the Bands' events, even those that don't pay. Building a fan base often means exposing the band for free. Whenever you do perform, have a designated leader, manager or friend who can hand out business cards with contact information, and try to develop a decent website so that your fans know the band's schedule. If you can attract a booking agent, pick one who knows your style and doesn't book you into places that aren't right for your music.

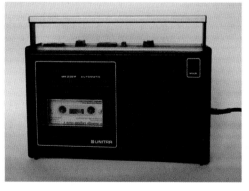

LEFT: **Don't want to splash out on a fancy digital audio recorder? Just dig out your old cassette player – as long as it has a record button, you're all set.**

Getting the Word Out

As you and your band mates develop your repertoire you should begin to think about the finer points of performing live. As previously discussed, you will have already thought about the kinds of places you would want to play and paid some attention to the business end of things. First, however, you must be sure that you are tying up any musical loose ends.

S
E
C
T
I
O
N

T
W
O

The Song List

As you rehearse, it's likely you'll have discussions, and probably an argument or two about which songs to play and which ones to avoid. If you're a cover band, the job is somewhat straightforward: you'll be looking for the best existing songs for the gigs you want to play. Whether your audience gathers in an auditorium, a dancehall or a mosh pit, you'll need the songs that please the crowd the most, thereby getting yourself asked back.

You'll need to pay attention to the bands or DJs that work those clubs or halls currently and watch how the most successful performers arrange their show for maximum impact. Then, as you rehearse the tunes, you'll have a clear idea of what works – and what might stall your performing career.

OF THE GIRL
EVOLUTION
ANIMAL
RED MOSQUITO
CORDUROY
LIGHT YEARS
NOTHING AS IT SEEMS
GIVEN TO FLY
EVEN FLOW
FAITHFUL
MFC
BREAKERFALL
WISHLIST
THIN AIR
DAUGHTER
EVACUATION
IMMORTALITY
BETTER MAN
BLACK
DON'T GO

ABOVE: **Deciding on a set list can be a fraught process, but it's vital for a successful gig. Pearl Jam opted for the tried-and-tested method of scribbling theirs on a scrap of paper for a Lisbon gig in 2000.**

Originals

If you're building a set that showcases you as an artist with original material, things are quite different. Here the focus must be on the songs that set you apart from the bands you admire and (within strict limits) emulate. You must build a show as an established star builds a concert, taking care of every detail of your performance, presentation and style. Is everyone in the band putting his or her best foot forward? Do all the arrangements support the songs, or are the lyrics buried under a sonic onslaught? Does your sequence of songs engage the audience and make them feel you have star power?

Image

Before you ever set foot on a stage, you can do a lot to build an image. Remember, many recording stars still have two albums out before they put together a tour. Anticipation is built and the audience's appetite is whetted while the act is rehearsed and promoted.

Promotion

If you're recording your rehearsals, you can use CDs to help promote the band. Many bands build full promotional packages with photos, bios and CDs for passing out to club owners and booking agents. These are essential tools that build word of mouth and continue promoting your act as you perform locally.

Find a good photographer whose work you like and who knows how to showcase musicians. Make sure your stage look is accurately represented in the photos. Prepare biographies of the band members but don't go overboard. Highlight any well-known groups with whom your band mates have performed.

If you can't make a quality recording of rehearsals, consider hiring a professional recording studio and make a two- or three-song demo for your 'press kit'. A well-recorded demo can open doors if the songs are played well, and give you another promotional tool for local radio or television shows. Be absolutely prepared and fully rehearsed before recording. Remember the cliché: you don't get a second chance to make a first impression.

LEFT: **One of David Bowie's greatest strengths throughout his career has been his ability to adapt his public image to fit, and even anticipate, the prevailing music trends.**

The Web

The Internet gives you an amazing number of resources for promoting yourself before you begin to play live. You can create a band page on social networking sites, such as MySpace or Facebook, participate on bulletin boards that attract fans of your musical style and upload your songs to any number of sites for easy download. On your main band page you can list upcoming gigs or projects, build a mailing list of fans and create an image that rivals established stars.

BELOW: **Recording a few quality tracks in a professional setting could make all the difference to your demo.**

Preparing for a Gig

There are almost as many kinds of gigs as there are kinds of musicians, even if the demand for live players has been greatly compromised in recent years by recorded music and computers. Electronics and DJs have taken over many of the live performance duties that were once handled by living, breathing musicians. However, opportunities still exist for the enterprising guitarist to ply his or her trade in front of an audience.

Clubs that cater to patrons who are more willing to listen to music will probably be as interested in your singing as in your guitar playing, and so if you can 'carry a tune' your chances of landing steady work are enhanced. If you can't sing a lick, then it may be time to consider finding a partner who can, and becoming a duo.

Going Solo

If you've built a large repertoire of pop songs, you may be able to build up a network of clubs, restaurants or special-event halls that will hire you to perform. These kinds of establishments are generally looking for soft, instrumental music, which, unfortunately, may make you a player of 'background' music, and, fortunately, may pay well. However, if you're serious about performing in many styles, or perhaps you're an aspiring jazz player, nothing will sharpen your skills better than playing two to four sets of music on your own several days a week.

ABOVE: **Open mic nights are a great way to gain experience performing in front of a live audience without the hassle of getting yourself booked by the club's management.**

Small-hall Gear

Making vocals part of your act will generally mean owning a small public-address (PA) system, which in its simplest form means two

speaker cabinets (placed on either side of the stage or playing area) and a powered mixer, which accepts microphones and drives the speakers. Many well-known companies like Mackie, Yamaha and Peavey make small PAs, some with built-in effects for small rooms.

Rocking the House

As a member of a band, your concerns about gigs become more complicated, and nothing is more complicated than the fact that you will make less money as a rock guitarist than as a 'pop' guitarist on a solo gig. However, your sacrifice has method to its madness: you're building the band's sound, image and fan base for the future – not to mention it's just a way cooler job!

Making a band successful takes years of dedication and hard work. The most successful bands get better at every gig and find ways to triumph over the inevitable squabbles among band members. Most important is that the band be exhaustively rehearsed, have a show or sets that build momentum, and execute their music like a well-oiled machine, even if they're cultivating an image of loose cannons.

Pre-emptive Strikes

The leader or manager of your band should book your first gig or tour as far in advance as possible. Observe the club or venue on its best nights. Check out their most popular (returning) act and pay attention to what works in their show and what doesn't. It's also a good idea to get to know the owner or manager of the venue (he or she should have already heard your demo). Pay close attention to the venue's sound system. Is the band running it from the stage? Does the club have its own system? Is there a sound crew? If all the bands bring their own sound

LEFT: **Smaller venues may not have a house PA system. If you find yourself with gigs rolling in, you may want to buy a small portable PA system, such as this Yamaha EMX620/AS108.**

company or engineer, you will need to do the same unless you know your system competes favourably.

Meanwhile, Back at Rehearsal

As a guitarist, your responsibilities are similar whether you're a solo jazzer or power-trio shredder: make sure you know your songs backwards and forwards; keep your gear in tip-top shape; and make sure your look is right for the audience you're seeking.

BELOW: **Try to keep feuding with your band mates to a minimum. If you're not careful you could end up like Eddie Van Halen and David Lee Roth, whose battles are legendary.**

Playing to an Audience

LEFT: The 'rules' of good stage presence don't exactly apply when you're as big as Led Zeppelin.

know if your audience will recognize that as acceptable behaviour. If they do, then turning your back won't hurt your performance. Generally, however, good stage presence still requires facing and making eye contact with your audience when possible.

If you're a singing guitarist, pick one face in the crowd and sing to that person. It's often more effective than trying to reach several people at once. Let the emotions in the song be reflected in your own visage as you sing. The same applies when you're soloing: let your body movements reflect the emotions evoked by the solo. Movement onstage is much more important today than it was in the 'classic rock' era. Perform like you're making your next video!

In many styles of music, audience participation is more than just a gimmick – it's a requirement. Whether chanting along to the chorus of your penultimate number or holding flames aloft during your most gut–wrenching ballad, the audience is signalling that it's on your side. Find the best opportunities within your show to encourage audience involvement. It's another sign to the club owner or booker that you're a professional.

Your first gigs will probably involve playing in front of friends at a house party. If you've prepared well, you won't have to worry about your playing as you get over the initial discomfort of being on stage. If you're ready to go in front of a paying audience, you should try to remember some of the time-honoured rules of show business.

Audience Dos

Relating to your audience is the first step in building an effective stage presence. For example, the oldest, common sense rule of performing is to face the audience when you play. This 'rule' has been tested and broken many times in the rock era, but you must

Audience Don'ts

You don't need this book to tell you not to play too loud; every bar owner and manager, if not every customer, will tell you as soon as you play your first note. Playing too loud in the wrong venue assaults the people you need most. Do sound checks with a technician, and listen to his or her advice.

ABOVE: **Getting the audience behind you is crucial. Ultimately, you are there to entertain them, so without their approval you're unlikely to get another shot.**

If you're in a heavy–metal band at a venue that has no restrictions on volume, then that 'other' boss – your ears – will have that same message for you, except that your ears can't fire you. They will simply deteriorate. (Just ask Pete Townshend, Jeff Beck, or Eric Clapton, all of whom have hearing loss associated with loud music.) If you play loud, get pro–level earplugs designed for musicians.

Don't solo inappropriately. Open-ended jams were great for the Grateful Dead and Phish, but they may not make sense in your situation. For every member of the audience who hangs on your every note, another may be putting on her coat.

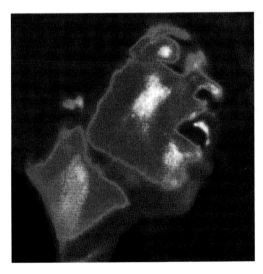

Most of the greatest solos in guitar history covered about eight or 16 bars, and the best solos build from something subtle to something powerful, whatever their duration. Try to build a solo like a mini–song, with a solid beginning, middle and end – and enjoy the applause as you settle back into the groove of the tune.

Two other fatal flaws of performing are 'dead air' and 'chatter'. Prepare for those times when something goes wrong and the band needs some time before it kicks off the next song. Whoever has the best 'vibe' with the audience should handle the mic and keep things flowing until the band is ready. Avoid long stretches of silence. As a last resort have a CD or DJ ready to take over.

LEFT: **Listen to Jimi Hendrix's cover of Dylan's 'All Along The Watchtower' from his 1968 *Electric Ladyland* album – that's how to perform a solo!**

Choosing Venues

All musicians must take care when deciding where and when to play. If you are booking yourself, then you are more likely to find the right place to perform. Things get more complicated when you turn your scheduling over to an agent or manager. The trade-off is that you may get many more gigs with less work. But even when you book yourself it can be tempting to take a job for the money, even if that job could harm your reputation.

Retaining Control

To book yourself effectively you must devote time to business, which takes time away from individual practise and group rehearsal. If you already have a regular job, this can be stressful. However, if you're a solo guitarist looking to play small clubs,

restaurants and parties, you may only need some business cards, a telephone number, and good word of mouth to keep working. Living in a large city also makes self-booking easier.

Research and networking are just as important in music as in business at large. Know your market – that is, all the possible venues in your town for your style of music. Talk to other guitarists who have played at the places in which you're interested. When you've determined the best candidates, drop off your promo package (press kit) and try to make an appointment with the person who books acts there.

BELOW: **For over 30 years the CBGB club in Manhattan was the world's most famous punk-rock club, playing host to giants like the Ramones and Patti Smith.**

LEFT: **London's Troubadour coffee house was one of the primary venues of the folk revival. Superstars like Bob Dylan, Joni Mitchell and Jimi Hendrix all played here early in their careers.**

Sales Pitch

When you get appointments with talent bookers, try to remember their motivations as well as your own. The booker is working for the club or event, not for you, and so your job is to explain why you should be invited to the 'party'. Mention any recommendations from other club owners, the size of your following, and any other data that makes you more attractive to a business.

Adverts

Although self-promotion is the practical way of exposing yourself to music buyers, traditional advertising may come in handy, especially for bands. Know the local music newspapers and their advertising rates. Duplicate your press kit and demo on your own website or a social network like MySpace Music, and include the web address (URL) for your page on any advert you distribute.

Booking Agents

If you've headlined every club in town and built a following, you may be ready to branch out with a regional tour. You or your manager should investigate booking agents who can get you into the right clubs and help organize the tour in a way that minimizes stress and monetary cost to you.

RIGHT: **A landmark of the London music scene, legendary jazz club Ronnie Scott's has been a Mecca for international jazz musicians since the 1960s.**

Your manager and agent should determine which clubs are the best fit for you. What is the distance between clubs and travel time? Is there any accommodation and is it acceptable? What are the club's rules regarding band behaviour and performance? When and how is the band paid, and what variables, such as a door or cover charge, can affect it? Be prepared to turn down venues that don't fit your goals. Performing there will probably not help you or the venue.

Ready for the Road

If you've done your homework and you and your agents are satisfied that a regional tour has been properly scheduled, then you can set about preparing to travel. Hauling equipment and people in a single bus or van can save transportation costs, but at a cost of personal freedom. Some bands prefer an equipment truck manned by roadies while the musicians travel more comfortably by car. Your financial situation will be your guide, but your goal should be a travel schedule that lets you conserve energy for the stage.

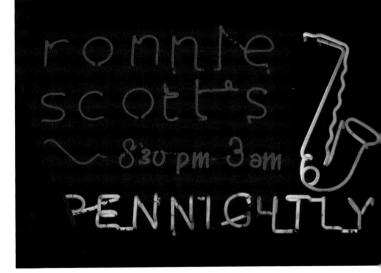

Life on the Road

Road gigs can make or break your band. They can make for some of the greatest or worst memories of your life. Good preparation can cut down the chances of the latter.

Protecting the Gear

What happens when you get to another town, open the back of your van, pull out a guitar case that's not where you packed it, and open it to find a crack between your headstock and neck? Not the way you'd hoped to kick off the tour, right? Yet this horror story has happened to plenty of unprepared bands starting life on the road.

Nothing is more important than ensuring your equipment gets from town to town safely. Invest in 'flight cases' for as much equipment as you can afford. Road Ready, SKB and many other companies make tough cases with metal hardware. Even your hard-shell guitar case should be replaced if it's not secured in a padded area.

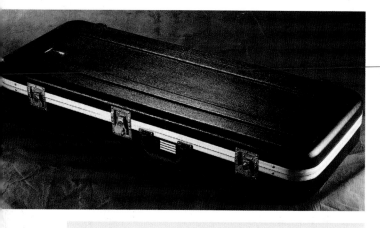

ABOVE: **Having a sturdy hard case for your guitar is vital when you're on the road.**

Pack your van intelligently, keeping heavier items towards the front to maintain the vehicle's centre of gravity. This is especially important if you're pulling a trailer. Use tie-down ropes to hold items in place. Always carry two- or four-wheel carts to help move things like speaker cabinets. Never pack things loosely that can shift positions when the vehicle starts or stops suddenly.

Next Stop, the Gig

Life on the road means late hours and 'sleeping in'. But driving late at night after a long and taxing show can be dangerous. Drive when you feel fresh and alert. When possible, get to the next town and club as soon as you can. That gives you plenty of time to get acclimated to the new town, set up, do a sound check, rehearse if necessary – oh, and to find a fix for that cracked headstock.

Taking Care of Business

When you or your roadies set up at the new venue, use the available space intelligently to allow yourself freedom of movement onstage and provide the audience with the best aural and visual experience you can give. Try to maintain your usual set-up, but be flexible if a new venue dictates a change.

Always be aware of safety conditions at unfamiliar clubs or halls, including fire exits and security procedures, and never leave your guitars and effects boxes, or any expensive and easily portable gear like microphones or laptop computers, in the club overnight. If you're playing out of doors be sure that your equipment is insulated from rain and heat at all times, and that technicians

RIGHT: **Don't be tempted to leave your effect pedals at the venue. An easy way to transport them is to convert an old flight case into a sturdy pedal board that can be packed up quickly.**

have handled electrical wiring and mains access properly. Never leave your guitar exposed to high humidity or extreme temperatures for long periods.

At any club, you're in a 'party' environment, and you want to interact with fans (unless you've reached a status that allows you to stay in your dressing room at the venue). Too much partying, though, and the band (also known as the business) will suffer. Pay attention to the rules and expectations of the club and club owner. As you build a bigger following and become an essential part of the club's entertainment schedule, the rules will be relaxed.

Moving On

Make sure you or your manager clears up any bar tabs, hotel bills or other expenses before leaving town, and be aware of the club's upcoming schedule and open dates. A good agent will ensure that subsequent tours are scheduled logically.

Hopefully, you will have built your reputation, fan base and recording career to the point where the next trip will be as an opening act or headliner on a major national or international tour!

BELOW: **For Iron Maiden there's only one way to travel between gigs, taking the concept of a tour bus to a whole new level.**

The Amplifier

The electric-guitar amplifier has generated almost as much mythology as the instrument itself. Amps began to take on their own unique aura, beginning with the radio-like amps of the 1940s, up through the Fender Tweed amps of the 1950s, and on to the coveted Blackface Fenders, Marshall combos or stacks and the Beatlesque Vox AC15s and 30s.

When it comes to playing electric guitar, the amplifier is an extension of the instrument itself. As the guitar replaced banjo in the dance bands of the 1930s and 1940s, guitarists began experimenting with pickups in order to equal and surpass the louder banjo, and ultimately to be able to solo above the horns and piano.

ABOVE: **The Vox AC30 is the amplifier that will forever be linked with the Beatles and the British Invasion of the 1960s.**

How Do They Work?

Firstly, you'll need to understand how a guitar pickup works (see page 258). In order for the relatively low electrical output generated by the coils of the pickup to drive the cone of a speaker (see page 196), the current must be increased – or 'amplified'. A guitar amplifier takes power from an external electrical source (outlet or battery) and controls the delivery of that power to the speaker according to the level of the voltage from the pickups. This can be accomplished by using valves (tubes), solid–state chips or a combination of both.

BELOW: **The hard-bop music of performers such as Wes Montgomery benefitted from the cleaner tone of a more powerful amp.**

RIGHT: **Mackie's UAD-1 digital signal processor (DSP) card comes with Nigel, a guitar-amp simulator and effects suite.**

The first amplifiers were of relatively low wattage (10–20 watts), while some of the early pickups were quite powerful, easily capable of driving those fledgling combos into a mild distortion. Tales of slashed speakers and loose tubes notwithstanding, you can hear Charlie Christian's Gibson guitar pushing his amplifier hard on his famous records with Benny Goodman. The guitars on blues and western-swing records from that era were also usually overdriving the amp to some degree. It was only later, as the amps got more powerful, and some of the single-coil pickups less so, that you began to hear cleaner tones in the surf music of the Ventures, the instrumental pop of the Shadows, the hard bop of Wes Montgomery and the country guitar of James Burton.

New Amp Technology

As popular music became more, well, popular, venues got larger and amplifiers continued to grow into the multiple stacks of heads and speakers that you sometimes see today. For over half a century after its invention, the guitar amplifier remained virtually unchanged. Only with the advent of cheap DSP (digital signal processing) chips have we started to see some new twists on the old formula. Multiple onboard effects and amp modelling have become possible, but certain things still remain the same: for the most part, more volume requires a bigger amplifier. The trend towards more power in smaller cheaper packages that has swept through most technologies has not quite overtaken the art of guitar amplification. In the quest for guitar tone, bigger still produces louder, and better usually means more expensive.

BELOW: **Although you may not need as many amplifiers as AC/DC, choose one that will suit your specific playing requirements.**

Tube (Valve) Amplifiers

In the beginning, there were only tube amplifiers. Initially they were adapted from radio and record players, though unlike hi-fi buffs and radio operators, guitarists were not concerned with strictly accurate transmission of sound. Instead they found that they liked the colouration and distortion that tubes added; this tone became the touchstone for years to come.

to the tubes to be amplified by the first stage of preamp tubes. It is then passed through (usually) passive tone controls that can roll off bass, treble and sometimes mid-range (some amplifiers have active tone controls that add as well as subtract these frequencies). The next stage of preamp tubes brings back the voltage lost in the passive tone roll-off. The power tubes then turn the increased voltage into current before sending it to the speakers.

How Does it Work?

In the simplest terms, a tube amplifier takes the electricity generated by your guitar's pickups into a control grid. The grid reads the fluctuations of electricity that represent your playing, and sends this voltage

Types of Tube Amplifiers

The sound of a tube amplifier can be determined by a number of factors. One is the type of power tubes used in the design. The four most common types used are the 6V6, the 6L6, the EL84 and the EL34; we will discuss the sonic differences later (see pages 202–03).

Pros and Cons

Even though the tube sound has been the industry standard for many years, tube amplifiers are far from a perfect solution. For starters, tubes are made of glass, making them somewhat fragile when it comes to road work; even if they don't actually break, the shock

LEFT: **Many guitarists prefer valve amps as they respond particularly well to playing dynamics. Companies such as Groove Tubes (see inset) currently produce sought-after valves for guitar amps.**

ABOVE: **The Ampeg J-20 Jet combo is a modern tube amp made with 6V6 power tubes to give it a vintage 1960s tone.**

you should shut it off between takes. You should try to replace all your tubes at the same time so that they match; if a tube goes out on an amplifier that has four tubes, and you are low on cash, you can replace the outside two or the inside two.

of bouncing up and down in the band bus can wear them out over time. They are also sensitive to heating up and cooling off, so it is best to leave the amplifier on during a gig rather than turning it off between sets; many amplifiers have standby switches that allow you to kill the sound without shutting down the tubes. That said, some amplifiers can also sound different after being left on for a length of time, so if you are trying to match sounds in the studio and your amplifier is one of these

Despite its faults, the tube amplifier is still the most popular amplifier design. Solid–state and digital amplifiers attempt to emulate it, and guitarists worldwide put up with its quirks in exchange for its warmth and character. As appealing as it sounds, playing through a great tube amplifier also has a great 'feel'.

The 'give' one experiences in reaction to a hard attack, and the natural tube compression that kicks in when the amplifier is pushed, are integral parts of the electric guitar experience.

LEFT: **The Vox company was started by Tom Jennings and Dick Denny, who manufactured small combo amps for the UK market.**

Solid-state Amplifiers

In the late 1960s solid-state technology replaced tubes in most electronic devices, and amplifier design got swept up in the trend. Despite some advantages, it was not universally welcomed as these fledgling designs suffered in the tone department. Solid-state has come a long way since then.

196

In solid-state amplifiers, transistors take over from tubes to convert the voltage from the pickups into the current necessary to drive the speakers. The elimination of tubes allows for lighter weight, cooler, more reliable amplifiers. In early designs this was weighed against the fact that transistors produce 'hard clipping', as opposed to the 'soft clipping' of tubes. This means that a solid-state amplifier would sound clean up to a certain volume and then suddenly begin to distort, whereas tubes gradually shift from a clean sound to a more distorted one. Once distorted, the quality of tube distortion was found to be much more pleasing by most guitarists. Later developments in solid-state design have led to a more tube-like response.

Today solid-state amplifiers are favoured by players seeking maximum clean headroom for jazz or funk, and some heavy-metal guitarists for the tightness of the low end when playing in drop-tunings. Jazz player George Benson still uses Polytone solid-state amplifiers for his music, while Jim Hall often used a small Walter Woods transistor amp. In proper hands, some solid-state amplifiers can produce a smooth distortion as well.

Speakers

An often-overlooked part of the tone chain is the guitar amplifier's speaker. Different speakers can alter your sound as much as changing guitars or even amplifiers. Speaker cabinet design can also influence the sound, so let's look at this important link.

A speaker works like a pickup in reverse: the fluctuating current created by the amplifier is passed through a coil and magnet – the 'voice coil' – that reacts with a magnet on the speaker diaphragm. As your playing causes the level of current to change, the diaphragm moves back and forth, moving air and creating sound.

The size of the speaker, the number of speakers, the size of the magnets, the design of the cabinets and the material of the

LEFT: **Early transistor amplifiers had a bad reputation for their limited dynamic range, but modern designs are much improved.**

ABOVE: **Over the years many jazz guitarists have favoured solid-state amps over tube amps. George Benson has always preferred Polytone amps, and even has his own signature model.**

diaphragm all influence the quality and volume of the sound produced by the speaker. Some speakers are more efficient than others; that is, they produce more volume from the same wattage amplifier. Guitar speakers tend to come in 10-in (25.4-cm) and 12-in (30.5-cm) diameters (and the occasional 15-in/38-cm). Speakers have impedance ratings, expressed in ohms – either 8 or 16. Sometimes the symbol W is used to represent ohms.

RIGHT: **Marshall speakers are iconic and have graced the stages of everyone from Eric Clapton to the Who.**

Speaker Wiring

Speakers can be wired together in series, parallel, or both.

1. Series doubles the impedance:
   8 ohms + 8 ohms in series = 16 ohms.
2. Parallel halves the impedance:
   8 ohms + 8 ohms in parallel = 4 ohms.
3. In a speaker cabinet with four or more speakers, both wirings are employed to bring the impedance back to the ohm-age of the original single speaker: 8 ohms + 8 ohms = 16 ohms. 16 ohms + 16 ohms in parallel = 8 ohms.
4. This impedance should be matched to the amplifier output ohms.

Classic Amplifiers

Despite advances in electronic technology, guitarists gravitate to the same basic tube-amplifier sounds. Most amplifiers are judged on how well they reproduce the sounds of a few classic archetypes from the 1950s and 1960s. The Big Three are Fender, Marshall and Vox.

Fender

Fender represents the 'American' sound: sparkling, full-range clean tones and smooth, warm distortion, suitable for blues, country, surf and jazz. Leo Fender began by developing amplifiers for lap-steel guitarists and his original tweed-covered amps from the late 1940s and early 1950s still sound great today, with tweed

Bassmans being sought after by rock and blues guitarists. Later models, covered in black Tolex, with black control panels, are called Blackface Fenders and are also prized. The Super Reverb was an integral part of Stevie Ray Vaughan's sound, and the Twin reverb helped define the country twang of James Burton and others. The powerful Showman models were developed for surf artists like Dick Dale, who loved to play clean but loud! Classic Fender amplifiers use 6V6 and 6L6 power tubes. Amplifiers like the affordable Peavey Classic series and the more expensive, early Mesa Boogies and boutique Victoria amplifiers are based upon Fender designs.

In the 1960s, Leo sold his company to CBS. During this period, the control panels changed to silver and the power of many models was increased. These Tweed, Blackface and early Silverface amps are all hand-wired (most current production amps use printed circuit boards), and are extremely rugged. Even at collectors' prices, they can still be cheaper than many boutique amplifiers.

Marshall

In the early 1960s Jim Marshall owned a music shop in London, where the Fender Bassman combo was a favourite amongst guitarists. As the sound of rock'n'roll was becoming louder and edgier, the players expressed a wish for 'dirtier' amplifiers. Marshall developed an amplifier based upon the Bassman, replacing the 12AY7 preamp tubes with the hotter 12AX7 model. In addition,

LEFT: **The legendary Blackface Super Reverb of the 1963–68 era featured built-in reverb and vibrato. This re-issue '65 Super Reverb was released by Fender in 2001.**

he moved the tone controls from before the preamp stage to after, and eventually began using EL34 tubes instead of Fender's 6L6s. Fortunately for him, in 1965 Eric Clapton and John Mayall's Bluesbreakers virtually invented the sound of modern rock guitar using a Marshall JTM45 2 x 12 combo (on the so-called *Beano* album). Marshall had originally designed the amplifier as a separate head and 4 x 12 cabinet combination. At the behest of Pete Townshend, Marshall

then created a 100-watt head, stacking a slanted 4 x 12 cabinet on top of a straight 4 x 12 cab. This 'stack' configuration became synonymous with the heavy-metal and hard-rock sounds of artists such as Jimi Hendrix, Deep Purple, Kiss and Joe Satriani. Amplifiers in the Marshall tradition include Soldano SLO, Mesa Boogie Rectifier and Peavey Triple XXX.

LEFT: **The pioneering sound of a Gibson Les Paul through an overdriven Marshall amp was first heard on John Mayall's 1966 album** *Blues Breakers* **(later nicknamed** *The Beano Album*).

to companies like Matchless, which were able to create workhorse amplifiers with the AC30 sound.

Other Classics

If you want a vintage amplifier and can't afford one of the Big Three, there are other vintage amplifiers that offer hand-wiring and classic tube tones of their own. Look out for old Ampeg Jets, Geminis and Rockets, as well as Silvertone and Supro amps, as played by Jimmy Page on Led Zeppelin records. Early Gibson amplifiers can also sound great. They are all increasing in value but are not yet priced like vintage Fender, Vox and Marshall amplifiers.

Vox

In the 1960s, a battle raged between Jim Marshall's new amplifiers and the Vox amplifiers being sold by the British Jennings Musical Industries. The Beatles were the most visible users of Vox amplifiers, but the company's classic AC30 2 x 12 combo was put to good use by Jeff Beck, the Rolling Stones and later by Queen's Brian May. The EL84-powered AC30 and AC15 combos remained fashionable among the pop and softer rock bands for a while but eventually the lower-priced and louder Marshalls gained sway. The AC30 regained popularity in the 1980s as artists like Tom Petty tried to recapture the sound of 1960s pop groups. The few available originals were notoriously unreliable, giving rise

RIGHT: **The popularity of Vox's classic AC30 combos has never waned. To commemorate their 50th anniversary, Vox produced this AC30 combo and amp head as part of a series of hand-wired editions of this classic amp.**

Amplifier Modelling

Having used various rented classic amplifiers for making a record, players find themselves unable to produce those sounds live. With the rise of home recording, many urban-dwelling guitarists own great amplifiers but risk eviction trying to record them in the usual fashion. Hence the rise of amplifier modelling.

Hardware

In 1982 Tom Scholz, guitarist for the band Boston, began manufacturing the Rockman, a device that permitted players to plug directly into a mixing board (desk) and still sound a bit like the guitar was plugged into a miked amplifier. In 1989, Tech 21 brought out the first SansAmp, an analogue, pedal-sized device that offered more varied and more realistic amp tones. In 1996, the company also began offering a line of amplifiers that incorporated their technology. Shortly afterwards, the Line 6 company began to make use of the increasingly powerful and increasingly inexpensive DSP technology in their amplifiers to create software that modelled the interaction of guitar–amp components and their effect on the signal. In the late 1990s, they placed this software in a red, kidney-shaped container called the POD. It gave guitarists emulations of numerous amplifier sounds, cabinet and speaker types, as well as a range of vintage and modern effects. Other companies followed suit, and soon Vox, DigiTech, Johnson, Fender, Behringer and others were offering tabletop modellers and/or amplifiers, making it possible to reproduce various sounds live without carting a van of amps.

ABOVE: **Known now as the SansAmp Classic, this pedal was the first analogue amplifier modeller available to guitarists.**

BELOW: **Amplifier simulators, such as the POD, are great for any guitarist who needs a wide variety of sounds.**

ABOVE: **Using a plug-in like Amp Farm allows you to record guitar parts and not commit until the final mix.**

ABOVE: **IK Multimedia AmpliTube is a popular amplifier simulator.**

Software

The first Line 6 product was actually Amp Farm, a plug-in for Pro Tools TDM recording systems (exclusively). Plug the guitar into the board, and Amp Farm displays pictures of virtual Fenders, Marshalls and Vox amplifiers as it changes straight guitar tone into a sound resembling the results of plugging into a miked amplifier. An advantage of software modelling is that it is possible to record guitar parts and not commit to the final amplifier, or tone, until the final mix. For other recording systems, there is now similar software available, like IK Multimedia's Amplitube and Native Instruments' Guitar Rig. In fact, modelling software has become a part of most recording packages, hardware or software.

The reaction to modelling has been much the same as the one to digital recording. Just as die-hard tape fanatics are yielding to the convenience and affordability of digital recording, amplifier aficionados have caved in to the convenience of modelling. Does it sound like the real thing? Played solo, head to head, few will contend that a modelled vintage amplifier sounds exactly like the original. But in a mix or played live with a band, it sounds close enough – at least millions think so.

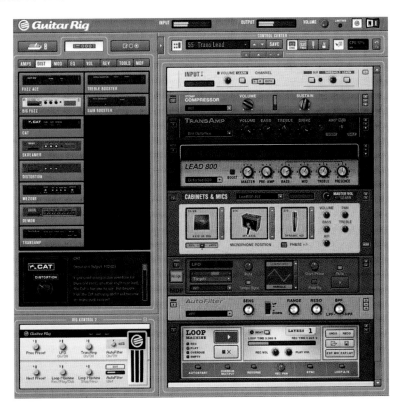

RIGHT: **Guitar Rig is a popular one-stop solution for guitarists, combining software with a foot controller to offer a host of classic and modern amps, microphones and effects**

Set-ups & Sounds

Which amplifier you buy depends on many factors. Do you have money, or room, for only one? Are you playing with a band or playing just for fun at home? Do you play just one kind of music or many?

What Sound Do You Want?

Different styles of music require different amplifiers. Country, jazz and funk need clean tones, often at high volume – an amplifier with plenty of 'headroom' (60–100 watts), such as Fender's Twin Reverb, works best. Rock or pop rock requires good crunch tones and warm distortion. The amp should clean up when guitar volume is backed off, and distort smoothly when it is turned up. Examples include the Fender Super Reverb, Vox AC30 and the

ABOVE: **Combo amplifiers are a combination of amplifier and loudspeaker and as a result are more portable and convenient.**

Marshall 50–watt heads or combos. For metal, especially live, you want high output and edgy distortion, so consider Marshall 100–watt stacks, Mesa Boogie Rectifiers or Peavey Triple XXX models.

Remember Your Guitar!

When shopping for an amplifier, be sure to bring the main guitar that you will be playing. You don't want to judge it with a guitar that doesn't sound like yours. If there is a return policy, try to play it in your rehearsal space or on a gig – you never really know how

BELOW: **A Fender Twin Reverb amplifier works best with any music that requires clean tones at high volumes.**

an amplifier sounds until you play it in context. If not, try to go to the shop early on a weekday – at a quiet shopping time they might let you crank up the volume a little.

Don't get hung up on price, brand or mystique. There are plenty of relatively inexpensive amplifiers, like Fender's Junior and Hot Rod series or Marshall and Vox's solid-state amplifiers that sound terrific at bargain prices. There are also pricey boutique amps that don't cut it.

LEFT: **For metal, a Peavey Triple XXX amplifier will provide the necessary high output and edgy distortion.**

Say No to Gimmicks

Remember that great basic tone is far more important than bells and whistles. You can always add distortion and other outboard effects later, but if the amplifier's unadorned sound doesn't do it for you, no amount of add-ons will make it better. Actually, the best test of an amplifier is to play through it clean, without any reverb or other effects. If you are not tempted to reach for the reverb knob, you have a winner.

Finally, trust your ears; if you think that it sounds good, it does sound good. There is no arbiter of tone. This is part of your musical voice and should reflect your particular taste, not some consensus.

BELOW: **Vox amps, used by everyone from Status Quo to Suede, range from the affordable to the pro.**

BELOW: **There's no need to spend a fortune – a Tone King Imperial (left), Fender Blues Junior (middle) or Fender Hot Rod Deluxe (right) won't break the bank, but will give you a terrific tone.**

Real World Rigs

Most professionals agree that the ideal guitar tone comes from owning the perfect amplifier for the music and playing it at its optimum volume. Ideally you would own amplifiers in different sizes and tonal colours, bring them all to each gig, and use the one that matches the tune and the venue. Unfortunately, few of us have that luxury.

204

LEFT: **Even a small practice amplifier can come to life with a microphone in front of it.**

If you play primarily only one style of music you should start with an amplifier that is best suited to that style. It is better to have too much headroom than too little; you don't want to be caught in a situation where the amp is distorting more than you wish.

use a cabinet with higher impedance than is recommended for the amp, this will act similarly to an attenuator. (NEVER use a cabinet rated lower than the amp.) If you tour with a band in a controlled sound situation, using a lower-wattage amp mixed through the PA will result in a better overall band sound, giving the engineer more control over the mix. Also, keep in mind that a small amp can sound huge in the studio.

Power Attenuator

Amplifiers – even solid-state ones – sound best when they are pushing their output stages. Sometimes achieving this requires louder volume than the venue permits. One solution is a Power Attenuator. This plugs in between your speaker output and your speakers, allowing you to push your output stage, then lower the final volume. If you use a separate amp head, another trick is to

RIGHT: **Combo amps, like this Carvin Bass model, are the most versatile amps around, offering an all-in-one package – amplifications, speakers, inputs and special effects.**

For players who cover many musical styles, manufacturers offer versatile amplifiers that can handle any and all of them, as well as many playing situations. They feature master volumes that permit high gain distortion sounds at low volumes, and plenty of effects options. As we have seen, modelling amplifiers also offer different amplifier tones in one package.

Most multi-purpose amplifiers feature multiple channels with control knobs marked gain, volume and/or master. Usually one channel will be optimized for clean sounds and the other for distortion. Sometimes the 'clean' channel has both gain and volume controls so that you can get mild distortion sounds from it as well, and still higher gain sounds from the overdrive channel.

BELOW: **A metal player, such as Steve Harris of Iron Maiden, would most likely select a clean or distorted channel on his amplifier.**

Sample Settings

Style: Country
Channel: Clean
Settings: Gain-3 Treble-7 Mid-5 Bass-5 Master-10

Style: Jazz
Channel: Clean
Settings: Gain-2 Treble-3 Mid-7 Bass-7 Master-10

Style: Funk
Channel: Clean
Settings: Gain-4 Treble-9 Mid-4 Bass-5 Master-10

Style: Rock
Channel: Clean
Settings: Gain-9 Treble-6 Mid-7 Bass-7 Master-8
Channel: Distortion
Settings: Gain-3 Treble-6 Mid-7 Bass-7 Master-6

Style: Pop
Channel: Clean
Settings: Gain-5 Treble-6 Mid-4 Bass-7 Master-10
Channel: Distortion
Settings: Gain-7 Treble-6 Mid-7 Bass-7 Master-8

Style: Metal
Channel: Clean
Settings: Gain-8 Treble-6 Mid-4 Bass-7 Master-10
Channel: Distortion
Settings: Gain-10 Treble-9 Mid-3 Bass-9 Master-10

These settings are all starting points – feel free to experiment. Virtually all major amplifier manufacturers offer a variety of channel-switching amplifiers, in all sizes, making it easy to find one to suit your needs.

Set-ups of the Stars

Below you will find information about the equipment used to help create the classic tones of some the world's most famous guitarists. Like the rest of us, these players often try out new and different rigs; but their signature tone came from a combination of this gear and their distinctive touch.

Jeff Beck

Beck has played Les Pauls, Stratocasters and Telecasters through very few effects, including a Pro-Co Rat, a delay, a wah–wah and either Fender or Marshall amplifiers.

Eric Clapton

Clapton has often changed musical styles, at times playing a Les Paul into a Marshall 2 x 12 combo, a Stratocaster through a Pignose portable amplifier and a Fender Champ ('Layla'), and in more recent years, a Stratocaster through Soldano and Fender–style amplifiers.

Kurt Cobain

Cobain's basic set-up consisted of plugging left–handed Fender Jaguars and Mustangs, with humbuckers installed at an angle to the bridge, into a Boss DS-2 Turbo Distortion and an

Electro–Harmonix Poly-Flange, Poly–Chorus or Small Clone. He used a Big Muff pedal for distortion. His amplification consisted of a Mesa Boogie Studio or Quad preamp set clean, wired into a Crest 4801 power amplifier and a number of 4 x 12 speakers.

The Edge

U2's The Edge used an Electro–Harmonix Deluxe Memory Man to add multiple rhythmic delays to the signal put out by his Gibson Explorers or Fender Strats. More recently, his huge rack has housed an array of analogue and digital effects, routed into multiple Vox AC30s.

Robben Ford

Robben originated the smooth LA guitar tone playing a Gibson Super 400 archtop through a Fender Bassman. He later switched to Gibson ES–335s, the Fender Robben Ford model and Baker guitars.

RIGHT: **Fender amplifiers have been used by many guitar legends.**

ABOVE: **Kurt Cobain was known to have smashed over 300 guitars on stage. In the beginning he played Epiphone SG or ET270 guitars, but his later preference was the Fender Mustang.**

These go through a wah-wah and a volume pedal into a T.C. Electronic 2290 for chorus and delay, and a Lexicon PCM-70 for reverb, into a Howard Dumble amplifier.

Jimi Hendrix

Jimi used his upside-down Fender Stratocaster through Fender, Sunn and Marshall amplifiers, creating an astonishing array of sounds with relatively few effects: Fuzz Face, Octavia, Uni-Vibe, wah-wah, tape delay and flanging among them.

Mark Knopfler

Mark Knopfler, associated with the 'out-of-phase' Stratocaster sound, used a stock Strat early on but has since employed Schecter Custom Shop Strat copies, Strat style Pensa-Suhr guitars and a Gibson Les Paul. He has used Fender, Soldano, Jim Kelly and other amplifiers over the years.

Pat Metheny

Metheny modernized jazz guitar by adding ambience. Using multiple delays and amplifiers, he spreads his sound across the stage. His guitar synthesizer used a Synclavier for his harmonica and trumpet sounds. Originally using Acoustic solid-state amplifiers, he now uses a Digitech multi-effects unit and his own monitors.

Andy Summers

Summers revolutionized pop-guitar tone with an Electro-Harmonix Electric Mistress flanger, a Memory Man and an MXR Dynacomp compressor through mostly Marshall amplifiers.

Eddie Van Halen

Eddie began playing his home-built guitars through Marshalls. Later he employed Peavey, Music Man and Charvel guitars bearing his name through Peavey 5150 amplifiers, along with MXR phasers and flangers.

Stevie Ray Vaughan

An important ingredient in SRV's sound was his use of heavy-gauge (.013–.058) strings on his '63 Strat. He tuned down to E♭, and ran his signal through a Fuzz Face, Octavia, Ibanez TS808 Tube Screamer, wah-wah and Leslie rotating speaker cabinets on its way to combinations of Fender Vibroverbs or Super Reverbs, Marshalls and Dumble amplifiers.

ABOVE: **Pat Metheny uses a Digitech multi-effects unit.**

To Begin

Whether your taste runs to Charlie Christian or Good Charlotte, there's a particular recording method that can make your guitar sound as good on playback as it does through your amplifier, though it will take practice and experience to achieve results similar to those of famous artists.

You probably first heard a guitar in a recording rather than a live performance. The second half of the twentieth century saw the guitar replace the piano as the dominant musical instrument in the western world, and the success of rock'n'roll ushered in the big business of creating as many different guitar 'tones' as there are colours in a paint store.

Many thousands of records exist with guitar sounds for you to study, emulate and duplicate. Of course, the great guitar heroes came up with their own unique sounds, and your primary task when you're ready to record is to accurately capture the sound you've already created with either your chosen acoustic guitar or your preferred combination of electric guitar, amplifier and effects.

Ear Training

Learning to recognize the relationship between notes on the scale by their sound is called ear training. But another kind of ear training is crucially important in becoming an accomplished guitar stylist, producer or recording engineer: learning to analyze the sound of your own gear and the guitar sounds you hear on records.

For example, you may know that Eric Clapton played a Gibson ES-335 when he was in Cream, but in later years he preferred the Fender Stratocaster. If you rush out and buy a 335 or a Strat 'off the shelf' and start recording with them, you'll have little chance of emulating Clapton's sound, let alone his reputation and success.

More study will inform you that the guitar sound of Cream came not only from the model of guitar, but also from the year it was made (1964), the type and design of its pickups, the string gauge,

LEFT: **Les Paul, guitar inventor and pioneer of multi-tracking recording techniques.**

LEFT: **A good producer can turn a lacklustre performance of a song into a polished gem.**

the artist created with his own gear. But the guitar sound you hear is influenced by other factors as well.

The Recording Chain

Because you know your favourite player best from his recordings, you must also factor in the equipment used at the recording sessions. This will include the type of microphone that captured the sound, the microphone preamp that was used to boost the level of the signal, the type of mixing console that was used to route the signal, and any number of outboard effects units used to enhance the sound's quality.

Clapton's preferred amplifier and of course the guitarist's style and technique. Repeated listening to the records of your favourite player will help train your ear to recognize the variety of tones

BELOW: **Listen to Eric Clapton's guitar work on Cream's *Disraeli Gears* (1967) and compare it to his work on later albums such as *Slowhand* (1977). Notice the difference?**

The system of electronic devices through which the signal flows on its journey from guitar to tape (or, more likely, computer) is called the recording chain. A chain is only as good as its weakest link, so attention must be paid at every stop along the signal's way. The first stop – the selection and maintenance of your instrument – is the most important stage of recording. You should make sure your sound is at its best before you get anywhere near a recording studio. The rules are different for each guitar, but we can take a general look at the recording challenges facing players of electric and acoustic guitars.

RIGHT: **Large-diaphragm condenser microphones are versatile and are often used for acoustic guitar and vocals, while dynamic mics are best for miking amps.**

Electric or Acoustic?

Although the acoustic guitar dates back centuries, the sound of electric guitar dominates modern records.

Electric-guitar sound, which is often heavily processed by stompboxes and outboard effects devices, can create a wide variety of tones, but acoustic guitar typically creates a wider frequency response – the range of sound to which our ears can respond. Generally, in an acoustic-guitar recording the 'lows' are lower and the 'highs' are higher. This is an important distinction when you begin to understand how recording engineers approach a mix.

Electric-guitar Sound

Electric guitar used to sound similar to acoustic guitar. The earliest electrics sported pickups designed simply to amplify the natural acoustic tone of the guitar. Pioneer recordings by Charlie Christian and Django Reinhardt exhibit the result of this early approach as well as primitive recording technology.

LEFT: Use your ear to decide how to mic an acoustic guitar.

Traditional jazz guitarists often play a semi-hollow-body archtop guitar that follows this tradition, such as the Gibson L-5. This type of guitar is usually matched with a simple amplifier designed to reproduce the rich archtop sound. It is almost never processed with extra effects, and emphasizes bass tones, sounding 'dark'. Classic examples can be heard on records by the jazz greats Joe Pass and Wes Montgomery.

LEFT: **A versatile industry-standard dynamic microphone like the Shure SM57 is an excellent investment.**

The vast majority of modern players, however, prefer the solid–body electric. Thousands of recordings illustrate the endless range of solid–body tones, from the sultry fire of Carlos Santana, to the bright plucking of Nashville 'chicken pickers' like Brent Mason, to the seven–string thunder of virtuosos like Steve Vai. Despite the wide range of tones these electric players create, the universally preferred way of capturing these sounds is to place a simple dynamic microphone in front of the amplifier's grille cloth.

Dynamic microphones work best with limited frequency ranges like those produced by snare drums and individual vocalists. Most modern electric-guitar tones occupy a similar space in the middle of the audible frequency spectrum. This keeps guitar chords from competing with lower-frequency sounds like bass or higher-frequency sounds like female vocals or cymbals. It also helps an electric guitar 'cut through' a mix during a solo.

ABOVE: **Steve Howe's impressive solo on 'Starship Trooper', from Yes's 1971 record *The Yes Album*, is an excellent example of the band's unique acoustic sound.**

guitarists, though typically with far less effects processing. Acoustic guitars can sound so thin and bright as to resemble an autoharp, an effect seemingly favoured by a number of Nashville producers, or comparatively dark, such as on classic rock recordings by the Beatles or Yes.

Acoustic-guitar Sound

Conversely, acoustic guitar is more like a piano in that its bass notes can be very bass–y indeed and its high notes can approach a frequency range only dogs can appreciate. Although the *pitch* of notes is the same in electric and acoustic guitar, the *tones* are very different.

The acoustic guitars of well-known players can sound as unique as those of electric

LEFT: **Many of Joe Pass's great tracks were recorded using the simple combination of archtop guitar and amplifier.**

The most popular method for recording an acoustic guitar is to place at least one condenser microphone in an effective area between the lower body and neck of the guitar. Condenser microphones are more sensitive to tones at the extreme ends of the frequency spectrum.

BELOW: **Small-diaphragm condenser mics record sensitive sounds.**

Home Recording

Guitar tracks are now frequently recorded in home studios, which provide relaxed, low-pressure environments for creating music.

In a home studio you can usually spend more time experimenting with various sounds, techniques and mix decisions. You can mix one section while you're tracking another. You can record whenever inspiration hits you rather than conform to a set schedule. Best of all, you can leave your Marshall stack set up and not have to haul it to another studio!

However, staying focused on an important project when the distractions of home and family are close by can be difficult. To be as efficient as possible, approach a home-recording project as you would a session at an outside studio.

Organize Your Workspace

It's easy to let your home studio become as dishevelled as your bedroom. But a messy, disorganized workspace inhibits the music–making process. You may feel completely at home with that old pizza box underfoot, but do your band mates or clients feel the same way?

ABOVE: **A computer with the appropriate sound card, sequencer software, virtual instruments and plug-in effects is essential.**

A knack for tidiness is even more important when it comes to session–critical items like computer files, CDs of important data, adaptor plugs and other recording paraphernalia. Designate an identifiable space for similar items (like a drawer for unlabelled CDs and tapes), and use it!

Control Your Room

Although a thorough discussion of studio design, acoustic treatments and soundproofing is beyond the scope of this book, an acceptable recording environment can be set up without your having to make a major investment in either labour or materials.

For starters, most residential living rooms and bedrooms are usable natural recording spaces. Rooms with carpets, couches, drapes and other absorbent materials control unwanted reflections and enable an average guitar or voice to sound pretty good.

Commercial recording studios have an advantage in the areas of sound isolation and treatments for problems like bass build-up in the corners of a room. Of course there are other reasons your

RIGHT: **If your room acoustics aren't as good as you'd like them to be, you could invest in some commercially available acoustic foam, which is made specifically to tame the responses of your room.**

bedroom won't sound as good as Abbey Road, but for recording demos, some simple tasks can improve the results:

1. Choose your work area wisely. If you're setting up a studio in a bedroom, use a corner (preferably against exterior walls) for your workstation and monitors. Try various placements for your amplifier, angling it up if necessary to hear its sound at ear level. Keep blankets handy to help isolate an amplifier microphone from any ambient noise in the room.

2. Find the 'sweet spot'. Keep your monitors at least a foot or two from surrounding walls. Listen to a familiar CD in various parts of the room. If the sound is different every few steps or in one particular area, experiment with workstation and furniture placement until you find the best spot for your monitors.

3. Use a small amplifier. These days, combo amps with one small speaker can sound frighteningly similar to concert stacks. Consider using a guitar processor such as the Line 6 POD to avoid miking an amplifier at all. Chances are the convenience and quality will more than make up for the loss of your beloved amplifier's sound.

For more on studio set-up techniques, see Flame Tree Publishing's *The Illustrated Home Recording Handbook*.

BELOW: **Commercial studios use professional gobos, but even hanging heavy blankets will help to keep signals in and noise out.**

Preparing for the Studio

The trick is to determine the type of project early on in the process, and your exact role as a guitar player. Are you a sideman who's been hired to enhance someone else's work? Are you adding a crucial guitar part to your own demo, which has to be in the record company's hands tomorrow morning? Are you sitting around your own studio informally jamming with friends?

Different mindsets are required for these varying roles. The first example in the list given above, recording guitar parts for a producer in an outside studio, requires the most preparation on your part. Look at yourself and your guitar as an element of the process known as pre-production.

Shipshape

If you've been hired to work on a commercial recording, in some ways you have the easiest role. You don't have to worry about engineering, studio mechanics or gear maintenance (other than

Recording a performance or a song you've composed can be one of the most rewarding experiences of your musical life. The process is fun, and the recorded result can be an accomplishment in which you take a lot of pride – if everything goes well.

ABOVE: Recording in a professional studio can be a great experience.

LEFT: **It's a good idea to take a spare pack of strings with you. A fast winder may also be useful – it could save valuable time.**

degradation and you have high-quality spares, as you do of picks, straps and strings. (It is not a pretty sight when a commercial recording session stops dead because a guitarist has no spare high E string, or has left his strap at home.)

Most importantly, you are ready to play. You have warmed up before arriving at the studio or have done so unobtrusively during other studio pre-session activity. If you're not already familiar with the material to be recorded you are looking over a chart (printed music) of the piece.

your own). In all likelihood you've been hired because your sound is good and the producer, songwriter or contractor who hired you likes your work.

In this case focus on your equipment and your playing. If you're an experienced session musician you're already prepared. Your guitar is in top shape, with new strings that are already stretched and broken in. The guitar's controls and pots are clean and noise-free. Your frets are well maintained, your neck is unbowed, and your head is on straight, so to speak.

Your guitar also stays in tune, and you can correct it quickly if it goes out. The poles of your pickups are matched, creating no uneven volumes between strings and no noise, other than what's expected with single-coil pickups. You may have even modified your guitar with hotter pickups or 'silent' single-coils from companies like EMG, Seymour Duncan or DiMarzio.

Once your amplifier has been positioned and miked by the assistant engineer, you have positioned yourself where you can hear your amplifier and play comfortably. You have indicated any adjustments that need to be made to the mix in the headphones you've been given for monitoring the other musicians or previously recorded tracks. You know and are ready for your cues. It's time for the engineer to start rolling and press record.

Ready Teddy

Your amplifier and accessories are also in top condition. Your amplifier sounds as clean and noise-free as the day it came off the assembly line. Your cables are short-run for the least signal

LEFT: **Ensure your pickups and rig are noise-free before entering the studio.**

BELOW: **Make sure that you have fully prepared for your session in the recording studio in order to get the most out of it.**

The Commercial Studio

the days when all recorded music required an orchestra, the live room is where musicians make noise. It is separated from the control room, where engineers can supposedly work in peace.

The band, ensemble or orchestra sets up in the live room; microphones are set up to capture the individual instruments; and the microphones' cables connect to a multi-connector 'mic box', usually mounted on a wall in the live room. The cables connect to the mixing console in the control room.

A professional recording studio offers every aid a guitarist needs to make his or her sound the best it can be.

Some guitarists are much more than sidemen, handling the roles of engineer or producer as well. Even if you only want to work in a modest home-recording studio, you'll want to know your way around a professional facility.

Usually, all the studio's microphone stands are kept in the live room, as is the studio's grand piano, if it owns one. Often, you'll find tall moveable baffles known as gobos, which are very important for controlling bleed

The Live Room

The live room – sometimes just called the studio – is a vanishing breed in the world of computer-based recording studios, but as long as live bands make records we'll still need the big galoots. Developed in

RIGHT: **You can make gobos out of foam or any other thick material.**

from, say, one extremely loud amplifier into the microphone of another extremely loud amplifier nearby. Since bleed can ruin a good recording, if a gobo doesn't provide enough isolation from other instruments a guitarist may have to set up in a different area, such as a vocal booth.

The Control Room

Every guitarist probably knows that the giant structure in the middle of a studio control room is the mixing console, or desk (see Signal Flow, page 220), but other elements in the control room are just as important to a successful guitar recording.

Outboard Gear

Usually housed in racks on a side wall or in an island, outboard gear includes the standard 19-in (48.3-cm) wide 'signal processors' that are used to enhance all audio signals. Rackmount effects include dynamics processors such as compressors and noise gates, along with effects such as reverbs and digital delay lines. You will also find instruments such as samplers and synthesizer modules, as well as power amplifiers and sometimes even modified computers in racks.

BELOW: **The computer is now at the heart of every commercial studio's control room.**

The Patch Bay

The patch bay lets the engineer connect ('patch') any audio signal in the control room or live room to any other device that can accept the signal. This means you can hear your sound through the megabucks outboard reverb in the control room instead of the cheap reverb in your amplifier, if you wish, without moving from your playing position. The patch bay makes things much more convenient; without it you'd have to crawl into the tight spaces behind those racks every time you wanted to plug in a different piece of gear.

ABOVE: **Even small studios may need a patch bay for routing signals.**

The Computer

The newest member of the standard studio control room – the computer – is now often the most important element of the commercial recording studio. Besides replacing the tape recorder, the computer stores sounds, automates the mixing console, saves all the settings of gear used in the session and provides fun and entertainment during 'down time'. It still doesn't make the coffee though; that's what assistant engineers are for.

Studio Recording

218

LEFT: **The DAW may alternatively be a dedicated personal digital workstation (PDW) such as the Roland VS-2400 CD, which can record up to 24 tracks of 24-bit/48-kHz audio simultaneously.**

Two methods of working have dominated the way guitarists record: working with engineers in a commercial studio and recording by themselves in a home studio. The environment may dictate the type of equipment you use.

If you have prepared wisely, your instrument, amplifier and effects already form an efficient system that sounds exactly the way you and the producer want it (see pages 226–27). It is now the recording engineer's job to get that sound on to a recording medium, most likely a digital audio recorder or workstation (DAW). Most likely, the DAW to which you'll record is a computer application with supporting hardware, such as one of Digidesign's Pro Tools systems, Steinberg's Cubase or Nuendo, or MOTU's Digital Performer.

Your role as a guitarist in a recording session may be as simple as adding a syncopated single-note background rhythm to a complex production, or it may be to perform multiple parts in a completely guitar-based arrangement. Either way, capturing the sound involves the same process.

With your equipment ready to go and the music in your head or in print on a music stand, you will begin recording at the beginning of the song or punch in (resume recording somewhere in the middle of a track you've already begun).

Going Digital

Any digital recording system converts the analogue signals created by your guitar rig into binary code, the ones and zeros that computers understand. These days that conversion may take place in the computer, in an add-on card, in a separate unit (audio interface) that is connected to the computer, or in the guitar rig itself.

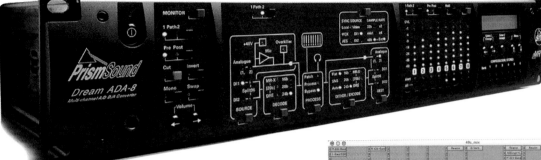

ABOVE: **This analogue–digital/digital–analogue converter turns analogue sound waves into computer-friendly codes.**

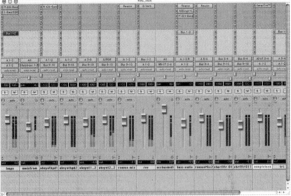

While you are playing along with the song, the digital converters are doing their job and the recording application is sending the converted data to the computer's hard drive. The recording application is designed to function just like a multi–track tape recorder, allowing you to record on individual tracks and perform overdubs as you listen to previously recorded tracks. The application also works like a conventional analogue mixer, allowing you to route individual tracks to digital signal processors (DSPs) called plug-ins, before combining these processed tracks into a final stereo or surround mix.

ABOVE: **Digidesign's Pro Tools is the market leader in digital recording systems, and is able to record and play back multiple audio tracks simultaneously.**

Sticking with Analogue

You might own or work at a studio that still uses an analogue recording system based upon a multi–track tape recorder. Many people feel that printing analogue signals on tape imparts a warm quality to the audio signal that is preferable to the sound created by digital recorders. However, the guitar sound you've created is more likely to become altered and possibly degraded by all but the most sophisticated (and increasingly rare) analogue recorders.

Successful analogue recording requires wide tape (2-in/5-cm tape for multi-track recording) and a fast tape speed (15 or 30 in/38 or 76 cm per second) or a noise-reduction system such as those made by Dolby or dbx to compensate for noise and loss of fidelity generated by thin, slow-moving tape. Maintenance issues and the high cost of supplies are all factors that have made analogue recording an unattractive option in an age of more affordable and pristine-sounding digital equipment.

LEFT: **Many professional engineers prefer the sound of tape reproduction to digital, as produced by the Otari MTR90 24-track tape recorder.**

Signal Flow

LEFT: **Understanding signal flow will help you to understand how a professional mixing console (or mixer) works.**

The various paths your guitar sound can take through a recording system before it becomes part of a final mix on a CD are determined by your mixing console or computer, depending on which one gets the signal from your guitar rig first.

Recording engineers must learn the concept of signal flow, which is crucial to understanding how a mixing console (or the mixing console simulation in your software) works.

The diagram on the next page shows how an audio signal like that from your guitar rig travels through a mixer and is routed to various destinations to enhance the signal's quality before being deposited on one or more tracks of a multi-track recorder. The same pathways are also options after recording, when the recorded signal is combined with other signals to produce a final mix.

If you are recording from the direct output of an amplifier or guitar processor, the line–level signal enters the input section

of a mixer channel. If your amplifier is miked the weaker microphone–level signal enters the mic–preamp section of that mixer channel, where the signal is boosted before continuing its journey. Some mixers provide an instrument–level input for plugging your guitar directly into the board. But most modern guitarists prefer some sort of extra processing of the sound before the signal reaches the mixer or computer, so this is a less–common option.

After you've chosen the correct output from your rig and connected the proper cable to it, the signal enters a channel of your mixer or the recording interface connected to your computer. If you're using a mixer, you have the option of further analogue processing before routing the signal to the recorder. If you're using a computer audio interface, the signal will be digitized at this point and all processing will now take place in the digital domain, usually through the use of plug–ins – small auxiliary programs that open within your recording application.

BELOW: **The Focusrite TrakMaster possesses both pre-amplifier and channel-strip functions.**

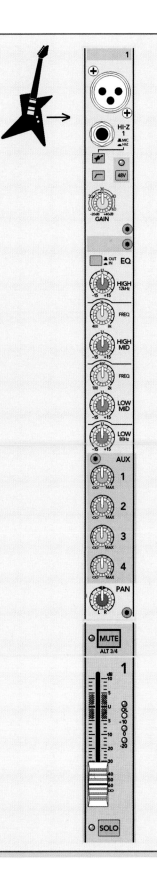

Preamp section

The signal from your guitar rig enters a mixer's preamp.

If a guitar or amplifier is miked, the signal enters a mixer channel at the 3-pin XLR input.

The signal from a guitar processor or amp's 'direct out' enters the channel's Line Input.

Some mixers have Instrument Inputs, into which a guitar can be plugged directly.

The incoming level can be boosted or cut on modern mixer channels.

EQ Section

After the preamp section, the signal enters the EQ section, where its tone can be adjusted.

Modern mixer channels allow control over several frequency bands to shape the sound of the guitar.

The EQ circuitry can usually be defeated or bypassed to ensure the cleanest possible signal.

Aux Section

At this point the signal can be sent out of the mixer along with signals from other channels.

This is usually done to send several channels to one device, such as a reverb unit or headphone amplifier.

This mixer can provide four different sub-mixes to external devices.

Output Section

The output section determines the final status of the signal before it reaches the main mix or 'stereo bus'.

The signal may be panned to position the sound in the stereo field, or it may be assigned to an 'aux bus', usually used to control the level being sent to an external recorder.

On this mixer, pressing the Mute button sends the signal to the aux bus.

Finally, the channel fader controls the level sent to the stereo bus or, on this mixer, to the aux bus when the Mute button is pressed.

Performing

S
E
C
T
I
O
N

222

T
W
O

The quality of your playing can sometimes suffer when you're also wearing the hats of producer and recording engineer. Simplify your recording system so it requires as little attention as possible when you're recording that important track.

Inexperienced guitarists often find the pro recording studio a daunting experience. But when you trade the pressure for the control you exercise in your own studio, another set of problems arises. How do you operate the controls of a recording system when you're playing your instrument? How can you hear the mix in your monitors when your amplifier is so loud? How do you communicate with your band and engineer at the same time?

BELOW: **Try not to be daunted by the recording-studio experience. A professional recording engineer could make your life easier and vastly improve the quality of your sound.**

On Location

The easy solution to most of these problems is to enlist the help of others. If you're a sideman working in an outside studio, let the engineer or producer handle the logistics of recording while you concentrate on your performance. Good preparation is the best prescription. Make sure you and your rig are ready to go, learn the material in advance, and set up your rig according to the engineer's instructions.

When recording, bear in mind that technical flaws like squeaky strings, noisy pots and badly voiced chords generate noises that will show up in the mix. These may not have been apparent when you were playing in your bedroom or jamming with the band. You don't want a producer, engineer or fellow musician staring at you wondering why all your retakes are slowing down the work and costing somebody (perhaps you) money. Thoroughly practising and preparing before the session starts avoids that nightmare.

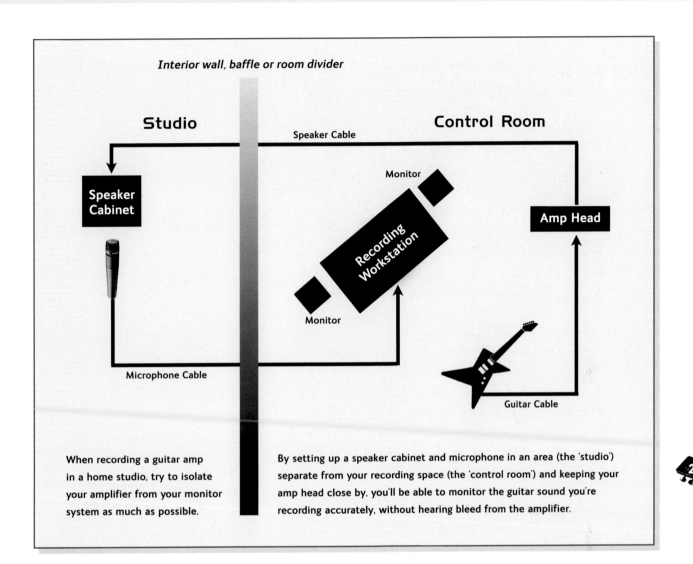

Interior wall, baffle or room divider

Studio

Control Room

Speaker Cable

Monitor

Speaker Cabinet

Recording Workstation

Amp Head

Monitor

Microphone Cable

Guitar Cable

When recording a guitar amp in a home studio, try to isolate your amplifier from your monitor system as much as possible.

By setting up a speaker cabinet and microphone in an area (the 'studio') separate from your recording space (the 'control room') and keeping your amp head close by, you'll be able to monitor the guitar sound you're recording accurately, without hearing bleed from the amplifier.

Home Sweet Home

If you are the producer and engineer you will not only have to get a good performance but also solve the technical problems that occur in the session.

Here are some tips for handling common challenges.

1. Use guitar processors or modellers for recording. Units like the Line 6 POD have revolutionized guitar recording by giving the player access to dozens of simulated guitars, amplifiers, speaker cabinets and effects in small desktop cases that can be transported anywhere. They generate great sounds that could take you days to duplicate when miking an amp in your home studio. It is easy to sit at your recording workstation and alternate between operating the recorder and playing.

2. Isolate your amplifier. If you're only happy with the sound of your own amp and speaker cabinet, you'll get the best results by placing the amp in a room separate from your recording area. This works best with a two-piece amp like a Marshall stack, because you can keep the head with you in the control room and run speaker cable to the cabinet. Place the speaker cabinet in a closet or bathroom, position microphones and run the cables back to your recorder or mixer. Now you can control the amplifier's sound by listening to it through your studio monitors. You'll only need to leave the control room if you have to reposition the microphone.

Mixing

Creating a final mix has always been more art than science, but the modern guitarist has more options than ever for getting his sound right before recording and during mixdown.

Assuming your sound was the best it could be before recording and you've executed your parts to your or the producer's satisfaction, what other options will be present for fine-tuning your sound after recording?

Plug-ins

Traditionally, guitarists got the best sound they could before recording, sometimes using stompbox versions of signal-processing tools like compression and gating to even out and clean up the signal. Although a more dramatic effect like phase shifting or flanging would be considered so crucial to the sound that it would be recorded with the guitar part, usually these effects would be reserved for mixdown, where they could be better controlled while maintaining the fundamental guitar part that was recorded.

Digital recording allows scores of effects to be auditioned and employed at any step of the process. (See pages 230–31.) A guitar can be recorded 'bone dry' into the computer and processed later by dynamics or effects plug-ins, completely altering the character of the original guitar sound.

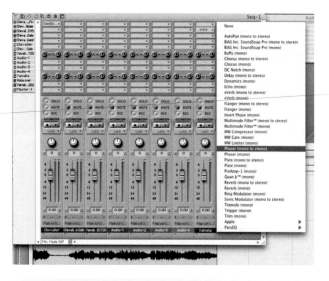

ABOVE: **A channel strip pull-down menu allows you to add any number of effects to your original recording.**

Because digital recording is a 'non-destructive' process, the original part can be referred to at any time. An effect will be accessed during a mix by selecting it from a list of effects that accompanies the guitar track in the recording application. A recordist has access to any effect imaginable without keeping a roomful of outboard effects on the premises.

LEFT: **Camel Crusher is a free multi-effects plug-in, one of the many available for download on the Internet.**

Re-amping

During mixdown, guitar tracks can also be routed back to amplifiers from a recorder. This is increasingly becoming a popular method for injecting a warmer sound created by analogue equipment into digitally recorded tracks. If the processing amp has digital inputs and outputs, re-amping means you can use a digital amplifier to reprocess a signal without converting it back to analogue, thereby maintaining the integrity of the digital signal. This might be a good option when taking previously recorded tracks to a different studio for mixing.

RIGHT: **A mixer, hard or soft, can be intimidating. Nuendo's mixer allows the user to configure it to his or her own needs.**

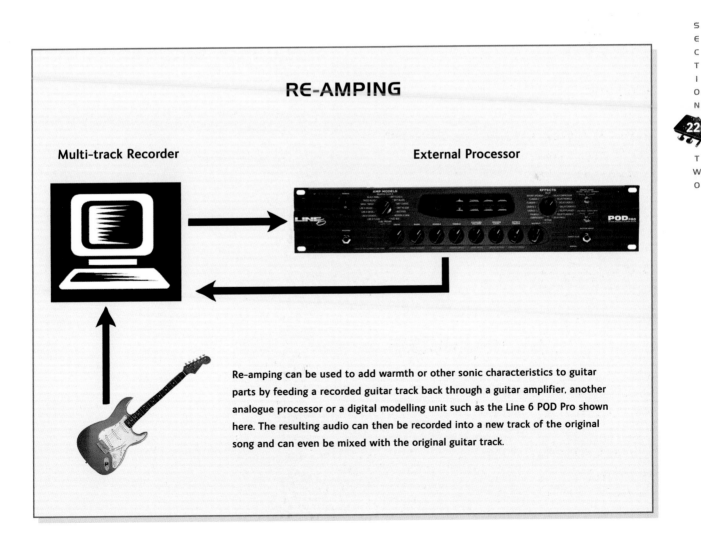

RE-AMPING

Multi-track Recorder

External Processor

Re-amping can be used to add warmth or other sonic characteristics to guitar parts by feeding a recorded guitar track back through a guitar amplifier, another analogue processor or a digital modelling unit such as the Line 6 POD Pro shown here. The resulting audio can then be recorded into a new track of the original song and can even be mixed with the original guitar track.

Getting a Good Sound

A successful recording session begins the same way as a successful performance – by getting not only a good sound but also a sound that's right for the project at hand.

As with any other technique related to guitar performance, a thorough command of your sound requires practice, and well-known recording stars who are guitarists have practised for years, honing their sound and making adjustments to enhance their identifiable style or to fit new music trends. Today, because of 'modelling' devices, a guitarist can have an unprecedented wealth of sounds for recording at his fingertips.

Acoustic Guitar

If you play acoustic guitar exclusively, you may own a collection of guitars with unique tones. That makes it much easier to pick the right sound for a recording session. Body size, body shape, type of strings and string gauge all affect the guitar's sound. Certain acoustic guitars are more 'boxy' sounding than others, which means that the guitar's tone exhibits greater response in the lower mid–range frequencies around 400 Hz. Other guitars, such as large dreadnoughts and jumbo models with a deeper bass, a brighter high-frequency response and a subdued mid–range can sound full and rich in a solo setting.

LEFT: **Acoustic artists such as James Taylor will have different guitars to suit different musical styles and playing requirements.**

However, the full, rich solo sound is not necessarily the best choice for recording with other instruments, a fact that illustrates one of the cardinal rules of recording: a sound that is beautiful by itself, or when 'soloed' in a mix, is not necessarily the best sound *in* the mix, where an instrument needs to occupy its own sonic 'space'. A guitar with lots of bass or high-frequency content can interfere with other instruments in those frequency ranges and turn the entire mix to mud!

If you don't own a collection of acoustic guitars, be prepared to modify your guitar's tone during the miking or mixdown process. Either process may require some trial and error to get the right sound for the job. The process starts with the guitar itself.

Acoustic-electric Guitar

Before you tackle the art and science of miking an acoustic guitar, consider an alternative that may provide the sound you want – the acoustic-electric guitar. These guitars have built-in electronics and an output jack that enables you to connect the guitar directly to a mixer or audio interface. The primary means of creating the signal is either through the use of a specialized magnetic pickup mounted in the guitar's soundhole or a piezo transducer mounted in the bridge.

The acoustic-electric is very popular for stage use because it allows the player freedom of movement from a microphone stand. Its unique character is often

ABOVE: **Acoustic-electric guitars have either a piezo transducer or a soundhole pickup, such as this Shadow SH 141 model.**

fine for recordings where an aggressive, biting acoustic sound is appropriate. However, many acoustic players, especially those playing traditional folk or country styles, would never consider an acoustic-electric for studio work.

Still, the convenience of a direct output, the ability to adjust EQ from the guitar itself, and its unique sound all add up to make the acoustic-electric a viable choice in many cases. It can work very well in mixes that require some acoustic guitar flavour rather than authenticity.

LEFT: **Acoustic-electric guitars produce a crisp, acoustic sound with plenty of sustain and little feedback.**

Acoustic Guitar Miking

The most important decision in recording acoustic guitar, besides picking the guitar itself, is choosing the right microphone.

There are as many ways to mic an acoustic guitar as there are guitars themselves. However, getting a pro-quality sound has become easier in recent years as the price of high-quality condenser microphones has come down.

Diaphragm Microphones

Condenser microphones in general capture a wide frequency response with excellent detail, and have traditionally been the preferred choice for acoustic guitars. A condenser with a small diaphragm (less than 1-in/2.5-cm diameter) generally has a

faster transient response than a microphone with a large one. Engineers associated the large-diaphragm microphone with a warmer sound, and those microphones became the most popular choice for vocals. Small-diaphragm condensers enjoy a similar popularity for recording acoustic guitar.

LEFT: **Condenser microphones are perfect for acoustic recordings.**

RIGHT: **Condenser microphones are far more sensitive than dynamic microphones and so are used to record quiet or subtle sounds.**

For many years Neumann was the acknowledged leader in producing high-quality small- and large-diaphragm condensers, such as the KM 184 and U 87, respectively. Today there are many high-quality, affordable alternatives including those from AKG, Audio-Technica, Shure, Soundeluxe, Studio Projects and many others. Both types of condenser can provide excellent results on acoustic guitar.

LEFT: **Choosing the right microphone is almost as important as choosing the right guitar.**

Positioning

The best microphone position for an acoustic guitar will depend on your style of playing, the ambience of the room and the guitar itself. Because you cannot totally isolate yourself from the guitar in order to monitor its sound in your control room, recording the acoustic guitar yourself is one of the most challenging tasks for the guitarist and/or engineer. Some trial and error is therefore unavoidable.

A standard procedure for miking acoustic guitar involves using two small-diaphragm condenser microphones. One microphone is placed about 6–8 in (15–20 cm) from, and pointed at, the soundhole. Another microphone is positioned opposite the neck and pointed towards the upper frets. If a third microphone is available, it can be placed 3 ft (1 m) or further away to pick up some of the natural reverberation in the room. All three microphones are mixed to create one composite signal that is recorded.

This is only a starting point. Most home recordists cannot dedicate three microphones to this task, and many have to use the same large-diaphragm condenser for acoustic guitar that they use for vocals. There is no magic 'sweet spot' for microphones. The most important job in placing the microphone is getting the sound as good as it can be in the room first. That may involve wall coverings to control reflections, several changes of playing position, and lubricants to control squeaky chairs, microphone stands or visitors.

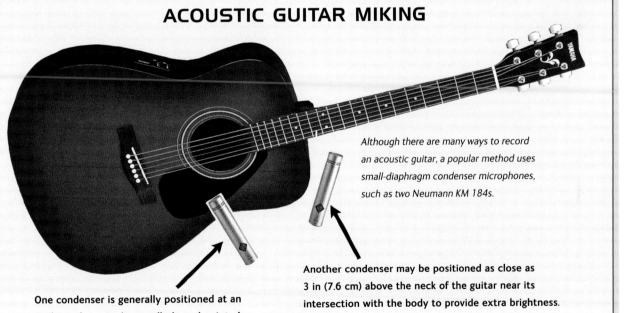

ACOUSTIC GUITAR MIKING

Although there are many ways to record an acoustic guitar, a popular method uses small-diaphragm condenser microphones, such as two Neumann KM 184s.

One condenser is generally positioned at an angle to the guitar's soundhole and pointed towards the lower bout of the guitar.

Another condenser may be positioned as close as 3 in (7.6 cm) above the neck of the guitar near its intersection with the body to provide extra brightness.

In some cases, a large-diaphragm condenser, such as a Neumann U 87 will be positioned 6 ft (1.8 m) or more away to capture room ambience. The signals from all three microphones can be mixed to create the recorded sound.

Electric Guitar Miking

Practice will introduce nuance into your playing and give you a range of tones that can be created by the simple interaction of your fingers, your pickups and your amplifiers. After that, it's stompbox time!

BELOW: **It's important to get your instrument doing what you want before putting a mic in front of it. Try moving the amp to a few different places around the room – you might find a 'sweet spot'.**

By now you have learned many different ways to start off with the guitar sound you want. Single–coil pickups with five–position selector switches on Stratocaster–style guitars sound very different from dual–humbucker Les Pauls and the model's various knockoffs, which in turn sound very different from single–pickup archtops.

But your chosen guitar does not start to shine until you've matched it with the right amplifier, solid–state or tube, piggyback or combo. Even with the right amplifier (see pages 192–207), your guitar sound will come alive when you begin to understand and develop a knack for using a whole range of effects, which might include compression, distortion and delay (see pages 162–73).

Of course, effects don't have to come from stompboxes like the popular ones made by BOSS and others. You can use a studio's outboard compressor or digital delay unit. Often, though, guitarists consider these units too clean and prefer to use an effect they've tailored to their playing style on live gigs. If that's your method (and if your amplifier is like one of your children, never to be separated from its instrument and effect siblings) then you'll want to mic the amplifier.

Miking Your Amp

Most studio engineers prefer to use a small dynamic microphone (or two), such as the hugely popular and time-tested Shure SM57 on a combo amp or cabinet stack. Dynamic microphones are rugged and are able to handle high sound–pressure levels (SPL), which make these mics well suited for loud sound sources like 1,000–watt amplifiers and 200–pound drummers! Though generally able to capture less detail than condenser microphones, dynamic microphones often don't need to. Heavily compressed and distorted lead–guitar sounds and crunchy rhythm parts tend to occupy a limited frequency range in the middle of the spectrum. Dynamic microphones seem to enhance the warmth and fire that most electric guitarists want.

Dynamic microphones like the SM57 are 'front address', meaning that the capsule points toward the end of the microphone. (Large diaphragm condensers like the Neumann U 87 or AKG C 414 models are 'side address' microphones.) Generally a dynamic microphone will be placed on a stand 6–12 in (15–30 cm) from

the amplifier or speaker cabinet's grille cloth. Best results are often obtained by angling the microphone toward the outside edge of a speaker's cone rather than dead centre, but once again, experimentation, trial and error and experience will be necessary to optimize your guitar sound in your studio.

Different styles of music create different amplifier requirements.

BELOW: **Most recording engineers get good results miking a combo amplifier such as the Fender Twin reverb with a single dynamic microphone, like a Shure SM57, positioned about 3 in (7.6 cm) in front of the amp's grille and pointed towards the outside area of the speaker's cones. With larger amplifiers, multiple-microphone set-ups may be used, and as with acoustic guitars, a condenser microphone may be used to capture some of the natural room ambience contributing to the amplifier's sound.**

The Final Mix

In the modern studio, many new options are available for creating an entirely unique sound that separates you from other guitarists.

Though traditional acoustic guitar and amp miking techniques still dominate record production, a guitarist has many new tools for modifying his or her sound and creating new ones.

Guitar Synthesizers and Controllers

For decades companies have sought to free creative guitarists from the sonic limitations of string vibrations. Early versions of guitar synthesizers suffered from tracking problems, the inherent latency in converting a string vibration into a signal (and later

a computer instruction) that could control the broad palette of sounds available through synthesizers. But Roland achieved the greatest refinement of the process and success with its GR series of guitar synthesizers. At the beginning of 2005, the company's GR–33 guitar synthesizers possessed the internal architecture of an entire JV–1080 synthesizer module.

Roland also developed emulation technology that brought the sounds of multiple guitars, amplifiers, speaker cabinets and even pickup models and alternate tunings to players using the company's VG (virtual guitar) line of processors and amps with the GK series add-on pickups.

RIGHT: A Roland GR-33 guitar synth deals with the problem of string vibrations in a very compact package.

LEFT: The built-in piezo bridge pickup of the Brian Moore iGuitar works with hardware that allows you to emulate the sound of any guitarist.

The VG devices could also be driven by the built-in piezo bridge pickup of other guitars with 13-pin outputs, such as the Brian Moore Guitars' iGuitar. This set-up enables you to summon up realistic versions of the sound of any guitarist from Jimi Hendrix to Joe Satriani and beyond while playing your favourite axe.

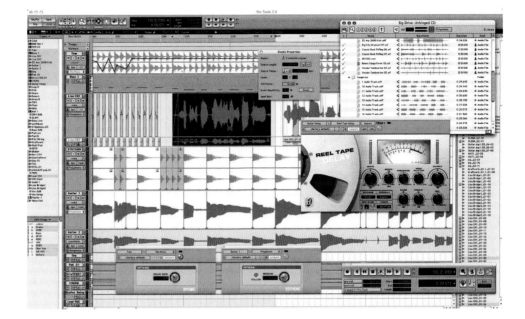

Software Heaven

Whether your recorded guitar sound comes from a miking job or a guitar processor or synthesizer, the development of digital processing gives the computer-savvy guitarist more tools than ever before. After concentrating on conventional effects like reverbs and delays, software programmers turned their attention to guitar-oriented plug-ins. Pro Tools, the first and most popular digital audio platform in commercial studios, led the way with Line 6's Amp Farm for Pro Tools TDM-based systems.

TDM requires costly external hardware, but many guitar plug-ins and stand-alone applications are now available for host-based audio programs such as Cubase, Logic and Digital Performer, which may be able to utilize various plug-in platforms such as VST, AU or MAS. These plug-ins include IK Multimedia's Amplitube, Native Instruments' Guitar Rig and Apple's Guitar Amp Pro.

These plug-ins allow you to bypass hardware amps and effects, and create or remix your sound using only the plug-ins'

ABOVE: Pro Tools has evolved from a high-end pro-studio investment dependent upon expensive custom hardware to a standard application available to all home studio owners in three different versions and supporting a wide range of compatible audio interfaces.

processing power either before or after recording. After assigning your guitar input to a track in the recording application, a pull-down menu is generally the means of selecting the plug-in you wish to use. You can also record a dry guitar signal and call up the plug-in during mixdown to select amp models, compression and distortion levels and other effects.

RIGHT: **Guitar amp plug-ins, such as Guitar Rig, give a technology-friendly guitarist more options then ever before.**

Getting Your Music Out There

Assuming you have successfully recorded a piece of music, you now have many more tools for getting it to the public than bands of earlier generations did. (For more detailed information on the recording process and distributing your music, see Flame Tree Publishing's *Illustrated Home Recording Handbook*.)

The Internet

The most popular and most easily accomplished method of distributing your music is on the Internet, and modern tools give you much of the reach and power previously reserved to record companies. You can create your own promotional space on popular social-networking websites like MySpace and Facebook. You can market finished CDs through companies like CD Baby, which handle the distribution and accounting. You can sell your CDs directly from your own website, or even interview or record videos of yourself performing and upload the results to YouTube.

Even a high-quality MP3 is up to 10 times smaller than uncompressed digital audio file. Almost all DAWs can now mix down your songs to the MP3 format. iTunes, of course, has conversion options built in, and can also play your original uncompressed audio files and burn CDs of those files.

ABOVE: **With Apple's free iTunes application, Mac and PC users can easily convert full-resolution audio files they've recorded to MP3 or AAC format for sharing on the Internet.**

Audio

The most popular audio file formats on the Internet are the MP3 (or MPEG 3) file and AAC (part of the MPEG 4 format) file used by Apple's QuickTime and iTunes. MP3 and AAC files are small and convenient.

ABOVE: **CD Baby is one of the largest sellers of independent music on the Web.**

Video

Video files are very large, but programs like Apple's iMovie (which is free with every new Mac computer) can reduce these files to a size compatible with YouTube and other sites that accept video files. PC users can choose programmes like Sony's Vegas Video Suite to prepare video files for Web compatibility. Check out the websites for audio and video requirements and submission guidelines.

Promoting Your Band

You might also want to employ some of the more traditional tools for marketing a band and getting noticed by record companies.

The Press Kit

The overall effect of a good press kit is to concisely and interestingly express the creative image and vision of the band, while describing who you are and what music you make. Traditionally, it contains three things: a press release, photos and a CD. A bonus would be a short DVD of the band in action.

Getting a Record Deal

This time-honored dream starts with identifying the record companies that specialize in your kind of music. This involves researching companies and making contact with A&R (Artists and Repertoire) representatives. However, identifying A&R people can be difficult. In the US, *Music Connection* and *Billboard* are publications that can help you understand the industry, and in the UK there is *Music Week*. A current A&R directory from www.musicregistry.com could also be a good purchase.

Apart from the direct approach, several avenues are open to expose you to labels' attention.

Getting a Manager

Lawyers, managers and other agents are easier to attract than record-company decision-makers, but bear in mind that all these business people are barraged with requests for attention. If you stand out, their influence, contacts

and negotiating powers can push you along to commercial success. Identify an agent based on his or her track record, and try to secure a meeting or attendance at a gig with your press kit.

ABOVE: **There are sites on the Internet to which you can upload your music for others to hear, such as this Internet radio station.**

Self-Promotion

A self-promotion strategy requires a lot of work, but it can bring you attention, if you have no other help. Here are some businesses to contact:

- Radio stations that play unsigned acts and feature similar artists;
- Music magazines and papers for free publicity;
- Distributors, who may like your music and talk you up to a record company.

LEFT: **The Arctic Monkeys' 2006 debut album *Whatever People Say I Am, That's What I'm Not* became the fastest-selling debut album in UK history, largely thanks to the word-of-mouth frenzy generated through the power of the Internet.**

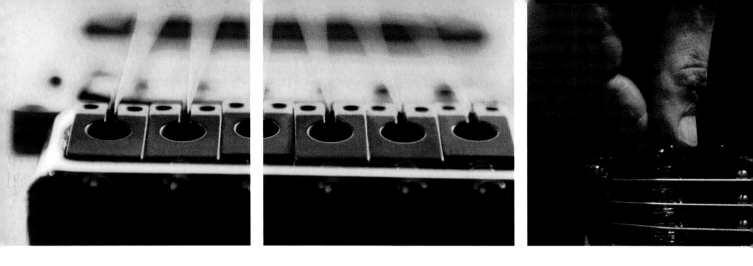

Maintenance & Customization

Your guitar needs care and feeding, just like you, and taking care of your instrument properly will bring you many years of happy playing with your axe. Understanding the various components of your guitar will help you understand the different approaches to care and maintenance that each requires. The next coolest thing to buying a bright, shiny guitar is putting a bright and shiny new part on to your existing guitar. And so this section shows you how to dress up and improve your guitar while you take care of it.

Choosing Strings

Strings are the voice of your guitar. The right strings will make your guitar sound great, feel fantastic and last much longer than a cheaper set. The wrong strings will sound terrible, will turn your expensive guitar into an unplayable plank and, worst of all, will break just at the worst moment. So buy the most expensive set you can afford. Your guitar and your ears will thank you for it.

Strings for electric and acoustic guitars are either 'wound' (rhymes with round) or 'plain'. The difference is that wound strings are in fact two separate strings, one wound around the other. Plain strings are simply a single length of wire. Both wound and plain strings have a ball attached to one end of the string. This enables the string to be attached to the guitar bridge. Nylon strings mostly do not have this ball end, although some beginner's sets do have a ball as it makes the string easier to attach.

ABOVE: **Having a metal ball on the end of each string makes it much easier to replace them.**

Strings are sold in packs of six and each string has a different 'gauge' (diameter in thousandths of an inch). Electric–guitar strings generally are of lighter gauge than acoustic–guitar strings. A 'regular gauge' set of electric–guitar strings will have diameters of (from high E to low E) .010, .013, .017, .026, .036 and .046. Players sometimes refer to this as a '10 set'.

Many electric players, though, prefer a lighter–gauge '9 set', which may be made up of strings with gauges .009, .011, .016, .024, .032 and .042. There are lighter– and heavier–gauge sets, and individual strings may be mixed and matched.

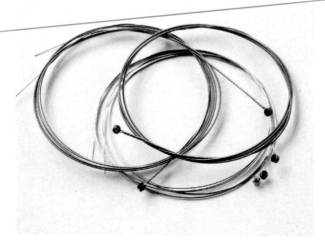

LEFT: **The gauge of a string is the technical term for its diameter.**

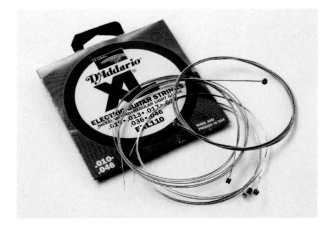

ABOVE: **'Light-gauge'** strings aren't the only size; try any set for a week or two to see if they are comfortable.

Strings for Electric Guitars

If you're starting out on electric guitar choose a lighter–gauge set of nickel–steel strings and play with them for a week or so. Then try other gauges to find the one that best suits your playing style and the tone you wish to achieve.

Ernie Ball and other manufacturers make hybrid sets. For instance, a 'heavy bottom/skinny top' set has the three highest strings from a light–gauge set (.008) and the lower strings from a heavier set. Some players like this bottom-heavy feel and sound. The trade-off is always feel against stability. Thinner .008 or even .007 strings feel easy on your fingers but quickly go out of tune and break. Heavier .010 or .011 strings are harder work but last much longer and sound louder. One thing that Jimi Hendrix, Stevie Ray Vaughan and many other fantastic players have in common is that they all had big, strong fingers and used heavy strings.

Strings for Acoustic Guitars

Acoustic–guitar strings are also sold in light, medium and heavy sets. However, acoustic sets are almost

always heavier than electric. (A '10 set' would be considered 'extra light gauge' for acoustic guitar.) Acoustic-string sets have two other major differences. Firstly, the wound strings are usually made of bronze and steel alloy instead of nickel silver. Bronze enhances an acoustic guitar's resonance, whereas electric–guitar sound is more dependent on the guitar's pickups. Secondly, the third string (G) is wound instead of the plain G in an electric set.

ABOVE: **Bronze strings are usually used with acoustic guitars.**

Nylon strings are used on classical guitars. Nylon produces a round, mellow sound, which is preferred for classical, Latin and

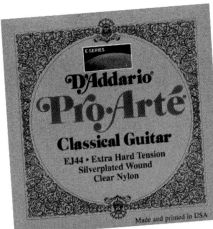

many pop/folk styles. This type of string requires a lower string tension and feels much smoother under the fingers, making a classical guitar easier to play than a steel-string acoustic. The longer string length from saddle to nut enhances the bass response and sustain.

LEFT: **Nylon strings are used on classical guitars for a softer tone.**

Fitting Strings

ACOUSTIC

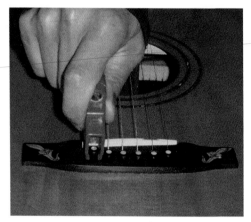

BELOW: **When changing a string on an acoustic guitar, first remove the pin that holds it in place.**

To fit new strings on an acoustic guitar, loosen the strings using the (tuning) machine heads until the end of the string can be pulled back through the centre hole. At the other end of the guitar remove the bridge pin using a bridge-pin remover. Be careful not to misplace the bridge pins. The ball end can now be pulled out of the bridge and the string is free from the guitar.

of the string. Aim for at least four windings on any plain string or two windings on any wound string. Ensure that the windings are neat and placed on top of each other; never leave so much loose that the new winding is lying on top of the string already wound round the post. Finally, when all the strings are fitted to the guitar take a pair of side cutters and trim the excess string.

Attach the String

Take the thickest string from the packet of new strings and uncoil. Bend the new string 30 degrees, one inch from the ball end and push the ball end into the first hole in the bridge. Seat the bridge pin in the hole and pull the string gently. If the pin keeps slipping out, buy a new set from your local guitar store. Wooden pins are always better than plastic.

Wind it Through

With the string attached under the bridge take the other end of the string and push it through the hole in the first machine head. Turn the machine-head key until the hole is pointing towards the string, then pass the first few inches of string through the head. The actual amount of string to pass through the head depends on which string it is in the set, the scale of your guitar and the weight

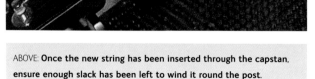

ABOVE: **Once the new string has been inserted through the capstan, ensure enough slack has been left to wind it round the post.**

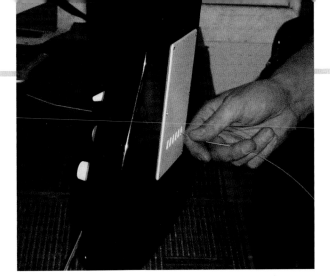

ABOVE: **If you have a Stratocaster, Telecaster or any other model with a through-body bridge, push the string through the bridge block in the back of the guitar and up through the hole in the centre of the saddle.**

ELECTRIC

Pass the ball end through the bridge of the guitar, either from the back or through the back of the bridge, depending on the model of your guitar. Tug the string firmly a couple of times to seat the ball end and pass the string up to the machine heads. As usual, turn the machine-head key until the hole in the shaft is pointing down at the string.

Wind it Through

Pass the string through the machine head but leave enough slack to enable the string to be pulled about 3 in (8 cm) from the fingerboard. Bring the loose end clockwise around the shaft and tuck it under the string as it enters the string post. Turn the key so the string is wound on to the post, trapping the loose end under the new winding. Repeat for each of the other strings. If your headstock is 'three a side', you'll need to pass the loose end clockwise around the post for the G, B and E strings to trap the end successfully.

ABOVE: **Fast winders can help you wind new strings round the post.**

BELOW: **Stretching new strings once fitted helps tuning stability.**

Stretch Your Strings

Stretch the new strings immediately after fitting. Place the guitar on your knee in the playing position and place the flat of your thumb under the low E string. Push the string firmly away from the guitar and repeat for each string. Now retune and stretch again. You should find that you can repeat this three or four times before the guitar remains roughly in tune after stretching.

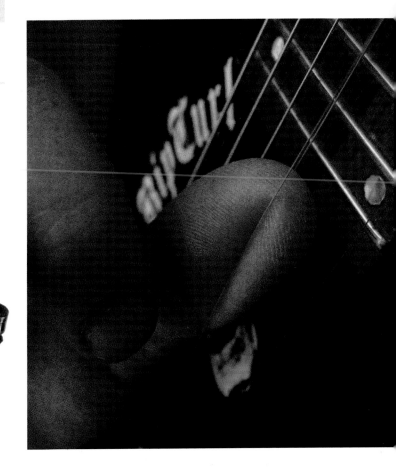

Making Strings Last Longer

When you have fitted the new strings, wipe a soft cloth dipped in three-in-one oil over the strings and saddle. This will prolong the life of your strings and also keep height adjustment screws from seizing up.

Setting the Action

Action is incorrectly known as the height of the string above the fingerboard. In truth, the 'action' of the guitar is a combination of string height, intonation and neck relief, and it refers to how the guitar feels when played.

The great majority of guitar players prefer a comfortable action, though some jazz players are proud of the difficult action of their instruments as it enables the purity of tone that jazz players prefer. Rock players could not use a heavily strung jazz instrument, as rock relies on fast soloing with hammering and pull-offs that are only possible on a guitar with a very low and comfortable action.

ABOVE: **The gap between the bottom of the low E string and the top of the seventh fret should be about 0.013 inches (0.33 mm).**

HIGH ACTION   **LOW ACTION**

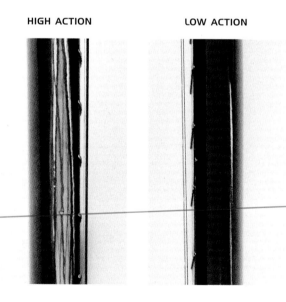

have the strings as close as possible to the fingerboard without the buzzing or false tones that are produced when the vibrating string meets the frets or even the top of the pickup.

Depending on the model of the guitar, the individual string saddles or even the whole bridge can be adjusted to whatever height is suitable. Adjustments should always be made with the guitar tuned to concert pitch. Make small changes to the height

String Height

String height on all electric and some acoustic guitars can be adjusted at the bridge. Optimum string height is dictated by player preference and the physical characteristics of the guitar, such as fret height or the angle of the neck. Generally, players prefer to

LEFT: **The action of a guitar significantly affects the sound – the higher the action, the louder the volume.**

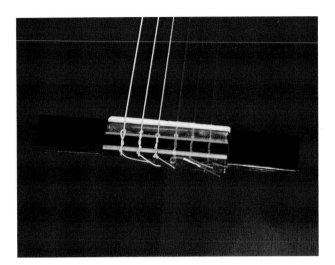

LEFT: **The saddle is the place on a guitar's bridge for supporting the strings. Acoustic guitars tend to have a one-piece saddle.**

about a more adjustable bridge for your guitar. Often the strings will appear to mysteriously rattle or buzz around the 13th or 14th fret. This is caused by fret wear or even a poorly fitted fret behind the point where the buzz is heard. If you do not have the tools or experience to correct this yourself, the only option is to raise the bridge until the string stops buzzing and make plans to have the guitar examined by a technician.

Guitar bridges trap muck and grease from your hands and if left for a while they will rust and eventually stick. Adjusting a stuck bridge saddle is difficult and sometimes destructive as the small grub screws inside the saddle are easily broken. Use a small amount of penetrating oil or 'Plus Gas' on the screws and other moving parts, then set aside for a couple of hours before trying again. A stuck bridge probably needs more maintenance than just a simple wipe over with a little oil, but a can of WD–40 in the guitar case comes in handy for emergencies.

of the bridge saddles before retuning and playing at the top of the neck close to the pickups. Listen closely for rattles caused by the strings meeting the frets and, if possible, listen with the guitar plugged into an amplifier. Stratocasters and other guitars with individual bridge saddles can be adjusted to produce a profile at the bridge that mirrors or closely resembles the camber (curved radius) of the fingerboard. Some guitars have bridges that may only be raised or lowered using wheels or screws at each bridge pillar. Height adjustment with this kind of bridge can only be a compromise and if you find that you are unable to get the adjustment you need it may be time to talk to a repairman

BELOW: **Electric-guitar saddles usually have six substructures, each with a groove over which a string passes.**

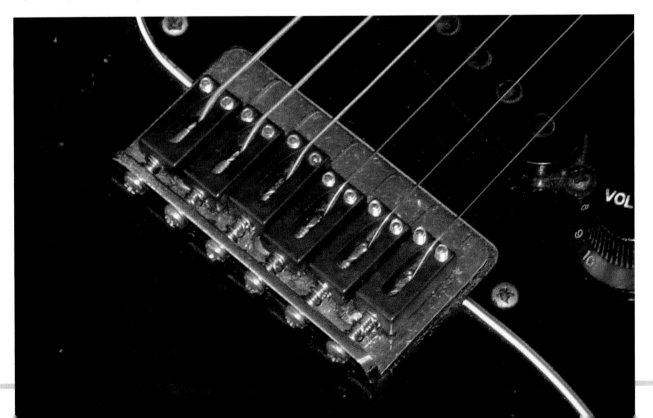

Setting the Bridge for Intonation

The electric-guitar bridge has a moveable string saddle under each string. These saddles can be adjusted in two ways – backwards or forwards for intonation or up and down for string height. Bridge adjustment involves correctly setting both string height and intonation for each string to make the guitar comfortable to play and to play in tune.

Some bridges do not have height–adjustable saddles. For these guitars the whole bridge must be moved up or down using screws set into the bridge posts. Height adjustment in this way is not as precise but it is easier than setting the height for each string.

ABOVE: **The saddles on this Fender have been adjusted for intonation. Notice how each saddle is set in a slightly different position.**

ABOVE: **Raise or lower the height of the bridge by turning the milled thumb wheel under the bass or treble sides.**

Different Bridges

Because each string is larger than the next, the distance between the string and the top of the fret is greater or smaller depending on the thickness of the string. This tiny difference causes the guitar to go gradually out of tune as the notes are fretted higher up the neck. Electric guitars have bridge saddles that can be moved forwards or backwards to compensate for this difference. Acoustic guitars have the same problem, but bridges with this kind of correction are not common on acoustic guitars as notes above the 12th fret are not as easy to play. It is important to correctly adjust the bridge as the guitar will permanently be 'out of tune' above the 12th fret if this is not done. This adjustment should also be checked each time the strings are changed as the new set may have different characteristics.

or the bridge is moved. Optimum bridge adjustment involves making tiny adjustments and then checking both height and intonation. Eventually the bridge will be balanced and your guitar will play in tune and feel great. It is a hassle, and it may take some time, but it will be worth the trouble.

BELOW: **Adjusting the intonation should be done whenever changes are made to string gauge, neck relief or string height.**

Check the Intonation

To check the intonation you will need an electronic tuner and a screwdriver or 'Allen wrench', depending on the model of bridge. Prepare to move the string saddle using the screwdriver or key to turn the adjustment screw behind each string saddle. Play the harmonic note at the 12th fret and note the reading on the tuner. Tune to concert pitch (a=440) if necessary and recheck the harmonic note – it should be reading dead centre on the tuner. Now play the fretted note at the 12th fret and check the reading. If the fretted note is lower (flat) the saddle must be moved forward by $1/16$ in (1–2 mm). If the fretted note is sharp, the saddle must be moved back towards the bottom of the guitar. Retune and check that the harmonic and fretted notes are the same; then move on to the next string.

Tiny Adjustments

Following this adjustment you may find that the string height has also changed. After adjusting the string height you will have to recheck the intonation. Either the string height or the intonation of the guitar will change each time the saddle

Adjusting the Neck Relief

The neck of the guitar has a slight concave bow in it. This bow is there by design to allow for the vibrating string at its widest excursion above the seventh fret. If the bow was not there, or if it was not deep enough, the vibrating string would catch on the frets, causing the guitar to rattle as it was played.

LEFT: **A Gibson Les Paul-style truss rod (pictured top) and a Fender Stratocaster-style truss rod (pictured bottom).**

The amount of bow set into the neck is called the 'relief'. The relief is held by a metal rod, which lies at tension under the fingerboard. This is called the truss rod. One end of the truss rod has a key or nut allowing for more or less tension to be applied to the neck. Neck relief is the third most important adjustment you have to make to your guitar. It must also be made in conjunction with string height and intonation and, most importantly, the bridge must be reset following adjustment of neck relief.

How Much Relief?

If your guitar is not rattling when played it may be that your neck relief is perfectly set. On the other hand if your guitar feels 'stiff' when playing around the seventh fret it may be that there is too much relief. To check the amount of relief you must tune the guitar to concert pitch and hold it in the playing position. Lay a steel ruler on its edge along the neck of the guitar between the low E and A strings. Examine the gap between the ruler and the seventh fret. There should be enough space to slip a thin piece of card or even a .010 flatpick between the ruler and the fret. Any thin material will do. If this gap appears to be too large you may be able to reduce the gap and so ease the playing of the guitar without causing string rattle.

Truss-rod Adjustment

Depending on the model of your guitar, use a nut spinner or Allen wrench to loosen the truss-rod adjustment screw by a very small amount. The adjustment screw is normally found at the headstock just behind the nut and is often covered with a plastic plate. Check the measurement again, play the guitar and see how it has reacted to this adjustment. You may have to adjust and play several times before you have the optimum neck relief. Check string height (action) and intonation at the bridge following the final adjustment.

ABOVE: **Check the tension of the neck by placing a straight edge along the frets between the 12th fret and the nut.**

The truss-rod adjustment key may be stiff and difficult to turn. This could indicate that the guitar neck has suffered some damage (maybe from extreme changes in heat or humidity, causing warping) or it may be that the truss rod is damaged. If you can't adjust the truss rod, then you should take the guitar to a professional repair shop. Always make adjustments with the guitar tuned to concert pitch and in the playing position. Allow for further changes in the neck in the hours following adjustment; if you're changing the gauge of your strings, adjust the truss rod after the new strings are on.

BELOW: **Measure the guitar's action with a ruler. It should be no more than 0.013 inches (0.33 mm).**

LEFT: **Gently turn the nut less than one-quarter turn in either direction (right to tighten or left to loosen).**

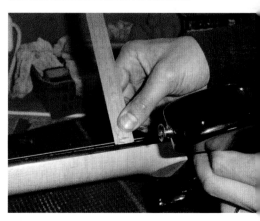

Guitar Care

S E C T I O N

T H R E E

Look at your guitar as a living, breathing instrument. The wood of your guitar is porous, with hundreds of thousands of tiny holes. These holes trap moisture, swell and contract, and can make your guitar change its mood overnight if not carefully looked after.

The golden rule is to never keep your guitar anywhere that you would not be happy yourself. That means not storing it under the bed, hung on a wall above a radiator or put at the back of the garage for the winter. Seasonal change spells danger for the guitar. Your instrument can experience extreme changes in temperature just on the journey from the house to the car. Invest in a moulded case with a waterproof seal to check the ingress of moisture into the case (SKB and Hiscox have a fine selection). A packet or two of silica gel can be placed inside the case to absorb the moisture

ABOVE: **A hard case is the heaviest but most sensible option for transporting your instrument safely.**

evaporating from the guitar. In winter, travel with your guitar in the car rather than the unheated boot or trunk.

Inside the house your guitar should be on a guitar stand away from radiators or sources of heat. In dry conditions place a glass of water near the guitar stand and, if you do have to leave the guitar in storage for more than a few months, do not take the strings off! Your guitar was made to be under tension and removing the strings will enable the neck to twist and warp. In short, make your guitar as comfortable as you would be yourself. But don't forget that the best thing you can do to keep your guitar in premium condition is to regularly pick it up and play it!

LEFT: **A glass of water left in a centrally heated room can stop guitars drying out.**

The plastic parts of your guitar can be treated with the same white automotive compound but may need a little silicone spray polish on a soft cloth when buffing back. Be careful with the control surfaces that may be screen-printed 'Rhythm/ Treble' or similar. The printed words can be rubbed off if you use too much force, and can't be rubbed back into view.

BELOW: **Wipe the strings down after every performance or practice.**

ABOVE: **Cleaning your guitar every time you play helps to prolong the life of your instrument.**

Keep it Clean

When cleaning your guitar, use as little domestic cleaning product (furniture spray or silicone-based polish) as possible. Use a little white automotive polishing compound to take off the grease and grime; then use clean cotton cutting cloth to bring up the original finish. Use a tack rag (a cotton cloth moistened with light machine oil) to wipe down the bridge and other hardware. The tack rag will also do a good job on the metal pickup covers, but watch out for metal pieces that will stick to the magnets and fur up your tone. A clean tack rag moistened with a little WD-40 is as good as any shop-bought product when used along a dirty string. Unfinished fingerboards of ebony or rosewood can be helped with a little lemon oil or olive oil rubbed well into the grain. Finished maple fingerboards can be treated like the body of the guitar.

RIGHT: **Care for the finish of your guitar by buffing immediately after each practice with a soft cloth.**

Fret Care

LEFT: **Frets are metal strips placed across the radius of a guitar's fingerboard to mark out notes a half-tone apart.**

Finish off with same fine steel wool. This process takes a lot of time and is not easy. The problem is that taking material off the fret means lowering its height. A string stopped at this fret will probably buzz on the fret in front because it can no longer clear it. If this is happening you have a choice. You could lower all the frets on the neck, but this is a bad choice as it will take a lot of time, is highly

Frets are both hardwearing and fragile at the same time. With normal use your guitar will last for years without needing a re-fret. Drop it on its face and those nickel frets will quickly acquire more grooves than your dad's record collection. Dented or badly worn frets can, with care, be brought back into line with a crowning file (available from any good luthier) and some fine needle files and steel wool.

BELOW: **Fret files are used to sand down uneven or protruding frets.**

Replacing Frets

The key is to carefully draw the needle files over the fret, taking as little material off the fret as possible. When the top of the fret is as smooth you can get it, take the crowning file over the top of the fret to bring back the rounded shoulder of the fret.

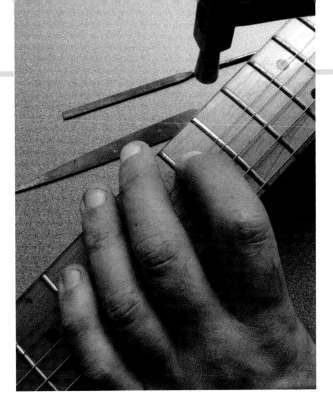

LEFT: **A loose fret can cause string buzzing. Tap the loose fret into place with a small hammer or remove carefully with pliers.**

and carefully polish the sides of each fret using a soft toothbrush if necessary. Do not be tempted to use any metal polish, particularly Brasso or anything with abrasive qualities. This kind of polish is too much for the nickel silver. Even worse, the residue will work its way on to the fingerboard – a nightmare on an open-grained rosewood board. Use only hard cotton cutting cloth and some firm rubbing to bring the nickel silver right up.

Remove the tape, wipe the fingerboard over with lemon oil and wipe down again. After you've thoroughly cleaned the frets and neck, re-string and check the guitar's action, intonation and relief.

ABOVE: **You can also use a proprietary string cleaner such as Fast-Fret, which conditions the fretboard and can stop the wood from drying out or warping.**

destructive, completely irreversible and will probably be disastrous for your guitar. The other thing to do is to raise or re-adjust the string height to clear all the frets. This is much simpler, is completely non-destructive and could even improve the sound of your guitar. It will be harder to play – but at least it will be playable and you can spend your time making enough money from all those gigs to pay for a complete re-fret.

Cleaning Frets

Polished frets are impressive and simple to achieve. Start by taping between the frets with low-tack masking tape until you can't see the wooden fingerboard and only the crowns of each fret are exposed. Use a pad of very fine 000-grade synthetic steel wool, available from many stores. Wipe (do not rub) over the tops of the frets along the length of the guitar neck, using minimal pressure. Brush off the grime that has collected by each fret

RIGHT: **Your guitar's fretboard can accumulate a lot of dirt and grease from your fingers, so it is important to clean it regularly.**

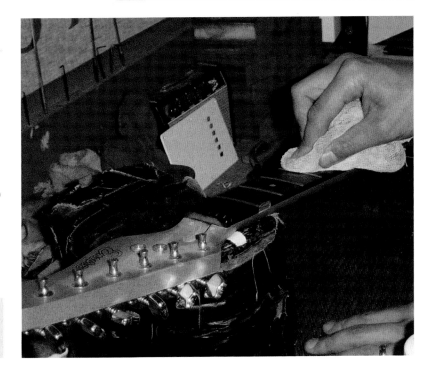

Customize Your Guitar

S
E
C
T
I
O
N

T
H
R
E
E

New Pickups

Pickups are simple to replace and offer the very best return for your money. Most stock guitars, including famous name models, aren't fitted with the very best pickups for a number of reasons. Replacing the stock pickups with beefed-up 'aftermarket' parts will give your guitar a better tone and provide you with a better experience. Replacement pickups are designed to slot straight into the holes left by the other pickups. You can often use the old screws and springs too. Stock single-coil pickups may be 'two-wire' pickups – hot and ground. Replacement pickups for the same guitar may be two- or even five-wire pickups. The latter can simply be attached using two-wire instructions. It's not necessary to use all five conductors if you do not want to. Choose a new pickup from Seymour Duncan, DiMarzio or one of the new manufacturers such as Bare Knuckle.

LEFT: **By changing your pickups you can change the tone of your guitar.**

Fitting is easy, but take your guitar to the dealer when you choose your bridge just in case there is a difference in dimensions. Guitars from the Far East often have parts that are slightly smaller than similar parts from Europe or the USA. A worthwhile alternative to a whole new bridge is a new set of bridge saddles. Special saddles are now available that will actually help your strings to last longer (String Savers), and they are well worth the minimal expense.

New Hardware

After pickups, the second most popular aftermarket part is a new bridge. Replacement bridges are available for all models of guitar and are very popular, which is surprising. After all – when did you last wear a hole in a solid steel bridge? Replacement bridges are popular because a new bridge can be easier to adjust and will probably hold the adjustment longer than a stock bridge.

RIGHT: **Bridges can be replaced fairly easily, but you should check with a professional that you have chosen the right size.**

Custom Control Knobs, Scratchplates and Other Hardware

Check out suppliers Pincotts, Stewart Macdonalds or Allparts for groovy multi-coloured control knobs and scratchplates (pickguards). Replacing a scratchplate takes about an hour of your time and the results can be truly spectacular.

ABOVE: **Scratchplates stop damage occurring to the guitar's body and can also add decoration to the instrument.**

A New Paint Job

An old Stratocaster–style guitar is like an artist's canvas just waiting to be turned into something beautiful. Take off all the hardware, remove the neck and rub down the old finish with very fine steel wool until the guitar is extremely smooth to the touch. Then attach the body to a piece of wood using the bolt holes in the heel, and let go with a few cans of your favourite automotive spray paint. Take a tip from the experts and always spray outside on a windless day (unless you have a very expensive custom spray booth in your house). Use short, even strokes and do anything to avoid drips or runs in the paint. Wait 12 hours between coats and at least 48 hours after the final coat before you go near it with

finishing compound. Practice makes perfect, so do not use your favourite guitar. Old American, English or Japanese guitars are also a bad choice for a re–spray, as the best–selling prices always go to un–refinished instruments.

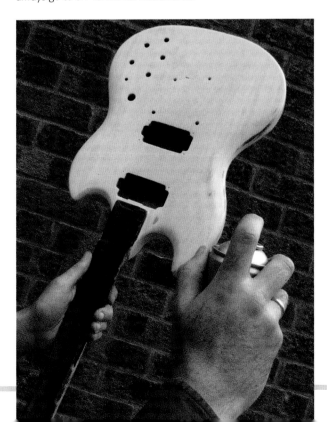

RIGHT: **Guitar bodies can be completely refinished using automotive spray paint.**

How the Electrics Work

The standard electric guitar contains a few relatively simple components. Electromagnetic pickups harness the vibrations of the metal string to produce energy, which is attenuated (made weaker) if desired by rotary controls called potentiometers further along the signal chain. These are called volume controls on the guitar.

Very similar potentiometers attached to capacitors bleed more energy from the signal in the form of tone controls. If the guitar has more than one pickup, a switch is placed in the path between the pickups and the tone and volume controls to enable the guitarist to select which pickup is activated. Finally, the signal appears at a jack socket which mates very closely with a jack or 'phone' plug, which is attached to high-quality copper strands protected by a rubber or cloth sleeve. The other end of the copper is attached to another phone plug, which connects the guitar to an amplifier. The purpose of the amplifier is to take the signals from the guitar and make them into something you want to hear.

ABOVE: **Most electric guitars have a selector switch that allows the player to choose whichever pickup is desired.**

Active Technology

Modern guitars take these basic principles and add more switching or tone controls to enable a wider range of tones to be achieved from the guitar. Active guitars boost the signal after it leaves the pickups using power from a battery situated in the guitar. Active pickups are fitted to non-active guitars to achieve the same thing. Some pickup manufacturers (for example EMG, Actodyne) use high technology to produce clean, glassy sounds from the guitar.

LEFT: **Switches and pickups are the basic electronic components of the electric guitar.**

ABOVE: **The EMG 81 and 85 pickups, seen here on a Gibson Explorer, are among the most popular active pickups on the market.**

the Variax offer so much in the way of convenience to the player that it is difficult to believe guitarists will lose sight of these instruments in the way that previous innovations have gone by the wayside. But however popular the Variax might get, it is still never going to be as easy to fix or as much fun to customize as an old electric guitar. The pickup isn't dead yet!

BELOW LEFT: **The Parker Fly Mojo guitar is made using an effective mix of traditional and modern.**

BELOW RIGHT: **The Variax 500 may be the future for guitarists, but don't write off the traditional axe just yet.**

Other pickup manufacturers (for example Seymour Duncan) pride themselves on using very old equipment and NOS (New Old Stock) components to produce brand-new pickups that look, sound and feel exactly like pickups made 40 years ago.

In With the New

During the Eighties some innovative manufacturers began to experiment with computer music technology to create guitars that were more like keyboards than stringed instruments (known as Bond guitars). In the early Eighties, Ned Steinberger produced the 'L-2' guitar with a wholly carbon-graphite composite body. Guitars such as the Parker Fly Mojo, featuring a mahogany body and composite neck, offer the best of traditional and modern.

In the new millennium the crown belongs to 'modelling' guitars such as the Line 6 Variax. These computer-aided instruments create convincing guitar sounds using the characteristics of sounds stored in their memory blended with the artist's own performance. Because the sounds are created from a list of instructions held in the computer's memory, the guitarist is able to produce a rock sound, then a country sound, even an acoustic guitar or banjo sound one after the other without having to put down a plectrum. Instruments like

Tools

Some say that all you need to fix an electric guitar is a sharp knife and a roll of gaffa tape. That's true up to a point, but lasting repairs are made by skilled technicians who need a few other simple tools to get the job done. Gather the following items, and you'll be ready for your own guitar-maintenance tasks.

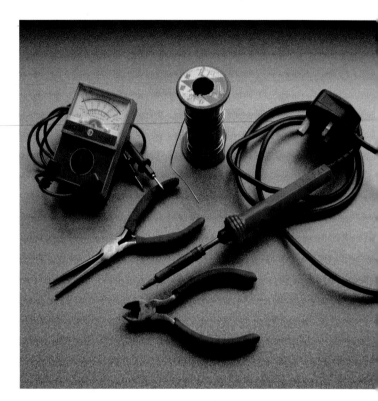

RIGHT: **It is possible to equip yourself to handle the majority of electrical tasks with just a few inexpensive tools.**

Screwdrivers

Get a Philips #2 and flat-bladed screwdriver with a high-quality tip that won't blunt and leave the tops of domed screws in a mess. Fender bolt-on necks need a larger Philips tip, while Gibson AB-1 bridges and stop-bar tailpieces need a large, good-quality flat-bladed tip. Use screwdrivers with rubber grips, which won't harm a glassy finish when the tool is dropped.

Keys

You will need a full set of 'Allen' or hex keys in US (inches) and European (metric) sizes. Allen keys hold everything together, from bridges to locking nuts to control knobs. Many guitars have hex nuts at the truss rod too. Many US guitars need a $1/2$-in (1.2-cm) key for bridge adjustment and a $1/8$-in (3-mm) hex key for truss-rod adjustment. A set of nut drivers or box spanners is also useful for truss-rod adjustments on Gibson guitars and some others.

LEFT: **Buying a full set of Allen or hex keys from a local home-improvement store can be a wise investment.**

ABOVE: **You may need an Exacto saw to deepen the B and E string slots when replacing a nut.**

Needle Files

A set of fine modeller's files is vital for removing burrs from bridges and nuts. Other abrasives such as 000–gauge synthetic steel wool and glass paper are also useful for fretwork and for removing very shallow scratches. Deeper scratches and dents require filling with specialist materials available from luthier suppliers. A very fine modeller's saw is also useful for cutting nut slots.

Fillers and Liquid Abrasives

On painted surfaces, holes can be filled with automotive fibreglass filler and then rubbed smooth before spraying. Liquid abrasives are good for cutting back around shallow scratches but should never be used on unfinished wood such as fingerboards.

Soldering Iron

A good–quality soldering iron with variable heat is vital for perfect solder joints on electrical components. Resin flux solder is required along with the hot iron to make the joint. Always use safety glasses when working with hot solder and a mask to avoid directly inhaling the fumes. If you are considering a lot of soldering, make a rig at the right height with enough light to see by, and ventilation to bring clean air into the room and to extract the fumes that may build up.

RIGHT: **Keep a good supply of tools on hand so you can make any vital repairs.**

Side Cutters and Thin Pliers or Pincers

Side (or wire) cutters are essential for trimming excess wire and snipping untidy guitar strings from the headstock. Needle nose pliers are useful if you have to hold cables within a cavity. Crocodile clips or locking clamps can make tricky wiring jobs much easier.

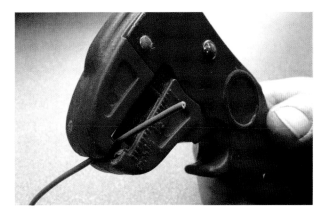

ABOVE: **A useful tool for cutting wires and trimming strings.**

Tape and Glues

Low–tack masking tape is essential for masking areas around the working point. High–speed glue is occasionally useful for repairs to pickups or other parts inside the body, but has very low shear strength and doesn't stand up well to handling or moisture. High–speed glue repairs are often highly visible as well. If you need to join two plastic parts use a high–quality epoxy and smooth the excess if you can with glass paper.

Pickups

HOW PICKUPS WORK

The function of the pickup is to detect the vibrating string of the guitar and turn the vibrations into electric current that can be amplified enough to move a speaker cone. The electric-guitar pickup does this by electro-magnetic induction.

Each pickup is a coil of some 7,000 turns of copper wire wrapped around a magnet. The vibrating metal strings of the guitar push and pull the magnetic field created by the magnet and so create an alternating electric current in the coil of wire. Stronger magnets, combined with a greater number of turns of wire, will produce a more powerful pickup. Smaller magnets and fewer turns produce a more musical sound but are lower in power. Pickup manufacturers use these characteristics to produce a range of pickups for country, rock or metal players.

Humbuckers

Electric guitar pickups have one or two coils of wire. Pickups with a single coil have a bright, clean sound which is full of detail and popular with country and blues players. Pickups with two coils are much more powerful and can overdrive an amplifier to produce the distorted sound that is associated

ABOVE: **The inside view of a humbucker pickup.**

with rock. Pickups are sensitive to electromagnetic noise or 'hum', which is amplified along with the strings. By reversing the polarity of one of the coils in a double-coil pickup, engineers virtually eliminated the hum. Thus was born the 'humbucking' pickup.

LEFT: **A humbucking pickup can translate vibrations into energy.**

Pickups for Acoustic Guitars

The sound of acoustic guitars, pianos, violins and every sort of acoustic instrument can also be amplified using transducers or contact microphones. This kind of pickup is placed against the instrument's soundboard. When the soundboard vibrates, the vibrations are converted by the electromagnet into small electric currents, which are amplified in the same way as electric guitar pickups.

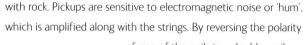

BELOW: **Piezo pickup systems are fitted to most electro-acoustic and some purely electric guitars.**

CUSTOMIZE YOUR ACTIVE ELECTRONICS

The best way to change the sound of your guitar and increase its value is to replace the factory pickups with high-output replacements. There are replacement pickups available for nearly every guitar, but all fit into just three general categories.

Single Coil

• Stratocaster, Telecaster and Other Models

Single-coil pickups have one coil for each pickup. Vintage-style replacement pickups have one single-coil but more windings and hotter magnets. Vintage-style pickups, such as Seymour Duncan's SSL-1, have similar staggered pole pieces and simple wiring like their factory equivalents – but they sound much better. Other options for single-coil replacements include pickups featuring long 'blade' style magnets such as Seymour Duncan's SHR-1 Hot Rails pickup. These have more output than vintage-style pickups and don't suffer from dropout as the blade magnet extends across all six strings.

Humbucking Pickups

• Les Paul and Other Similar Models

Humbucking pickups have two coils arranged to reduce noise and produce a hotter output than single-coil pickups. Humbucking pickups have five-conductor wiring (four conductors and ground). Switches can be placed between the conductors and the guitar electronics to enable one of the coils to be switched off (coil tapping) or the polarity of pickups to be reversed. By replacing your pickups you can also increase the range of sounds available from your guitar.

RIGHT: **The Patent Applied For (PAF) humbucker pickup is perhaps the most sought-after of all Gibson electric guitar pickups.**

ABOVE: **Before fitting new pickups to Stratocaster-style guitars, you should first remove the scratchplate.**

Hum-cancelling Pickups for Stratocaster and Telecaster

Engineers have developed hum-cancelling pickups that fit single-coil body cavities without the need for additional routing or woodwork. Hum-cancelling pickups are miniature humbucking pickups in single-coil shapes. These pickups offer full four-conductor wiring and high output without the requirement for destructive work on your guitar.

Other options for customizing your guitar electronics include active preamp kits for enhanced and expanded tone.

- Active kits need a battery, which requires additional circuitry being installed into the guitar.
- Consider additional switching for the pickups already in place.
- A simple 'on-off' mini-toggle switch can produce the 'missing' pickup combination of all pickups on neck and bridge only. Connect one side of the switch to the pickup selector switch at the connection for the hot wire from the treble pickup. Connect the other side to the hot connection leading to the volume control. Use the switch to turn the bridge pickup on or off independently of the pickup selector switch.

Troubleshooting

Guitar electronics lend themselves to simple troubleshooting. Here are a few common problems and remedies....

Noisy Switching

Pickup selector switches fail over time as the point of contact inside the switch becomes dirty or broken. This usually results in pickups not seeming to work, a big problem but one that can easily be resolved. Spray contact cleaner (Servisol) inside the switch and move the selector to work the fluid into the contacts.

ABOVE: **Having a few spare selector switches and other commonly broken or lost parts saves wasting valuable playing time visiting the repair shop.**

If the problem doesn't go away you will have to remove the rear cover or scratchplate and examine the switch. Check for loose or missing wiring. Finally, consider having the switch replaced with a new one.

Problems with the Jack Socket

The jack socket is a weak point on the guitar. If the instrument appears to work only when the barrel of the jack plug is pushed to one side you have a bent or corroded socket. Remove the control plate or scratchplate and gently squeeze the long spring arm towards the centre hole. Gently rub with a little fine glass paper to remove corrosion; then test.

BELOW: **The jack sockets are the parts of your guitar most vulnerable to damage and should be replaced whenever necessary.**

Dull or Scratchy Volume and Tone Control

Carbon tracks inside the tone control become worn with age and use. Remove the scratchplate or rear cover and apply contact cleaner to the inside of the potentiometer through the small space in the metal can above the solder connections. Work the control backwards and forwards to ease the fluid along the track. The pot will have to be replaced if this procedure fails to solve the problem.

Humming or Noise that Stops when the Strings of the Guitar are Touched

This problem indicates poor grounding of the guitar. Remove the rear cover or scratchplate and look for a grounding wire connecting the metal can of the volume pot to the bridge of your guitar. Replace if this connection is missing or broken on your Stratocaster or Telecaster guitar. This ground wire is missing on Les Paul-style guitars. Unfortunately most Les Paul guitars have a hum problem because the electronics in these instruments are shielded with a metal 'can'. Les Paul copies don't have the can and also don't have the ground wire.

Dab Blu Tack around the pickups to remove accumulated metal particles.

BELOW: **Copper tape can be used to deal with humming or any other noise that stops when the strings are touched.**

Adding a ground wire between the bridge and ground will help protect your Les Paul-style guitar from noise. Electric foil or conductive paint should completely cover the walls of the cavity containing the electronics. A few strips attached to the scratchplate won't be enough. Check out Stewart-Macdonald or any good electronic parts supplier. Some players also add a 0.022uF capacitor to the ground wire. This will help to protect you from lethal mains voltage if your amplifier should have a poor or missing ground. Ensure that the capacitor is taped or wrapped in bubble wrap to avoid touching and shorting on any other components. If in doubt as to these procedures, consult a qualified guitar technician.

'Furry' Pickups

Pickups attract metal particles from strings and other metal parts of the guitar. Over time these can cause the sound from the pickup to lose definition. Use Blu Tack to remove the metal particles by dabbing around the pickups, paying attention to the small gaps between the cover and the pole pieces.

Cables

The electric guitar and amplifier are usually connected by a guitar lead or cable. The typical guitar cable has a stranded copper core screened with stranded or braided steel wire, called a 'screen', as a protection against atmospheric radio waves.

The screen is always connected to a solid pathway to ground through the metal chassis of the amplifier and the ground wire of the electric cord connecting the amp to the power supply. The small amount of energy created when the stray radio waves reach the screen is channelled to ground rather than being amplified along with the guitar signal. It is vitally important to make sure that your amplifier has a good-quality earth connection. Doing so will clean up your tone and may also save your life.

Copper Cables

The 'hot' stranded copper-wire core of the guitar cable needs to be both flexible and high quality. Treble sounds can quickly be degraded by passing the signal through poor-quality cable, so the guitar lead must use high-purity copper for the signal path. Some manufacturers, such as Planet Waves, sell guitar cables with two very high-quality cores. The central cores overlap to encourage

LEFT: **The sound from a typical guitar-and-amplifier setup such as this relies on good-quality cables being used.**

LEFT: **Most guitar cables have a stranded copper core screened with stranded or braided steel wire.**

noise cancellation along the length of the cable. Planet Waves also has cables with connectors labelled 'guitar' and 'amp'. When connected as directed the guitar cable is almost noise–free and will reject noise created by 'earth loops'.

ABOVE: **Jack plugs: the standard cable connection for most effects and guitars.**

Jack Plugs

Each end of the guitar cable is terminated with a metal connector called a 'jack plug'. These connectors have two signal paths: the ground connection is made along the shaft of the jack plug, while signal connections are made through the very tip of the plug. The dark band between the shaft and the tip is insulating material separating the signal from the ground. A short circuit would be created if these were to be connected, and the guitar cord would stop working. Some bass guitars use 'balanced' leads terminating in a round connector with three pins. These leads are for use with special 'low–impedance' instruments or microphones. A balanced cable has two signal wires and a ground wire, sometimes with an additional screen. These cables are able to carry a high-quality signal along a longer distance than a normal guitar cable with very little signal loss.

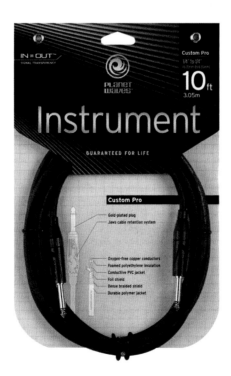

Fixing Broken Cables

Guitar cables fail either because one or more of the jack connectors has been damaged or because the wire itself is broken. It's simple to check the plugs by unscrewing the metal barrel and examining the connections. If the hot connection has come away it will need to be soldered back on or else a new lead must be obtained. A broken wire is more difficult to detect as the connections will be fine even though the lead appears to be broken. Sometimes 'waggling' or stretching the cable will tell you where the break is. In this case the cable could be cut behind the break and a new plug fitted. However, it's usually more efficient to simply buy a new cable. Guitar cables with moulded plugs cannot be repaired without replacing the jack plugs and are usually discarded after breaking.

LEFT: **Spending a bit more on good-quality cables may not seem like a priority, but given that some of the newest releases are guaranteed for life, it could be money well spent.**

The Innovators

Excellence and renown in guitar performance come from the perfect melding of player and instrument. In the history of music few artists have become legendary without their signature instruments at their side. In this section are the players, the icons and legends of guitar, and also their instruments – the powerful tools and symbols of their art that made guitar the most popular and emotive musical instrument of the last century. From Maybelle Carter with her Martin to Steve Vai with his JEM and through all the greats in between, these innovators reign supreme.

The Guitarists

Chet Atkins

Chester Burton 'Chet' Atkins (1924–2001) developed
his legendary right-hand finger-picking style while still
in high school. He made his first appearance at the Grand
Ole Opry in 1946. In 1947 Atkins was signed by RCA and
played with Mother Maybelle & the Carter Sisters. He had
his first hit single with 'Mr. Sandman' (1954), and became
a design consultant for Gretsch, who manufactured a
popular Chet Atkins line of electric guitars from 1955–80.

The Nashville Sound

In 1957, Atkins was put in charge of RCA's Nashville division. With
country-music record sales slumping, Atkins and others eliminated
fiddles and steel guitar from productions in an attempt to appeal
to pop fans. The result was known as the Nashville Sound, a label
Atkins did not like. By 1968 Atkins had become vice-president
of RCA's country division, and he brought Waylon Jennings, Willie
Nelson and Dolly Parton, amongst others, to the label during that
decade. Atkins' own biggest hit single was 'Yakety Axe' (1965).

By the Seventies Atkins was tiring of executive duties. He produced
fewer records but still had successes, like Perry Como's 'And I Love
You So'. He recorded extensively with Jerry Reed and Les Paul,
with whom Atkins won a Grammy for Best Country Instrumental
Performance on *Chester And Lester* (1976). At the end of the
decade, Atkins left RCA and withdrew authorization for Gretsch
to use his name. He signed with Columbia Records, for whom he
produced a debut album in 1983, and designed guitars for Gibson.
In the Nineties he continued to release albums, and performed
with orchestras and with friends. He died of colon cancer in 2001.

Atkins' awards included 11 Grammies and nine Country Music
Association Instrumentalist of the Year awards. *Billboard* magazine
awarded him their Century Award in 1997. In 2002, Atkins was
posthumously inducted into the Rock And Roll Hall Of Fame.

Jeff Beck

The most mercurial guitarist of his generation, Jeff Beck (b. 1944) has never conformed to the conventional image of a guitar hero. He has left or broken up bands before their commercial potential could be realized; he changes style from one album to the next; and his live appearances are intermittent. But despite these idiosyncrasies, he is widely acclaimed as a genius.

Beck's virtuoso qualities became apparent soon after he joined the Yardbirds in 1965 to replace Eric Clapton. His vibrant playing was a major element of the band's biggest hits: 'Heart Full Of Soul', 'Evil Hearted You', 'Shapes Of Things' and 'Over Under Sideways Down'. But towards the end of 1966 he quit the band, which had recently added guitarist Jimmy Page, at the start of an American tour.

Causing a Riot

Early in 1967 Beck scored a solo hit single with 'Hi Ho Silver Lining', an unabashed pop song that he has disowned ever since. But the instrumental flip side, 'Beck's Bolero', a riotous swirl of feedback, overdubbing and backwards guitar, has become something of a signature tune. He then formed the Jeff Beck Group with Rod Stewart on vocals and Ron Wood on bass. Their first album, *Truth* (1968), saw Beck taking the blues to excess. But internal tensions broke the group apart after they recorded their second album, *Beck-Ola* (1969).

Beck's career went on hold for 18 months after a car crash in 1969. He returned with a new group that included Bobby Tench (vocals), Max Middleton (keyboards) and Cozy Powell (drums), blending rock with funk on *Rough And Ready* (1972). When *Beck Bogert & Appice* was finally recorded in 1973, it was suitably bombastic but lacked a singer to match the instrumental pyrotechnics and by early 1974 Beck was on his own again.

After another hiatus Beck re-emerged with the all-instrumental, funk-infused jazz-rock of George Martin-produced *Blow By Blow* (1975), his most successful album. For the follow up,

LEFT: **As a member of the Yardbirds, Beck pioneered the use of several new guitar techniques, such as the use of feedback and distortion, which influenced generations of guitarists to come.**

ABOVE: **On 1975's *Blow By Blow* Beck displayed some skilful lead-guitar work, lyrical solos with tasteful bends, unique nuances and brilliant harmonics.**

Wired (1976), Beck brought in Mahavishnu Orchestra keyboard player Jan Hammer and drummer Narada Michael Walden and took the jazz–rock fusion a stage further. Hammer also was featured on *There And Back* (1980).

His own albums have continued to take bold and diverse directions. *Flash* (1985), produced by Nile Rodgers, confronted the Eighties style of rock guitar as well as disco. *Guitar Shop* (1989) won a Grammy for Best Instrumental Rock Album. *Crazy Legs* (1993) was a tribute to Gene Vincent's guitarist Cliff Gallup. *Who Else!* (1999), *You Had It Coming* (2001) and *Jeff* (2003) all set Beck's guitar against a varying backdrop of techno beats and electronica. His two most recent releases, *Live Beck!* (2006) recorded in 2003 and *Live Bootleg USA 06* (2006), finally do justice to his concert performances.

Be My Guest

While Beck's solo career was becoming less prolific, he was making guest appearances on Stevie Wonder's *Talking Book* (1972), Stanley Clarke's *Journey To Love* (1975) and *Modern Man* (1978), Tina Turner's *Private Dancer* (1984), Mick Jagger's *She's The Boss* (1985), Roger Waters' *Amused To Death* (1992) and Kate Bush's *The Red Shows* (1993). He also took part in the 1993 ARMS benefit shows with Eric Clapton and Jimmy Page – the only time all three legendary Yardbirds guitarists have appeared on the same stage together.

Beck's preferred guitar is a Fender Telecaster, although in the Yardbirds he played a Fender Esquire. He gets his distinctive sound by using his fingers rather than a plectrum and using the tremolo arm and a wah–wah pedal.

LEFT: **Beck is one of the most admired guitarists in the world, drawing equal respect from rock, blues and jazz musicians.**

Maybelle Carter

As a member of the first family of country music, Maybelle Carter (1909–78) distinguished herself far beyond her role as accompanist to her brother-in-law A.P. Carter and his wife Sara in the Carter Family.

Born Maybelle Addington in Nickelsville, Virginia, she married Ezra J. Carter in 1926. The Carter Family was formed in 1927, and Maybelle (pictured seated) was the guitarist. She also doubled on autoharp and banjo. Her unique style involved using her thumb (with thumb-pick) to play bass and melody while her index finger filled out the rhythm on the higher strings – a technique that became known as the 'Carter scratch'.

In 1927, A.P. convinced Sara (Maybelle's cousin) and a pregnant Maybelle to travel from Virginia to Tennessee, where they would audition for record producer Ralph Peer. That year, the Victor recording company released a 78-RPM record of the group performing 'Wandering Boy' and 'Poor Orphan Child'. But it was 1928's release of 'The Storms Are On The Ocean' and 'Single Girl, Married Girl' that boosted the family's popularity.

Country Standards

The Carter Family performed together on radio shows and records until the breakup of A.P. and Sara's marriage in 1942. Many of the Carters' recordings, such as 'Can The Circle Be Unbroken' and 'Cannonball Blues' became country-music standards. After the breakup, Maybelle continued to perform with her daughters Anita, June and Helen as Mother

Maybelle & the Carter Sisters. Daughter June would eventually marry country legend Johnny Cash, and Mother Maybelle & the Carter Sisters would be regulars on Cash's television show.

The Carter Family was elected to the Country Music Hall Of Fame in 1970, and in 1988, they were inducted into the Grammy Hall Of Fame. In 2001, Maybelle was initiated into the International Bluegrass Music Hall Of Honour. Mother Maybelle died in October 1978, in Nashville.

Charlie Christian

Charlie Christian (1916–42) was born in Texas but moved to Oklahoma with his family. He picked up the guitar from his father, and began playing around Oklahoma City, learning from guitarist 'Bigfoot' Ralph Hamilton. By 1936, he was playing electric guitar and would jam with stars travelling through Oklahoma City. It was jazz pianist Mary Lou Williams who told producer John Hammond about Christian.

Topping the Polls

Christian auditioned for Hammond, who became convinced that Christian would be a perfect fit for Benny Goodman's new sextet. On hearing Christian, Goodman hired him on the spot and he became a star of the Benny Goodman Sextet. With the later additions of Count Basie, trumpeter Cootie Williams and tenor saxophonist Georgie Auld, the Goodman Sextet was an all-star band that dominated the jazz polls in 1941.

Christian was influenced more by horn players such as Lester Young and Herschel Evans than by early acoustic guitarists like Eddie Lang and jazz-bluesman Lonnie Johnson, and Christian admitted he wanted his guitar to sound like a tenor saxophone. By 1939 several players had adopted electric guitar, but Christian was the first great soloist on the amplified instrument.

Christian's participation in after-hours jam sessions, in which he created flights of improvisational fancy on extended solos, helped spur the developing form of bebop. Two recordings from a 1941 session, 'Blues In B' and 'Waiting For Benny', foreshadow the bop-jam sessions of the late Forties. Other Goodman Sextet records that foretell bop are *Seven Come Eleven* (1939) and *Air Mail Special* (1940 and 1941).

Christian was a habitual drinker and marijuana user and contracted tuberculosis in the late Thirties. After hospital treatment, he resumed his hectic lifestyle, but died in March 1942.

Most of Christian's recorded works are available on CD, including *Selected Broadcasts & Jam Sessions* (2002), *The Genius Of The Electric Guitar* (1989) and *Featuring Charlie Christian 1939–41* (1989).

Eric Clapton

Eric Clapton's (b. 1945) career has passed through an extraordinary series of highs and lows during his five decades as a guitar hero. He has also experimented with stylistic changes but always returned to his first love, the blues.

Clapton started playing guitar aged 13 and in 1963 joined the Yardbirds, establishing his reputation on *Five Live Yardbirds* (1964). He quit the band in 1965 after recording their first hit, 'For Your Love', and joined John Mayall's Bluesbreakers. *Blues Breakers* (1966) is still regarded as one of the seminal blues–guitar albums. But before it was released, Clapton left to form Cream with Jack Bruce (bass) and Ginger Baker (drums).

Cream of the Crop

Cream became superstars as a result of *Fresh Cream* (1966), *Disraeli Gears* (1967) and *Wheels Of Fire* (1968), and a series of American tours. But within two years the band was worn out and Clapton joined keyboard player and singer Steve Winwood to form Blind Faith, which also included Baker. Unfortunately, *Blind Faith* (1969) could not live up to the hype surrounding the group, and they soon split.

BELOW: **With John Mayall's Bluesbreakers, Eric Clapton redefined electric blues guitar.**

LEFT: **Clapton's blues-style solos and memorable riffs have been hugely influential to many rock musicians.**

His appearance at Live Aid in 1985 and his duet with Tina Turner on 'Tearing Us Apart' in 1987 raised his profile further. *Crossroads* (1988) and *Journeyman* (1989) were both hugely successful.

Got the Blues

But it was the blues that set the seal on Clapton's career. In 1992 he played the first *Unplugged* show for MTV, performing an acoustic version of 'Layla', 'Tears In Heaven' and a selection of blues songs. *MTV Unplugged* (1992) sold over 12 million copies. *From The Cradle* (1994) topped the UK and US charts, selling 10 million copies – unprecedented for a blues album.

Since then Clapton has balanced contemporary albums, such as *Pilgrim* (1998) and *Reptile* (2001), with blues albums *Riding With The King* (2001) – recorded with B.B. King – and *Me And Mr Johnson* (2004) – featuring songs by Clapton's hero Robert Johnson. As well as extensive touring, Clapton revisited his past, joining John Mayall for his 70th birthday concert in 2003, reuniting with Cream in 2005 and teaming up with Winwood in 2008.

In his early years Clapton favoured Gibson guitars, starting with a Les Paul Sunburst, followed by a Gibson Firebird, a Gibson ES–335 and a Gibson SG, before moving to Fender Stratocasters in 1969.

Blind Faith's support group, Delaney & Bonnie, helped Clapton to record his first solo album, *Eric Clapton* (1970) and provided him with the musicians for his next group. Derek & the Dominos recorded *Layla And Other Assorted Love Songs* (1970), on which Clapton was joined by guitarist Duane Allman, and the band toured Britain and America before imploding in a maelstrom of drug use. Clapton was left with a heroin dependency, and after appearing at *Concert For Bangladesh* (1971) he retreated from view to return, clean and rejuvenated with *461 Ocean Boulevard* (1974). This contained Clapton's version of 'I Shot The Sheriff', the US No. 1 hit that introduced the world to Bob Marley.

He also began songwriting, notably on *Slowhand* (1977) with 'Wonderful Tonight' and 'Lay Down Sally'. Extensive touring maintained his popularity, but by the late Seventies alcohol dependency was hampering his playing. By 1983 he was sober, and *Money And Cigarettes* (1983) and *Behind The Sun* (1985) confirmed his return to form.

His most famous Stratocaster, 'Blackie', was sold at auction in 2004 to raise money for his Crossroads Centre for drug and alcohol addictions. In 1988 Fender inaugurated their signature range of guitars with an Eric Clapton Stratocaster model.

LEFT: **Eric Clapton has enjoyed a hugely successful solo career. 1992's acoustic *Unplugged* album sold millions.**

Paco de Lucía

Spanish composer and guitarist Paco de Lucía (b. 1947), born Francisco Sánchez Gómez, is a proponent of the modern flamenco style and one of the very few flamenco guitarists who has successfully crossed over into other genres of music, including jazz, funk, classical and world music. The son of Gypsy flamenco guitarist Antonio Sánchez, he adopted the stage name Paco de Lucía in honour of his Portuguese gypsy mother, Lucía Gomes.

In 1958, aged 11, De Lucía made his first public appearance on Radio Algeciras; a year later he won a special prize in the Jerez flamenco competition. In 1961, he toured with the flamenco troupe of dancer José Greco. In 1964 de Lucía met Madrilenian guitarist Ricardo Modrego, with whom he recorded *Dos Guitarras Flamencas* (1965) and *Doce Canciones De Federico García Lorca Para Guitarra* (1965). Between 1968 and 1977 he enjoyed a fruitful collaboration with fellow new-flamenco innovator Camarón de la Isla, with whom he recorded 10 albums.

Radical Innovator

In 1979, De Lucía, John McLaughlin and Larry Coryell formed the Guitar Trio and briefly toured Europe. Coryell was later replaced by Al Di Meola, and the trio have recorded two albums, *Friday Night In San Francisco* (1980) and *The Guitar Trio* (1996), with that line-up. His band, the Paco De Lucía Sextet, released the first of their three albums that same year. De Lucia has released several albums encompassing traditional and modern flamenco styles. He introduced instruments, techniques and variations that shocked flamenco purists yet became accepted elements of the modern musical form.

De Lucia's work has led to a new understanding of flamenco and advanced the technical and musical boundaries of his instrument. De Lucia's *Antologia*, volumes 1 and 2, are good starting points to explore the master's range. Other important works include *Almoraima* (1976), *Siroco* (1988) and *Luzia* (1998).

David Gilmour

The teenage David Gilmour (b. 1946) was a friend of Syd Barrett, with whom he learned to play guitar, and Roger Waters. Barrett and Waters formed Pink Floyd in the early Sixties with Richard Wright and Nick Mason, and in 1968 asked Gilmore to cover for Barrett, whose performances and behaviour were becoming increasingly erratic. Within weeks Barrett left the group and Gilmour became lead guitarist.

Setting the Atmosphere

Gilmour's guitar parts and solos on the band's defining album, *The Dark Side Of The Moon* (1973), were a distinctive element of the Pink Floyd sound. Gilmour focused on getting a strong, clean tone from his guitar that he then blended with an increasing variety of effects pedals. He developed his sound further on *Wish You Were Here* (1975). His evocative, melancholic playing on 'Shine On You Crazy Diamond' centred on a sublime, introductory four-note riff.

By the time of *The Wall* (1979) Waters had assumed complete control over Pink Floyd and Gilmour's expressive scope was limited. Nevertheless, his guitar break on 'Another Brick In The Wall Part 2' is often cited as the best example of his 'clean' tone. He released two solo albums, *David Gilmour* (1978) and *About Face* (1984).

In 1986 Waters quit Pink Floyd, but Gilmour and the others continued. They embarked on a world tour that ran for three years and yielded *Delicate Sound Of Thunder* (1988). After *The Division Bell* (1994) and *Pulse* (1995), Gilmour then resumed his solo career. In 2005 Waters rejoined Gilmour, Mason and Wright for Live 8, and in 2006 Gilmour released his third solo album, *On An Island*.

Throughout his career Gilmour has generally played a Fender Stratocaster. He also has an extensive collection of guitars, including a Gibson Les Paul, a Gretsch Duo-Jet and a Gibson EH1 50 lap steel guitar. His acoustic guitars include models by Gibson, Ovation and Martin.

Jonny Greenwood

Jonny Greenwood (b. 1971) met the other members of Radiohead (singer Thom Yorke, guitarist Ed O'Brien and drummer Phil Selway) through his brother Colin.

Originally called On A Friday, the band changed their name to Radiohead after signing a record deal with EMI.

Pablo Honey (1993) blended guitar-led anthemic rock with atmospheric instrumental passages. *The Bends* (1995) was a low-key album of melancholic grandeur with Yorke's vocals set against dense guitar arrangements. *OK Computer* (1997) was a minimalist art-rock album on which Greenwood used a wide range of sounds and effects to enhance the songs.

Unconventional and Virtuosic

Kid A (2000) deliberately moved away from conventional melodies or commercial sounds. Guitars were less in evidence and Greenwood also played the Theremin-like ondes martenot and arranged a string orchestra. *Amnesiac* (2001) had a lighter feel, but the guitars were mostly used for ambient textures, and *Hail To The Thief* (2003) remained complex, although some of Radiohead's earlier energy returned. After a lengthy hiatus, *In Rainbows* (2007) restored the passion in the studio that they had never lost on stage, with guitars coming back into favour.

Greenwood became the first member of Radiohead to release a solo album, *Bodysong* (2003), a film soundtrack that featured guitars on just two tracks, as he focused on his multi-instrument and arranging skills. In 2004 he was appointed composer in residence at the BBC and composed several pieces for orchestra, piano and ondes martenot. Some of this work later appeared in his *There Will Be Blood* (2007) soundtrack album.

Greenwood has generally favoured Fender Telecaster guitars that have been customized and rewired, although he also has a number of Gibson electric and acoustic guitars as well as a Gretsch. He uses a Vox AC30 amplifier for clean tones. For distorted tones he uses effects pedals and a Fender Deluxe 85.

Steve Hackett

Steve Hackett (b. 1950) taught himself guitar as a teenager. After leaving school at 16, he was approached by Genesis, who were looking for a new guitarist. He joined singer Peter Gabriel, keyboard player Tony Banks, bassist Mike Rutherford and drummer Phil Collins.

Part of the Musical Tapestry

His introspective manner suited Genesis' style on *Nursery Cryme* (1971), and the line-up gelled more effectively on *Foxtrot* (1972), with Hackett's acoustic and electric guitars blending with the tight arrangements. On *Selling England By The Pound* (1973) Hackett made some of his strongest contributions yet, with controlled guitar effects and an epic solo. *The Lamb Lies Down On Broadway* (1974) was a complex concept album on which Hackett's guitar was fed through a range of distortion devices.

Gabriel left the band in 1975, and Hackett recorded his first solo album, *Voyage Of The Acolyte* (1975). Hackett contributed some strident playing and atmospheric effects to Genesis' next album, *A Trick Of The Tail* (1976). But despite several co-writing credits on *Wind And Wuthering* (1977), he was dissatisfied with the level of his contribution and left Genesis while they were preparing *Seconds Out* (1977).

Hackett's second solo album, *Please Don't Touch* (1978) was deliberately diverse, and *Spectral Mornings* (1979) featured some powerful guitar playing. *Cured* (1981) and *Highly Strung* (1983) moved closer to the pop mainstream, and throughout the Eighties Hackett consciously varied the style of his albums. In 1986 he joined guitarist Steve Howe for the GTR project. They recorded one self-titled album and undertook a world tour, but disbanded soon afterwards. His first live album, *Timelapse* (1992), used material from his entire career, and since then his albums have switched between acoustic and electric.

Hackett's favourite guitar is a 1957 Gibson Les Paul Goldtop. He also plays a Fernandes Monterey Elite, an Ovation UK2, a Yairi Classical and a 1975 Zemaitis acoustic 12–string.

SECTION FOUR

277

Jimi Hendrix

Jimi Hendrix (1942–70) remains the most innovative and influential rock guitarist in the world. He changed the way the guitar was played, transforming its possibilities and its image. Other guitarists had toyed with feedback and distortion but Hendrix turned these and other effects into a controlled, personalized sound that generations of guitarists since have emulated and embellished.

He was left-handed and played his favourite guitar, a right-handed Fender Stratocaster, upside down and re-strung, giving him a different perspective on the Fender's tremolo arm and enabling him to bend notes and chords without the strings going out of tune. He continually looked for ways to get new sounds out of the guitar, from electronic gadgets to experimental techniques.

A New Experience

Hendrix was born in Seattle in 1942 and moved to England in 1966 after being spotted in a New York club by Chas Chandler, bassist with the recently disbanded Animals. Arriving in England, Hendrix formed the Jimi Hendrix Experience with bassist Noel Redding and drummer Mitch Mitchell. He recorded a version of 'Hey Joe', creating a buzz that launched his career. His second single, 'Purple Haze', early in 1967, galvanized the music scene. *Are You Experienced* (1967) was an audacious debut album, drawing on a range of styles and opening up a new world of sounds that included flanging, double-tracking and variable recording speeds.

Hendrix returned to America in summer 1967 to play the Monterey Pop Festival. Before he returned to England he recorded 'Burning Of The Midnight Lamp', which showcased the recently introduced wah-wah pedal. Barely six months after his first album, *Axis Bold As Love* (1967) pushed the sonic innovations, particularly the phasing technique, still further and fused his rhythm-and-blues influences with the music he had heard in England. An instant hit in the UK, the album also spent a year on the American charts.

LEFT: **Hendrix backed the Isley Brothers and Little Richard before forming his own band.**

ABOVE: **The ultimate showman, Hendrix embellished his performances with long improvisations.**

A Rising Star

Electric Ladyland (1968) was his most ambitious and successful record. ranging from the futuristic funk of 'Crosstown Traffic' to the emblematic style of 'Voodoo Chile (Slight Return)'. But if Hendrix's music was peaking, tensions were growing within his band. As Hendrix jammed with a widening circle of musicians in the studio, Redding in particular became irritated. In June 1969 Hendrix disbanded the Experience and formed a new band called Gypsy Sun And Rainbow. They made a tentative debut at the Woodstock Festival in August, notable for Hendrix's unaccompanied rendition of 'The Star Spangled Banner', performed against a sustained wall of feedback.

Within a month the band had disintegrated and little was heard from Hendrix until the end of 1969, when he played two nights at New York's Fillmore

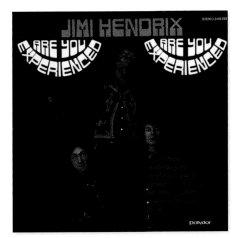

East with a new trio called the Band Of Gypsys. *Band Of Gypsys* (1970) was the last Hendrix album released before he died.

The Band Of Gypsys lasted no longer than Gypsy Sun And Rainbow, and Hendrix reverted to the Experience. The first half of 1970 was divided between recording and touring, and the next album was largely complete when Hendrix died of an overdose of sleeping tablets in London in August 1970 after playing a European tour that included a headlining appearance at the Isle Of Wight Festival.

In the aftermath of his death, unreleased studio recordings were hurriedly released, bearing no relation to the album he had been planning. It wasn't until 1997 that *First Rays Of The New Rising Sun*, roughly corresponding to a suggested track-listing Hendrix had scrawled on a tape box, was released. It is a tribute to Hendrix's genius that his status as the ultimate guitar hero remains undiminished.

LEFT: *Are You Experienced* was one of only five albums released in Hendrix's lifetime.

Eric Johnson

Defying categorization with his blend of rock, blues, country and melodic pop styles, Eric Johnson (b. 1954) is highly revered by guitarists of all genres for his skill and perfectionism on stage and in the studio, and for his uniquely rich, overdriven tone.

Encouraged by his parents, Johnson started playing guitar aged 11. After hearing Jimi Hendrix's *Are You Experienced* (1967) he began experimenting with new sounds on the guitar. He formed a fusion band, the Electromagnetics, in the mid–Seventies, but his prospects were badly damaged when he signed a six–year contract with a production company that failed to release his album, *Seven Worlds*, recorded in 1977, and effectively buried his career.

Playing local gigs and recording sessions with Cat Stevens, Carole King and Christopher Cross, Johnson resumed his career in 1984, signing to Warner Brothers and releasing his first album, *Tones* (1986). Despite critical praise, the album did not succeed commercially.

Success at Last

Johnson spent four years recording his next album, *Ah Via Musicom* (1990), and this time the sales matched the reviews. He even won a Grammy for Best Instrumental with 'White Cliffs Of Dover'. However, it was another six years before he released *Venus Isle* (1996), featuring more rock instrumentals, blues and jazz. In 1996 he was part of the first G3 guitarists tour of North America with Joe Satriani and Steve Vai. Johnson has subsequently taken part in G3 tours of Asia (2000) and South America (2006).

Johnson's obsessive quest for perfection has restricted his career, although it has enhanced his cult status. *Live & Beyond* (2000), recorded with power trio Alien Love Child, was a blues-

oriented album. *Bloom* (2005) was a reflection of his continuingly nomadic musical styles. Johnson mostly plays a Stratocaster, although he also plays vintage Gibson guitars and a Flying V.

Robert Johnson

Robert Johnson (1911–38) died relatively unknown aged 27, having recorded just 29 songs. But those songs of dreams and nightmares, crossroads and hellhounds revealed a darkness at the heart of Johnson's blues, expressed with a chilling eloquence that has never been matched.

Johnson's legend was fostered by the Sixties generation of British blues guitarists, led by Eric Clapton and Keith Richards, who were in thrall to *King Of The Delta Blues Singers* (1962), a collection of Johnson's songs that personified the iconic image of a blues singer. Clapton recorded 'Rambling On My Mind' with John Mayall and merged 'Cross Road Blues' and 'Travelling Riverside Blues' into 'Crossroads', a cornerstone of Cream's career, while the Rolling Stones' version of 'Love In Vain' was a crucial part of their late–Sixties reinvention.

A Living Legend

As a teenager Johnson learned guitar and harmonica, hanging around with Charley Patton, Son House and Willie Brown. He disappeared for two years, and when he returned the dramatic improvement in his playing led to speculation that he had sold his soul to the devil. Songs like 'Cross Road Blues', 'Preaching Blues (Up Jumped The Devil)', 'Stones In My Passway', 'Hellhound On My Trail' and 'Me And The Devil Blues' did nothing to dispel those notions. Even today, guitarists struggle to master Johnson's technique.

Johnson recorded twice, in 1936 and 1937, and had 11 records released, the most popular of which was the bawdy 'Terraplane Blues'. Famously, he was poisoned by a jealous husband while playing a juke joint in 1938. As befits his legend, he has three marked burial sites. While his ardent disciples have left some of his most haunting songs alone, others like 'I Believe I'll Dust My Broom', 'Sweet Home Chicago', 'Come On In My Kitchen' and 'Walking Blues' have become a standard part of the blues repertoire.

B.B. King

The bluesman who took the blues into the mainstream, B.B. King (b. 1925) is also its ambassador to the world. His style draws on the Mississippi blues of Elmore James and Muddy Waters, the Chicago blues of Buddy Guy and Magic Sam, and the West-Coast blues of T-Bone Walker and Lowell Fulsom, all filtered through his distinctive vibrato and the phrases that flow out of his beloved Lucille.

King found his voice in a gospel choir and started playing the guitar in his teens, moving to Memphis in his early twenties after securing a sponsored radio spot. Recruiting a band, he embarked on the 'chitlin' touring circuit around the American South, honing his style and arrangements.

An Instinctive Bluesman

King scored a No. 1 rhythm-and-blues record with 'Three O'Clock Blues' in 1952 and followed it with a string of hits during the rest of the decade. In the Sixties, as his blues waned in favour of soul and Motown, King signed to major label MCA to broaden his audience. *Live At The Regal* (1964) failed in that respect, although it has been acclaimed as one of the greatest blues albums ever recorded. But later in the Sixties he found an appreciative audience in the rock scene, scoring a Top 20 hit with 'The Thrill Is Gone' in 1970.

Through the Seventies King regularly toured Europe, taking on the ambassadorial role that enabled him to survive passing fashions and occasionally hitting the spotlight – like his collaboration with U2 in 1988 on 'When Love Comes To Town'. In 2006 he undertook a farewell world tour but he was still making appearances in 2007.

King's constant companion since 1950 has been Lucille, originally a Gibson ES-335 model but for the past 25 years a solid-body Gibson ES-355.

Mark Knopfler

Born in Glasgow in 1949, Knopfler spent his teenage years in Newcastle, playing in a number of local schoolboy bands. After attending colleges in Harlow and Leeds he came to London and formed Dire Straits in 1977 with his brother David on rhythm guitar, bassist John Illsley and drummer Pick Withers, and took to playing the pub circuit. A demo tape of 'Sultans Of Swing' sent to DJ Charlie Gillett stirred up interest and the band secured a contract with Vertigo Records.

Unassuming but Compelling

Dire Straits (1978), recorded on a shoestring, attracted little attention in Britain but took off in Europe, followed by America, where 'Sultans Of Swing' was a No. 2 hit. *Communiqué* (1979), recorded in Nassau with Barry Beckett and Jerry Wexler producing, maintained the stripped-down sound, while *Making Movies* (1980) and *Love Over Gold* (1982) stretched out their country-rock groove. But it was 1985's *Brothers In Arms* that hit the zeitgeist, becoming the first-ever million-selling CD, propelled by the hit 'Money For Nothing' and a massive world tour. Afterwards Knopfler switched to solo projects, including soundtracks (having had success with *Local Hero* in 1983) and the low-key Notting Hillbillies. Dire Straits' only appearance for the rest of the decade was at the Nelson Mandela Tribute Concert in 1988.

Dire Straits reformed for *On Every Street* (1991) and played another world tour that produced a live album, *On The Night* (1993), before Knopfler dissolved the band for good and pursued a solo career that has included *Golden Heart* (1996), *Sailing To Philadelphia* (2000), *The Ragpicker's Dream* (2002) and *Shangri-La* (2006).

Although Knopfler is left-handed, he plays right-handed guitars, usually Fender Stratocasters and Telecasters. He famously used a National Steel Resonator Guitar on 'Romeo & Juliet' (pictured on the cover of *Brothers In Arms*).

Yngwie Malmsteen

A leading figure of Eighties 'neo-classical' rock guitarists, Yngwie Malmsteen (b. 1963) learned his breakneck arpeggios and baroque composing style from classical composers as well as rock artists. His sweep-picking technique, use of harmonic scales and pedal tones, and aggressive playing all helped create his distinctive style.

Born in Stockholm, Sweden, Malmsteen's interest in the guitar started with the death of Jimi Hendrix in 1970. Also influenced by Ritchie Blackmore's style, which was influenced by the classics, Malmsteen studied composers like Bach and flamboyant violinist Niccolò Paganini. Malmsteen practised intently and by the age of 18 was playing in various bands around Sweden.

A Rising Force

A demo tape that Malmsteen unsuccessfully sent around to Swedish record companies was picked up by US label Shrapnel, and he was invited over to join metal band Steeler. He played on their self-titled debut album (1983) before moving on to Alcatrazz, where he recorded *No Parole For Rock & Roll* (1984) and *Live Sentence* (1984). However, he still felt stifled, so he formed his own band, Rising Force, with keyboard player Jens Johansson.

Rising Force (1984) showcased Malmsteen's writing and playing abilities and charted in the US. The band toured extensively and released *Marching Out* (1985), *Trilogy* (1986) and *Odyssey* (1988), each of which expanded his following. Malmsteen disbanded the group and recruited Swedish musicians for his next band. *Eclipse* (1990), *Fire & Ice* (1992), *The Seventh Sign* (1994) and *Magnum Opus* (1995) were major successes in Japan. *Inspiration* (1996) paid tribute to Malmsteen's influences, covering songs by Deep Purple, Hendrix, Rush and the Scorpions. In 1998 he recorded the 'Concerto Suite For Electric Guitar And Orchestra' with the Czech Philharmonic Orchestra. He also revived Rising Force for *Unleash The Fury* (2005).

Malmsteen's best-known guitar is his 1972 blond Fender Stratocaster, which he bought when he was a teenager in Sweden.

Juan Martín

Juan Cristóbal Martín (b. 1948) started learning the guitar aged six. In his early twenties he studied under Nino Ricardo and Paco de Lucía. Martín was influenced by classic flamenco and the Spanish classical guitar tradition. His major influences included De Lucía, Tomatito and Andrés Segovia. But Martín's work evokes jazz guitarists like Joe Pass as well, and even the style of the late Brazilian guitar virtuoso Laurindo Almeida, one of the first guitarists to combine samba with cool jazz and a major influence on Martín.

One of Martín's early recordings was *Picasso Portraits* (1981). Martín composed the pieces, and each section is an audio depiction of a painting by Pablo Picasso. Although it was not released until the Nineties, he recorded a track with Rory Gallagher in 1984 (on the album *Wheels Within Wheels*). He recorded with Herbie Hancock in 1987 and played on stage with Miles Davis.

Playing With the Best

Martín began his record career in the Eighties, when he recorded a few albums for RCA's Novus label, including *Through The Moving Window* and *Painter In Sound* (both 1990). He crossed paths with jazz greats ranging from tenor and soprano saxophonist Wayne Shorter to Brazilian singer Flora Purim and her percussionist husband, Airto Moreira. Martín recorded for the Alex label in the early to mid–Nineties, and in the late Nineties and early Noughties recorded extensively for the independent Flamenco Vision label. By early 2005 Martín had recorded at least 16 albums.

Martín also released a successful instructional book *Juan Martín's Guitar Method El Arte Flamenco De La Guitarra*, which was printed in both English and Spanish.

Martín has been voted in the top three guitarists in the world by the magazine *Guitar Player*. His latest albums have flamenco dancers on the soundtrack, adding the sounds of flamenco *zapateado* dancing to the music.

Brian May

Queen guitarist Brian May (b. 1947) is among the most recognizable players in the world. His distinctive tones, created by the home-made guitar he built when he was 16 and has used throughout his career, are integral to Queen's sound.

May started playing guitar aged seven. Academically gifted, particularly in physics, he made his own guitar with help from his father when he was unable to afford the Fender Stratocaster he wanted. The Red Special (also known as the Fireplace Guitar, because the mahogany neck was carved from a 200-year-old fireplace) took 18 months to build at a cost of £18 ($30), and he played it with a sixpence rather than a plectrum.

Queen is Born

May formed 1984 with bassist friend Tim Staffels prior to entering Imperial College, London in 1965. After 1984 broke up, May and Staffels formed the trio Smile with drummer Roger Taylor.

Staffels left in 1969, and his flatmate Freddie Mercury approached May and Taylor about forming another band. Bassist John Deacon joined in 1971, completing the Queen line-up. Their debut album, *Queen* (1973), included their first May-composed single, 'Keep Yourself Alive'. *Queen II* (1974) reached No. 5 in the UK charts.

Sheer Heart Attack (1974) brought their stylish hard rock into focus, with May's guitar showcased on the opening 'Brighton Rock'. *A Night At The Opera* (1975) moved Queen into a category of their own, a theatrical pop dominated by multi-layered guitars and vocals. The operatic 'Bohemian Rhapsody', with May's memorable solo, became a global hit.

A Day At The Races (1976) saw May drawing on Queen's hard roots for 'Tie Your Mother Down' and contributing one of his finest solos on 'Somebody To Love'. There was a rockier edge to *News Of The World* (1977), opening with May's anthemic 'We Will Rock You', and a broader sweep to *Jazz* (1978), featuring the May-penned 'Fat Bottomed Girls'. May contributed two ballads to *The Game* (1980): 'Sail Away Sweet Sister', which featured a rare acoustic guitar solo, and the poignant 'Save Me'.

The band took an extended break in 1983, and May recorded a solo project with guitarist Eddie Van Halen that was released as a mini-album, *Star Fleet Project*, later that year. Queen reconvened to record *The Works* (1984), which was pop-oriented, although May's two songs, 'Hammer To Fall' and 'Tear It Up', maintained the band's hard-rock stance.

ABOVE: **Aided by his unique home-made guitar, May was able to create some unusual sound effects, ranging from orchestral tones on 'Procession' to mimicking a trombone and piccolo on 'Good Company'.**

ABOVE: **By the mid-Seventies Queen had developed a unique sound based around Freddie Mercury's quasi-operatic vocals and May's rich, multi-layered guitar parts.**

(1989) and *Innuendo* (1991) saw all tracks credited to the band, although May was largely responsible for 'Scandal' and 'I Want It All' on the former and 'Headlong' and 'I Can't Live With You' on the latter. The band continued recording until Mercury's death from AIDS at the end of 1991.

May's first solo album, *Back To The Light* (1992) featured the hit singles 'Too Much Love Will Kill You' and 'Driven By You', and embarked on a world tour. He then worked with Deacon and Taylor, completing songs for which Mercury had already recorded vocals, on *Made In Heaven* (1995). A second solo album, *Another World* (1998), was followed by another world tour.

In 2004 May and Taylor began working with former Free and Bad Company vocalist Paul Rodgers, making their debut at Nelson Mandela's 46664 AIDS Awareness Concert in South Africa in 2005 as Queen + Paul Rodgers. They toured in 2005 and 2006, and entered the studio in 2007 to record with Rodgers as lead vocalist.

The Show Must Go On

A Kind Of Magic (1986) followed Queen's show–stopping appearance at Live Aid in 1985 with May writing and arranging the orchestra parts for 'Who Wants To Live Forever'. *The Miracle*

BELOW: **With a set list that mainly focused on Queen's best-known hits, Brian May returned to the main stage for the Queen + Paul Rodgers tour in 2005.**

Jimmy Page

Jimmy Page (b. 1944) became an icon of rock guitarists in the Seventies with Led Zeppelin. Elements of his playing style have been copied to the point of cliché in the years since Led Zeppelin dominated the rock world, but as the originator Page developed the heavy-metal blueprint for all the guitarists who followed.

His first electric guitar was a 1949 Gibson Les Paul, the guitar with which he became associated throughout his career. After leaving school at 16 he played briefly with Neil Christian & the Crusaders before becoming an in-demand session musician. Between 1962 and 1968 Page played on sessions for bands including the Rolling Stones, the Who, the Kinks, Donovan, Them, Cliff Richard and Burt Bacharach, and was often hired as an insurance policy in case the band's guitarist couldn't cut it in the studio.

In With the New

But the joy of sessions was already fading by 1966 when Page joined the Yardbirds, for whom Jeff Beck was lead guitarist. A short but exciting experiment with Beck and Page as twin lead guitarists ended when Beck abruptly left the band. Page found himself carrying a disillusioned band, and after *Little Games*'s (1967) commercial failure, he started planning a new band, encouraged by Yardbirds' road manager Peter Grant.

Page, Robert Plant, John Paul Jones and John Bonham came together as the Yardbirds were disintegrating in 1968, and recorded *Led Zeppelin I* (1969) before manager Peter Grant secured a record contract with Atlantic. The album's raw sound and Page's dynamic range, along with innovative techniques,

LEFT: **As a producer, composer and guitarist for Led Zeppelin, Page became one of the driving forces of the Seventies rock sound.**

RIGHT: **Widely regarded as one of Led Zeppelin's defining works, *Physical Graffiti* (1975) was a massive critical and commercial success, selling over 16 million copies in the US alone.**

made a resounding impact. *Led Zeppelin I* spent 18 months in the charts in the US and UK, as the band toured incessantly.

An Unstoppable Force

One-off Led Zeppelin reunions at Live Aid (1985) and Atlantic Records' twenty-fifth anniversary (1988) proved unsatisfactory, but towards the end of 2007 the band reformed with Bonham's son Jason on drums to play a spectacular show at London's O2 Arena to benefit the late Atlantic founder Ahmet Ertegun's charitable trust.

Led Zeppelin II (1969) topped the charts on both sides of the Atlantic, propelled by Page's signature riff on 'Whole Lotta Love'. The band broadened their scope with *Led Zeppelin III* (1970), adding more folk-influenced acoustic songs between the rock and blues numbers. This approach paid off on *Led Zeppelin IV* (1971), which featured the bombastic 'Black Dog', the more restrained 'Misty Mountain Hop', and the monumental 'Stairway To Heaven', which drew on elements of both.

Through the mid-Seventies Led Zeppelin swept all before them with *Houses Of The Holy* (1973), *Physical Graffiti* (1975), *Presence* (1976) and an epic live show that was captured on the film and soundtrack album *The Song Remains The Same* (1976). But in the summer of 1977 the band's career came to a sudden halt when Plant's son died during a successful American tour. They returned in 1979 at the Knebworth Festival, but the following year, Bonham died after a drinking binge and Led Zeppelin was at an end.

During the Eighties Page occupied himself with the film soundtracks *Death Wish II* (1982) and *Lucifer Rising* (1987), a solo album *Outrider* (1988), the Robert Plant collaboration *The Honeydrippers Volume One* (1984), and *The Firm* project with singer Paul Rodgers (formerly of Free). In the Nineties he worked with former Deep Purple singer David Coverdale on *Coverdale Page* (1993) before reuniting with Plant for the re-styled Zeppelin-esque albums *No Quarter* (1994) and *Walking Into Clarksdale* (1998). The turn of the century found him working with American band the Black Crowes on *Live At The Greek* (2000).

ABOVE: **Page's monumental solo on 'Stairway To Heaven' is still considered one of the best guitar solos of all time.**

Django Reinhardt

Django Reinhardt (1910–53) was born in Belgium to gypsy parents and his mother's tribe settled near Paris. The French Gypsies, or Manouches, were medieval in their beliefs, and distrustful of modern science. But Django grew up exposed to Paris while living the life of the nomadic gypsy.

He learned to play the banjo/guitar aged 12, by mimicking the fingerings of musicians he watched. Before he was 13 he began his musical career playing in dance halls. After a fire in his caravan in 1928 that left him with severe burns, the 18–year–old Django was bedridden for 18 months. Given a guitar, he created a whole new fingering system built around the two fingers on his left hand that had full mobility.

A Highly Influential Sound

In 1934 the Quintet Of The Hot Club Of France was formed by a chance meeting of Django and violinist Stéphane Grappelli. A small record company Ultraphone recorded the Hot Club's first sides, including 'Dinah' and 'I Saw Stars'. These first records made a big impression, and the Quintet went on to record hundreds of sides. Django played and recorded with many American jazz legends such as Coleman Hawkins, Benny Carter, Rex Stewart and Louis Armstrong.

In 1939 the Quintet was touring in England when war broke out. Django returned to Paris, and played and recorded throughout the war years. After the war he rejoined Grappelli, and they again played and recorded. He toured briefly with Duke Ellington in America and returned to Paris, where he continued his career until retirement in 1951.

In May 1953 Django suffered a brain haemorrhage and died. He is well represented on CD with *The Classic Early Recordings In Chronological Order* (2000), *Quintette Du Hot Club De France: 25 Classics 1934–1940* (1998), the remastered *Djangology* (2002) and others.

Keith Richards

**Keith Richards (b. 1943) attended Sidcup Art College,
which was crucial to his development, as he was able
to nurture his passion for rhythm and blues. He bought
an acoustic guitar and mastered it by listening to
records. Chuck Berry was a defining influence, and
he soon began playing a cheap electric guitar.**

A Two-guitar Band

A chance meeting with Mick Jagger revealed a shared interest in
the blues. In 1962, Richards and Jagger attended an audition for
a rhythm and blues outfit that Brian Jones was putting together,
which evolved into the Rolling Stones. Richards and Jones spent
days together trying to achieve the sounds of bluesmen like
Robert Johnson, Elmore James and Muddy Waters. '... the whole
secret ... behind the sound of the Rolling Stones, is the way we
work two guitars together,' said Richards. The interlocking lead
and rhythm guitars can be heard to good effect on *Rolling Stones*
(1964), *Rolling Stones No.2* (1965) and *Out Of Our Heads* (1965).

The recruitment of Bill Wyman (bass) and Charlie Watts (drums)
completed the line-up. Richards was at his most creative on
Beggars Banquet (1968), playing almost all the guitar parts on the
album. Jones was replaced in 1969 by Mick Taylor. The high point
of Taylor's time in the Stones was *Exile On Main Street* (1972),
on which the two guitars combined and interplayed effortlessly.
Ronnie Wood was recruited after Taylor's departure in 1974, and
proved the ideal foil for Richards.

Richards is an innovative player, claiming the first chart hit to
feature a fuzzbox, '(I Can't Get No) Satisfaction' (1965), while
his use of open tunings became a trademark. He has a collection
of over 1,000 guitars and was often associated with the Fender
Telecaster, although in 1964 he was one of the first stars in Britain
to own a Les Paul. Recently, he has favoured the Gibson ES–345.

Joe Satriani

Joe Satriani (b. 1956) played piano and drums until he heard Jimi Hendrix's 'Purple Haze' and picked up the guitar. He acquired a Hagstrom III solid-body guitar and, although he never had any formal lessons, by the age of 17 he was giving guitar lessons to students, one of whom was his classmate Steve Vai. In the mid-Seventies he was on a Rolling Stones list of possible replacements for Mick Taylor before they opted for Ron Wood. In 1977 he settled in Berkeley, California, and resumed teaching.

In 1986 he released his first album, *Not Of This Earth*, focusing on sound textures rather than technique. *Surfing With The Alien* (1987) was his major breakthrough, highlighting his composing, production and playing talents.

A Master Rock Instrumentalist

Flying In A Blue Dream (1989) had a more experimental feel, introducing Satriani's vocals on a number of tracks, exploring harmony and counterpoint. *The Extremist* (1992) put more emphasis on melodic rock. In the early Nineties Satriani guested on albums by Alice Cooper and Spinal Tap, and in 1993 he joined Deep Purple at short notice in the middle of a tour. *Time Machine* (1993) consisted of studio tracks together with live material, while *Joe Satriani* (1995) took a more relaxed, bluesier approach.

In 1996 Satriani set up the first G3 tour with Steve Vai and Eric Johnson. The success of the tour and subsequent CD/DVD *G3: Live In Concert* (1997) ensured that G3 became a regular event. Meanwhile Satriani continued his own career. *Crystal Planet* (1998) contained power ballads, anthems and rockers, while *Engines Of Creation* (2000) was more experimental, incorporating techno and electronica. *Strange Beautiful Music* (2002), *Is There Love In Space* (2004) and *Super Colossal* (2006) have all brought the guitar back to the fore.

Satriani has had a long association with Ibanez guitars (with DiMarzio pick-ups) and Peavey amplifiers, and both companies have made customized equipment for him.

Andrés Segovia

When Andrés Segovia (1894–1987), who had been tutored in piano and violin, heard the guitar for the first time, he was hooked. Disregarding familial objections, Segovia persisted in learning to play.

He plucked the strings with a combination of his fingernails and fingertips, producing a sharper sound than many of his contemporaries. With this technique, he could create a wider range of tones. As his talent developed, so did his reputation, and at the age of 15, in 1909, he made his public debut in Granada. Numerous concerts followed. In Madrid he acquired a guitar from the craftsman Manuel Ramírez that he played for many years. In the mid-Thirties he began using an instrument made by Hermann Hauser of Munich.

The Beginning of a Legend

In 1919 Segovia toured South America, where he gained an enthusiastic reception. He returned to Europe in 1923 and won over critics at his London and Paris debuts, and a successful Berlin debut in 1924 cemented his international reputation.

As there was a limited repertoire for guitar, Segovia transcribed works written for other instruments. He relied on Renaissance and Baroque pieces, and adapted works by Sylvius Leopold Weiss and J.S. Bach. Segovia's growing fame ushered in a rising interest in the guitar. During his career it became one of the world's most popular instruments, and leading composers began to write for it.

The outbreak of the Spanish Civil War forced Segovia to leave Spain in 1936. He toured extensively in Central and South America before returning to the United States in 1943. Over the next 20 years, Segovia secured his place as the pre-eminent classical guitarist of the modern age. Segovia died of a heart attack aged 94.

The boxed set *The Segovia Collection* (2002) is a widely praised remastering of the guitarist's 1952–69 performances for Decca. The set's discs are also available as individual volumes.

Pete Townshend

Pete Townshend's (b. 1941) first instrument was the banjo, which he played in the Dixieland outfit the Confederates with school friend John Entwistle. When bassist Entwistle joined the Detours, a rhythm-and-blues group fronted by singer Roger Daltrey, Townshend, who had switched to guitar at the age of 12, followed him. With the recruitment of drummer Keith Moon, the classic Who line-up was complete.

The Who's first album *My Generation* (1965) was a mix of rhythm and blues and pop, while the follow-up *A Quick One* (1966) contained Townshend's first conceptual piece in the title track. *Tommy* (1969) was hailed as the first rock opera, and *Live At Leeds* (1970, reissued with extra tracks in 1995) captured the original line-up at its peak.

A Force to be Reckoned With

The Who consolidated their position as a major player in Seventies rock with the acclaimed *Who's Next* (1971) and a second rock opera *Quadrophenia* (1973). In between, Townshend made his first solo album, *Who Came First* (1972). Shortly after *Who Are You* (1978), Moon died, but the band continued with Kenney Jones. Townshend pursued a parallel solo career, achieving notable success with *Empty Glass* (1980). In 1983 the Who split, although they reunited for occasional live performances, including Live Aid, in the Eighties. Townshend has continued to work with various incarnations of the band. With Daltrey, Townshend made the first new Who album in 24 years, *Endless Wire* (2006).

Townshend's early inspirations included John Lee Hooker, Bo Diddley and Eddie Cochran. His use of the guitar as a sonic tool as much as a melodic device was influential to many punk guitarists. In the Who's early days he played an Emile Grimshaw SS Deluxe, plus six- and 12-string Rickenbackers. From the late Sixties,

he favoured Gibson guitars for live work, using a Gretsch in the studio. Since the late Eighties he has preferred the Fender Eric Clapton Stratocaster to his own signature model.

Steve Vai

Steve Vai (b. 1960) began taking guitar lessons from his schoolmate Joe Satriani when he was 14. He attended the Berklee College of Music, where he developed an obsession with transcribing Frank Zappa guitar solos. Zappa hired him in 1979, and he appeared on many of his albums, including *Tinsel Town Rebellion* (1981), *You Are What You Is* (1981) and *The Man From Utopia* (1983).

Vai left Zappa's band in 1982 and recorded his first solo album, *Flex-Able* (1984). That year he joined Alcatrazz, replacing Yngwie Malmsteen. After *Disturbing The Peace* (1985) Vai accepted an offer to join David Lee Roth's post-Van Halen band with bassist Billy Sheehan and drummer Greg Bissonette. *Eat 'Em And Smile* (1986) and *Skyscraper* (1988) combined the band's fire with Roth's showmanship, and both albums went platinum.

Becoming a Virtuoso

Vai left Roth's band in 1989 and temporarily joined Whitesnake before recording a solo album, *Passion And Warfare* (1990), which went gold, splicing reflective compositions with bursts of intense guitar. He formed a conventional rock band for *Sex & Religion* (1993) but returned to his standard format for *Alien Love Secrets* (1995) and *Fire Garden* (1996). That same year he also took part in the first G3 tour with Satriani and Eric Johnson, and has played on almost every tour since.

Vai has continued to release studio albums like *Real Illusions: And Reflections* (2005); live albums like *Alive In An Ultra World* (2001); and compilations like *Elusive Light And Sound* (2002), which featured his film work for *Crossroads*, *PCU*, and *Bill And Ted's Excellent Adventure*. He has also taken part in classical projects with the Tokyo Metropolitan Symphony Orchestra and the Netherlands Metropole Orchestra.

Like Satriani, Vai favours Ibanez guitars with a DiMarzio pick-up. In the Nineties he pioneered the use of seven-string guitar, which was used by Korn and other bands to create the nu-metal sound.

Eddie Van Halen

Eddie Van Halen (b. 1955) redefined the sound of heavy metal at the end of the Seventies. His high-velocity solos, distinguished by his fingertapping technique and tremolo bar effects, on Van Halen's 1978 debut album heralded a new era in hard-rock guitar that rejected the clichés of a jaded genre. His solo on Michael Jackson's 'Beat It' in 1982, which effectively compressed his style into one 30-second explosive burst, took Van Halen's guitar sound into the mainstream.

Eddie, who had been playing guitar since the age of 12, and his brother Alex, who played drums, formed a band in 1972, recruiting bassist Michael Anthony and singer David Lee Roth. They played the competitive Los Angeles rock scene as Mammoth until the band changed its name to Van Halen.

Runaway Success

The album *Van Halen* (1978) made an immediate impact on the heavy-metal scene. Eddie poured 10 years of obsessive practising into his solo instrumental, 'Eruption', with its innovative use of two-handed tapping, high-speed fretwork, vibrato and tremolo picking. His 'Frankenstrat' guitar, made from a Charvel body and neck with a modified Gibson humbucker pickup and Fender tremolo arm, provided his distinctive tone. The band's high-energy rock style was displayed on 'Running With The Devil', a cover of the Kinks' 'You Really Got Me', and the album went platinum.

BELOW: **Rock legend Eddie Van Halen (right) reinvented how to play the electric guitar.**

Van Halen II (1979) capitalized on their initial success with Eddie's singular riff on 'Dance The Night Away' – their first hit single – while his acoustic playing on the instrumental 'Spanish Fly' and use of harmonics in 'Women In Love' broadened his scope. *Women And Children First* (1980) and *Fair Warning* (1981) consolidated Van Halen's position as a guaranteed Top 10 album band in America – as well as a stadium–filling live act – and *Diver Down* (1982) brought them another hit single with a cover of Roy Orbison's '(Oh) Pretty Woman', while Eddie refined and developed his own style on the instrumentals 'Cathedral' and 'Intruder'.

LEFT: **Van Halen revived the rock-music genre with this eponymous 1978 debut album.**

Roth was recalled to sing two new tracks for a Greatest Hits collection (1996), but the band then replaced him with Extreme vocalist Gary Cherone for *Van Halen III* (1998). The album also featured Eddie taking lead vocals on one track, 'How Many Say I'.

In March 2007 Van Halen were inducted into the Rock And Roll Hall Of Fame, and in September 2007 Van Halen with Roth (but without Anthony, who was replaced by Eddie's son Wolfgang) began an American tour, which continued into 2008.

Jump To It

Following Eddie's groundbreaking solo on Michael Jackson's 'Beat It', the album *1984* (1984) propelled Van Halen to superstardom with their No. 1 hit 'Jump', featuring a trademark guitar solo. He also expanded his repertoire of riffs and runs on 'Panama' and 'Hot For Teacher'. The simmering competitive tension that had been growing between Eddie and Roth led to the singer's departure in 1985.

Van Halen's success continued with new vocalist Sammy Hagar. The album *5150* (1986) finally gave them a No. 1 album. The band overhauled their sound mix, and the chemistry between Eddie's riffs and Hagar's vocals was evident on 'Best Of Both Worlds' and the hit singles 'Why Can't This Be Love', 'Dreams' and 'Love Walks In'. The discs *OU812* (1988) and *For Unlawful Carnal Knowledge* (1991) also hit No. 1, along with the live *Right Here, Right Now* (1993). The studio rapport between Eddie and Hagar was still strong on *Balance* (1995), but personality clashes eventually led to Hagar's departure.

RIGHT: **Eddie Van Halen's speciality is virtuoso soloing, using wide stretches, tapping, hammer-ons and pull-offs.**

The Guitars

Fender Stratocaster

GUITAR SPEC	
Model Pictured: Daphne Blue Stratocaster	
Pickups: Three	
Controls: Three-way (later five-way) switch, volume, two tone	
Characteristics: Wide tonal range, versatile, vibrato arm	
Played by: Jeff Beck, Buddy Guy, Jimi Hendrix, Mark Knopfler, Stevie Ray Vaughan	

While Fender's Telecaster was an extremely popular model, some criticized the instrument for its 'Plain Jane' appearance and for its sharp edges, which could be uncomfortable to hold. Heeding these complaints, Leo Fender and colleague Freddie Tavares went back to the drawing board, introducing the Stratocaster in 1954.

The Construction

The Stratocaster was designed with a sleek body, smoothly contoured for the player's comfort. Its double-cutaway style afforded players access to high notes while adding visual appeal. The Stratocaster had advanced electronics; it was the first solid-body to incorporate three pickups. The pickups possessed staggered polepieces, providing for even volume levels across all six strings. Furthermore, players discovered that the instrument's three-way switch could be set in between positions, which created a unique 'out-of-phase' sound, exploited to excellent effect by Jeff Beck and Jimi Hendrix, among others. Five-way switches were later introduced to make this sound easily accessible.

Another Fender first was represented by the Stratocaster's all-in-one bridge, tailpiece and tremolo bar. With its six individual saddles – one for each string – moveable in both height and length directions, the new bridge portion was fully adjustable. By releasing tension on the strings, the tremolo bar allowed a player to bend notes with the pick hand, resulting in a shimmering sound effect. Inside the body, the strings were accessible under a plastic cover at the back of the guitar.

Cars and Guitars

Stratocasters are among the most coveted guitars on the vintage market. Most desirable are the late-1950s Custom Color models. Inspired by the paint jobs on automobiles, these finishes – including Fiesta Red, Lake Placid Blue, Foam Green and Shoreline Gold – are rare; a Custom Color Stratocaster can now command over 20 per cent more than its sunburst- or blonde-coloured counterpoint in identical condition.

LEFT: **Jeff Beck** plays a signature Strat built according to his specifications, with a particularly thick neck. He uses minimal effects and plucks the strings with his fingers.

Fender Telecaster

GUITAR SPEC

Model Pictured: 1950s Telecaster

Pickups: Two

Controls: Three-way switch, tone, volume

Characteristics: Versatile, bright, twangy sound

Played by: Jimmy Bryant, Roy Buchanan, James Burton, Danny Gatton, Albert Lee, Keith Richards, Muddy Waters

In the late 1940s, inventor Leo Fender set about making an electric guitar that would be resistant to the feedback associated with amplified hollow-bodies. His concept was realized in 1950 with the Fender Esquire, a single-pickup solid-body guitar, followed shortly after by the Broadcaster, a twin-pickup version.

In 1951, the name of the latter guitar was changed to Telecaster, in order to avoid infringing on the Gretsch Company's drum line, as well as to suggest state-of-the-art technology, similar to the name television.

The Construction

In making the Telecaster, Fender set out to create a dependable, minimalist guitar – one that would sound excellent while being cheaply and efficiently manufactured. Accordingly, the Telecaster was devoid of the select tone-woods characteristic of acoustic guitars, stripped of superfluous ornamentation, and constructed from easy-to-assemble parts.

Yet the Telecaster featured a number of innovations in addition to its solid ash body. Its bolt-on, one-piece maple neck could easily be replaced,

and the neck's truss rod allowed for precision adjustment. The guitar's 21 frets were set directly into the neck, precluding the need for a separate fretboard and, to some ears, enhancing the sound. The Telecaster's fully adjustable metal bridge, the first of its kind, could be tweaked lengthwise as well as raised or lowered. Furthermore, the bridge allowed the strings to pass through the body, arguably enhancing the tone.

The Legacy

Initially, western-swing players were drawn to the instrument's cutting, twangy tone. As the Telecaster's reputation spread, it became the country-music guitarist's instrument of choice. But the instrument came to be associated with a variety of genres. Bluesman Muddy Waters used a Telecaster to create his signature electric sound, as did a diverse set of other legends including modern jazzman Mike Stern and punk rocker Joe Strummer, frontman for the Clash.

LEFT: **After tuning his Telecaster to open G, Keith Richards explored this alternative tuning and created a whole new style of guitar playing.**

Gibson Les Paul

Les Paul had been experimenting with solid-body guitars since the 1930s. Two of his handmade, experimental solid-bodies – the 'Log' and the 'Clunker' – led to the 1952 release of the Les Paul model, Gibson's first solid-body, which was to become one of the world's most influential guitar designs.

The Construction

The Les Paul's construction was complex. A two-pickup guitar, it was built from a mahogany neck with a rosewood fingerboard, set into a mahogany body with an arched, carved maple top, distinguishing it from the flat-top Fender models. The Les Paul's controls – two tone, two volume and selector switch – were mounted on to the top and accessed by two separate plastic covers

BELOW: **Al Di Meola uses his Les Paul to great effect.**

in the back. The set-neck construction and choice tonewoods, in conjunction with hardware that was screwed directly into the top, made for a warm, creamy tone with considerable sustain. The original Les Paul was completed with a lavish gold-coloured metallic finish, earning it the nickname 'Gold Top', although some models had gold-coloured sides and backs as well.

Gibson created several Les Paul variations, including the fancy custom no-frills Les Paul Junior. The most coveted Les Paul is the Standard, introduced in 1958. On that model, the original gold finish was replaced with a transparent cherry sunburst finish – which graduated from red to orange – revealing the instrument's maple top; this was sometimes covered with spectacular 'flames' or figuring in the grain. The Standard featured two powerful humbucking pickups.

The Standard was discontinued in 1960, but as players like Clapton and Page picked up the instrument later that decade, it essentially became the first collectible electric guitar. Owing to its quality and rarity – only 643 models were produced in 1959 – the original Standard is now considered the Holy Grail of electric guitars, with clean examples currently fetching more than $200,000.

Martin D-45

<table>
<tr><td>GUITAR SPEC</td><td>
Model Pictured: 1988 D-45

Construction: Rosewood body, spruce top, mahogany neck with ebony fretboard

Characteristics: Excellent bass response, full tone, loud, well-balanced, magical sound

Played by: Gene Autry, Stephen Stills, Neil Young
</td></tr>
</table>

The Martin guitar company was founded in 1833, when German immigrant Christian Frederick Martin set up shop in the US. Martin's first instruments were modelled after those made by Johann Stauffer, an Austrian builder under whom he had apprenticed in the 1820s.

Soon, however, Martin began to experiment with his own construction ideas, and created the design principles that would result in the modern flat-top acoustic guitar.

The Dreadnought Line

Launched in 1931, Martin's dreadnought line of guitars was named after the hulking British battleship of the First World War. With its wide, deep body, the dreadnought was designed with volume, tone and projection in mind. The first Martin dreadnoughts were called D-1 and D-2, changed to D-18 and D-28 respectively in 1932. While the plainer D-18 had a mahogany body and the fancier D-28 had a rosewood body, both had a neck that joined the body at the 12th fret; beginning in 1934, the neck joined the body at the 14th fret, effectively extending the guitar's range by a whole step.

The D-28 first gained acceptance amongst country and bluegrass guitarists, who needed a big sound to compete with fiddlers and banjoists. The D-28 eventually became the benchmark for flat-top guitar design.

The Singing Cowboy

In 1933, country singer Gene Autry approached Martin with a special request – he wanted a guitar like his hero Jimmie Rodgers' small-bodied 000-45, but with the larger, dreadnought body style. This resulted in the first D-45, an ultra-swanky guitar with intricate abalone trim and Autry's name inlaid in pearl script on the fretboard. The D-45 proved too expensive to manufacture, and it was temporarily discontinued in 1942; only 91 had been made. Pre-war versions are the most desirable of all flat tops, currently fetching upwards of $100,000.

LEFT: Neil Young playing a Martin dreadnought, a guitar favoured by folk musicians for the full, expressive sound it produces.

Benedetto La Cremona Azzurra

LA CREMONA AZZURRA

Robert Benedetto is a premier luthier of modern archtops who has been building instruments for over four decades.

His exquisite instruments have been played by such jazz–guitar heavyweights as Johnny Smith, Kenny Burrell and Howard Alden. Among Benedetto's most striking guitars is his Cremona Azzurra (Blue Cremona), commissioned in 1995 for the Blue Guitar project of the late instrument collector Scott Chinery.

The Blue Cremona was built from materials selected for both their sound and beauty. Its wide top and back were made from old European cello wood; the two–piece neck from well–seasoned American maple; and the fingerboard, bridge, truss–rod cover and finger rest all hand–sculpted from select solid ebony.

The instrument was finished in a striking blue stain and has a minimalist, modern appearance. It sports unconventional floral–shaped sound openings – as opposed to conservative f–holes – resulting in both a graceful design and a loud, well–balanced instrument.

GUITAR SPEC
Model Pictured: La Cremona Azzurra
Construction: Fine spruce, maple and ebony
Characteristics: Elegant modernist design, outstanding tone and projection

Danelectro Convertible

GUITAR SPEC
Model Pictured: 1960s Convertible
Pickups: One
Controls: Volume, tone
Characteristics: Retro vibe, quirky tone

In the 1950s many aspiring rockers picked up Silvertone guitars, manufactured for Sears, Roebuck and Company by Nathan Daniel, whose instruments were distributed under the name Danelectro beginning in 1956. 'Danos' were made from inexpensive materials – often Masonite tops affixed to pine frames – but were undeniably cool, and occasionally were used by pros, like Jimmy Page.

Named for its purported adaptability as an acoustic or electric guitar, Danelectro's Convertible had a hollow, double–horned Masonite body with a bolt–on maple neck. The Convertible could be ordered with pre–drilled notches so that electronics could be installed later, or with a single–coil 'lipstick–tube' pickup, the cover of which was made from an actual cosmetics casing.

The Convertible did not quite cut it as an acoustic guitar. When plugged in, though, its single pickup helped produce a wonderfully distinctive tone – halfway between a resonator guitar and a Stratocaster.

D'Angelico New Yorker

In 1932 John D'Angelico set up shop in New York City, repairing stringed instruments. He also began building archtops that were patterned after Gibson's L-5 before developing his own design.

D'Angelico became a pre-eminent jazz-guitar luthier, known for his craftsmanship; he hand-built more than 1,100 guitars. D'Angelico's most identifiable design, the New Yorker, was introduced in the late 1930s.

When Gibson unveiled its top-of-the-line Super 400 in 1934, D'Angelico followed suit with his New Yorker, an archtop with a body of the same spec, X-pattern bracing, and split-block fretboard inlays. D'Angelico's handcrafted New Yorker received the sort of attention to detail unobtainable by a large manufacturer such as Gibson.

His guitars were breathtaking, both as musical instruments and as works of art. With its ornate, gold stair-step tailpiece, Art-Deco style inlay and fancy binding, the New Yorker ranks among the most beautiful guitars ever created.

Epiphone Sheraton

In the 1930s the Epiphone Company was the leading manufacturer of archtops. In 1957, Gibson bought the company and moved it to Kalamazoo, Michigan.

Gibson president Ted McCarty decided to create a new line of Epiphone guitars, which could be built with Gibson's existing tooling and production lines, thus relieving the overwhelming dealer demand for Gibson instruments.

Introduced in 1958, a stellar example of a Kalamazoo Epiphone was the Sheraton, essentially a dressed-up version of Gibson's dot-neck ES-335. The early Sheraton had the then-new Gibson semi-hollow-body construction, combined with distinctive Epiphone touches: multi-ply binding, pearl/abalone block-and-triangle

fingerboard markers, gold hardware, a split-level 'Frequensator' tailpiece and a floral headstock inlay. Despite it being made alongside Gibsons, the Sheraton never enjoyed the ES-335's elevated status. A fine vintage Epiphone semi-hollow can now be had for a fraction of the price of its Gibson counterpart.

Fender Precision Bass

Model Pictured: Precision Bass

Pickups: One   **Controls:** Volume, tone

Characteristics: Versatile, crisp, clear tone in all registers

Played by: James Jamerson, Monk Montgomery, Jaco Pastorius, Sting

In the early 1950s, having created and mass-produced the solid-body Telecaster guitar, Leo Fender realized that a bass version was in order.

Introduced in 1952, Fender's Precision bass marked the birth of the electric bass guitar, and forever altered the landscape of popular music. The instrument became so commonplace that for many years all electric basses – regardless of make – became known as 'Fender Basses'.

With its double-cutaway body, manageable 34-inch (83-cm) fretted neck and powerful pickup, the radical Precision bass – named for its ease of intonation and clear tone – freed bassists from the problems associated with the upright (double) bass.

The P Bass, as it is known, has a round, crisp sound in all its registers. It works well in a variety of genres, including blues, country and jazz. Much popular music in the second half of the twentieth century was indebted to the P Bass's colourful bottom end.

Gibson L-5

In 1922, Gibson introduced the 'Master Line Guitar L-5 Professional Grand Concert Model'. Priced at $275, this elegant, top-of-the-line model was by far Gibson's most expensive guitar, and its revolutionary design represented the birth of the f-hole archtop jazz box.

Model Pictured: 1924 L-5

Construction: Arched spruce top, maple back and neck, ebony fingerboard

Characteristics: Classic jazz sound, pristine tone and excellent projection

Played by: Eddie Lang, Russell Malone, Wes Montgomery

Finished in a Cremona brown sunburst, the debut L-5 had a 16 $\frac{1}{4}$-in (41-cm) wide, 3 $\frac{1}{2}$-in (9-cm) deep body with an arched spruce top and birch back (replaced by maple in 1924); a maple neck with an ebony fingerboard; and a metal tailpiece, which added sustain. The L-5 was the first guitar to feature violin-style f-holes – as opposed to an oval soundhole – which provided a unique tonal response. With its huge, well-balanced sound, the L-5 was essentially America's first orchestra guitar.

The L-5 has gone through numerous alterations – both cosmetic and structural – throughout the years, and remains one of the most revered jazz guitars.

Gibson ES-150

The ES-150 (ES for 'Electric Spanish', 150 for the model's price – $150 with amplifier, case and cord) was effectively the first mass-produced electric guitar, and was made famous by Charlie Christian.

With its 16-in (40-cm) carved spruce top, maple back, mahogany neck and rosewood fretboard, the ES-150 was an amped-up version of Gibson's mid-level L-50 archtop. The 150's pickup had one solid, straight pole piece and two magnets.

A matching amplifier, the EH-150, was a six-tube, 15-watt unit wired to a 10-inch (25-cm) speaker, the High Fidelity Ultrasonic Reproducer. This package was a bold, state-of-the-art rig in the late 1930s.

Charlie Christian was quick to exploit the ES-150's capabilities. 'Amplifying my instrument has made it possible for me to get a wonderful break,' he told *Down Beat* magazine. Whereas previous ensemble guitarists largely had been relegated to accompaniment chores, Christian was able to pioneer the horn-like, single-note soloing guitar style.

GUITAR SPEC	
Model Pictured: Charlie Christian's 1930s ES-150	
Pickups: One	
Controls: Volume, tone	
Characteristics: Historically significant, warm rich tone	
Played by: Charlie Christian	

Gibson SJ-200

In the 1930s, as the flat-top acoustic guitar gained popularity, players demanded improved features. The Martin company responded by introducing big, loud 'dreadnought' models and, in 1934, Gibson followed suit with its first line of jumbo flat-tops, the most fancy of which – the SJ-200 – was introduced in 1938.

One of the earliest singing-cowboy film stars, Ray Whitley, provided Gibson with the ideas – a deeper body, relocated bridge and increased scale length – that resulted in the Super Jumbo model. This advanced flat-top had a 17-in (43-cm) wide spruce top with a new narrow-waist shape. Its 4 ½-in (11-cm) deep body, combined with a 26-in (66-cm) scale-length fretboard, provided a deep sound well suited to

cowboy strumming, blues riffing and other applications. The Super Jumbo was available in two versions: a fairly simple, mahogany-bodied SJ-100 and the fancier SJ-200, with a rosewood (later replaced with maple) body, which has remained in continuous production.

GUITAR SPEC	
Model Pictured: Emmylou Harris's 1952 SJ-200	
Construction: Rosewood body, spruce top, maple neck with ebony fretboard	
Characteristics: Versatile, excellent bass response, loud, well-balanced sound	
Played by: Reverend Gary Davis, Emmylou Harris, Ray Whitley	

Gibson ES-335

In 1958, Gibson unveiled another innovation – the ES-335 TD. In continuous production since its introduction, the ES-335 has proven one of Gibson's most enduring designs.

In the late 1950s, solid-body electrics were becoming increasingly popular as they offered sustaining tone and resistance to feedback. Hollow-body electrics, on the other hand, possessed a certain tonal warmth. So Gibson created a neat hybrid;

the ES-335 was built from a laminated, 16-in (40-cm) wide, 1¾-in (4-cm) thick hollow maple body with a solid maple block in its centre.

The guitar's semi-solid, double-cutaway construction allowed its mahogany neck (with rosewood fingerboard) to be joined to the body at the 19th fret, which permitted access to the uppermost registers. Two humbuckers, controlled by a three-way switch, afforded a number of timbral possibilities. The ES-335 had the best of both worlds – the warmth of a hollow-body with the sustain and feedback resistance of a solid-body.

GUITAR SPEC

Model Pictured: ES-335 TDN
Pickups: Two
Controls: Three-way selector, two volume, two tone
Characteristics: Versatile, hollow-body warmth with solid-body sustain
Played by: B.B. King, Eric Clapton, Larry Carlton

Gibson Flying V & Explorer

GUITAR SPEC

Model Pictured: 1950s Flying V
Pickups: Two
Controls: Two volume, one tone
Characteristics: Bold design, classic humbucker tone
Played by: Dave Davies, Rick Derringer, Lonnie Mack

With the rise of rock'n'roll in the late 1950s, Gibson began to lag behind as players gravitated towards Fender's more radical designs like the Stratocaster and the Jazzmaster.

Gibson responded in 1958 by supplementing its line with audacious 'modernistic' models, breaking away from

conventional curves with oddly shaped guitars, including the Flying V and the Explorer. Gibson's Ted McCarty, in conjunction with a local Michigan artist, designed several unconventional guitars; one was fashioned after an arrow, but a staff member at Gibson thought it looked more like a 'flying v', hence the name.

Initially, the guitars were commercial disasters; players found the instruments too radical. Only 98 Flying Vs were shipped in 1958–59, and fewer than 25 Explorers were made during the same period. Nonetheless, these guitars, which have been continuously reissued, inspired radical shapes by later manufacturers. Today, they are among the most collectible of electric guitars.

Gibson SG

By 1960, sales of the now iconic Les Paul Standard had become sluggish. So in 1961, Gibson gave the instrument a thorough redesign.

With its double-cutaway, light, thin mahogany body, long-looking mahogany neck, twin humbuckers, vibrato unit and deep cherry finish, the new Les Paul was at first known as the new Standard. It was renamed the SG (solid guitar) in 1963, when Paul's contract with Gibson expired.

Paul was not impressed with his new namesake guitar; he called Gibson and had his name removed from the instrument. Despite his disapproval, the SG has remained in continuous production since 1961. The guitar is now a rock'n'roll icon. Its pointy, devil-horned silhouette and raw sound have proved indispensable for heavy acts such as AC/DC and Black Sabbath. A comfortable, versatile instrument, the SG has also been employed to excellent effect by slide guitarists such as Duane Allman and Derek Trucks.

> **GUITAR SPEC**
>
> **Model Pictured:** SG   **Pickups:** Two
> **Controls:** Three-way switch, two volume, two tone
> **Characteristics:** Lightweight and versatile, powerful, honking sound
> **Played by:** Duane Allman, George Harrison, Tony Iommi, Derek Trucks, Angus Young

Gretsch White Falcon

Founded by Friedrich Gretsch in New York in 1883, Gretsch Guitars is best known for its instruments of the 1950s and 1960s. By far the flashiest was the White Falcon.

Originally a promotional item, the White Falcon was so spectacular that it was demanded as a production model. In 1955, the ultra-expensive ($600) White Falcon was commercially introduced; this mono guitar featured a hollow, single-cutaway 17-in (43-cm) wide body, twin DeArmond pickups, Cadillac-inspired tailpiece and a falcon-emblazoned pickguard. Lacquered in white and trimmed in gold, complemented by 24-K hardware, this was a showpiece. While maintaining its opulent appearance, there were a number of variations: in 1959, a stereo version; the 1963 model was a double-cutaway; and in 1965, a number of knobs and switches were added, affording access to new tonal variations.

> **GUITAR SPEC**
>
> **Model Pictured:** 1950s White Falcon   **Pickups:** Two
> **Controls:** Three-way selector, volume for each pickup, master volume, master tone
> **Characteristics:** Flashiness, classic Gretsch twang
> **Played by:** Stephen Stills, John Frusciante, Neil Young

Hofner 500/1 Bass

In their eight years together, the Beatles amassed many fabulous instruments, the most famous of which was Paul McCartney's violin-shaped electric bass guitar. McCartney played a 500/1 throughout the Beatles' career, and the instrument became known as the 'Beatle' or 'Cavern' bass, after the Liverpool club where the Beatles got their start.

In the early 1960s, Paul McCartney apparently couldn't afford a Fender bass and opted for the less expensive, more distinctive Hofner 500/1. With its symmetrically shaped body, the 500/1 looked normal when played left-handed.

Made from a small, hollow spruce/maple body and a thin maple neck with a short-scale (30-in/76-cm) rosewood fretboard, the 500/1 has two pickups (controlled by individual on/off switches),

volume knobs and a master boost knob. The 500/1's basic tone is rich and round, with a pronounced mid-range; in its upper register, the instrument sounds especially heavy, as on the Beatles' 'Come Together' (1969).

GUITAR SPEC	
Model Pictured: Paul McCartney's 1960s 500/1	
Pickups: Two	
Controls: Two on-off switches, two volume, master boost	
Characteristics: Excellent playability, warm, round tone	

Ibanez JEM

In the 1980s the over-the-top 'shred' style necessitated specialized instruments. Guitar hero Steve Vai collaborated with the Ibanez company to produce the JEM – a 'Superstrat' based upon traditional Fender principles, coupled with modern advances.

First available in 1987, the JEM was built to Vai's exacting specifications – a contoured, lightweight basswood body with

a 'monkey grip'; high-output DiMarzio pickups and a 24-fret rosewood fingerboard. The guitar also featured a recessed Ibanez 'Edge' whammy bar with locking nut, so that pitch could be radically lowered and raised without creating any tuning problems.

Early, limited editions of the JEM models, painted green with tiny drawings by Vai, became instant collector's items. Regular production versions included a yellow model with pink pickups, a shocking-pink one with pyramid inlays and a floral-patterned one with vine inlays. JEMs have proved to be wildly successful over the years, and they're still in production today.

GUITAR SPEC	
Model Pictured: 1980s JEM	**Pickups:** Two
Controls: Five-way selector, volume, tone	
Characteristics: Versatile, crisp, clear tone in all registers, advanced tremolo bar	
Played by: Steve Vai	

Kay Barney Kessel Artist

Based in Chicago, the Kay company manufactured affordable guitars in all styles – including a number of archtop variations – from the 1930s through to the 1960s. In the late 1950s, in an attempt to bolster its chintzy image, Kay teamed up with leading jazz guitarist Barney Kessel to create several artist models.

Made from 1957–60, Kay's three Kessels included the 13-in (33-cm), semi-solid Pro ($200), the 15½-in (39-cm), single-cutaway

Artist ($300) and the 17-in (43-cm) single-cutaway Jazz Special ($400). Each version had a number of fun touches, including Kessel's gold signature on the pickguard, and an Art-Deco style 'Kelvinator' headstock overlay, named after a similar-looking refrigerator.

While outfitted with good hardware, the Kessels were all made from inexpensive veneered bodies and therefore lacked the full tone of a traditional archtop. Yet these striking instruments tend to have an attractive punch and an indisputably cool vintage vibe.

GUITAR SPEC

Model Pictured: Kay Barney Kessel Artist **Pickups:** Two

Controls: Three-way switch, two volume, two tone

Characteristics: Vintage vibe, punchy tone

Played by: Sarah McLachlan

S
E
C
T
I
O
N

310

F
O
U
R

National Style O

In the mid-1920s, the guitarist George Beauchamp had an idea for an 'ampliphonic system', which he took to John Dopyera and his brother Rudy, Czechoslovakian immigrants known for their sonic improvement of banjos. From this meeting came the National Triple Resonator – a guitar amplified by three metal cones and enhanced by a metal body – which debuted in 1927, followed several years later by a single-cone version, the Style O.

On a tri-cone guitar, three thin, 6-in (15-cm) aluminium speaker cones are arranged in a triangle. A T-shaped bridge connects the centre of each cone. The strings' vibrations excite the saddle and the bridge and cones vibrate, creating a sweet, sustaining tone well suited to Hawaiian-style slide guitar.

Single-resonator models feature a 9½-in (24-cm) cone topped with a maple 'biscuit'; the strings pass over a wooden saddle attached to the biscuit. The design makes a single-resonator guitar a louder instrument than the tri-cone version.

GUITAR SPEC

Model Pictured: Style O

Construction: Brass alloy body, mahogany neck, cone resonator

Characteristics: Loud, aggressive tone

Played by: Son House, Tampa Red, Bukka White

Ovation Adamas

GUITAR SPEC

Model Pictured: Adamas
Construction: Lyrachord bowl body, birch/carbon top
Characteristics: Bright tone, exceptional projection
Played by: Glen Campbell, Al Di Meola, Rick Nielsen

One of the most visible guitar innovations was the rounded back of the Ovation guitar, developed by Charles H. Kaman.

An engineer who had founded an aircraft company, Kaman introduced his first round–back guitar in 1966. After many experiments with high-tech sonic equipment, Kaman devised a one-piece body shell, or Lyrachord bowl, made from fibres that were also used to cover helicopter blades. Coupled with a solid spruce top, one of Ovation's first models, the Balladeer, was an effective marriage of radical and traditional design.

Introduced in 1976, the Adamas was Ovation's top-of-the-line guitar. Its synthetic top was made of a thin $1/_{32}$-in (0.8-mm) birch core, with thinner layers of carbon graphite fibres. A series of small soundholes at the body's top end facilitated greater projection than a traditional, centred round hole. A wooden epaulette in the shape of leaves added a rustic touch to this space-age instrument.

Parker Fly

Introduced in 1992, the Parker Fly embodied a complete rethinking of the electric guitar. Developed over a decade of experiments by luthier Ken Parker and electronics guru Larry Fishman, the innovative Fly incorporated a number of new ideas in a streamlined, space-age design.

The Fly possesses a slender poplar body and a lightweight basswood neck. But, departing from tradition, the neck is reinforced with a skin of glass/carbon epoxy. Another revolutionary feature is that the instrument's hardened stainless-steel frets are resistant to the wear and tear associated with traditional nickel/steel fretwire.

The Fly combines two magnetic humbucking pickups with a bridge-mounted piezo-electric unit (fed to an active stereo preamp), for access to a full range of electric tones and an amplified-acoustic guitar simulation. These sounds can be blended to create a unique electric/acoustic tone, and the guitar's split-stereo output allows for further depth of sound.

GUITAR SPEC

Model Pictured: Fly **Pickups:** Two magnetic, one piezo
Controls: Three-way switch, two volume, two tone, master volume
Characteristics: Versatile, edgy, immediate tones, bright, spirited and funky
Played by: The Edge, Eddie Van Halen, Joni Mitchell, Keith Richards

PRS Custom 24

In the summer of 1975, Paul Reed Smith set up a workshop in his parents' home and began making guitars.

Before long, he was peddling his creations at local concerts. By the mid-1980s, Smith had begun creating his own strikingly modern designs. Basically the same instrument that Smith first shopped in 1985, the Custom 24 combines elements of Gibson- and Fender-style design: its double-cutaway silhouette was inspired by Gibson's Les Paul Special, and its mahogany body with maple top and mahogany neck is informed by the Les Paul Standard. The Custom 24's vibrato bar updates that of the Fender Stratocaster. A five-way pickup selector includes coil-tap positions, facilitating both Gibson- and Fender-like tones.

The Custom 24 has been offered in a dazzling array of finishes, and a number of other special touches. The rosewood fretboard can be inlaid with abalone birds in flight, and the top can be upgraded to figured maple.

GUITAR SPEC

Model Pictured: Custom 24
Pickups: Two
Controls: Five-way rotary selector, volume, tone
Characteristics: Versatile, robust creamy tone
Played by: Nils Lofgren, Al Di Meola, Carlos Santana

Rickenbacker 360-12

Overshadowed by Fenders and Gibsons, Rickenbacker electrics were obscure until the early 1960s, when the Beatles' John Lennon picked up his 325 model. Soon after, band mate George Harrison got an early 12-string version, as did the Byrds' Roger McGuinn, who used a 360-12 to create his trademark jingle-jangle sound.

First made in 1964, the 360-12 was a deluxe mono/stereo guitar, constructed of a slender, semi-hollow maple body and a set-in maple neck with rosewood fretboard, inlaid with white triangles. Commonly sprayed with a Fireglo (pink-to-red sunburst) finish, the guitar was outfitted with twin high-output 'Toaster Top' pickups, a two-tiered white pickguard, and a custom 'R' tailpiece.

GUITAR SPEC

Model Pictured: 1964 360-12 **Pickups:** Two
Controls: Three-way selector, two volume, two tone, one balance
Characteristics: Jangly, shimmering tone
Played by: George Harrison, Roger McGuinn, Peter Buck

The 360-12 employs an unconventional tuning-knob configuration – its machine heads are alternately placed slotted (classical-guitar style) and in the regular perpendicular fashion. This allows for a conventionally sized headstock, ensuring that the instrument is balanced.

Steinberger GL

GUITAR SPEC

Model Pictured: Steinberger GL

Pickups: Two

Controls: Three-way switch, volume, tone

Characteristics: Clear and resonant, piano-like attack

Played by: Allan Holdsworth, Mike Rutherford, Eddie Van Halen

In 1981, the industrial designer Ned Steinberger introduced the sleek, unconventional L-2 electric bass, the most radical update of the instrument since its introduction by Leo Fender three decades earlier.

A six-string guitar version, the GL, followed in 1983. Initially Steinberger's instruments were objects of ridicule, but they soon came to be praised by both musicians and design journals.

The GL's conventionally sized neck and diminutive body were made from a lightweight composite of epoxy resin, carbon graphite and glass fibres – twice as strong and 10 times denser than wood. The GL's most striking element was its lack of a headstock; the tuners were relocated to the end of the body (necessitating double-ball-ended strings), creating a total physical balance. Many top players, including Eddie Van Halen, were drawn to the GL. But perhaps due to its disorientating shape, the guitar did not achieve widespread appeal.

Vox Mk VI

GUITAR SPEC

Model Pictured: 1960s Mk VI

Pickups: Three

Controls: Five-way switch, volume, two tone

Characteristics: Bright, clear tone; novel body shape

Played by: Ian Curtis, Tony Hicks, Brian Jones

In the 1960s, England's guitar manufacturers had difficulty competing with American brands like Fender, Gibson and Gretsch. One British company to achieve a measure of success was Vox, which in addition to a fine line of valve amplifiers, made guitars in England between 1961 and 1964. Perhaps the best-known design from the Vox guitar range was the Vox Mark VI.

With its bolt-on maple neck, three single-coil pickups, five-way switch, and vibrato unit, the Mk VI was clearly inspired by Fender's Stratocaster. But with its egg-shaped body and headstock, the instrument, nicknamed the 'Teardrop', was one of the most unconventional-looking guitars of the early 1960s.

The Mk VI gained considerable exposure when a rare, two-pickup white version was seen being played by Rolling Stones guitarist Brian Jones on *The Ed Sullivan Show*. The guitar steadily gained interest amongst players and collectors alike; since the 1980s the Mk VI has been reissued in several different versions, and original 1960s models perform well on the vintage market.

Chord Dictionary

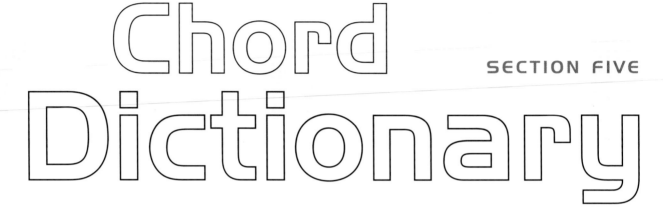

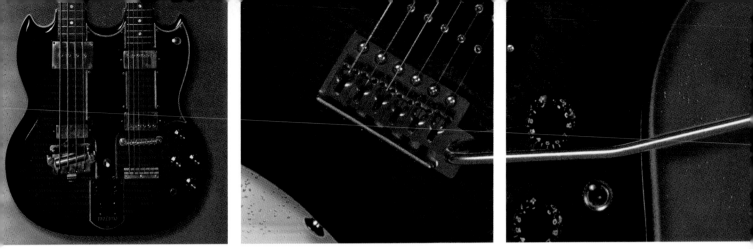

Chords are the harmonic building blocks that let a guitarist stand alone – to make exciting or plaintive music unaccompanied. Simple chords let you get a fast start on the road to making music, and complex chords take you into the exotic worlds of jazz and cutting-edge music. Understanding the right chord, and when and where to play it in a band or ensemble, is what makes you an accomplished guitarist, with chops a saxophonist or trumpet player will never master. The following pages illustrate every chord you need to build a guitar vocabulary for any occasion – or musical style.

Introduction

The chord fretboxes in this section will help you to learn the shapes of hundreds of chords, and will be a useful reference guide when you are playing and composing your own music. These next few pages are by no means comprehensive, but should contain enough chord formations for you, whatever your needs.

While learning the fingerings might not seem particularly interesting, you should remember that the wider your chord vocabulary becomes, the more you will be able to vary your compositions and your playing style. If you jam with other musicians, it is very important to know your chords – you don't want to be struggling to find the right fingering when the leader shouts 'G'!

The chords are divided by key, from A to G♯, with the key's notes shown at the top of the right-hand page. There is one double-page spread devoted to each key. The first page outlines the main chords you will need to learn, each shown in three different fingerings or positions. It can be useful to know a variety of positions for each chord, especially when fitting them into a progression – when you are playing in high fingerboard positions, you do not want to have to stop and scramble about, trying to find a chord position back on the first few frets.

The second page shows some of the more advanced chords that can be useful when playing progressions, for linking chords

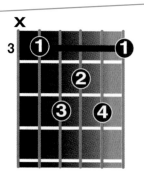

Cmaj7   C Major 7th
1st (C), 3rd (E), 5th (G), 7th (B)

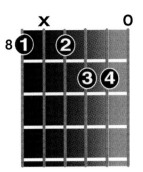

C7#5 C Dominant 7th #5
1st (C), 3rd (E), #5th (G#), b7th (Bb)

or for use when you are improvising. There are only two positions shown for these, so as to include a greater variety of chords.

All the diagrams show the guitar fretboard in an upright position, with high E on the right. The nut appears at the top if the chord is played on the lower frets. If the chord is in a higher position, the fret number on which it begins is given to the left of the diagram.

The notes to be played are shown as circles, with the finger number that should be used for each note (❶ = index finger; ❷ = middle finger; ❸ = ring finger; ❹ = little finger). An **X** above the string

indicates that the string should not be played in the chord and should be muted to prevent it from sounding accidentally. An **O** above the string shows that it should be played as an open string.

This section should not be difficult to use. Where there is a choice of note name (e.g. C# or Db) we have selected the one that you are more likely to come across in your playing.

Where a chord contains a flattened (b) or sharpened (#) interval (e.g. #5th), you can find the notes by playing a fret lower (for a flat) or a fret higher (for a sharp) than the interval note indicated at the bottom of the right-hand page. In the keys that contain a large number of sharps or flats, double flats (bb) and double sharps (x) sometimes occur in the augmented or diminished chords. A double flat is the note two frets below the named note, while a double sharp is two frets up.

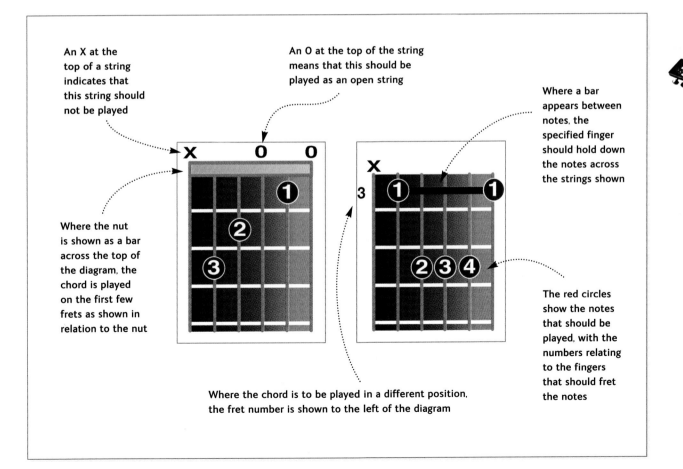

An X at the top of a string indicates that this string should not be played

An O at the top of the string means that this should be played as an open string

Where a bar appears between notes, the specified finger should hold down the notes across the strings shown

Where the nut is shown as a bar across the top of the diagram, the chord is played on the first few frets as shown in relation to the nut

The red circles show the notes that should be played, with the numbers relating to the fingers that should fret the notes

Where the chord is to be played in a different position, the fret number is shown to the left of the diagram

A

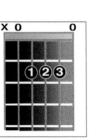

A A Major
1st (A), 3rd (C#), 5th (E)

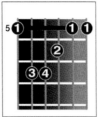

A A Major
1st (A), 3rd (C#), 5th (E)

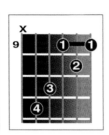

A A Major
1st (A), 3rd (C#), 5th (E)

Am A Minor
1st (A), ♭3rd (C), 5th (E)

Am A Minor
1st (A), ♭3rd (C), 5th (E)

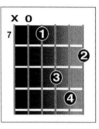

Am A Minor
1st (A), ♭3rd (C), 5th (E)

Amaj7 A Major 7th
1st (A), 3rd (C#), 5th (E), 7th (G#)

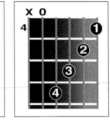

Amaj7 A Major 7th
1st (A), 3rd (C#), 5th (E), 7th (G#)

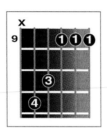

Amaj7 A Major 7th
1st (A), 3rd (C#), 5th (E), 7th (G#)

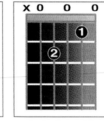
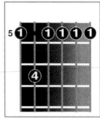

Am7 A Minor 7th
1st (A), ♭3rd (C), 5th (E), ♭7th (G)

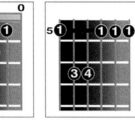

Am7 A Minor 7th
1st (A), ♭3rd (C) 5th (E), ♭7th (G)

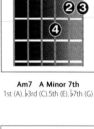

Am7 A Minor 7th
1st (A), ♭3rd (C), 5th (E), ♭7th (G)

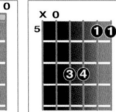
Asus4 A Suspended 4th
1st (A), 4th (D), 5th (E)

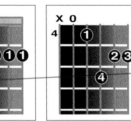

Asus4 A Suspended 4th
1st (A), 4th (D), 5th (E)

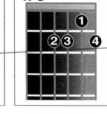

Asus4 A Suspended 4th
1st (A), 4th (D), 5th (E)

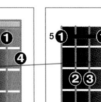

A7sus4 A Dominant 7th sus4
1st (A), 4th (D), 5th (E), ♭7th (G)

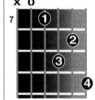
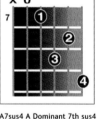

A7sus4 A Dominant 7th sus4
1st (A), 4th (D), 5th (E), ♭7th (G)

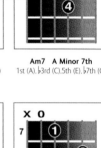

A7sus4 A Dominant 7th sus4
1st (A), 4th (D), 5th (E), ♭7th (G)

A6 A Major 6th
1st (A), 3rd (C#), 5th (E), 6th (F#)

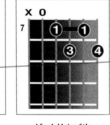
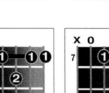

A6 A Major 6th
1st (A), 3rd (C#), 5th (E), 6th (F#)

A6 A Major 6th
1st (A), 3rd (C#), 5th (E), 6th (F#)

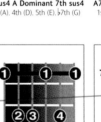

Am6 A Minor 6th
1st (A), ♭3rd (C), 5th (E), 6th (F#)

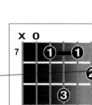
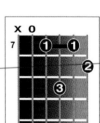

Am6 A Minor 6th
1st (A), ♭3rd (C), 5th (E), 6th (F#)

Am6 A Minor 6th
1st (A), ♭3rd (C), 5th (E), 6th (F#)

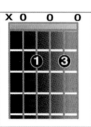

A7 A Dominant 7th
1st (A), 3rd (C#), 5th (E), ♭7th (G)

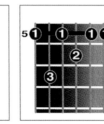

A7 A Dominant 7th
1st (A), 3rd (C#), 5th (E), ♭7th (G)

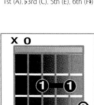

A7 A Dominant 7th
1st (A), 3rd (C#), 5th (E), ♭7th (G)

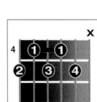

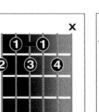

A9 A Dominant 9th
1st (A), 3rd (C#), 5th (E), ♭7th (G), 9th (B)

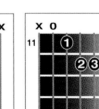
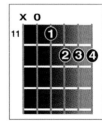

A9 A Dominant 9th
1st (A), 3rd (C#), 5th (E), ♭7th (G), 9th (B)

A9 A Dominant 9th
1st (A), 3rd (C#), 5th (E), ♭7th (G), 9th (B)

Scale of A major

A	B	C#	D	E	F#	G#
1st	2nd	3rd	4th	5th	6th	7th
	9th		11th		13th	

A5 A 5th (power chord)
1st (A), 5th (E)

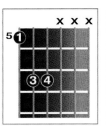

A5 A 5th (power chord)
1st (A), 5th (E)

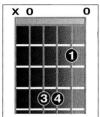

A 6/9 A Major 6th add 9th
1st (A), 3rd (C#), 5th (E).
6th (F#), 9th (B)

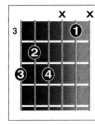

A 6/9 A Major 6th add 9th
1st (A), 3rd (C#), 5th (E).
6th (F#), 9th (B)

A11 A Dominant 11th
1st (A), 3rd (C#), 5th (E), b7th
(G), 9th (B), 11th (D)

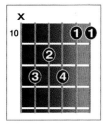

A11 A Dominant 11th
1st (A), 3rd (C#), 5th (E), b7th
(G), 9th (B), 11th (D)

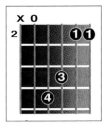

A13 A Dominant 13th
1st (A), 3rd (C#), 5th (E), b7th
(G), 9th (B), 13th (F#)

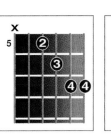

A13 A Dominant 13th
1st (A), 3rd (C#), 5th (E), b7th
(G), 9th (B), 13th (F#)

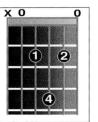

Aadd9 A Major add 9th
1st (A), 3rd (C#), 5th (E), 9th (B)

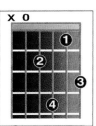

Aadd9 A Major add 9th
1st (A), 3rd (C#), 5th (E), 9th (B)

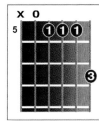

Am9 A Minor 9th
1st (A), b3rd (C), 5th (E), b7th
(G), 9th (B)

Am9 A Minor 9th
1st (A), b3rd (C), 5th (E), b7th
(G), 9th (B)

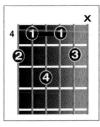

Amaj9 A Major 9th
1st (A), 3rd (C#), 5th (E).
7th (G#), 9th (B)

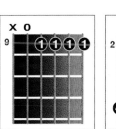

Amaj9 A Major 9th
1st (A), 3rd (C#), 5th (E).
7th (G#), 9th (B)

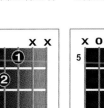

A+ A Augmented
1st (A), 3rd (C#), #5th (E#)

A+ A Augmented
1st (A), 3rd (C#), #5th (E#)

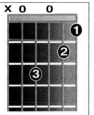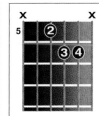

A7#5 A Dominant 7th #5
1st (A), 3rd (C#), #5th (E#),
b7th (G)

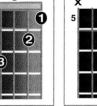

A7#5 A Dominant 7th #5
1st (A), 3rd (C#), #5th (E#),
b7th (G)

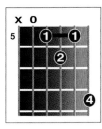

A7#9 A Dominant 7th #9
1st (A), 3rd (C#),
5th (E), b7th (G), #9th (B#)

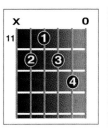

A7#9 A Dominant 7th #9
1st (A), 3rd (C#),
5th (E), b7th (G), #9th (B#)

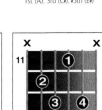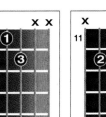

A07 A Diminished 7th
1st (A), b3rd (C), b5th (Eb),
bb7th (Gb)

A07 A Diminished 7th
1st (A), b3rd (C), b5th (Eb),
bb7th (Gb)

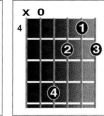

A0 A Diminished triad
1st (A), b3rd (C), b5th (Eb)

A0 A Diminished triad
1st (A), b3rd (C), b5th (Eb)

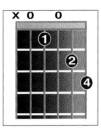

A7b5 A Dominant 7th b5
1st (A), 3rd (C#), b5th (Eb),
b7th (G)

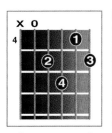

A7b5 A Dominant 7th b5
1st (A), 3rd (C#), b5th (Eb),
b7th (G)

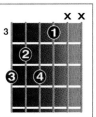

A7b9 A Dominant 7th b9
1st (A), 3rd (C#), 5th (E),
b7th (G), b9th (Bb)

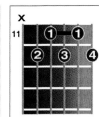

A7b9 A Dominant 7th b9
1st (A), 3rd (C#), 5th (E), b7th
(G), b9th (Bb)

A9b5 A Dominant 9th b5th
1st (A), 3rd (C#), b5th (Eb), b7th
(G), 9th (B)

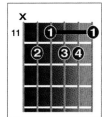

A9b5 A Dominant 9th b5th
1st (A), 3rd (C#), b5th (Eb), b7th
(G), 9th (B)

B♭/A♯

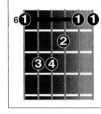
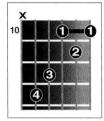

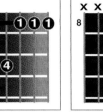

B♭ B♭ major
1st (B♭), 3rd (D), 5th (F)

B♭ B♭ major
1st (B♭), 3rd (D), 5th (F)

B♭ B♭ major
1st (B♭), 3rd (D), 5th (F)

B♭m B♭ Minor
1st (B♭), ♭3rd (D♭), 5th (F)

B♭m B♭ Minor
1st (B♭), ♭3rd (D♭), 5th (F)

B♭m B♭ Minor
1st (B♭), ♭3rd (D♭), 5th (F)

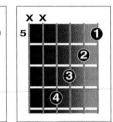
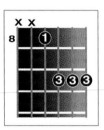
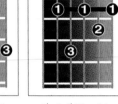
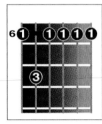

B♭maj7 B♭ Major 7th
1st (B♭), 3rd (D), 5th (F), 7th (A)

B♭maj7 B♭ Major 7th
1st (B♭), 3rd (D), 5th (F), 7th (A)

B♭maj7 B♭ Major 7th
1st (B♭), 3rd (D), 5th (F), 7th (A)

B♭m7 B♭ Minor 7th
1st (B♭), ♭3rd (D♭), 5th (F), ♭7th (A♭)

B♭m7 B♭ Minor 7th
1st (B♭), ♭3rd (D♭), 5th (F), ♭7th (A♭)

B♭m7 B♭ Minor 7th
1st (B♭), ♭3rd (D♭), 5th (F), ♭7th (A♭)

320

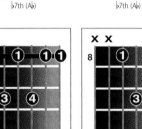
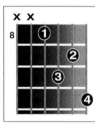

B♭sus4 B♭ Suspended 4th
1st (B♭), 4th (E♭), 5th (F)

B♭sus4 B♭ Suspended 4th
1st (B♭), 4th (E♭), 5th (F)

B♭sus4 B♭ Suspended 4th
1st (B♭), 4th (E♭), 5th (F)

B♭7sus4 B♭ Dominant 7th sus4
1st (B♭), 4th (E♭), 5th (F), ♭7th (A♭)

B♭7sus4 B♭ Dominant 7th sus4
1st (B♭), 4th (E♭), 5th (F), ♭7th (A♭)

B♭7sus4 B♭ Dominant 7th sus4
1st (B♭), 4th (E♭), 5th (F), ♭7th (A♭)

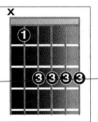
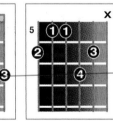
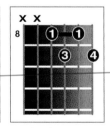
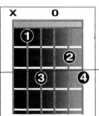
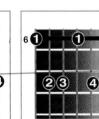
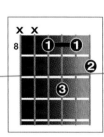

B♭6 B♭ Major 6th
1st (B♭), 3rd (D), 5th (F), 6th (G)

B♭6 B♭ Major 6th
1st (B♭), 3rd (D), 5th (F), 6th (G)

B♭6 B♭ Major 6th
1st (B♭), 3rd (D), 5th (F), 6th (G)

B♭m6 B♭ Minor 6th
1st (B♭), ♭3rd (D♭), 5th (F), 6th (G)

B♭m6 B♭ Minor 6th
1st (B♭), ♭3rd (D♭), 5th (F), 6th (G)

B♭m6 B♭ Minor 6th
1st (B♭), ♭3rd (D♭), 5th (F), 6th (G)

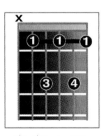

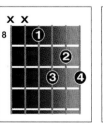
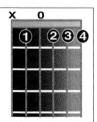

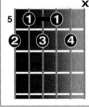
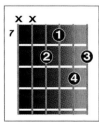

B♭7 B♭ Dominant 7th
1st (B♭), 3rd (D), 5th (F), ♭7th (A♭)

B♭7 B♭ Dominant 7th
1st (B♭), 3rd (D), 5th (F), ♭7th (A♭)

B♭7 B♭ Dominant 7th
1st (B♭), 3rd (D), 5th (F), ♭7th (A♭)

B♭9 B♭ Dominant 9th
1st (B♭), 3rd (D), 5th (F), ♭7th (A♭), 9th (C)

B♭9 B♭ Dominant 9th
1st (B♭), 3rd (D), 5th (F), ♭7th (A♭), 9th (C)

B♭9 B♭ Dominant 9th
1st (B♭), 3rd (D), 5th (F), ♭7th (A♭), 9th (C)

Scale of B♭/A♯ major

B♭	C	D	E♭	F	G	A
1st	2nd	3rd	4th	5th	6th	7th
	9th		11th	13th		

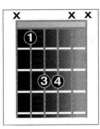

B♭5 B♭ 5th (power chord)
1st (B♭). 5th (F)

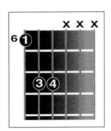

B♭5 B♭ 5th (power chord)
1st (B♭). 5th (F)

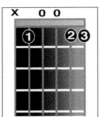

B♭6/9 B♭ Major 6th add 9th
1st (B♭). 3rd (D). 5th (F).
6th (G). 9th (C)

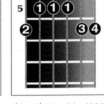

B♭6/9 B♭ Major 6th add 9th
1st (B♭). 3rd (D). 5th (F).
6th (G). 9th (C)

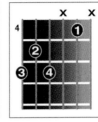

B♭11 B♭ Dominant 11th
1st (B♭). 3rd (D). 5th (F).
♭7th (A♭). 9th (C). 11th (E♭)

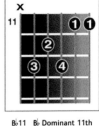

B♭11 B♭ Dominant 11th
1st (B♭). 3rd (D). 5th (F).
♭7th (A♭). 9th (C). 11th (E♭)

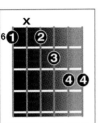

B♭13 B♭ Dominant 13th
1st (B♭). 3rd (D). 5th (F).
♭7th (A♭). 9th (C). 13th (G)

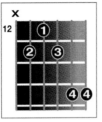

B♭13 B♭ Dominant 13th
1st (B♭). 3rd (D). 5th (F).
♭7th (A♭). 9th (C). 13th (G)

B♭add9 B♭ Major add 9th
1st (B♭). 3rd (D). 5th (F). 9th (C)

B♭add9 B♭ Major add 9th
1st (B♭). 3rd (D). 5th (F). 9th (C)

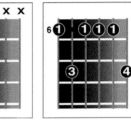

B♭m9 B♭ Minor 9th
1st (B♭). ♭3rd (D♭). 5th (F).
♭7th (A♭). 9th (C)

B♭m9 B♭ Minor 9th
1st (B♭). ♭3rd (D♭). 5th (F).
♭7th (A♭). 9th (C)

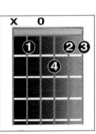

B♭maj9 B♭ Major 9th
1st (B♭). 3rd (D). 5th (F).
7th (A). 9th (C)

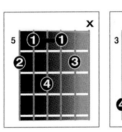

B♭maj9 B♭ Major 9th
1st (B♭). 3rd (D). 5th (F).
7th (A). 9th (C)

B♭+ B♭ Augmented
1st (B♭). 3rd (D). ♯5th (F♯)

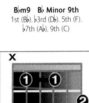

B♭+ B♭ Augmented
1st (B♭). 3rd (D). ♯5th (F♯)

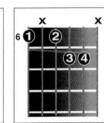

B♭7♯5 B♭ Dominant 7th ♯5
1st (B♭). 3rd (D). ♯5th (F♯).
♭7th (A♭)

B♭7♯5 B♭ Dominant 7th ♯5
1st (B♭). 3rd (D). ♯5th (F♯).
♭7th (A♭)

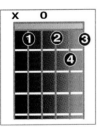

B♭7♯9 B♭ Dominant 7th ♯9
1st (B♭). 3rd (D). 5th (F).
♭7th (A♭). ♯9th (C♯)

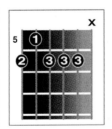

B♭7♯9 B♭ Dominant 7th ♯9
1st (B♭). 3rd (D). 5th (F).
♭7th (A♭). ♯9th (C♯)

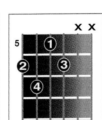

B♭o7 B♭ Diminished 7th
1st (B♭). ♭3rd (D♭). ♭5th (F♭).
♭♭7th (A♭♭)

B♭o7 B♭ Diminished 7th
1st (B♭). ♭3rd (D♭). ♭5th (F♭).
♭♭7th (A♭♭)

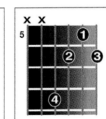

B♭o B♭ Diminished triad
1st (B♭). ♭3rd (D♭). ♭5th (F♭)

B♭o B♭ Diminished triad
1st (B♭). ♭3rd (D♭). ♭5th (F♭)

B♭7♭5 B♭ Dominant 7th ♭5
1st (B♭). 3rd (D). ♭5th (F♭).
♭7th (A♭)

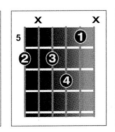

B♭7♭5 B♭ Dominant 7th ♭5
1st (B♭). 3rd (D). ♭5th (F♭).
♭7th (A♭)

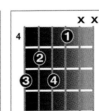

B♭7♭9 B♭ Dominant 7th ♭9
1st (B♭). 3rd (D). 5th (F).
♭7th (A♭). ♭9th (C♭)

B♭7♭9 B♭ Dominant 7th ♭9
1st (B♭). 3rd (D). 5th (F).
♭7th (A♭). ♭9th (C♭)

B♭9♭5 B♭ Dominant 9th ♭5
1st (B♭). 3rd (D). ♭5th (F♭).
♭7th (A♭). 9th (C)

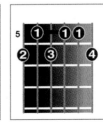

B♭9♭5 B♭ Dominant 9th ♭5
1st (B♭). 3rd (D). ♭5th (F♭).
♭7th (A♭). 9th (C)

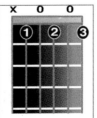

B

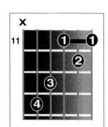
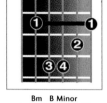
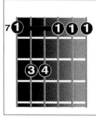
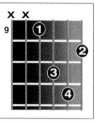

B   B Major
1st (B), 3rd (D♯), 5th (F♯)

B   B Major
1st (B), 3rd (D♯), 5th (F♯)

B   B Major
1st (B), 3rd (D♯), 5th (F♯)

Bm   B Minor
1st (B), ♭3rd (D), 5th (F♯)

Bm   B Minor
1st (B), ♭3rd (D), 5th (F♯)

Bm   B Minor
1st (B), ♭3rd (D), 5th (F♯)

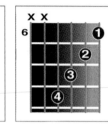
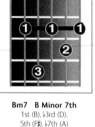
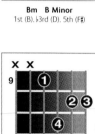

Bmaj7   B Major 7th
1st (B), 3rd (D♯),
5th (F♯), 7th (A♯)

Bmaj7   B Major 7th
1st (B), 3rd (D♯),
5th (F♯), 7th (A♯)

Bmaj7   B Major 7th
1st (B), 3rd (D♯),
5th (F♯), 7th (A♯)

Bm7   B Minor 7th
1st (B), ♭3rd (D),
5th (F♯), ♭7th (A)

Bm7   B Minor 7th
1st (B), ♭3rd (D),
5th (F♯), ♭7th (A)

Bm7   B Minor 7th
1st (B), ♭3rd (D),
5th (F♯), ♭7th (A)

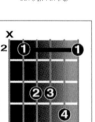
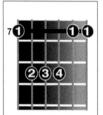

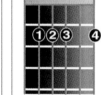
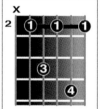

Bsus4   B Suspended 4th
1st (B), 4th (E), 5th (F♯)

Bsus4   B Suspended 4th
1st (B), 4th (E), 5th (F♯)

Bsus4   B Suspended 4th
1st (B), 4th (E), 5th (F♯)

B7sus4   B Dominant 7th sus4
1st (B), 4th (E), 5th (F♯), ♭7th (A)

B7sus4   B Dominant 7th sus4
1st (B), 4th (E), 5th (F♯), ♭7th (A)

B7sus4   B Dominant 7th sus4
1st (B), 4th (E), 5th (F♯), ♭7th (A)

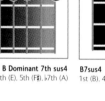

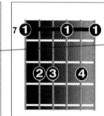

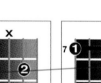

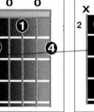
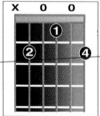

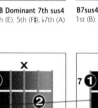

B6   B Major 6th
1st (B), 3rd (D♯), 5th (F♯), 6th (G♯)

B6   B Major 6th
1st (B), 3rd (D♯), 5th (F♯), 6th (G♯)

B6   B Major 6th
1st (B), 3rd (D♯), 5th (F♯), 6th (G♯)

Bm6   B Minor 6th
1st (B), ♭3rd (D), 5th (F♯), 6th (G♯)

Bm6   B Minor 6th
1st (B), ♭3rd (D), 5th (F♯), 6th (G♯)

Bm6   B Minor 6th
1st (B), ♭3rd (D), 5th (F♯), 6th (G♯)

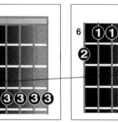
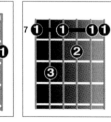
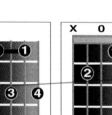

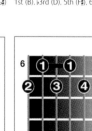
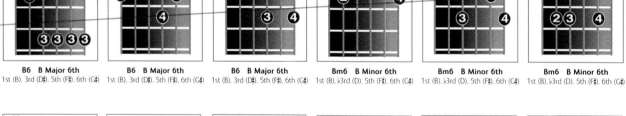

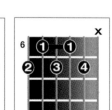
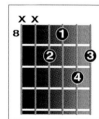

B7   B Dominant 7th
1st (B), 3rd (D♯), 5th (F♯), ♭7th (A)

B7   B Dominant 7th
1st (B), 3rd (D♯), 5th (F♯), ♭7th (A)

B7   B Dominant 7th
1st (B), 3rd (D♯), 5th (F♯), ♭7th (A)

B9   B Dominant 9th
1st (B), 3rd (D♯), 5th (F♯),
♭7th (A), 9th (C♯)

B9   B Dominant 9th
1st (B), 3rd (D♯), 5th (F♯),
♭7th (A), 9th (C♯)

B9   B Dominant 9th
1st (B), 3rd (D♯), 5th (F♯),
♭7th (A), 9th (C♯)

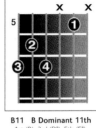

Scale of B major						
B	**C#**	**D#**	**E**	**F#**	**G#**	**A#**
1st	2nd	3rd	4th	5th	6th	7th
	9th		11th		13th	

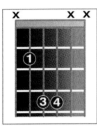  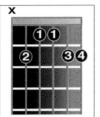 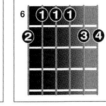 

B5 B 5th (power chord)
1st (B), 5th (F#)

B5 B 5th (power chord)
1st (B), 5th (F#)

B 6/9 B Major 6th add 9th
1st (B), 3rd (D#), 5th (F#),
6th (G#), 9th (C#)

B 6/9 B Major 6th add 9th
1st (B), 3rd (D#), 5th (F#),
6th (G#), 9th (C#)

B11 B Dominant 11th
1st (B), 3rd (D#), 5th (F#),
♭7th (A), 9th (C#), 11th (E)

B11 B Dominant 11th
1st (B), 3rd (D#), 5th (F#),
♭7th (A), 9th (C#), 11th (E)

B13 B Dominant 13th
1st (B), 3rd (D#), 5th (F#),
♭7th (A), 9th (C#), 13th (G#)

B13 B Dominant 13th
1st (B), 3rd (D#), 5th (F#),
♭7th (A), 9th (C#), 13th (G#)

Badd9 B Major add 9th
1st (B), 3rd (D#), 5th (F#), 9th (C#)

Badd9 B Major add 9th
1st (B), 3rd (D#), 5th (F#), 9th (C#)

Bm9 B Minor 9th
1st (B), ♭3rd (D), 5th (F#),
♭7th (A), 9th (C#)

Bm9 B Minor 9th
1st (B), ♭3rd (D), 5th (F#),
♭7th (A), 9th (C#)

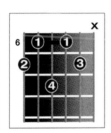  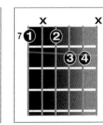

Bmaj9 B Major 9th
1st (B), 3rd (D#), 5th (F#),
7th (A#), 9th (C#)

Bmaj9 B Major 9th
1st (B), 3rd (D#), 5th (F#),
7th (A#), 9th (C#)

B+ B Augmented
1st (B), 3rd (D#), #5th (Fx)

B+ B Augmented
1st (B), 3rd (D#), #5th (Fx)

B7#5 B Dominant 7th #5
1st (B), 3rd (D#), #5th (Fx), ♭7th (A)

B7#5 B Dominant 7th #5
1st (B), 3rd (D#), #5th (Fx), ♭7th (A)

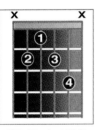 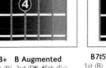 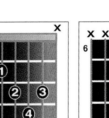 

B7#9 B Dominant 7th #9
1st (B), 3rd (D#), 5th (F#),
♭7th (A), #9th (Cx)

B7#9 B Dominant 7th #9
1st (B), 3rd (D#), 5th (F#),
♭7th (A), #9th (Cx)

B07 B Diminished 7th
1st (B), ♭3rd (D), ♭5th (F), ♭♭7th (A♭)

B07 B Diminished 7th
1st (B), ♭3rd (D), ♭5th (F), ♭♭7th (A♭)

B0 B Diminished triad
1st (B), ♭3rd (D), ♭5th (F)

B0 B Diminished triad
1st (B), ♭3rd (D), ♭5th (F)

 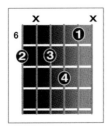 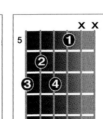 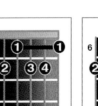 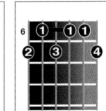 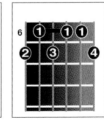

B7♭5 B Dominant 7th ♭5
1st (B), 3rd (D#), ♭5th (F), ♭7th (A)

B7♭5 B Dominant 7th ♭5
1st (B), 3rd (D#), ♭5th (F), ♭7th (A)

B7♭9 B Dominant 7th ♭9
1st (B), 3rd (D#), 5th (F#),
♭7th (A), ♭9th (C)

B7♭9 B Dominant 7th ♭9
1st (B), 3rd (D#), 5th (F#),
♭7th (A), ♭9th (C)

B9♭5 B Dominant 9th ♭5
1st (B), 3rd (D#), ♭5th (F),
♭7th (A), 9th (C#)

B9♭5 B Dominant 9th ♭5
1st (B), 3rd (D#), ♭5th (F),
♭7th (A), 9th (C#)

 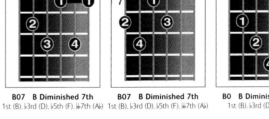   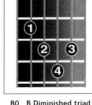 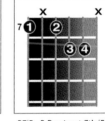   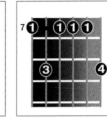

C

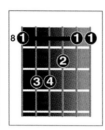
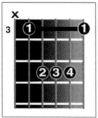
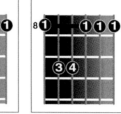
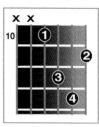

C   C Major
1st (C), 3rd (E), 5th (G)

C   C Major
1st (C), 3rd (E), 5th (G)

C   C Major
1st (C), 3rd (E), 5th (G)

Cm   C Minor
1st (C), b3rd (Eb), 5th (G)

Cm   C Minor
1st (C), b3rd (Eb), 5th (G)

Cm   C Minor
1st (C), b3rd (Eb), 5th (G)

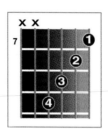
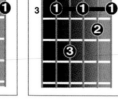
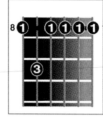
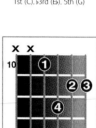

Cmaj7   C Major 7th
1st (C), 3rd (E), 5th (G), 7th (B)

Cmaj7   C Major 7th
1st (C), 3rd (E), 5th (G), 7th (B)

Cmaj7   C Major 7th
1st (C), 3rd (E), 5th (G), 7th (B)

Cm7   C Minor 7th
1st (C), b3rd (Eb),
5th (G), b7th (Bb)

Cm7   C Minor 7th
1st (C), b3rd (Eb),
5th (G), b7th (Bb)

Cm7   C Minor 7th
1st (C), b3rd (Eb),
5th (G), b7th (Bb)

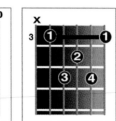
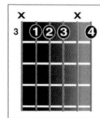
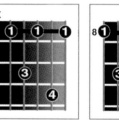
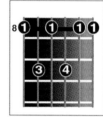

Csus4   C Suspended 4th
1st (C), 4th (F), 5th (G)

Csus4   C Suspended 4th
1st (C), 4th (F), 5th (G)

Csus4   C Suspended 4th
1st (C), 4th (F), 5th (G)

C7sus4   C Dominant 7th sus4
1st (C), 4th (F), 5th (G), b7th (Bb)

C7sus4   C Dominant 7th sus4
1st (C), 4th (F), 5th (G), b7th (Bb)

C7sus4   C Dominant 7th sus4
1st (C), 4th (F), 5th (G), b7th (Bb)

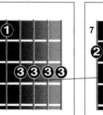
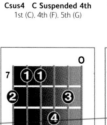

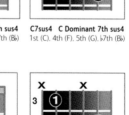

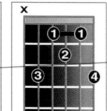
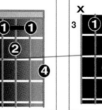
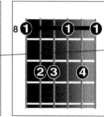

C6   C Major 6th
1st (C), 3rd (E), 5th (G), 6th (A)

C6   C Major 6th
1st (C), 3rd (E), 5th (G), 6th (A)

C6   C Major 6th
1st (C), 3rd (E), 5th (G), 6th (A)

Cm6   C Minor 6th
1st (C), b3rd (Eb), 5th (G), 6th (A)

Cm6   C Minor 6th
1st (C), b3rd (Eb), 5th (G), 6th (A)

Cm6   C Minor 6th
1st (C), b3rd (Eb), 5th (G), 6th (A)

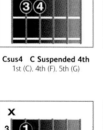
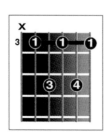

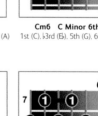

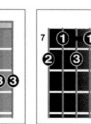
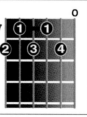
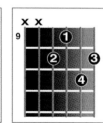

C7   C Dominant 7th
1st (C), 3rd (E), 5th (G), b7th (Bb)

C7   C Dominant 7th
1st (C), 3rd (E), 5th (G), b7th (Bb)

C7   C Dominant 7th
1st (C), 3rd (E), 5th (G), b7th (Bb)

C9   C Dominant 9th
1st (C), 3rd (E), 5th (G),
b7th (Bb), 9th (D)

C9   C Dominant 9th
1st (C), 3rd (E), 5th (G),
b7th (Bb), 9th (D)

C9   C Dominant 9th
1st (C), 3rd (E), 5th (G),
b7th (Bb), 9th (D)

Scale of C major

C	D	E	F	G	A	B
1st	2nd	3rd	4th	5th	6th	7th
	9th		11th		13th	

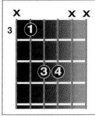

C5 C 5th (power chord)
1st (C), 5th (G)

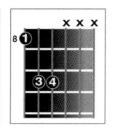

C5 C 5th (power chord)
1st (C), 5th (G)

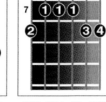

C 6/9 C Major 6th add 9th
1st (C), 3rd (E), 5th (G),
6th (A), 9th (D)

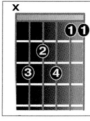

C 6/9 C Major 6th add 9th
1st (C), 3rd (E), 5th (G),
6th (A), 9th (D)

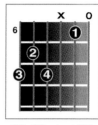

C11 C Dominant 11th
1st (C), 3rd (E), 5th (G),
♭7th (B♭), 9th (D), 11th (F)

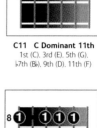

C11 C Dominant 11th
1st (C), 3rd (E), 5th (G),
♭7th (B♭), 9th (D), 11th (F)

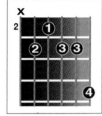

C13 C Dominant 13th
1st (C), 3rd (E), 5th (G),
♭7th (B♭), 9th (D), 13th (A)

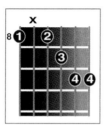

C13 C Dominant 13th
1st (C), 3rd (E), 5th (G),
♭7th (B♭), 9th (D), 13th (A)

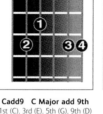

Cadd9 C Major add 9th
1st (C), 3rd (E), 5th (G), 9th (D)

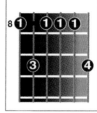

Cadd9 C Major add 9th
1st (C), 3rd (E), 5th (G), 9th (D)

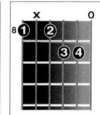

Cm9 C Minor 9th
1st (C), ♭3rd (E♭), 5th (G),
♭7th (B♭), 9th (D)

Cm9 C Minor 9th
1st (C), ♭3rd (E♭), 5th (G),
♭7th (B♭), 9th (D)

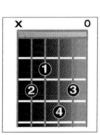

Cmaj9 C Major 9th
1st (C), 3rd (E), 5th (G),
7th (B), 9th (D)

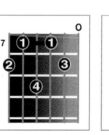

Cmaj9 C Major 9th
1st (C), 3rd (E), 5th (G),
7th (B), 9th (D)

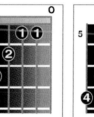

C+ C Augmented
1st (C), 3rd (E), ♯5th (G♯)

C+ C Augmented
1st (C), 3rd (E), ♯5th (G♯)

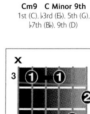

C7♯5 C Dominant 7th ♯5
1st (C), 3rd (E), ♯5th (G♯), ♭7th (B♭)

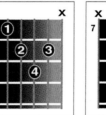

C7♯5 C Dominant 7th ♯5
1st (C), 3rd (E), ♯5th (G♯), ♭7th (B♭)

C7♯9 C Dominant 7th ♯9
1st (C), 3rd (E), 5th (G),
♭7th (B♭), ♯9th (D♯)

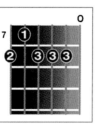

C7♯9 C Dominant 7th ♯9
1st (C), 3rd (E), 5th (G),
♭7th (B♭), ♯9th (D♯)

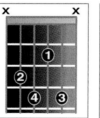

C07 C Diminished 7th
1st (C), ♭3rd (E♭), ♭5th (G♭), ♭♭7th (B♭♭)

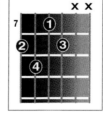

C07 C Diminished 7th
1st (C), ♭3rd (E♭), ♭5th (G♭), ♭♭7th (B♭♭)

C0 C Diminished triad
1st (C), ♭3rd (E♭), ♭5th (G♭)

C0 C Diminished triad
1st (C), ♭3rd (E♭), ♭5th (G♭)

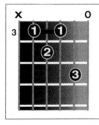

C7♭5 C Dominant 7th ♭5
1st (C), 3rd (E), ♭5th (G♭), ♭7th (B♭)

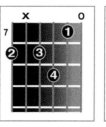

C7♭5 C Dominant 7th ♭5
1st (C), 3rd (E), ♭5th (G♭), ♭7th (B♭)

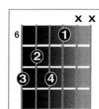

C7♭9 C Dominant 7th ♭9
1st (C), 3rd (E), 5th (G),
♭7th (B♭), ♭9th (D♭)

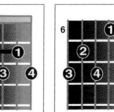

C7♭9 C Dominant 7th ♭9
1st (C), 3rd (E), 5th (G),
♭7th (B♭), ♭9th (D♭)

C9♭5 C Dominant 9th ♭5th
1st (C), 3rd (E), ♭5th (G♭),
♭7th (B♭), 9th (D)

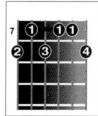

C9♭5 C Dominant 9th ♭5th
1st (C), 3rd (E), ♭5th (G♭),
♭7th (B♭), 9th (D)

C♯/D♭

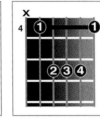

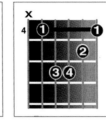

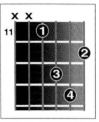

C♯ C♯ Major
1st (C♯), 3rd (E♯), 5th (G♯)

C♯ C♯ Major
1st (C♯), 3rd (E♯), 5th (G♯)

C♯ C♯ Major
1st (C♯), 3rd (E♯), 5th (G♯)

C♯m C♯ Minor
1st (C♯), ♭3rd (E), 5th (G♯)

C♯m C♯ Minor
1st (C♯), ♭3rd (E), 5th (G♯)

C♯m C♯ Minor
1st (C♯), ♭3rd (E), 5th (G♯)

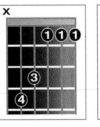
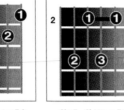
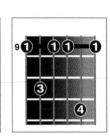

C♯maj7 C♯ Major 7th
1st (C♯), 3rd (E♯), 5th (G♯), 7th (B♯)

C♯maj7 C♯ Major 7th
1st (C♯), 3rd (E♯), 5th (G♯), 7th (B♯)

C♯maj7 C♯ Major 7th
1st (C♯), 3rd (E♯), 5th (G♯), 7th (B♯)

C♯m7 C♯ Minor 7th
1st (C♯), ♭3rd (E), 5th (G♯), ♭7th (B)

C♯m7 C♯ Minor 7th
1st (C♯), ♭3rd (E), 5th (G♯), ♭7th (B)

C♯m7 C♯ Minor 7th
1st (C♯), ♭3rd (E), 5th (G♯), ♭7th (B)

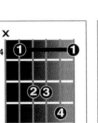
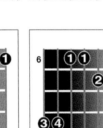
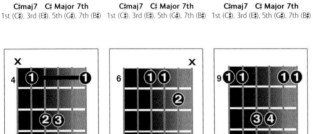

C♯sus4 C♯ Suspended 4th
1st (C♯), 4th (F♯), 5th (G♯)

C♯sus4 C♯ Suspended 4th
1st (C♯), 4th (F♯), 5th (G♯)

C♯sus4 C♯ Suspended 4th
1st (C♯), 4th (F♯), 5th (G♯)

C♯7sus4 C♯ Dominant 7th sus4
1st (C♯), 4th (F♯), 5th (G♯), ♭7th (B)

C♯7sus4 C♯ Dominant 7th sus4
1st (C♯), 4th (F♯), 5th (G♯), ♭7th (B)

C♯7sus4 C♯ Dominant 7th sus4
1st (C♯), 4th (F♯), 5th (G♯), ♭7th (B)

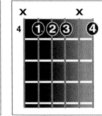

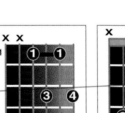
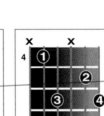
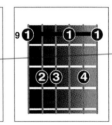

C♯6 C♯ Major 6th
1st (C♯), 3rd (E♯), 5th (G♯), 6th (A♯)

C♯6 C♯ Major 6th
1st (C♯), 3rd (E♯), 5th (G♯), 6th (A♯)

C♯6 C♯ Major 6th
1st (C♯), 3rd (E♯), 5th (G♯), 6th (A♯)

C♯m6 C♯ Minor 6th
1st (C♯), ♭3rd (E), 5th (G♯), 6th (A♯)

C♯m6 C♯ Minor 6th
1st (C♯), ♭3rd (E), 5th (G♯), 6th (A♯)

C♯m6 C♯ Minor 6th
1st (C♯), ♭3rd (E), 5th (G♯), 6th (A♯)

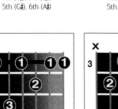

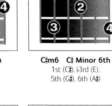
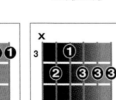
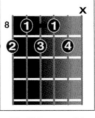
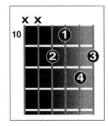

C♯7 C♯ Dominant 7th
1st (C♯), 3rd (E♯), 5th (G♯), ♭7th (B)

C♯7 C♯ Dominant 7th
1st (C♯), 3rd (E♯), 5th (G♯), ♭7th (B)

C♯7 C♯ Dominant 7th
1st (C♯), 3rd (E♯), 5th (G♯), ♭7th (B)

C♯9 C♯ Dominant 9th
1st (C♯), 3rd (E♯), 5th (G♯), ♭7th (B), 9th (D♯)

C♯9 C♯ Dominant 9th
1st (C♯), 3rd (E♯), 5th (G♯), ♭7th (B), 9th (D♯)

C♯9 C♯ Dominant 9th
1st (C♯), 3rd (E♯), 5th (G♯), ♭7th (B), 9th (D♯)

Scale of C#/Db major

C#	D#	E#	F#	G#	A#	B#
1st	2nd	3rd	4th	5th	6th	7th
	9th		11th		13th	

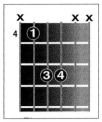

C#5   C# 5th (power chord)
1st (C#). 5th (G#)

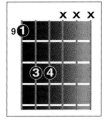

C#5   C# 5th (power chord)
1st (C#). 5th (G#)

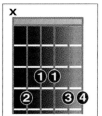

C# 6/9   C# Major 6th add 9th
1st (C#). 3rd (E#). 5th (G#).
6th (A#). 9th (D#)

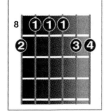

C# 6/9   C# Major 6th add 9th
1st (C#). 3rd (E#). 5th (G#).
6th (A#). 9th (D#)

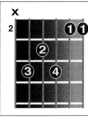

C#11   C# Dominant 11th
1st (C#). 3rd (E#). 5th (G#).
b7th (B). 9th (D#). 11th (F#)

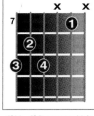

C#11   C# Dominant 11th
1st (C#). 3rd (E#). 5th (G#).
b7th (B). 9th (D#). 11th (F#)

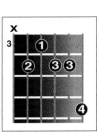

C#13   C# Dominant 13th
1st (C#). 3rd (E#). 5th (G#).
b7th (B). 9th (D#). 13th (A#)

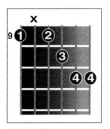

C#13   C# Dominant 13th
1st (C#). 3rd (E#). 5th (G#).
b7th (B). 9th (D#). 13th (A#)

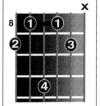

C#add9   C# Major add 9th
1st (C#). 3rd (E#). 5th (G#).
9th (D#)

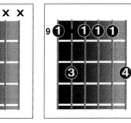

C#add9   C# Major add 9th
1st (C#). 3rd (E#). 5th (G#).
9th (D#)

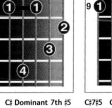

C#m9   C# Minor 9th
1st (C#). b3rd (E). 5th (G#).
b7th (B). 9th (D#)

C#m9   C# Minor 9th
1st (C#). b3rd (E). 5th (G#).
b7th (B). 9th (D#)

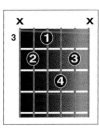

C#maj9   C# Major 9th
1st (C#). 3rd (E#). 5th (G#).
7th (B#). 9th (D#)

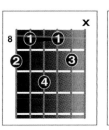

C#maj9   C# Major 9th
1st (C#). 3rd (E#). 5th (G#).
7th (B#). 9th (D#)

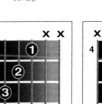

C#+   C# Augmented
1st (C#). 3rd (E#). #5th (Gx)

C#+   C# Augmented
1st (C#). 3rd (E#). #5th (Gx)

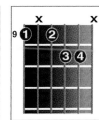

C#7#5   C# Dominant 7th #5
1st (C#). 3rd (E#). #5th (Gx).
b7th (B)

C#7#5   C# Dominant 7th #5
1st (C#). 3rd (E#). #5th (Gx).
b7th (B)

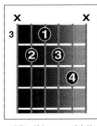

C#7#9   C# Dominant 7th #9
1st (C#). 3rd (E#). 5th (G#).
b7th (B). #9th (Dx)

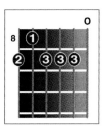

C#7#9   C# Dominant 7th #9
1st (C#). 3rd (E#). 5th (G#).
b7th (B). #9th (Dx)

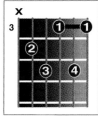

C#07   C# Diminished 7th
1st (C#). b3rd (E). b5th (G).
bb7th (Bb)

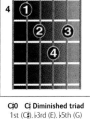

C#07   C# Diminished 7th
1st (C#). b3rd (E). b5th (G).
bb7th (Bb)

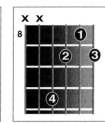

C#0   C# Diminished triad
1st (C#). b3rd (E). b5th (G)

C#0   C# Diminished triad
1st (C#). b3rd (E). b5th (G)

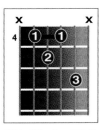

C#7b5   C# Dominant 7th b5
1st (C#). 3rd (E#). b5th (G).
b7th (B)

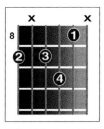

C#7b5   C# Dominant 7th b5
1st (C#). 3rd (E#). b5th (G).
b7th (B)

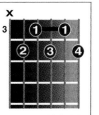

C#7b9   C# Dominant 7th b9
1st (C#). 3rd (E#). 5th (G#).
b7th (B). b9th (D)

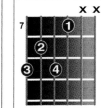
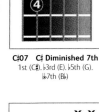

C#7b9   C# Dominant 7th b9
1st (C#). 3rd (E#). 5th (G#).
b7th (B). b9th (D)

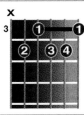
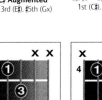
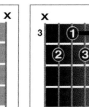

C#9b5   C# Dominant 9th b5th
1st (C#). 3rd (E#). b5th (G).
b7th (B). 9th (D#)

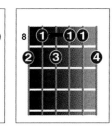

C#9b5   C# Dominant 9th b5th
1st (C#). 3rd (E#). b5th (G).
b7th (B). 9th (D#)

D

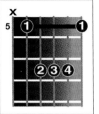
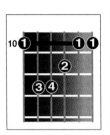
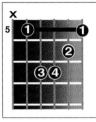
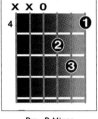

D D Major
1st (D), 3rd (F#), 5th (A)

D D Major
1st (D), 3rd (F#), 5th (A)

D D Major
1st (D), 3rd (F#), 5th (A)

Dm D Minor
1st (D), ♭3rd (F), 5th (A)

Dm D Minor
1st (D), ♭3rd (F), 5th (A)

Dm D Minor
1st (D), ♭3rd (F), 5th (A)

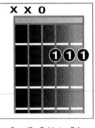
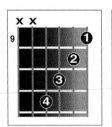
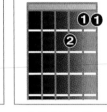
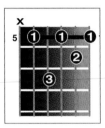
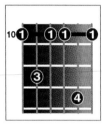
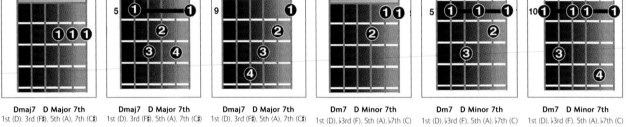

Dmaj7 D Major 7th
1st (D), 3rd (F#), 5th (A), 7th (C#)

Dmaj7 D Major 7th
1st (D), 3rd (F#), 5th (A), 7th (C#)

Dmaj7 D Major 7th
1st (D), 3rd (F#), 5th (A), 7th (C#)

Dm7 D Minor 7th
1st (D), ♭3rd (F), 5th (A), ♭7th (C)

Dm7 D Minor 7th
1st (D), ♭3rd (F), 5th (A), ♭7th (C)

Dm7 D Minor 7th
1st (D), ♭3rd (F), 5th (A), ♭7th (C)

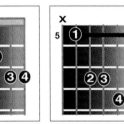
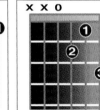
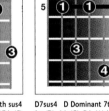

Dsus4 D Suspended 4th
1st (D), 4th (G), 5th (A)

Dsus4 D Suspended 4th
1st (D), 4th (G), 5th (A)

Dsus4 D Suspended 4th
1st (D), 4th (G), 5th (A)

D7sus4 D Dominant 7th sus4
1st (D), 4th (G), 5th (A), ♭7th (C)

D7sus4 D Dominant 7th sus4
1st (D), 4th (G), 5th (A), ♭7th (C)

D7sus4 D Dominant 7th sus4
1st (D), 4th (G), 5th (A), ♭7th (C)

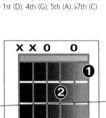

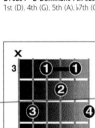
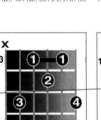

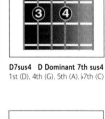

D6 D Major 6th
1st (D), 3rd (F#), 5th (A), 6th (B)

D6 D Major 6th
1st (D), 3rd (F#), 5th (A), 6th (B)

D6 D Major 6th
1st (D), 3rd (F#), 5th (A), 6th (B)

Dm6 D Minor 6th
1st (D), ♭3rd (F), 5th (A), 6th (B)

Dm6 D Minor 6th
1st (D), ♭3rd (F), 5th (A), 6th (B)

Dm6 D Minor 6th
1st (D), ♭3rd (F), 5th (A), 6th (B)

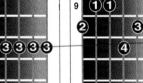

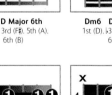

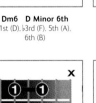
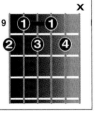
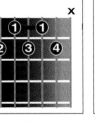

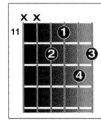

D7 D Dominant 7th
1st (D), 3rd (F#), 5th (A), ♭7th (C)

D7 D Dominant 7th
1st (D), 3rd (F#), 5th (A), ♭7th (C)

D7 D Dominant 7th
1st (D), 3rd (F#), 5th (A), ♭7th (C)

D9 D Dominant 9th
1st (D), 3rd (F#), 5th (A), ♭7th (C), 9th (E)

D9 D Dominant 9th
1st (D), 3rd (F#), 5th (A), ♭7th (C), 9th (E)

D9 D Dominant 9th
1st (D), 3rd (F#), 5th (A), ♭7th (C), 9th (E)

Scale of D major

D	E	F#	G	A	B	C#
1st	2nd	3rd	4th	5th	6th	7th
	9th		11th		13th	

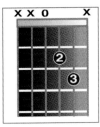
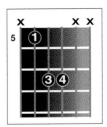
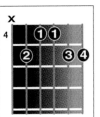
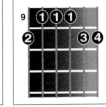
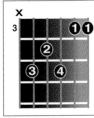
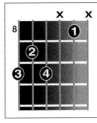

D5 D 5th (power chord)
1st (D). 5th (A)

D5 D 5th (power chord)
1st (D). 5th (A)

D 6/9 D Major 6th add 9th
1st (D). 3rd (F#). 5th (A). 6th (B). 9th (E)

D 6/9 D Major 6th add 9th
1st (D). 3rd (F#). 5th (A). 6th (B). 9th (E)

D11 D Dominant 11th
1st (D). 3rd (F#). 5th (A). b7th (C). 9th (E). 11th (G)

D11 D Dominant 11th
1st (D). 3rd (F#). 5th (A). b7th (C). 9th (E). 11th (G)

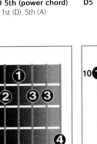
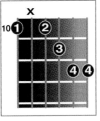
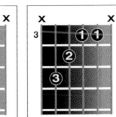
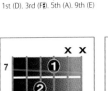
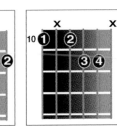
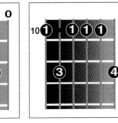

D13 D Dominant 13th
1st (D). 3rd (F#). 5th (A). b7th (C). 9th (E). 13th (B)

D13 D Dominant 13th
1st (D). 3rd (F#). 5th (A). b7th (C). 9th (E). 13th (B)

Dadd9 D Major add 9th
1st (D). 3rd (F#). 5th (A). 9th (E)

Dadd9 D Major add 9th
1st (D). 3rd (F#). 5th (A). 9th (E)

Dm9 D Minor 9th
1st (D). b3rd (F). 5th (A). b7th (C). 9th (E)

Dm9 D Minor 9th
1st (D). b3rd (F). 5th (A). b7th (C). 9th (E)

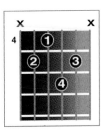

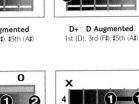
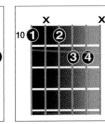
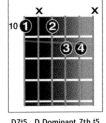

Dmaj9 D Major 9th
1st (D). 3rd (F#). 5th (A). 7th (C#). 9th (E)

Dmaj9 D Major 9th
1st (D). 3rd (F#). 5th (A). 7th (C#). 9th (E)

D+ D Augmented
1st (D). 3rd (F#). #5th (A#)

D+ D Augmented
1st (D). 3rd (F#). #5th (A#)

D7#5 D Dominant 7th #5
1st (D). 3rd (F#). #5th (A#). b7th (C)

D7#5 D Dominant 7th #5
1st (D). 3rd (F#). #5th (A#). b7th (C)

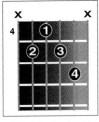

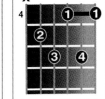
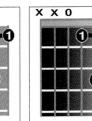
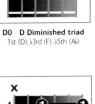
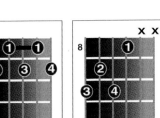

D7#9 D Dominant 7th #9
1st (D). 3rd (F#). 5th (A). b7th (C). #9th (E#)

D7#9 D Dominant 7th #9
1st (D). 3rd (F#). 5th (A). b7th (C). #9th (E#)

Dº7 D Diminished 7th
1st (D). b3rd (F). b5th (Ab). bb7th (Cb)

Dº7 D Diminished 7th
1st (D). b3rd (F). b5th (Ab). bb7th (Cb)

Dº D Diminished triad
1st (D). b3rd (F). b5th (Ab)

Dº D Diminished triad
1st (D). b3rd (F). b5th (Ab)

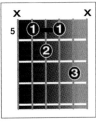
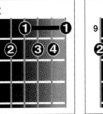
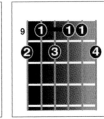

D7b5 D Dominant 7th b5
1st (D). 3rd (F#). b5th (Ab). b7th (C)

D7b5 D Dominant 7th b5
1st (D). 3rd (F#). b5th (Ab). b7th (C)

D7b9 D Dominant 7th b9
1st (D). 3rd (F#). 5th (A). b7th (C). b9th (Eb)

D7b9 D Dominant 7th b9
1st (D). 3rd (F#). 5th (A). b7th (C). b9th (Eb)

D9b5 D Dominant 9th b5th
1st (D). 3rd (F#). b5th (Ab). b7th (C). 9th (E)

D9b5 D Dominant 9th b5th
1st (D). 3rd (F#). b5th (Ab). b7th (C). 9th (E)

E♭/D♯

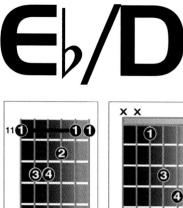

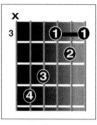
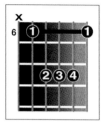

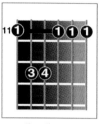

E♭ E♭ Major
1st (E♭), 3rd (G), 5th (B♭)

E♭ E♭ Major
1st (E♭), 3rd (G), 5th (B♭)

E♭ E♭ major
1st (E♭), 3rd (G), 5th (B♭)

E♭m E♭ Minor
1st (E♭), ♭3rd (G♭), 5th (B♭)

E♭m E♭ Minor
1st (E♭), ♭3rd (G♭), 5th (B♭)

E♭m E♭ Minor
1st (E♭), ♭3rd (G♭), 5th (B♭)

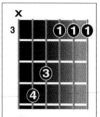
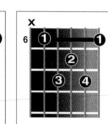
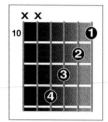
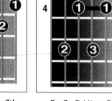
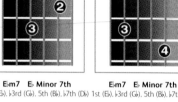

E♭maj7 E♭ Major 7th
1st (E♭), 3rd (G), 5th (B♭), 7th (D)

E♭maj7 E♭ Major 7th
1st (E♭), 3rd (G), 5th (B♭), 7th (D)

E♭maj7 E♭ Major 7th
1st (E♭), 3rd (G), 5th (B♭), 7th (D)

E♭m7 E♭ Minor 7th
1st (E♭), ♭3rd (G♭), 5th (B♭), ♭7th (D♭)

E♭m7 E♭ Minor 7th
1st (E♭), ♭3rd (G♭), 5th (B♭), ♭7th (D♭)

E♭m7 E♭ Minor 7th
1st (E♭), ♭3rd (G♭), 5th (B♭), ♭7th (D♭)

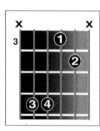
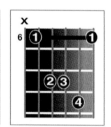

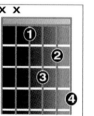

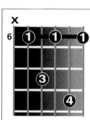
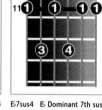

E♭sus4 E♭ Suspended 4th
1st (E♭), 4th (A♭), 5th (B♭)

E♭sus4 E♭ Suspended 4th
1st (E♭), 4th (A♭), 5th (B♭)

E♭sus4 E♭ Suspended 4th
1st (E♭), 4th (A♭), 5th (B♭)

E♭7sus4 E♭ Dominant 7th sus4
1st (E♭), 4th (A♭), 5th (B♭), ♭7th (D♭)

E♭7sus4 E♭ Dominant 7th sus4
1st (E♭), 4th (A♭), 5th (B♭), ♭7th (D♭)

E♭7sus4 E♭ Dominant 7th sus4
1st (E♭), 4th (A♭), 5th (B♭), ♭7th (D♭)

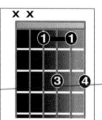
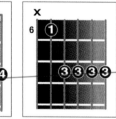
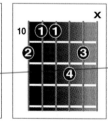
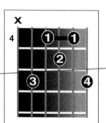
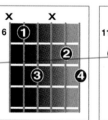
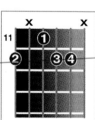

E♭6 E♭ Major 6th
1st (E♭), 3rd (G), 5th (B♭), 6th (C)

E♭6 E♭ Major 6th
1st (E♭), 3rd (G), 5th (B♭), 6th (C)

E♭6 E♭ Major 6th
1st (E♭), 3rd (G), 5th (B♭), 6th (C)

E♭m6 E♭ Minor 6th
1st (E♭), ♭3rd (G♭), 5th (B♭), 6th (C)

E♭m6 E♭ Minor 6th
1st (E♭), ♭3rd (G♭), 5th (B♭), 6th (C)

E♭m6 E♭ Minor 6th
1st (E♭), ♭3rd (G♭), 5th (B♭), 6th (C)

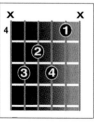
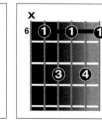
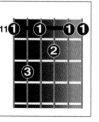
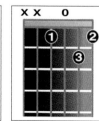
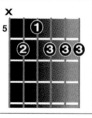
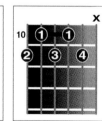

E♭7 E♭ Dominant 7th
1st (E♭), 3rd (G), 5th (B♭), ♭7th (D♭)

E♭7 E♭ Dominant 7th
1st (E♭), 3rd (G), 5th (B♭), ♭7th (D♭)

E♭7 E♭ Dominant 7th
1st (E♭), 3rd (G), 5th (B♭), ♭7th (D♭)

E♭9 E♭ Dominant 9th
1st (E♭), 3rd (G), 5th (B♭), ♭7th (D♭), 9th (F)

E♭9 E♭ Dominant 9th
1st (E♭), 3rd (G), 5th (B♭), ♭7th (D♭), 9th (F)

E♭9 E♭ Dominant 9th
1st (E♭), 3rd (G), 5th (B♭), ♭7th (D♭), 9th (F)

Scale of E♭/D♯ major

E♭	F	G	A♭	B♭	C	D
1st	2nd	3rd	4th	5th	6th	7th
	9th		11th		13th	

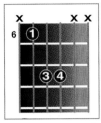

E♭5   E♭ 5th (power chord)
1st (E♭), 5th (B♭)

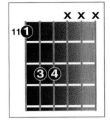

E♭5   E♭ 5th (power chord)
1st (E♭), 5th (B♭)

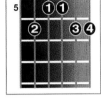

E♭6/9   E♭ Major 6th add 9th
1st (E♭), 3rd (G), 5th (B♭),
6th (C), 9th (F)

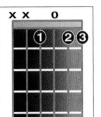

E♭6/9   E♭ Major 6th add 9th
1st (E♭), 3rd (G), 5th (B♭),
6th (C), 9th (F)

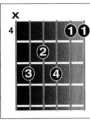

E♭11   E♭ Dominant 11th
1st (E♭), 3rd (G), 5th (B♭),
♭7th (D♭), 9th (F), 11th (A♭)

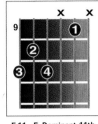

E♭11   E♭ Dominant 11th
1st (E♭), 3rd (G), 5th (B♭),
♭7th (D♭), 9th (F), 11th (A♭)

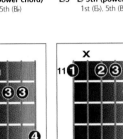

E♭13   E♭ Dominant 13th
1st (E♭), 3rd (G), 5th (B♭),
♭7th (D♭), 9th (F), 13th (C)

E♭13   E♭ Dominant 13th
1st (E♭), 3rd (G), 5th (B♭),
♭7th (D♭), 9th (F), 13th (C)

E♭add9   E♭ Major add 9th
1st (E♭), 3rd (G), 5th (B♭), 9th (F)

E♭add9   E♭ Major add 9th
1st (E♭), 3rd (G), 5th (B♭), 9th (F)

E♭m9   E♭ Minor 9th
1st (E♭), ♭3rd (G♭), 5th (B♭),
♭7th (D♭), 9th (F)

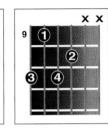

E♭m9   E♭ Minor 9th
1st (E♭), ♭3rd (G♭), 5th (B♭),
♭7th (D♭), 9th (F)

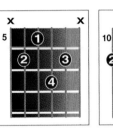

E♭maj9   E♭ Major 9th
1st (E♭), 3rd (G), 5th (B♭),
7th (D), 9th (F)

E♭maj9   E♭ Major 9th
1st (E♭), 3rd (G), 5th (B♭),
7th (D), 9th (F)

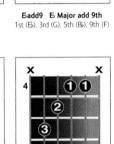

E♭+   E♭ Augmented
1st (E♭), 3rd (G), ♯5th (B)

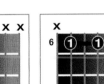

E♭+   E♭ Augmented
1st (E♭), 3rd (G), ♯5th (B)

E♭7♯5   E♭ Dominant 7th ♯5
1st (E♭), 3rd (G),
♯5th (B), ♭7th (D♭)

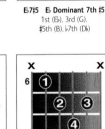

E♭7♯5   E♭ Dominant 7th ♯5
1st (E♭), 3rd (G),
♯5th (B), ♭7th (D♭)

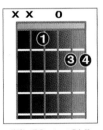

E♭7♯9   E♭ Dominant 7th ♯9
1st (E♭), 3rd (G), 5th (B♭),
♭7th (D♭), ♯9th (F♯)

E♭7♯9   E♭ Dominant 7th ♯9
1st (E♭), 3rd (G), 5th (B♭),
♭7th (D♭), ♯9th (F♯)

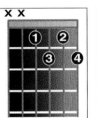
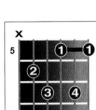
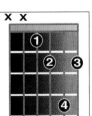

E♭○7   E♭ Diminished 7th
1st (E♭), ♭3rd (G♭),
♭5th (B♭♭), ♭♭7th (D♭♭)

E♭○7   E♭ Diminished 7th
1st (E♭), ♭3rd (G♭),
♭5th (B♭♭), ♭♭7th (D♭♭)

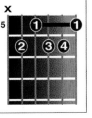

E♭○   E♭ Diminished triad
1st (E♭), ♭3rd (G♭), ♭5th (B♭♭)

E♭○   E♭ Diminished triad
1st (E♭), ♭3rd (G♭), ♭5th (B♭♭)

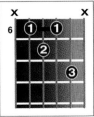

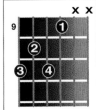
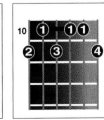

E♭7♭5   E♭ Dominant 7th ♭5
1st (E♭), 3rd (G), ♭5th (B♭♭), ♭7th (D♭)

E♭7♭5   E♭ Dominant 7th ♭5
1st (E♭), 3rd (G), ♭5th (B♭♭), ♭7th (D♭)

E♭7♭9   E♭ Dominant 7th ♭9
1st (E♭), 3rd (G), 5th (B♭),
♭7th (D♭), ♭9th (F♭)

E♭7♭9   E♭ Dominant 7th ♭9
1st (E♭), 3rd (G), 5th (B♭),
♭7th (D♭), ♭9th (F♭)

E♭9♭5   E♭ Dominant 9th ♭5th
1st (E♭), 3rd (G), ♭5th (B♭♭),
♭7th (D♭), 9th (F)

E♭9♭5   E♭ Dominant 9th ♭5th
1st (E♭), 3rd (G), ♭5th (B♭♭),
♭7th (D♭), 9th (F)

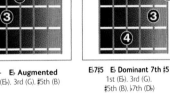
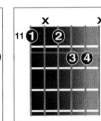

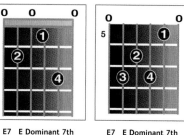

E

 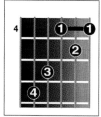 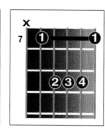 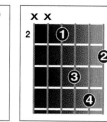 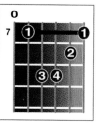

E   E Major
1st (E), 3rd (G♯), 5th (B)

E   E Major
1st (E), 3rd (G♯), 5th (B)

E   E Major
1st (E), 3rd (G♯), 5th (B)

Em   E Minor
1st (E), ♭3rd (G), 5th (B)

Em   E Minor
1st (E), ♭3rd (G), 5th (B)

Em   E Minor
1st (E), ♭3rd (G), 5th (B)

 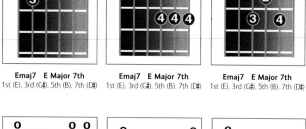 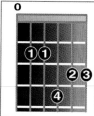 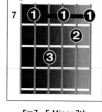

Emaj7   E Major 7th
1st (E), 3rd (G♯), 5th (B), 7th (D♯)

Emaj7   E Major 7th
1st (E), 3rd (G♯), 5th (B), 7th (D♯)

Emaj7   E Major 7th
1st (E), 3rd (G♯), 5th (B), 7th (D♯)

Em7   E Minor 7th
1st (E), ♭3rd (G),
5th (B), ♭7th (D)

Em7   E Minor 7th
1st (E), ♭3rd (G),
5th (B), ♭7th (D)

Em7   E Minor 7th
1st (E), ♭3rd (G),
5th (B), ♭7th (D)

  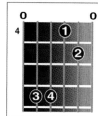 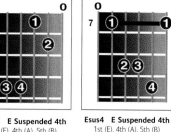 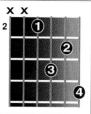 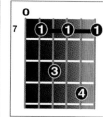

Esus4   E Suspended 4th
1st (E), 4th (A), 5th (B)

Esus4   E Suspended 4th
1st (E), 4th (A), 5th (B)

Esus4   E Suspended 4th
1st (E), 4th (A), 5th (B)

E7sus4   E Dominant 7th sus4
1st (E), 4th (A), 5th (B), ♭7th (D)

E7sus4   E Dominant 7th sus4
1st (E), 4th (A), 5th (B), ♭7th (D)

E7sus4   E Dominant 7th sus4
1st (E), 4th (A), 5th (B), ♭7th (D)

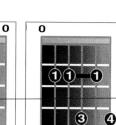 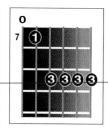 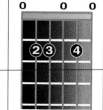  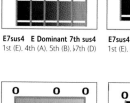 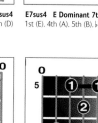 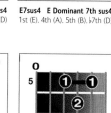 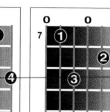

E6   E Major 6th
1st (E), 3rd (G♯),
5th (B), 6th (C♯)

E6   E Major 6th
1st (E), 3rd (G♯),
5th (B), 6th (C♯)

E6   E Major 6th
1st (E), 3rd (G♯),
5th (B), 6th (C♯)

Em6   E Minor 6th
1st (E), ♭3rd (G), 5th (B), 6th (C♯)

Em6   E Minor 6th
1st (E), ♭3rd (G), 5th (B), 6th (C♯)

Em6   E Minor 6th
1st (E), ♭3rd (G), 5th (B), 6th (C♯)

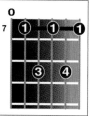 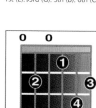 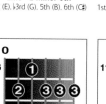

E7   E Dominant 7th
1st (E), 3rd (G♯),
5th (B), ♭7th (D)

E7   E Dominant 7th
1st (E), 3rd (G♯),
5th (B), ♭7th (D)

E7   E Dominant 7th
1st (E), 3rd (G♯),
5th (B), ♭7th (D)

E9   E Dominant 9th
1st (E), 3rd (G♯), 5th (B),
♭7th (D), 9th (F♯)

E9   E Dominant 9th
1st (E), 3rd (G♯), 5th (B),
♭7th (D), 9th (F♯)

E9   E Dominant 9th
1st (E), 3rd (G♯), 5th (B),
♭7th (D), 9th (F♯)

Scale of E major

E	F#	G#	A	B	C#	D#
1st	2nd	3rd	4th	5th	6th	7th
	9th		11th		13th	

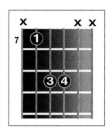

E5 E 5th (power chord)
1st (E), 5th (B)

E5 E 5th (power chord)
1st (E), 5th (B)

E 6/9 E Major 6th add 9th
1st (E), 3rd (G#), 5th (B), 6th (C#), 9th (F#)

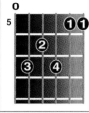

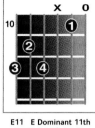

E 6/9 E Major 6th add 9th
1st (E), 3rd (G#), 5th (B), 6th (C#), 9th (F#)

E11 E Dominant 11th
1st (E), 3rd (G#), 5th (B), ♭7th (D), 9th (F#), 11th (A)

E11 E Dominant 11th
1st (E), 3rd (G#), 5th (B), ♭7th (D), 9th (F#), 11th (A)

E13 E Dominant 13th
1st (E), 3rd (G#), 5th (B), ♭7th (D), 9th (F#), 13th (C#)

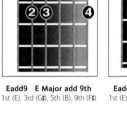

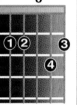
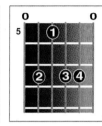

E13 E Dominant 13th
1st (E), 3rd (G#), 5th (B), ♭7th (D), 9th (F#), 13th (C#)

Eadd9 E Major add 9th
1st (E), 3rd (G#), 5th (B), 9th (F#)

Eadd9 E Major add 9th
1st (E), 3rd (G#), 5th (B), 9th (F#)

Em9 E Minor 9th
1st (E), ♭3rd (G), 5th (B), ♭7th (D), 9th (F#)

Em9 E Minor 9th
1st (E), ♭3rd (G), 5th (B), ♭7th (D), 9th (F#)

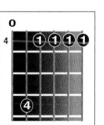

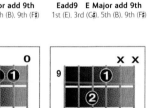
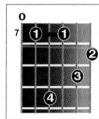

Emaj9 E Major 9th
1st (E), 3rd (G#), 5th (B), 7th (D#), 9th (F#)

Emaj9 E Major 9th
1st (E), 3rd (G#), 5th (B), 7th (D#), 9th (F#)

E+ E Augmented
1st (E), 3rd (G#), #5th (B#)

E+ E Augmented
1st (E), 3rd (G#), #5th (B#)

E7#5 E Dominant 7th #5
1st (E), 3rd (G#), #5th (B#), ♭7th (D)

E7#5 E Dominant 7th #5
1st (E), 3rd (G#), #5th (B#), ♭7th (D)

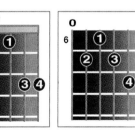
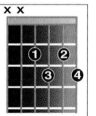

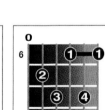
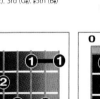

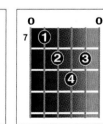

E7#9 E Dominant 7th #9
1st (E), 3rd (G#), 5th (B), ♭7th (D), #9th (Fx)

E7#9 E Dominant 7th #9
1st (E), 3rd (G#), 5th (B), ♭7th (D), #9th (Fx)

E07 E Diminished 7th
1st (E), ♭3rd (G), ♭5th (B♭), ♭♭7th (D♭)

E07 E Diminished 7th
1st (E), ♭3rd (G), ♭5th (B♭), ♭♭7th (D♭)

E0 E Diminished triad
1st (E), ♭3rd (G), ♭5th (B♭)

E0 E Diminished triad
1st (E), ♭3rd (G), ♭5th (B♭)

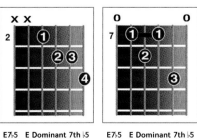
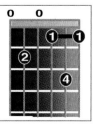
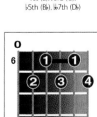
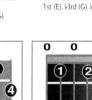

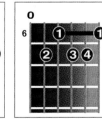

E7♭5 E Dominant 7th ♭5
1st (E), 3rd (G#), ♭5th (B♭), ♭7th (D)

E7♭5 E Dominant 7th ♭5
1st (E), 3rd (G#), ♭5th (B♭), ♭7th (D)

E7♭9 E Dominant 7th ♭9
1st (E), 3rd (G#), 5th (B), ♭7th (D), ♭9th (F)

E7♭9 E Dominant 7th ♭9
1st (E), 3rd (G#), 5th (B), ♭7th (D), ♭9th (F)

E9♭5 E Dominant 9th ♭5th
1st (E), 3rd (G#), ♭5th (B♭), ♭7th (D), 9th (F#)

E9♭5 E Dominant 9th ♭5th
1st (E), 3rd (G#), ♭5th (B♭), ♭7th (D), 9th (F#)

F

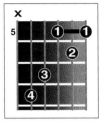

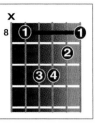
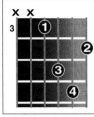

F F Major
1st (F), 3rd (A), 5th (C)

F F Major
1st (F), 3rd (A), 5th (C)

F F Major
1st (F), 3rd (A), 5th (C)

Fm F Minor
1st (F), b3rd (Ab), 5th (C)

Fm F Minor
1st (F), b3rd (Ab), 5th (C)

Fm F Minor
1st (F), b3rd (Ab), 5th (C)

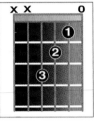
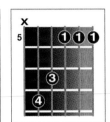
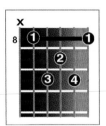
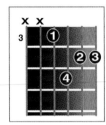
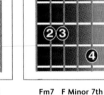
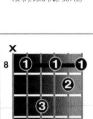

Fmaj7 F Major 7th
1st (F), 3rd (A), 5th (C), 7th (E)

Fmaj7 F Major 7th
1st (F), 3rd (A), 5th (C), 7th (E)

Fmaj7 F Major 7th
1st (F), 3rd (A), 5th (C), 7th (E)

Fm7 F Minor 7th
1st (F), b3rd (Ab), 5th (C), b7th (Eb)

Fm7 F Minor 7th
1st (F), b3rd (Ab), 5th (C), b7th (Eb)

Fm7 F Minor 7th
1st (F), b3rd (Ab), 5th (C), b7th (Eb)

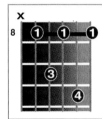
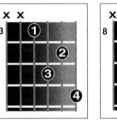
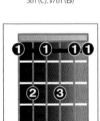

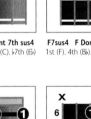

Fsus4 F Suspended 4th
1st (F), 4th (Bb), 5th (C)

Fsus4 F Suspended 4th
1st (F), 4th (Bb), 5th (C)

Fsus4 F Suspended 4th
1st (F), 4th (Bb), 5th (C)

F7sus4 F Dominant 7th sus4
1st (F), 4th (Bb), 5th (C), b7th (Eb)

F7sus4 F Dominant 7th sus4
1st (F), 4th (Bb), 5th (C), b7th (Eb)

F7sus4 F Dominant 7th sus4
1st (F), 4th (Bb), 5th (C), b7th (Eb)

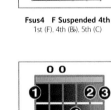
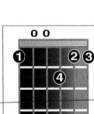
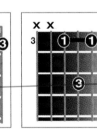
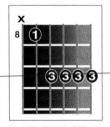
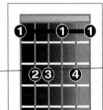
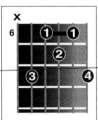
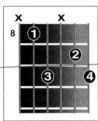

F6 F Major 6th
1st (F), 3rd (A), 5th (C), 6th (D)

F6 F Major 6th
1st (F), 3rd (A), 5th (C), 6th (D)

F6 F Major 6th
1st (F), 3rd (A), 5th (C), 6th (D)

Fm6 F Minor 6th
1st (F), b3rd (Ab), 5th (C), 6th (D)

Fm6 F Minor 6th
1st (F), b3rd (Ab), 5th (C), 6th (D)

Fm6 F Minor 6th
1st (F), b3rd (Ab), 5th (C), 6th (D)

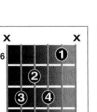

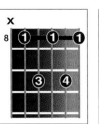
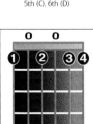

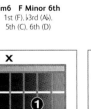

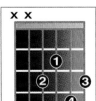
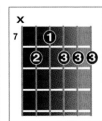

F7 F Dominant 7th
1st (F), 3rd (A), 5th (C), b7th (Eb)

F7 F Dominant 7th
1st (F), 3rd (A), 5th (C), b7th (Eb)

F7 F Dominant 7th
1st (F), 3rd (A), 5th (C), b7th (Eb)

F9 F Dominant 9th
1st (F), 3rd (A), 5th (C), b7th (Eb), 9th (G)

F9 F Dominant 9th
1st (F), 3rd (A), 5th (C), b7th (Eb), 9th (G)

F9 F Dominant 9th
1st (F), 3rd (A), 5th (C), b7th (Eb), 9th (G)

Scale of F major						
F	G	A	B♭	C	D	E
1st	2nd	3rd	4th	5th	6th	7th
	9th		11th		13th	

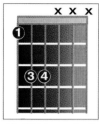

F5 F 5th (power chord)
1st (F), 5th (C)

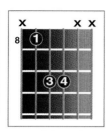

F5 F 5th (power chord)
1st (F), 5th (C)

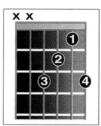

F 6/9 F Major 6th add 9th
1st (F), 3rd (A), 5th (C),
6th (D), 9th (G)

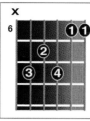

F 6/9 F Major 6th add 9th
1st (F), 3rd (A), 5th (C),
6th (D), 9th (G)

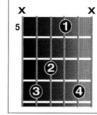

F11 F Dominant 11th
1st (F), 3rd (A), 5th (C),
♭7th (E♭), 9th (G), 11th (B♭)

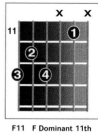

F11 F Dominant 11th
1st (F), 3rd (A), 5th (C),
♭7th (E♭), 9th (G), 11th (B♭)

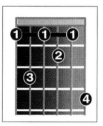

F13 F Dominant 13th
1st (F), 3rd (A), 5th (C),
♭7th (E♭), 9th (G), 13th (D)

F13 F Dominant 13th
1st (F), 3rd (A), 5th (C),
♭7th (E♭), 9th (G), 13th (D)

Fadd9 F Major add 9th
1st (F), 3rd (A), 5th (C), 9th (G)

Fadd9 F Major add 9th
1st (F), 3rd (A), 5th (C), 9th (G)

Fm9 F Minor 9th
1st (F), ♭3rd (A♭), 5th (C),
♭7th (E♭), 9th (G)

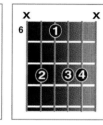

Fm9 F Minor 9th
1st (F), ♭3rd (A♭), 5th (C),
♭7th (E♭), 9th (G)

Fmaj9 F Major 9th
1st (F), 3rd (A), 5th (C),
7th (E), 9th (G)

Fmaj9 F Major 9th
1st (F), 3rd (A), 5th (C),
7th (E), 9th (G)

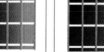

F+ F Augmented
1st (F), 3rd (A), ♯5th (C♯)

F+ F Augmented
1st (F), 3rd (A), ♯5th (C♯)

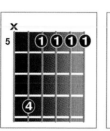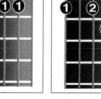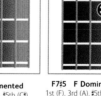

F7♯5 F Dominant 7th ♯5
1st (F), 3rd (A), ♯5th (C♯), ♭7th (E♭)

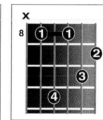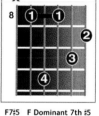

F7♯5 F Dominant 7th ♯5
1st (F), 3rd (A), ♯5th (C♯), ♭7th (E♭)

F7♯9 F Dominant 7th ♯9
1st (F), 3rd (A), 5th (C),
♭7th (E♭), ♯9th (G♯)

F7♯9 F Dominant 7th ♯9
1st (F), 3rd (A), 5th (C),
♭7th (E♭), ♯9th (G♯)

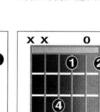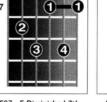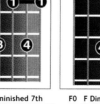

F07 F Diminished 7th
1st (F), ♭3rd (A♭), ♭5th (C♭), ♭♭7th (E♭♭)

F07 F Diminished 7th
1st (F), ♭3rd (A♭), ♭5th (C♭), ♭♭7th (E♭♭)

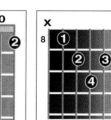

F0 F Diminished triad
1st (F), ♭3rd (A♭), ♭5th (C♭)

F0 F Diminished triad
1st (F), ♭3rd (A♭), ♭5th (C♭)

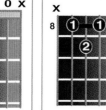

F7♭5 F Dominant 7th ♭5
1st (F), 3rd (A), ♭5th (C♭), ♭7th (E♭)

F7♭5 F Dominant 7th ♭5
1st (F), 3rd (A), ♭5th (C♭), ♭7th (E♭)

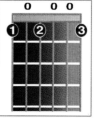

F7♭9 F Dominant 7th ♭9
1st (F), 3rd (A), 5th (C),
♭7th (E♭), ♭9th (G♭)

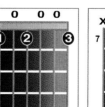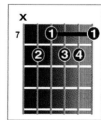

F7♭9 F Dominant 7th ♭9
1st (F), 3rd (A), 5th (C),
♭7th (E♭), ♭9th (G♭)

F9♭5 F Dominant 9th ♭5th
1st (F), 3rd (A), ♭5th (C♭),
♭7th (E♭), 9th (G)

F9♭5 F Dominant 9th ♭5th
1st (F), 3rd (A), ♭5th (C♭),
♭7th (E♭), 9th (G)

F#/Gb

 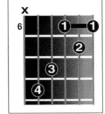 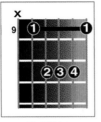 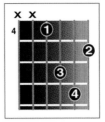  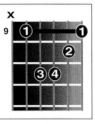

F# F# Major
1st (F#), 3rd (A#), 5th (C#)

F# F# Major
1st (F#), 3rd (A#), 5th (C#)

F# F# Major
1st (F#), 3rd (A#), 5th (C#)

F#m F# Minor
1st (F#), b3rd (A), 5th (C#)

F#m F# Minor
1st (F#), b3rd (A), 5th (C#)

F#m F# Minor
1st (F#), b3rd (A), 5th (C#)

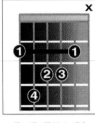 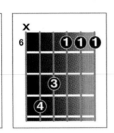 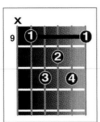 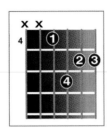 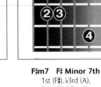 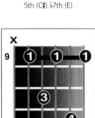

F#maj7 F# Major 7th
1st (F#), 3rd (A#), 5th (C#), 7th (E#)

F#maj7 F# Major 7th
1st (F#), 3rd (A#), 5th (C#), 7th (E#)

F#maj7 F# Major 7th
1st (F#), 3rd (A#), 5th (C#), 7th (E#)

F#m7 F# Minor 7th
1st (F#), b3rd (A), 5th (C#), b7th (E)

F#m7 F# Minor 7th
1st (F#), b3rd (A), 5th (C#), b7th (E)

F#m7 F# Minor 7th
1st (F#), b3rd (A), 5th (C#), b7th (E)

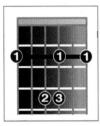 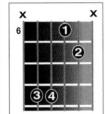 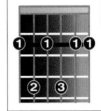 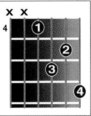 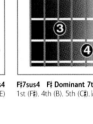 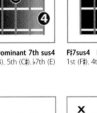

F#sus4 F# Suspended 4th
1st (F#), 4th (B), 5th (C#)

F#sus4 F# Suspended 4th
1st (F#), 4th (B), 5th (C#)

F#sus4 F# Suspended 4th
1st (F#), 4th (B), 5th (C#)

F#7sus4 F# Dominant 7th sus4
1st (F#), 4th (B), 5th (C#), b7th (E)

F#7sus4 F# Dominant 7th sus4
1st (F#), 4th (B), 5th (C#), b7th (E)

F#7sus4 F# Dominant 7th sus4
1st (F#), 4th (B), 5th (C#), b7th (E)

    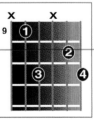 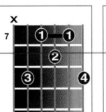

F#6 F# Major 6th
1st (F#), 3rd (A#), 5th (C#), 6th (D#)

F#6 F# Major 6th
1st (F#), 3rd (A#), 5th (C#), 6th (D#)

F#6 F# Major 6th
1st (F#), 3rd (A#), 5th (C#), 6th (D#)

F#m6 F# Minor 6th
1st (F#), b3rd (A), 5th (C#), 6th (D#)

F#m6 F# Minor 6th
1st (F#), b3rd (A), 5th (C#), 6th (D#)

F#m6 F# Minor 6th
1st (F#), b3rd (A), 5th (C#), 6th (D#)

  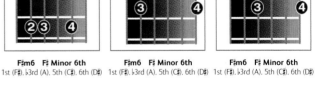 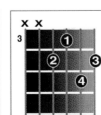 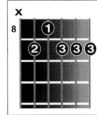

F#7 F# Dominant 7th
1st (F#), 3rd (A#), 5th (C#), b7th (E)

F#7 F# Dominant 7th
1st (F#), 3rd (A#), 5th (C#), b7th (E)

F#7 F# Dominant 7th
1st (F#), 3rd (A#), 5th (C#), b7th (E)

F#9 F# Dominant 9th
1st (F#), 3rd (A#), 5th (C#), b7th (E), 9th (G#)

F#9 F# Dominant 9th
1st (F#), 3rd (A#), 5th (C#), b7th (E), 9th (G#)

F#9 F# Dominant 9th
1st (F#), 3rd (A#), 5th (C#), b7th (E), 9th (G#)

Scale of F♯/G♭ major

F♯	G♯	A♯	B	C♯	D♯	E♯
1st	2nd	3rd	4th	5th	6th	7th
	9th		11th		13th	

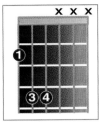
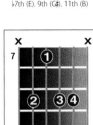
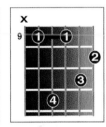
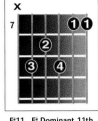
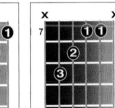
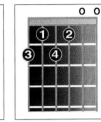
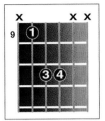

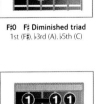

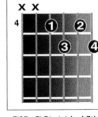

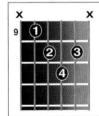
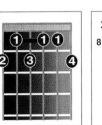
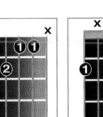

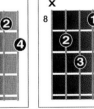
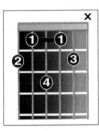
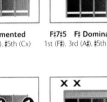
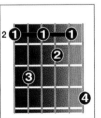
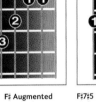

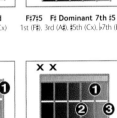
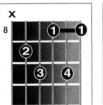
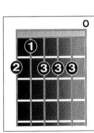

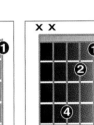
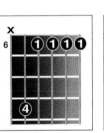
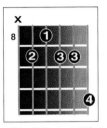
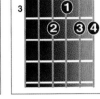

F♯5 F♯ 5th (power chord)
1st (F♯), 5th (C♯)

F♯5 F♯ 5th (power chord)
1st (F♯), 5th (C♯)

F♯ 6/9 F♯ Major 6th add 9th
1st (F♯), 3rd (A♯), 5th (C♯),
6th (D♯), 9th (G♯)

F♯ 6/9 F♯ Major 6th add 9th
1st (F♯), 3rd (A♯), 5th (C♯),
6th (D♯), 9th (G♯)

F♯11 F♯ Dominant 11th
1st (F♯), 3rd (A♯), 5th (C♯),
♭7th (E), 9th (G♯), 11th (B)

F♯11 F♯ Dominant 11th
1st (F♯), 3rd (A♯), 5th (C♯),
♭7th (E), 9th (G♯), 11th (B)

F♯13 F♯ Dominant 13th
1st (F♯), 3rd (A♯), 5th (C♯),
♭7th (E), 9th (G♯), 13th (D♯)

F♯13 F♯ Dominant 13th
1st (F♯), 3rd (A♯), 5th (C♯),
♭7th (E), 9th (G♯), 13th (D♯)

F♯add9 F♯ Major add 9th
1st (F♯), 3rd (A♯), 5th (C♯), 9th (G♯)

F♯add9 F♯ Major add 9th
1st (F♯), 3rd (A♯), 5th (C♯), 9th (G♯)

F♯m9 F♯ Minor 9th
1st (F♯), ♭3rd (A), 5th (C♯),
♭7th (E), 9th (G♯)

F♯m9 F♯ Minor 9th
1st (F♯), ♭3rd (A), 5th (C♯),
♭7th (E), 9th (G♯)

F♯maj9 F♯ Major 9th
1st (F♯), 3rd (A♯), 5th (C♯),
7th (E♯), 9th (G♯)

F♯maj9 F♯ Major 9th
1st (F♯), 3rd (A♯), 5th (C♯),
7th (E♯), 9th (G♯)

F♯+ F♯ Augmented
1st (F♯), 3rd (A♯), ♯5th (Cx)

F♯+ F♯ Augmented
1st (F♯), 3rd (A♯), ♯5th (Cx)

F♯7♯5 F♯ Dominant 7th ♯5
1st (F♯), 3rd (A♯), ♯5th (Cx), ♭7th (E)

F♯7♯5 F♯ Dominant 7th ♯5
1st (F♯), 3rd (A♯), ♯5th (Cx), ♭7th (E)

F♯7♯9 F♯ Dominant 7th ♯9
1st (F♯), 3rd (A♯), 5th (C♯),
♭7th (E), ♯9th (Gx)

F♯7♯9 F♯ Dominant 7th ♯9
1st (F♯), 3rd (A♯), 5th (C♯),
♭7th (E), ♯9th (Gx)

F♯○7 F♯ Diminished 7th
1st (F♯), ♭3rd (A), ♭5th (C), ♭♭7th (E♭)

F♯○7 F♯ Diminished 7th
1st (F♯), ♭3rd (A), ♭5th (C), ♭♭7th (E♭)

F♯○ F♯ Diminished triad
1st (F♯), ♭3rd (A), ♭5th (C)

F♯○ F♯ Diminished triad
1st (F♯), ♭3rd (A), ♭5th (C)

F♯7♭5 F♯ Dominant 7th ♭5
1st (F♯), 3rd (A♯), ♭5th (C), ♭7th (E)

F♯7♭5 F♯ Dominant 7th ♭5
1st (F♯), 3rd (A♯), ♭5th (C), ♭7th (E)

F♯7♭9 F♯ Dominant 7th ♭9
1st (F♯), 3rd (A♯), 5th (C♯),
♭7th (E), ♭9th (G)

F♯7♭9 F♯ Dominant 7th ♭9
1st (F♯), 3rd (A♯), 5th (C♯),
♭7th (E), ♭9th (G)

F♯9♭5 F♯ Dominant 9th ♭5th
1st (F♯), 3rd (A♯), ♭5th (C),
♭7th (E), 9th (G♯)

F♯9♭5 F♯ Dominant 9th ♭5th
1st (F♯), 3rd (A♯), ♭5th (C),
♭7th (E), 9th (G♯)

G

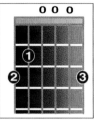
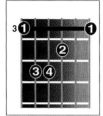
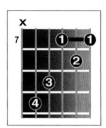
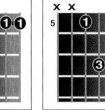
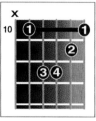

G G Major
1st (G), 3rd (B), 5th (D)

G G Major
1st (G), 3rd (B), 5th (D)

G G Major
1st (G), 3rd (B), 5th (D)

Gm G Minor
1st (G), b3rd (Bb), 5th (D)

Gm G Minor
1st (G), b3rd (Bb), 5th (D)

Gm G Minor
1st (G), b3rd (Bb), 5th (D)

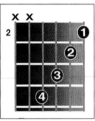
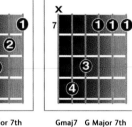
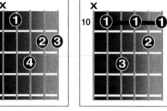

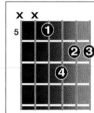
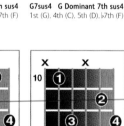

Gmaj7 G Major 7th
1st (G), 3rd (B), 5th (D), 7th (F#)

Gmaj7 G Major 7th
1st (G), 3rd (B), 5th (D), 7th (F#)

Gmaj7 G Major 7th
1st (G), 3rd (B), 5th (D), 7th (F#)

Gm7 G Minor 7th
1st (G), b3rd (Bb), 5th (D), b7th (F)

Gm7 G Minor 7th
1st (G), b3rd (Bb), 5th (D), b7th (F)

Gm7 G Minor 7th
1st (G), b3rd (Bb), 5th (D), b7th (F)

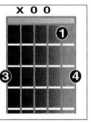

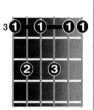
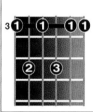
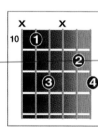

Gsus4 G Suspended 4th
1st (G), 4th (C), 5th (D)

Gsus4 G Suspended 4th
1st (G), 4th (C), 5th (D)

Gsus4 G Suspended 4th
1st (G), 4th (C), 5th (D)

G7sus4 G Dominant 7th sus4
1st (G), 4th (C), 5th (D), b7th (F)

G7sus4 G Dominant 7th sus4
1st (G), 4th (C), 5th (D), b7th (F)

G7sus4 G Dominant 7th sus4
1st (G), 4th (C), 5th (D), b7th (F)

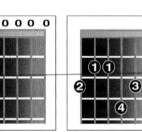
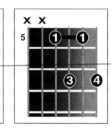
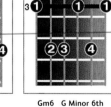
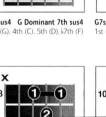

G6 G Major 6th
1st (G), 3rd (B), 5th (D), 6th (E)

G6 G Major 6th
1st (G), 3rd (B), 5th (D), 6th (E)

G6 G Major 6th
1st (G), 3rd (B), 5th (D), 6th (E)

Gm6 G Minor 6th
1st (G), b3rd (Bb), 5th (D), 6th (E)

Gm6 G Minor 6th
1st (G), b3rd (Bb), 5th (D), 6th (E)

Gm6 G Minor 6th
1st (G), b3rd (Bb), 5th (D), 6th (E)

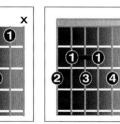

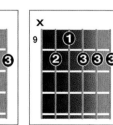
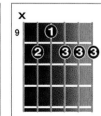

G7 G Dominant 7th
1st (G), 3rd (B), 5th (D), b7th (F)

G7 G Dominant 7th
1st (G), 3rd (B), 5th (D), b7th (F)

G7 G Dominant 7th
1st (G), 3rd (B), 5th (D), b7th (F)

G9 G Dominant 9th
1st (G), 3rd (B), 5th (D), b7th (F), 9th (A)

G9 G Dominant 9th
1st (G), 3rd (B), 5th (D), b7th (F), 9th (A)

G9 G Dominant 9th
1st (G), 3rd (B), 5th (D), b7th (F), 9th (A)

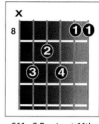

Scale of G major

G	A	B	C	D	E	F#
1st	2nd	3rd	4th	5th	6th	7th
	9th		11th		13th	

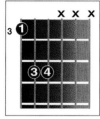 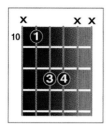  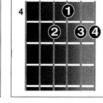 

G5 G 5th (power chord)
1st (G), 5th (D)

G5 G 5th (power chord)
1st (G), 5th (D)

G 6/9 G Major 6th add 9th
1st (G), 3rd (B), 5th (D),
6th (E), 9th (A)

G 6/9 G Major 6th add 9th
1st (G), 3rd (B), 5th (D),
6th (E), 9th (A)

G11 G Dominant 11th
1st (G), 3rd (B), 5th (D),
♭7th (F), 9th (A), 11th (C)

G11 G Dominant 11th
1st (G), 3rd (B), 5th (D),
♭7th (F), 9th (A), 11th (C)

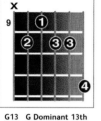 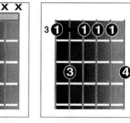

G13 G Dominant 13th
1st (G), 3rd (B), 5th (D),
♭7th (F), 9th (A), 13th (E)

G13 G Dominant 13th
1st (G), 3rd (B), 5th (D),
♭7th (F), 9th (A), 13th (E)

Gadd9 G Major add 9th
1st (G), 3rd (B), 5th (D), 9th (A)

Gadd9 G Major add 9th
1st (G), 3rd (B), 5th (D), 9th (A)

Gm9 G Minor 9th
1st (G), ♭3rd (B♭), 5th (D),
♭7th (F), 9th (A)

Gm9 G Minor 9th
1st (G), ♭3rd (B♭), 5th (D),
♭7th (F), 9th (A)

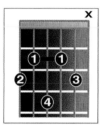 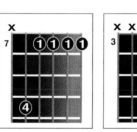 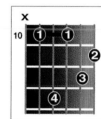 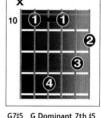

Gmaj9 G Major 9th
1st (G), 3rd (B), 5th (D),
7th (F#), 9th (A)

Gmaj9 G Major 9th
1st (G), 3rd (B), 5th (D),
7th (F#), 9th (A)

G+ G Augmented
1st (G), 3rd (B), #5th (D#)

G+ G Augmented
1st (G), 3rd (B), #5th (D#)

G7#5 G Dominant 7th #5
1st (G), 3rd (B), #5th (D#), ♭7th (F)

G7#5 G Dominant 7th #5
1st (G), 3rd (B), #5th (D#), ♭7th (F)

 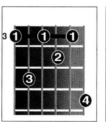 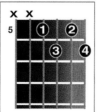 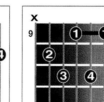 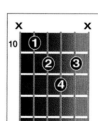

G7#9 G Dominant 7th #9
1st (G), 3rd (B), 5th (D),
♭7th (F), #9th (A#)

G7#9 G Dominant 7th #9
1st (G), 3rd (B), 5th (D),
♭7th (F), #9th (A#)

G07 G Diminished 7th
1st (G), ♭3rd (B♭), ♭5th (D♭), ♭♭7th (F♭)

G07 G Diminished 7th
1st (G), ♭3rd (B♭), ♭5th (D♭), ♭♭7th (F♭)

G0 G Diminished triad
1st (G), ♭3rd (B♭), ♭5th (D♭)

G0 G Diminished triad
1st (G), ♭3rd (B♭), ♭5th (D♭)

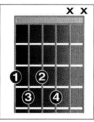 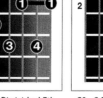  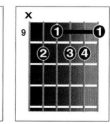

G7♭5 G Dominant 7th ♭5
1st (G), 3rd (B), ♭5th (D♭), ♭7th (F)

G7♭5 G Dominant 7th ♭5
1st (G), 3rd (B), ♭5th (D♭), ♭7th (F)

G7♭9 G Dominant 7th ♭9
1st (G), 3rd (B), 5th (D),
♭7th (F), ♭9th (A♭)

G7♭9 G Dominant 7th ♭9
1st (G), 3rd (B), 5th (D),
♭7th (F), ♭9th (A♭)

G9♭5 G Dominant 9th ♭5
1st (G), 3rd (B), ♭5th (D♭),
♭7th (F), 9th (A)

G9♭5 G Dominant 9th ♭5
1st (G), 3rd (B), ♭5th (D♭),
♭7th (F), 9th (A)

A♭/G♯

340

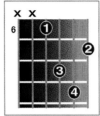
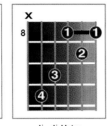
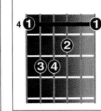
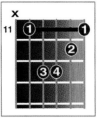

A♭ A♭ Major
1st (A♭), 3rd (C), 5th (E♭)

A♭ A♭ Major
1st (A♭), 3rd (C), 5th (E♭)

A♭ A♭ Major
1st (A♭), 3rd (C), 5th (E♭)

A♭m A♭ Minor
1st (A♭), ♭3rd (C♭), 5th (E♭)

A♭m A♭ Minor
1st (A♭), ♭3rd (C♭), 5th (E♭)

A♭m A♭ Minor
1st (A♭), ♭3rd (C♭), 5th (E♭)

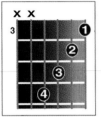
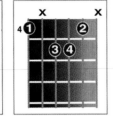
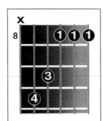
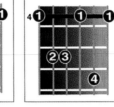
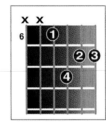

A♭maj7 A♭ Major 7th
1st (A♭), 3rd (C),
5th (E♭), 7th (G)

A♭maj7 A♭ Major 7th
1st (A♭), 3rd (C),
5th (E♭), 7th (G)

A♭maj7 A♭ Major 7th
1st (A♭), 3rd (C),
5th (E♭), 7th (G)

A♭m7 A♭ Minor 7th
1st (A♭), ♭3rd (C♭),
5th (E♭), ♭7th (G♭)

A♭m7 A♭ Minor 7th
1st (A♭), ♭3rd (C♭),
5th (E♭), ♭7th (G♭)

A♭m7 A♭ Minor 7th
1st (A♭), ♭3rd (C♭),
5th (E♭), ♭7th (G♭)

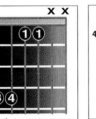
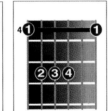
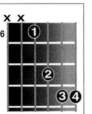

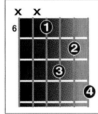
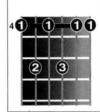

A♭sus4 A♭ Suspended 4th
1st (A♭), 4th (D♭), 5th (E♭)

A♭sus4 A♭ Suspended 4th
1st (A♭), 4th (D♭), 5th (E♭)

A♭sus4 A♭ Suspended 4th
1st (A♭), 4th (D♭), 5th (E♭)

A♭7sus4 A♭ Dominant 7th sus4
1st (A♭), 4th (D♭), 5th (E♭),
♭7th (G♭)

A♭7sus4 A♭ Dominant 7th sus4
1st (A♭), 4th (D♭), 5th (E♭),
♭7th (G♭)

A♭7sus4 A♭ Dominant 7th sus4
1st (A♭), 4th (D♭), 5th (E♭),
♭7th (G♭)

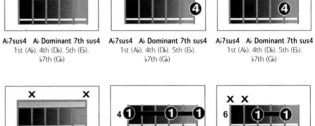
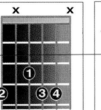
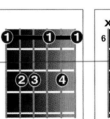
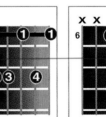
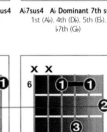

A♭6 A♭ Major 6th
1st (A♭), 3rd (C), 5th (E♭),
6th (F)

A♭6 A♭ Major 6th
1st (A♭), 3rd (C), 5th (E♭),
6th (F)

A♭6 A♭ Major 6th
1st (A♭), 3rd (C), 5th (E♭),
6th (F)

A♭m6 A♭ Minor 6th
1st (A♭), ♭3rd (C♭), 5th (E♭),
6th (F)

A♭m6 A♭ Minor 6th
1st (A♭), ♭3rd (C♭), 5th (E♭),
6th (F)

A♭m6 A♭ Minor 6th
1st (A♭), ♭3rd (C♭), 5th (E♭),
6th (F)

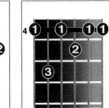
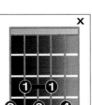
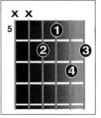
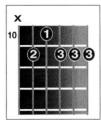

A♭7 A♭ Dominant 7th
1st (A♭), 3rd (C), 5th (E♭),
♭7th (G♭)

A♭7 A♭ Dominant 7th
1st (A♭), 3rd (C), 5th (E♭),
♭7th (G♭)

A♭7 A♭ Dominant 7th
1st (A♭), 3rd (C), 5th (E♭),
♭7th (G♭)

A♭9 A♭ Dominant 9th
1st (A♭), 3rd (C), 5th (E♭),
♭7th (G♭), 9th (B♭)

A♭9 A♭ Dominant 9th
1st (A♭), 3rd (C), 5th (E♭),
♭7th (G♭), 9th (B♭)

A♭9 A♭ Dominant 9th
1st (A♭), 3rd (C), 5th (E♭),
♭7th (G♭), 9th (B♭)

Scale of A♭/G♯ major						
A♭	B♭	C	D♭	E♭	F	G
1st	2nd	3rd	4th	5th	6th	7th
	9th		11th		13th	

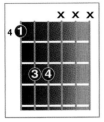

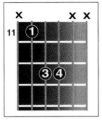

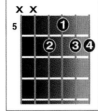

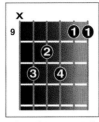

A♭5 A♭ 5th (power chord)
1st (A♭), 5th (E♭)

A♭5 A♭ 5th (power chord)
1st (A♭), 5th (E♭)

A♭6/9 A♭ Major 6th add 9th
1st (A♭), 3rd (C), 5th (E♭),
6th (F), 9th (B♭)

A♭6/9 A♭ Major 6th add 9th
1st (A♭), 3rd (C), 5th (E♭),
6th (F), 9th (B♭)

A♭11 A♭ Dominant 11th
1st (A♭), 3rd (C), 5th (E♭),
♭7th (G♭), 9th (B♭), 11th (D♭)

A♭11 A♭ Dominant 11th
1st (A♭), 3rd (C), 5th (E♭),
♭7th (G♭), 9th (B♭), 11th (D♭)

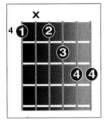

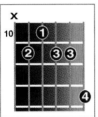

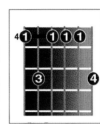

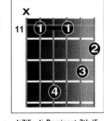

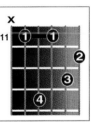

A♭13 A♭ Dominant 13th
1st (A♭), 3rd (C), 5th (E♭),
♭7th (G♭), 9th (B♭), 13th (F)

A♭13 A♭ Dominant 13th
1st (A♭), 3rd (C), 5th (E♭),
♭7th (G♭), 9th (B♭), 13th (F)

A♭add9 A♭ Major add 9th
1st (A♭), 3rd (C), 5th (E♭), 9th (B♭)

A♭add9 A♭ Major add 9th
1st (A♭), 3rd (C), 5th (E♭), 9th (B♭)

A♭m9 A♭ Minor 9th
1st (A♭), ♭3rd (C♭), 5th (E♭),
♭7th (G♭), 9th (B♭)

A♭m9 A♭ Minor 9th
1st (A♭), ♭3rd (C♭), 5th (E♭),
♭7th (G♭), 9th (B♭)

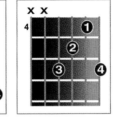

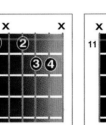

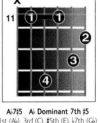

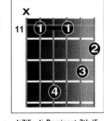

A♭maj9 A♭ Major 9th
1st (A♭), 3rd (C), 5th (E♭),
7th (G), 9th (B♭)

A♭maj9 A♭ Major 9th
1st (A♭), 3rd (C), 5th (E♭),
7th (G), 9th (B♭)

A♭+ A♭ Augmented
1st (A♭), 3rd (C), ♯5th (E)

A♭+ A♭ Augmented
1st (A♭), 3rd (C), ♯5th (E)

A♭7♯5 A♭ Dominant 7th ♯5
1st (A♭), 3rd (C), ♯5th (E), ♭7th (G♭)

A♭7♯5 A♭ Dominant 7th ♯5
1st (A♭), 3rd (C), ♯5th (E), ♭7th (G♭)

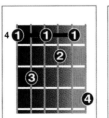

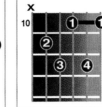

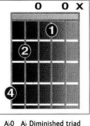

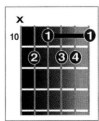

A♭7♯9 A♭ Dominant 7th ♯9
1st (A♭), 3rd (C), 5th (E♭),
♭7th (G♭), ♯9th (B)

A♭7♯9 A♭ Dominant 7th ♯9
1st (A♭), 3rd (C), 5th (E♭),
♭7th (G♭), ♯9th (B)

A♭°7 A♭ Diminished 7th
1st (A♭), ♭3rd (C♭), ♭5th (E♭♭),
♭♭7th (G♭♭)

A♭°7 A♭ Diminished 7th
1st (A♭), ♭3rd (C♭), ♭5th (E♭♭),
♭♭7th (G♭♭)

A♭° A♭ Diminished triad
1st (A♭), ♭3rd (C♭), ♭5th (E♭♭)

A♭° A♭ Diminished triad
1st (A♭), ♭3rd (C♭), ♭5th (E♭♭)

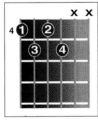

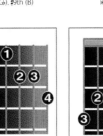

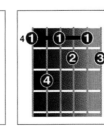

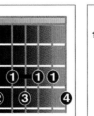

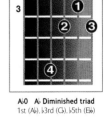

A♭7♭5 A♭ Dominant 7th ♭5
1st (A♭), 3rd (C), ♭5th (E♭♭), ♭7th (G♭)

A♭7♭5 A♭ Dominant 7th ♭5
1st (A♭), 3rd (C), ♭5th (E♭♭), ♭7th (G♭)

A♭7♭9 A♭ Dominant 7th ♭9
1st (A♭), 3rd (C), 5th (E♭),
♭7th (G♭), ♭9th (B♭♭)

A♭7♭9 A♭ Dominant 7th ♭9
1st (A♭), 3rd (C), 5th (E♭),
♭7th (G♭), ♭9th (B♭♭)

A♭9♭5 A♭ Dominant 9th ♭5th
1st (A♭), 3rd (C), ♭5th (E♭♭),
♭7th (G♭), 9th (B♭)

A♭9♭5 A♭ Dominant 9th ♭5th
1st (A♭), 3rd (C), ♭5th (E♭♭),
♭7th (G♭), 9th (B♭)

Glossary

Action

The 'action' of a guitar is commonly considered to be the height of the strings from the fingerboard, which determines how much pressure you have to put on the strings in order to play them. Technically, the 'action' of the guitar is a combination of string height, intonation and neck relief.

Active Electronics

Active electronics refers to battery-powered circuitry that boosts a guitar signal to make it easier to drive an amplifier into distortion. It can also be used to change the tone of the guitar.

Archtop

An archtop guitar is an instrument with an arched (curved) top and back. Such guitars, carved from solid pieces of wood, became hugely popular during the 1920s because they were louder than the previously used classical guitars. They are now associated mostly with jazz players.

Arpeggio

An arpeggio is the sounding of the notes of a chord in succession rather than all simultaneously. These can be played individually while holding a chord down or by picking out the notes separately on the fingerboard, just as you would when playing a scale.

Barre Chord

A barre chord is a chord where one of a guitarist's fretting fingers (usually the first finger) is held down across many or all of the strings in addition to other fingers holding down separate notes. Barre chords can be used in all of the 12 different keys simply by moving them up or down the fingerboard.

Bend

One of the most common lead guitar techniques is string bending, where a player plays a note on a string and pushes it up towards the next string while still holding the note down. You can bend one, two or even three strings at the same time.

Bottleneck

A technique where a player moves a glass or metal bar up and down the guitar neck while playing to produce sliding pitches. Famous bottleneck players include Robert Johnson, Muddy Waters, Eric Clapton and Ry Cooder.

Box-shape

Most guitarists normally learn scales as box-shapes, which show the finger positions for notes in a particular region of the fingerboard. The pentatonic scale, for example, can be played using five box-shapes that cover the whole guitar neck.

Bridge

This part of the guitar, along with the saddle, transmits energy from the string vibrations to the body of a guitar. It also spreads the mechanical tension of the strings. There are two main types of bridge: a fixed bridge is glued to the top of the soundboard with the strings anchored to it; and a floating bridge is held in place only by the tension in the strings that pass over it.

Classical Guitar

The classical guitar is a large acoustic guitar with a wide neck over which metal-wound silk or bronze bass strings and gut or nylon treble strings are usually strung. It was the first type of guitar to feature struts – pieces of wood attached to the inside of the body to improve volume and tonal response – and is almost always played finger-style.

Comping

'Comping' is a jazz term for accompanying. It usually means playing rhythm chords while a vocalist is singing or a lead performer is playing a solo.

Crown

The crown is the top of a fret on the guitar fingerboard. Crowns vary in width and curvature, and these differences influence the tone of a vibrating string: a thin crown tends to give a crisp treble edge to a string's tone, while a thicker one produces a more mellow sound that would appeal to a jazz player.

Cutaway

This is a rounded area cut out of a guitar's body next to the neck so that a player can comfortably reach further up the neck. Guitars such as Gibson Les Pauls and Fender Telecasters have cutaways underneath the neck, while others including the Gibson SG, Gibson 335, Fender Stratocaster and numerous Paul Reed Smith models have cutaways above and below the neck.

Dot Marker

Most guitars have these markers along the neck to help players navigate the fingerboard. They are usually behind the 3rd, 5th, 7th, 9th, 12th, 15th, 17th, 19th and 21st frets of the fingerboard. Other common markers are blocks (commonly found on Gibson and Ibanez guitars) and 'shark-tooths' (used on rock guitar models such as the Jackson Soloist). These markers are usually made out of abalone or plastic.

Double-stop

A two-note chord, melody or phrase.

Electro-acoustic (or Acoustic-electric)

An electro-acoustic guitar is an acoustic or semi-acoustic guitar fitted with a 'piezo-electric' transducer (usually under the bridge saddle) and an on-board pre-amplifier. When plugged into a suitable amp, this produces a crisp acoustic sound with plenty of sustain and little feedback.

EQ

EQ is short for equalization, a term describing the sound spectrum or parts of the sound spectrum of an audio signal. All audible sounds are pitched somewhere between 20 Hz (the lowest) and 20 KHz (the highest). An equalizer is a tone control that uses capacitors or other devices to cut or boost frequencies within this range.

342

F-hole

F-holes are ornamental sound holes found on a number of acoustic and electric guitars.

Finger-style

While most rock and pop guitarists play their instruments with a plectrum, all classical and flamenco guitar players articulate their notes with the separate fingers and thumb of their right hand (or left hand if they're left-handed). These players use their thumb to play the bass notes, usually with downstrokes on the bottom three strings, and their first, second and third fingers to play the other strings.

Flamenco

A popular folk music style from Andalucía in southern Spain.

Flatpicking

Flatpicking is a style where all notes, scalar and chordal, are articulated with a plectrum.

Footswitch

A footswitch is a device that allows you to change guitar sounds during a live performance without having to stop playing.

Fret

Frets are metal strips placed across the radius of a guitar's fingerboard to mark out notes a semitone apart. They make it easy for a guitarist to find precise notes in scales and chords. Frets come in all shapes and sizes: some are narrow while others are wide; and some are flat at the top while others are rounded.

Glissando

When a guitarist plays a glissando, he or she is sliding up or down the guitar neck in such a way that every note under the left-hand finger is articulated. This is different from a basic slide where the only notes that can be clearly heard are the first and last notes played by the left-hand finger.

Guitar, 7-string

The seven-string guitar is like a standard six-string instrument with an additional low string, usually tuned down to a low A. It was first used by jazzers such as George Van Eps and has since been used by various Nu Metal artists.

Guitar, 12-string

These guitars have 12 strings arranged into pairs (courses) so that a 6-string player can easily handle them. Six of the strings are tuned identically to those on a 6-string instrument, while the other six are tuned as follows; the lowest four are usually tuned an octave above the conventional E, A, D and G strings, while the other two are tuned the same as the conventional B and E strings.

Hammer-on

A hammer-on is a technique where you play a note behind a fret on the fingerboard and then hammer one of your other fingers down behind another fret higher up on the same string. It is one of the most common lead guitar techniques used by blues, rock, jazz and even classical players.

Headstock

The headstock is a wooden structure attached to the end of a guitar's neck on which the machine heads or tuning pegs are mounted. It is also usually the part of the guitar that carries the manufacturer's name and logo plus any other significant details of the guitar model.

Humbucking Pickup

Humbucking pickups have two coils instead of just one. These coils are wired in such a way that any electrical hum produced by one is cancelled out by the other. The result is a 'fatter' sound with less background noise. Humbuckers were originally launched by Gibson in 1955 and soon became a standard feature on their Les Paul, Explorer, Flying V, Firebird and SG guitars.

Intonation

The intonation of a guitar is correct when the notes behind every fret of the fingerboard all have the right pitch when the guitar is in tune. To check the intonation of your guitar, tune it up accurately and then listen to each note on each string. If any notes on any string are out of tune, you should be able to make intonation adjustments on the bridge screw that controls the vibrating length of that string.

Lick

A lick is a small musical motif such as a phrase or riff that can be incorporated into a lead guitar solo. All good soloists have a vocabulary of licks that they use in their lead lines.

Luthier

A luthier is a guitar maker. Originally the term was only used to describe lute and classical-guitar makers but now it is generally considered to apply to builders of all kinds of guitars and fretted instruments.

Nut

The nut is a structure at the headstock end of the fingerboard over which the strings pass before they reach the machine heads or pegs. The strings lean on the nut and all string vibrations occur between it and the guitar's bridge.

Palm-muting

You can mute a guitar's strings by placing your right hand lightly across them. This is very useful if you're playing at high volume and don't want the strings to ring out unnecessarily. It can also be used to add more colour and texture to a rhythm or solo.

Pickup Selector

A switch that allows a guitar player to choose between different pickups.

Pre-amp

A pre-amplifier (or pre-amp), is a device that strengthens and shapes audio signals before further routing or final amplification to drive a speaker. In guitar amps, volume and tone controls are in the pre-amp section.

Pre-bend

A pre-bend is when you bend a note before you actually play it. In this situation you play the string from the top of the bend and then let it fall back into its original position.

Pull-off

A pull-off can be seen as the reverse of a hammer-on. In this case, a note is played and then the finger playing that note is pulled off the string to sound a lower note that is either an open string or one fretted by another finger.

Rake

A rake is an interesting effect a guitarist can produce by rubbing one of their fingers or hands along one or several of the guitar strings. A harsher raking effect can be created by performing it with a hard object such as a plectrum.

Rasgueado

Rasgueado (also spelt Rascuedo) is an instantly recognizable flamenco technique where the fingers of the right hand (or left hand if the player is left-handed) individually strum across the strings in rapid succession.

Riff

A riff is a short series of chords or notes that can be repeated to form a catchy sequence. Some riffs are so effective that they more or less take up a whole song!

Saddle

The saddle is the place on a guitar's bridge for supporting the strings. The distance between it and the nut determines the scale length (length of vibrating open string) of a guitar.

Scratchplate (or Pickguard)

A scratchplate is a plastic plate that is fixed to the lower front part of a guitar's body (underneath the soundhole on an acoustic steel-string instrument) to protect the body from wear and tear caused by the player's plectrums or finger picks.

Semi-solid

In the late 1950s, Gibson introduced a range of semi-acoustic guitars that didn't suffer from the feedback problems that traditional 'electro-acoustic' models produced. These guitars, including the ES-355, ES-345, and the now famous ES-335, had thin hollow bodies with f-holes to let the sound out, a design which increased sustain and greatly reduced feedback.

Semitone

The smallest interval between two notes on a fretted guitar is called a semitone (S). Notes on either side of a fret are separated by a semitone. An interval of two semitones is called a tone (T).

Slide

This effect is produced when you play one note on the guitar and, while still holding the note down, slide up or down the guitar neck to another note. In a true slide, the only two notes

you can hear clearly are the first and last notes, at the beginning and end of the slide, whereas a glissando is a sliding effect that is played in such a way that every note under the finger is articulated.

Solid-body

A solid-body guitar is a guitar with a body that has no cavities other than those used for inserting pickups and other electrical components. Solid-body electric guitar prototypes were developed in the 1920s and 1930s when amplified acoustic guitars gave musicians too much feedback.

Soundhole

The soundhole is the hole in the front of the guitar body through which sound projects from the sound chamber. Most acoustic guitar soundholes are round, although some are oval (as on early Gibson acoustics), D-shaped (as on Maccaferri guitars), or violin-like f-holes (as on the Gibson ES-350).

Sweep-picking

Sweep-picking is an advanced technique where a guitarist plays notes across the neck with economic pick movements. In some ways it is similar to the way a violinist will sustain a note with the bow by bowing in both directions at a consistent speed. This technique can be used to facilitate execution of ultra-fast arpeggios.

Sympathetic Strings

Sitars and some specialist lutes and guitars have sympathetic strings which are not played but sound 'in sympathy' with strings that are. The sympathetic strings are tuned to particular notes and when those notes are played on the instrument, the corresponding strings start to vibrate and thus 'sing in sympathy'.

Thumbpick

Thumbpicks are often used by finger-style players who want to play the guitar forcefully without risk of damaging their thumbnails. A thumbpick fits over the end of the thumb with the pick protruding to strike the strings.

Time Signature

A time signature is a sign placed after the clef at the beginning of a piece of music to indicate its metre.

Tremolando

Tremolando is a classical and flamenco guitar technique in which the first, second and third fingers of the right hand (or left hand for a left-handed player) play a continuous, repeating pattern on one note.

Tremolo Arm

A tremolo arm (also known as a 'whammy bar') is a mechanical arm attached to the bridge of an electric guitar that can alter the pitch of the strings; as the arm is depressed, the pitch of a note played drops, and when the arm is let go, the altered pitch returns back to normal.

Triad

Triads are basic three-note chords that are also the building blocks of most other chords. There are four basic triads: a major triad is the first, third and fifth notes of the diatonic major scale (C, E and G in the key of C); a minor triad is the first, third and fifth notes of the natural minor scale (C, E♭ and G in the key of C); an augmented triad is a major triad with a sharpened fifth note (C, E and G# in the key of C); and a diminished triad is a minor triad with a flattened fifth note (C, E♭ and G♭ in the key of C).

Truss Rod

The truss rod is a metal bar used for reinforcing and adjusting a steel-strung guitar's neck. It can be adjusted to keep the neck straight if the tension in it changes when different gauge strings are used.

Vibrato

Vibrato is a left-hand technique (or right hand if you're left-handed) where a played note is moved rapidly to produce a fluctuation in pitch that gives more richness to the tone. Vibrato can be applied vertically (across the neck) or horizontally (along the neck). Vibrato is used extensively in classical guitar music, and in blues, jazz and rock solos.

Violining

Violining is an effect where you use a guitar's volume control (or a volume pedal) to fade notes or chords in from nothing to get a nice, smooth effect. Rock legends such as Gary Moore, Jimmy Page and Mark Knopfler have used violining to great effect.

Further Reading

Books

Amelar, C., *The Guitar F/X Cook Book*, Hal Leonard, 1997

Bacon, T., *History of the American Guitar*, Backbeat UK, 2001

Bacon T. and Day P., *The Fender Book: A Complete History of Fender Electric Guitars* (2nd ed.), Backbeat UK, 1999

Bennett, J. (ed.), *Guitar Facts*, Flame Tree Publishing, 2002

Brosnac, D., *Guitar Electronics for Musicians*, Music Sales Ltd, 1983

Carter, W., *Gibson Guitars: 100 Years of an American Icon*, General Publishing Group, 1994

Chappell, J., *Scales and Modes*, Cherry Lane Music, 1994

Chappell, J. and Verheyen, C., *Rock Guitar for Dummies*, Hungry Minds Inc., 2001

Cutchin, R., *Guitar Heroes*, Flame Tree Publishing, 2008

Cutchin, R. (ed.) and Macdonald, R. (ed.), *The Illustrated Home Recording Handbook* (2nd ed.), Flame Tree Publishing, 2007

Denyer, R., *The Guitar Handbook*, Alfred A. Knopf, 1992

Douse, C., *Really Easy Riffs*, Wise Publications, 2003

Duchossoir, A.R., *Gibson Electrics: The Classic Years*, Hal Leonard, 1981

Fliegler, R., *AMPS!: The Other Half of Rock'n'Roll*, Hal Leonard, 1993

Goodrick, M., *The Advancing Guitarist*, Music Sales Ltd, 1987

Gruhn. G. and Carter, W., *Electric Guitars and Basses: A Photographic History*, Omnibus Press, 1994

Guitar Chords, Flame Tree Publishing, 2006

Hall, J., *Exploring Jazz Guitar*, Hal Leonard, 1991

Hart, C., *Routes to Sight Reading*, Registry Publications, 2004

Heatley, M. and Brown, A., *How to Play Hard, Metal & Nu Rock*, Flame Tree Publishing, 2008

Heatley, M. and Brown, A., *How to Play Rock Rhythm, Riffs & Lead*, Flame Tree Publishing, 2008

Heatley, M. and Brown, A., *Play Flamenco*, Flame Tree Publishing, 2007

Iwanade, Y., *The Beauty of the 'Burst': Gibson Sunburst Les Pauls from 1958 to 1960*, Hal Leonard, 1999

Kamimoto, H., *Electric Guitar Setups*, Music Sales Ltd, 1996

Kempster G. *Guitars: Sounds, Chrome & Stars*, Flame Tree Publishing, 2007

Koch, G., *Rhythm Riffs*, Hal Leonard, 2003

Latarski, D., *First Chords*, Warner Bros., 1999

Menasché, E., *The Desktop Studio*, Hal Leonard, 2003

Philips, M. and Chappell, J., *Guitar for Dummies*, Hungry Minds Inc., 1998

Pinksterboer, H., *Rough Guide to Electric and Bass Guitar*, Rough Guides, 2000

Rooksby, R., *First Guitar Rhythm Patterns*, Wise Publications, 1998

Ross, M., *Getting Great Guitar Sounds*, Hal Leonard, 1998

Schmidt, P.W., *Acquired of the Angels: The Lives and Works of Master Guitar Makers John D'Angelico and James L. D'Aquisto*, Scarecrow Press, 1991

Sicard, A., *Instant Lead Guitar*, Mel Bay, 1993

Skinner, T., *Electric Guitar Playing Grade 1*, Registry Publications, 2004

Skinner, T., *Improvising Lead Guitar*, Registry Publications, 2004

Wheeler, T., *American Guitars: An Illustrated History*, HarperCollins Publishers, 1992

Wheeler, T., *The Stratocaster Chronicles: Celebrating 50 Years of the Fender Strat*, Hal Leonard, 2004

Wyatt, K., *Electric Guitar Basics*, Warner Bros., 1996

Magazines

20th Century Guitar: www.tcguitar.com

Acoustic Guitar: www.acguitar.com

Bass Guitar Magazine: www.bassguitarmagazine.com

Classical Guitar Magazine: www.classicalguitarmagazine.com

Electronic Musician: www.emusician.com

Flatpicking Guitar Magazine: www.flatpick.com

Guitarist: www.guitarist.co.uk

Guitar Player: www.guitarplayer.com

Guitar Techniques: www.guitartechniques.com

Guitar World: www.guitarworld.com

Total Guitar: www.totalguitar.co.uk

Vintage Guitar Magazine: www.vintageguitar.com

DVD

Home Recording Magazine's 100 Recording Tips and Tricks, Cherry Lane Music, 2003

Learning Guitar for Dummies, Jon Chappell, 2001

Websites

www.analogman.com: this is a site dedicated to analogue and vintage effects, including pedals.

www.BooksForGuitar.com: this site specializes in guitar education, with all titles being reviewed for quality before inclusion.

http://guitar.about.com/od/bluesjazzmetalmore/: this site has links to resources that give advice on how to play in styles such as blues, funk and jazz.

www.guitar.com: an online magazine including interviews, reviews, MP3 downloads, links to educational resources and a guitarist's forum.

www.guitarinstructor.com: a site featuring online video guitar lessons, video song lessons and advice from professional guitar instructors.

www.guitarists.net: this site is for players of all ages, styles and abilities. Take part in a guitar-related discussion, look up some lessons and a lot more.

www.guitar-player-resources.com: a site giving advice to acoustic, electric and bass guitarists on everything from choosing a guitar, to guitar lessons and repairs.

www.guitartips.addr.com: this site is a day-to-day resource for acoustic players, with tips and advice on care, preservation and maintenance of instruments, plus guitar chords.

www.harmony-central.com: this is a leading online resource for musicians, with everything from news and product reviews, to classified ads and chat rooms.

www.musicfirebox.com: a lo-fi music information site.

www.projectguitar.com: this site includes tutorials, projects, links and further information to help you get the most out of playing solid-body electric guitar.

www.RegistryOfGuitarTutors.com: this site includes the only database of formally registered guitar tutors across the UK and overseas.

www.tonequest.com: The ToneQuest Report is a monthly newsletter published by and for guitarists.

www.truefire.com: an extensive site dedicated to guitar education, offering thousands of free guitar lessons and interactive video courses available as downloads, video or CD-ROM.

345

Acknowledgements

Contributor Biographies

Rusty Cutchin (General Editor; Rehearsing; Playing Live; Recording; The Guitarists)

Rusty Cutchin has been a musician, recording engineer, producer and journalist for over 25 years. He has been technical editor and a columnist for *GuitarOne* magazine as well as an associate editor of *Electronic Musician* magazine and editor in chief of *Home Recording* magazine. Prior to that he was a recording engineer with credits on albums by Mariah Carey, Richie Sambora, Yoko Ono and many others. Cutchin has been a consultant editor and contributor to nine books on subjects such as the guitar, computer recording technology and rock history, including *The Illustrated Encyclopedia of Guitar Heroes* and *The Illustrated Home Recording Handbook*.

Paco Peña (Foreword)

Paco Peña made his first professional appearance at the age of 12. He has played in Ronnie Scott's Jazz Club, the Royal Albert Hall in London, New York's Carnegie Hall and the Concertgebouw in Amsterdam. He has shared the stage with fellow guitarists, singers and instrumental groups, bridging diverse musical genres, including classical, jazz, blues, country and Latin American. *Guitar* magazine judged him Best Flamenco Guitarist of the Year for five consecutive years. In 1981 he founded the Centro Flamenco Paco Peña in Córdoba, later becoming Artistic Director of the Córdoba International Guitar Festival. In 1985 he became the world's first Professor of Flamenco Guitar at Rotterdam Conservatory in the Netherlands. Since 1970, the Paco Peña Flamenco Dance Company has taken flamenco into the realm of music-theatre with regular seasons in London and many festival appearances world-wide. Productions include *Misa Flamenca* (1991) and *Musa Gitana* (1999); he has further plans to marry flamenco with the forms and forces of classical music. Paco Peña is based in London, but still spends a significant part of the year in his native Andalucía. In 1997 he was named Oficial de la Cruz de la Orden del Mérito Civil, an honour bestowed by King Juan Carlos of Spain.

Michael Leonard (Consultant Editor)

Michael Leonard began playing guitar at the age of 12, inspired by his elder brother's budget-priced but very fine Yamaha acoustic. He's worked in the music press since 1990, and has edited *The Guitar Magazine*, *Guitar Techniques* and Europe's longest-established musicians' magazine, *Guitarist*. As a freelance writer, he has contributed to *Q*, *Mojo*, *Blender* and many others. He lives with his wife and two children in Bath, England.

Cliff Douse (Musical Styles; Glossary)

Cliff Douse is a music author, editor and composer based in the UK. His first book, *Scales & Modes for Guitar*, was published in 1990 with an endorsement from the legendary rock guitarist, Pete Townshend, and he has since written a number of other books and countless articles for some of the UK's foremost music and computer magazines. Cliff also recently edited *Guitar Techniques* magazine and the *Guitarist Icons* series for Future Publishing in England.

Hugh Fielder (The Guitarists)

Hugh Fielder can remember the 1960s even though he was there. He can remember the 1970s and 1980s because he was at *Sounds* magazine (RIP) and the 1990s because he was editor of Tower Records' *TOP* magazine. He has shared a spliff with Bob Marley, a glass of wine with David Gilmour, a pint with Robert Plant, a cup of tea with Keith Richards and a frosty stare with Axl Rose. He has watched Mike Oldfield strip naked in front of him and Bobby Womack fall asleep while he was interviewing him.

Mike Gent (The Guitarists)

Nurturing an obsession with pop music, which dates back to first hearing Slade's 'Gudbuy T'Jane' in 1972, Mike Gent remains fixated, despite failing to master any musical instrument, with the possible exception of the recorder. A freelance writer since 2001, he has contributed to *Writers' Forum*, *Book and Magazine Collector*, *Record Buyer*, *When Saturday Comes*, *Inside David Bowie and the Spiders* (DVD), *The Kinks 1964–1978* (DVD), *The Beatles 1962–1970* (DVD), *Remember the Eighties, Where Were You When? – Music That Changed Our Lives*, *The Definitive Illustrated Encyclopedia of Rock* and *The Illustrated Encyclopedia of Guitar Heroes*.

Adam Perlmutter (The Guitars)

Adam Perlmutter has music degrees from the University of North Carolina at Greensboro and the New England Conservatory. He was a senior editor of *GuitarOne* magazine, and has authored several guitar instruction books and transcribed/arranged numerous folios.

Richard Riley
(The Story of the Guitar; Maintenance & Customization)

Richard Riley is a guitar player and writer. He has recorded and performed with a wide range of artists and is a long-time contributor to many of the UK's leading music technology publications. As an artist and musician he is regularly seen in the mp3.com charts.

Michael Ross (Effects; Amplification)

Michael Ross is a freelance guitarist/producer/writer/editor living in New York. He is the author of *Getting Great Guitar Sounds* (Hal Leonard). He has been gear editor for *GuitarOne* magazine, and a contributor to amazon.com, *What Guitar*, *No Depression*, puremusic.com and others. He would like to remind guitarists that it is 90% in the fingers.

Tony Skinner
(The Beginner; The Harmonic Guitarist; The Rhythm Guitarist; The Melodic Guitarist; Basic Techniques; Advanced Techniques)

Tony Skinner is widely respected as one of the UK's premier music educators. He is the director of the Registry of Guitar Tutors – the world's foremost organization for guitar education. He is also the principal guitar examiner for London College of Music Exams and has compiled examination syllabi in electric, bass and classical guitar playing, as well as popular music theory, rock/pop band and popular music vocals. He has written and edited over 50 music-education books, and is the editor of *Guitar Tutor* magazine and a columnist for *Total Guitar* magazine.

Picture Credits

Index

349